Anglo-German Foundation for the Study of Industrial Society

The Anglo-German Foundation for the Study of Industrial Society was established by an agreement between the British and German governments after a state visit to Britain by the late President Heinemann, and incorporated by Royal Charter in 1973. Funds were initially provided by the German government; since 1979 both governments have been contributing.

The Foundation aims to contribute to the knowledge and understanding of industrial society in the two countries and to promote contacts between them. It funds selected research projects and conferences in the industrial, economic and social policy areas designed to be of practical use to policy-makers.

Titles include:

Bernhard Blanke and Randall Smith (*editors*)
CITIES IN TRANSITION
New Challenges, New Responsibilities

John Bynner and Rainer K. Silbereisen (*editors*)
ADVERSITY AND CHALLENGE IN LIFE IN THE NEW GERMANY AND IN ENGLAND

Maurie J. Cohen (*editor*)
RISK IN THE MODERN AGE
Social Theory, Science and Environmental Decision-Making

Dagmar Ebster-Grosz and Derek Pugh (*editors*)
ANGLO–GERMAN BUSINESS COLLABORATION
Pitfalls and Potentials

Rainer Emig (*editor*)
STEREOTYPES IN CONTEMPORARY ANGLO–GERMAN RELATIONS

Karen Evans, Martina Behrens and Jens Kaluza
LEARNING AND WORK IN THE RISK SOCIETY
Lessons for the Labour Markets of Europe from Eastern Germany

Stephen F. Frowen and Jens Hölscher (*editors*)
THE GERMAN CURRENCY UNION OF 1990
A Critical Assessment

Stephen F. Frowen and Francis P. McHugh (*editors*)
FINANCIAL COMPETITION, RISK AND ACCOUNTABILITY
British and German Experiences

Jens Hölscher (*editor*)
50 YEARS OF THE GERMAN MARK
Essays in Honour of Stephen F. Frowen

Jens Hölscher (*editor*)
GERMANY'S ECONOMIC PERFORMANCE
From Unification to Euroization

Jens Hölscher and Horst Tomann (*editors*)
GLOBALIZATION OF CAPITAL MARKETS AND MONETARY POLICY

Eva Kolinsky (*editor*)
SOCIAL TRANSFORMATION AND THE FAMILY IN POST-COMMUNIST GERMANY

Mairi Maclean and Jean-Marc Trouille (*editors*)
FRANCE, GERMANY AND BRITAIN
Partners in a Changing World

William J. V. Neill and Hanns-Uve Schwedler (*editors*)
URBAN PLANNING AND CULTURAL INCLUSION
Lessons from Belfast and Berlin

Laura J. Spence, André Habisch and René Schmidpeter (*editors*)
RESPONSIBILITY AND SOCIAL CAPITAL
The World of Small and Medium Sized Enterprises

Howard Williams, Colin Wight and Norbert Kapferer (*editors*)
POLITICAL THOUGHT AND GERMAN REUNIFICATION
The New German Ideology?

Rüdiger Wink (*editor*)
ACADEMIA–BUSINESS LINKS
European Policy Strategies and Lessons Learnt

Anglo-German Foundation
Series Standing Order ISBN 0–333–71459–8
(*outside North America only*)

You can receive future titles in this series as they are published by placing a standing order. Please contact your bookseller or, in case of difficulty, write to us at the address below with your name and address, the title of the series and the ISBN quoted above.

Customer Services Department, Macmillan Distribution Ltd, Houndmills, Basingstoke, Hampshire RG21 6XS, England

Germany's Economic Performance

From Unification to Euroization

Edited by

Jens Hölscher

palgrave
macmillan

First published 2007 by
PALGRAVE MACMILLAN
Houndmills, Basingstoke, Hampshire RG21 6XS and
175 Fifth Avenue, New York, N.Y. 10010
Companies and representatives throughout the world

PALGRAVE MACMILLAN is the global academic imprint of the Palgrave Macmillan division of St. Martin's Press, LLC and of Palgrave Macmillan Ltd. Macmillan® is a registered trademark in the United States, United Kingdom and other countries. Palgrave is a registered trademark in the European Union and other countries.

ISBN-13: 978–1–4039–9950–4
ISBN-10: 1–4039–9950–3

This book is printed on paper suitable for recycling and made from fully managed and sustained forest sources.

A catalogue record for this book is available from the British Library.

Library of Congress Cataloging-in-Publication Data
Germany's economic performance: from unification to Euroization/edited by Jens Hölscher.
p. cm. — (Anglo-German Foundation)
Includes bibliographical references and index.
ISBN 1–4039–9950–3
1. Germany—Economic conditions—1990—Congresses.
2. Germany—Economic policy—1990—Congresses I. Hölscher, Jens.
II. Series: Anglo-German Foundation series.
HC286.8.G4785 2007
330.943′0887—dc22 2006046443

10 9 8 7 6 5 4 3 2 1
16 15 14 13 12 11 10 09 08 07

Printed and bound in Great Britain by
Antony Rowe Ltd, Chippenham and Eastbourne

To the memory of the late
Norbert Kloten
with great admiration

Photograph by Manfred Grohe

Contents

Part II Macroeconomic Performance

Part III Structural Developments

Part IV East Germany

Part V Conclusion

List of Tables

List of Figures

Notes on the Contributors

Joerg Bibow is Assistant Professor of Economics at Skidmore College, New York, USA. He holds a PhD in Economics from the University of Cambridge, UK. Previously he held lecturing positions at the University of Cambridge, Hamburg University, and at Franklin College Switzerland. He is a Research Associate at the Levy Economics Institute, New York. He is the author of numerous articles and co-authored volumes published in Europe and the US on European integration, central banking, financial systems, and the history of thought.

Iris Biefang-Frisancho Mariscal is a Senior Lecturer in economics at the University of the West of England. She wrote her PhD thesis in ecomomics at the Westfaelische Wilhelmsuniversitaet in Münster (Germany), where she was also senior academic assistant in the Department of Econometrics and Business Statistics. Subsequently she taught at the University of East London, UK. Her main research interests are in applied econometrics, unemployment and monetary economics. She has published in journals such as *Economics Letters*, *Scottish Journal of Political Economy*, *Journal of Post Keynesian Economics*, *Applied Economics*, *Empirica* and *Structural Change and Economic Dynamics*.

Horst Feldmann is a Lecturer in Economics in the Department of Economics and International Development at the University of Bath, UK. He received his PhD in Economics from the University of Hamburg, Germany, in 1990. From 1991 to 2005 he worked in the Department of Economics at the University of Tübingen, Germany, where he was also awarded the title 'Privatdozent' in 1998. His publications include three books, fifty-one articles in refereed journals, fourteen chapters in edited volumes and five contributions to encyclopaedias. His articles have been published in, *inter alia*, *Public Choice*, *Kyklos*, *Comparative Economic Studies*, *Journal of European Integration*, *Post-Communist Economies* and *Southern Economic Journal*.

Stephen F. Frowen is Honorary Research Fellow in the Department of Economics, University College London, and Senior Research Associate at the Von Hügel Institute at St Edmund's College, University of Cambridge, of which he is also Fellow Commoner. He was a Research Officer at the National Institute of Economic and Social Research, London, and editor of the world's oldest banking journal, *The Bankers' Magazine* (now *Financial World*), established in 1844. Following senior teaching posts at the University of Greenwich and the University of Surrey, he held, after a Visiting

Chair at the Johann Wolfgang Goethe-University Frankfurt am Main, the new Bundesbank Chair of Monetary Economics in the Free University of Berlin as its first incumbent. From 1994 to 2004 he was also Honorary Professor at the Institute for German Studies, University of Birmingham. He has published extensively on monetary economics, international monetary economics, banking and the methodology of economics, and is the editor of a number of collective works, including *Financial Competition, Risk and Accountability: British and German Experiences* (2001, with Francis McHugh). His 40-year correspondence with G. L. S. Shackle, *Economists in Discussion*, appeared in 2004. In 1993, he was awarded the Commander's Cross of the Order of Merit of the Federal Republic of Germany, and in 1996 was honoured with a Papal Knighthood (KSG).

Lothar Funk is Professor of International Economics at the University of Applied Sciences, Düsseldorf, Germany. Until mid-2005, he was also responsible for research in International Labour Relations at the Cologne Institute for Economic Research, where he is now an Associated Research Fellow. He is also Visiting Fellow at the Institute for German Studies, European Research Institute, University of Birmingham, UK.

Walter W. Heering is Senior Lecturer in Financial Economics at the Brighton Business School, University of Brighton. He holds a PhD in Economics from the Free University, Berlin. Until 2001 he taught Political Economy in the Department of Political Science, at the Free University, Berlin. He has published on monetary theory and policy, political economics of transition, European integration, and economics of the welfare state.

Eckhard Hein is a Senior Researcher for Macroeconomic Policies at the Macroeconomic Policy Institute (IMK) in the Hans Boeckler Foundation, Düsseldorf and a Visiting Lecturer at Carl von Ossietzky University, Oldenburg, Germany. He studied economics at the University of Bremen and at the New School for Social Research, New York, received a doctoral degree from the Free University of Berlin in 1996 and a post-doctoral degree (Habilitation) from Carl von Ossietzky University, Oldenburg in 2005. Among his most recent publications are co-edited books *Wages, Distribution, Employment and Growth – International Perspectives* (2006, Palgrave Macmillan) and *Macroeconomic Policy Coordination in Europe and the Role of the Trade Unions* (2005, ETUI), as well as (co-)authored papers on post-Keynesian theories of distribution and growth, and on German and European macroeconomics in *Banca Nazionale del Lavoro Quarterly Review, International Review of Applied Economics, Metroeconomica* and *Structural Change and Economic Dynamics*.

Jens Hölscher is Reader in Economics at the University of Brighton, UK and Vice-President of the European Association for Comparative Economic

Studies. Previously he taught at the Universities of Berlin, Swansea, Birmingham and Chemnitz. He has held Visiting Professorships at the Universities of Halle (IWH), Bonn (ZEI), Bozen, New Brunswick in Cairo, Almaty (KIMEP) and the Centre of Economic Research at the Deutsche Bundesbank. Currently he is on a mission for the London School of Economics, to the Kazack-British Technical University in Almaty. He is interested in monetary and transition economics, both areas in which he published widely. He is the co-editor of Palgrave Macmillan's book series 'Studies in Economic Transition'.

Peter Howells is Reader in Economics at the University of the West of England, Bristol. Formerly Professor of Economics at the University of East London, he has published widely on issues of money and central banking. He is the co-author of the standard undergraduate textbook on money, banking and finance, and a major text on monetary economics. His research interests lie in monetary issues and economics, and he has published extensively in a range of journals. At present he is concerned with several issues in central banking, including the optimum design of monetary policy. With Iris Biefang-Frisancho Mariscal he is the author of several papers which use evidence from the behaviour of money market interest rates to cast doubt on the widely held view that statutory rules necessarily improve the transparency of central bank decision-making and the outcomes of monetary policy. Dr Howells is a council member of the European Association for Evolutionary Political Economy (EAEPE) and editor of the Royal Economic Society's *Newsletter*.

Michael Kaser is Honorary Professor in the Institute for German Studies, University of Birmingham, and Emeritus Fellow of St Antony's College, Oxford University, where he was Professorial Fellow and University Reader in Economics until 1993. He was born in London in 1926 and, after graduating in economics at Cambridge University, he served successively in the British Foreign Service (1947–51) and the Secretariat of the UNECE, Geneva (1951–63). The latter included a mission to the then GDR, renewed from time to time for his research at Oxford. Among publications to which these contributed were to Edwina Moreton (ed.), *Germany between East and West* (CUP, 1987); *Post-Communist Privatization – Flaws in the Treuhand Model* (IGS, 1996); and to Jens Hölscher and Anja Hochberg (eds), *East Germany's Economic Development since Unification* (Palgrave Macmillan, 1998). He has been General Editor of the International Economic Association since 1986, and is a member of the Steering Committee for South-East European Studies at Oxford. He is author and/or editor of twenty-three books and 370 articles in journals on the East European and ex-Soviet economies, both under the Soviet-type system and in transition to the market.

Norbert Kloten was President of the Land Central Bank in Baden-Württemberg and an *ex officio* member of the German policy-making Central Bank Council from 1976 to 1992. Since 1967 he was also a member of the Economic Advisory Council at the Federal Ministry of Economics (Chairman from 1992 to 1996). Other activities included membership of the Board of Academic and Non-Academic Associations and the Trilateral Commission. His Professorship at the University of Tübingen (1960–76) was combined with membership of the German Council of Economic Experts (Sachverständigenrat) from 1969 to 1976, being its Chairman from 1970 to 1976. He published extensively on the principles of economic policy and in the area of monetary and international monetary economics, on the theory and policy of transition and development, and on the methodology of economics. He held two honorary doctorates, from the University of Karlsruhe (1980) and the University of Stuttgart (1993) respectively, and was the bearer of the Commander's Cross with Badge and Star of the Order of Merit of the Federal Republic of Germany.

Waltraud Schelkle studied economics at the Free University of Berlin and Duke University, North Carolina, USA. She worked for a development policy think tank before returning to the Free University as an Assistant and later Visiting Professor of International Economic Relations. Since October 2001, she has been a political economist at the European Institute of the London School of Economics, working on monetary integration and enlargement, fiscal policy co-ordination and welfare state reforms in Europe.

Eric Owen Smith, since his retirement, has retained research and teaching interests in German and EU economic affairs. His main part-time undergraduate and postgraduate teaching commitments are in the Department of Economics at Loughborough University. He has contributed to three previous Palgrave Macmillan/Anglo-German Foundation volumes, as well as to three books on German unification. A third edition of his *German Economy* (this time with Lothar Funk as a co-author) is planned for 2006/7.

Khaled Soufani is an Associate Professor of Financial Economics in the John Molson School of Business at Concordia University, Montréal, Canada, he is also a visiting academic at Brighton Business School, UK, and a visiting fellow at the University of Cambridge, UK. He lectures in Financial and Business Economics with emphasis on finance theory, corporate finance, and monetary economics. His area of research focuses on the economics and financial affairs of small and medium-sized enterprises (SMEs), and has various publications in academic journals such as the *Journal of Economics and Business, Managerial and Decision Economics, the International Journal of the Economics of Business, Environment and Planning: Journal of Government and Policy*. In addition he has contributed to numerous books including the *Globalization and Entrepreneurship: Policy and Strategy Perspectives and International*

Entrepreneurship: Globalization of SME's Orientation, Environment and Strategy. He is on the editorial board and served as guest editor for the topics of finance and economics in journals on small business.

Johannes Stephan is Head of the Department for Industrial Organization and Regulatory Economics at the Halle Institute for Economic Research (IWH), Germany. He studied economics at the Freie Universität Berlin and completed an economics PhD at the Institute for German Studies, University of Birmingham (UK). In 1997, he was awarded a senior research post at the IWH, where he has successfully applied for and managed two large EU-funded projects and participated in one smaller one. His research activities are focused upon various conditions for economic development, including the monetary sphere, competition, productivity, and knowledge transfer.

Achim Truger is a Senior Researcher on Public Finance and Taxation at the Macroeconomic Policy Institute (IMK) in the Hans Boeckler Foundation, Düsseldorf, Germany. He studied economics at the University of Cologne, where he received a doctoral degree in 1997. Among his most recent publications are co-edited books *Wages, Distribution, Employment and Growth – International Perspectives* (forthcoming, Palgrave Macmillan) and *Macroeconomic Policy Coördination in Europe and the Role of the Trade Unions* (2005), as well as (co-)authored papers on German and European macroeconomics in *International Review of Applied Economics* and *Structural Change and Economic Dynamics*. He is (co-)author or (co-)editor of eighteen books and has published forty-seven papers in research journals and collected volumes on fiscal policy, taxation, German and European macroeconomic policies, and on post-Keynesian macroeconomics.

Norbert Walter is Chief Economist of Deutsche Bank Group and CEO of Deutsche Bank Research. Before his current position he was a professor and director at the renowned Kiel Institute for World Economics and was a John J. McCloy Distinguished Research Fellow at the American Institute for Contemporary German Studies at the Johns Hopkins University in Washington, DC (1986–87). He holds a PhD in economics from the Johann-Wolfgang-Goethe University in Frankfurt am Main. As Chief Economist of Deutsche Bank Group, Norbert Walter is responsible for a globally integrated approach to economic research. He manages Deutsche Bank Research, Deutsche Bank's think tank, which covers a wide spectrum of issues ranging from economic forecasting to country rating and sector analysis. Services are rendered to the Bank's board, staff, customers and the general pubic. In addition to these responsibilities at Deutsche Bank, Professor Walter is a member of the Board of Directors of the American Chamber of Commerce, a member of the Council of Reutlingen University and a member of the Executive Committee of the Central Committee of German Catholics.

Obituary:[1] Professor Norbert Kloten – Liberal Conservative Economist

Stephen F. Frowen

Norbert Kloten was one of the most influential economists of the Federal Republic of Germany – as scholar, economic adviser and central banker contributing decisively to the country's reconstruction after the Second World War and to turning Germany into one of the world's leading industrial nations.

He was born in 1926 in Sinzig, where his family had been running their estate for generations, and grew up in the neighbouring more up-market town of Bad Honnef. After graduating from the University of Bonn in 1948 with the degree of Diplom-Volkswirt, he took his doctorate there under the supervision of Professor Erwin von Beckerath and Professor Matthias Ernst Kamp, and then, in 1956, his *Habilitation* (higher doctorate) under Professor Erwin von Beckerath. A short spell followed as Visiting Lecturer at the Bologna Center of the School of Advanced International Studies at Johns Hopkins University in Baltimore. During the summer of 1958 he replaced the academic teacher Erwin von Beckerath, and then for the winter semester 1959/60 Professor Hans Peters at the University of Tübingen – after which he was appointed to a permanent professorship there at the early age of 33 (a chair once held by the political economist Friedrich List).

Kloten first devoted himself to biography and the history of economic ideas, to the early Italian school, Enrico Barone and Vilfredo Pareto, and then Jean-Baptiste Say, William Stanley Jevons and, especially, John Stuart Mill, as well as Alfred Marshall, Gustav Cassel, and (working with von Beckerath) Lorenz von Stein. The ideas of these economists remained a lasting influence.

His active mind kept him abreast of developments in economics, but he remained a liberal conservative in economic theory, very much in the tradition of Walter Eucken and von Beckerath. His conviction of the importance of monetary stability dates from these early teachers. It coloured his whole approach to his support for the establishment of European Monetary Union and the European Central Bank, which reflected, as it turned out, the Bundesbank model.

When in 1976 he accepted the offer of the presidency of the Land Central Bank in Baden-Württemberg, the University of Tübingen made him an Honorary Professor, a position he held until his death. Running concurrently with his responsibilities as academic and central banker, Kloten pursued a third major activity, as an adviser – which proved to be his particular talent.

Since 1967 he had been a member of the Economic Advisory Council of the Federal Ministry of Economics and he served as its Chairman from 1992 to 1996. He was a member also, from 1969, of the Sachverständigenrat, the body that advises the Federal Government in Germany. This responsibility lasted until 1976 when he took over the presidency of the Land Central Bank; and he was its Chairman from 1970 until 1976. In addition, he acted in an advisory capacity to African and Asian governments, and latterly spent much time in China, too.

He was offered many other professorships – including one at Munich that would have meant taking over the Ifo Institute. He was tempted, but decided on the Central Bank offer, principally because it made him an *ex officio* member of the policy-making Central Bank Council of the Deutsche Bundesbank at a time when the Bundesbank was, for all practical purposes, determining not only German but European monetary policy. This powerful position he held until 1992 when he reached retirement age.

Kloten hardly retired, however. He remained President of the Institute of Applied Economics in Tübingen until 2003, and played an active part as a Curator of the Thyssen Stiftung and the Volkswagen Stiftung encouraging research on system transformations. He also continued to attend meetings of the Trilateral Commission, which he regarded as an outstanding international body.

In England he contributed ten papers to volumes edited or co-edited by me between 1983 and 2001, with a further paper, 'Aftermath of the Reunification of Germany', to be published later this year.[2] A Roman Catholic, he felt close to the Von Hügel Institute at St. Edmund's College, Cambridge, and its then Director, the Rev. Dr F. P. McHugh, and I were happy to get him actively involved in several of their conferences, at which he was one of the most stimulating participants. Most of his English papers are concerned with issues such as the impact of innovations and globalization of financial markets on monetary policy, the role of central banks in a global competitive environment, the German reunification and currency reform of 1990, and, most of all, aspects of the European Monetary and Political Union. As a serious and unusual interest Kloten explored the role of ethics in the regulation of globalised markets.

To celebrate Norbert Kloten's 80th birthday last month, the University of Tübingen and the Deutsche Bundesbank jointly arranged a *Festakt* at Tübingen University at which the Bundesbank President Professor Axel Weber and Professor Hermann Albeck were the main speakers. Most remarkable was the fact that Norbert Kloten, close to death with cancer, still managed to write his '*Reflexionen*', a detailed account and assessment of his professional life. Sadly, he was too ill to present these 'Reflections' himself to his 350 guests, and they had to be read by his daughter Ilka Kloten.

It was a moving moment when, at the end of the paper, he was helped up from his wheelchair to address just a few words of greeting. He received a standing ovation.

***Norbert Wilhelm Kloten**, economist and banker: born Sinzig, Germany 12 March 1926; Professor of Economics, University of Tübingen 1960–76; Honorary Professor 1976–2006; Chairman, Sachverständigenrat 1970–76; President, Land Central Bank, Baden-Württemberg 1976–92, President, Institute of Applied Economics, Tübingen 1979–2003, Honorary President 2003–06; Chairman, Economic Advisory Council, Federal Ministry of Economics 1992–96; married 1953 Annemie Münzel (one son, two daughters); died Tübingen, Germany 5 April 2006.*

Notes

1. *The Independent*, 24 April 2006, pp. 54–5. Permission to reprint the Obituary is gratefully acknowledged.
2. This paper is in fact published in this volume on pages 15–21. [Editor]

Introduction

Jens Hölscher

This book is based on the papers presented at a conference held at the Anglo-German Foundation on 29 and 30 April 2005. There were close to thirty participants at each of the sessions. The rationale behind the conference was to deepen understanding of Germany's economic performance at the turn of the twenty-first century. The period under observation stretched from Germany's unification in 1990 to the death of the German Mark and first experiences with the euro.[1] Particular attention was paid to East Germany.[2] The performance of the German economy is under vigorous debate in Germany, but is less well known to an English-speaking readership. The conference aimed to bring together academics who had demonstrated their expertise in fields related to the subject. The contributors also represent the spectrum of the current academic debate as it is reflected in the public sphere in German politics and business.

In his keynote address (Chapter 1 here) Stephen Frowen summarized the dramatic economic developments that have taken place in Germany since 1946. He highlighted the way that the monumental task of rebuilding the eastern part of the country had transformed public finances, and the impact of the introduction of the European single currency and the replacement of the Bundesbank as the monetary authority by the European Central Bank. Stephen Frowen argues that the task of bringing the two parts of the country together had proved to be too great to be mastered within the confines of the euro system. This, he said, supported the arguments previously made in an open letter that he and 155 other German-speaking economics professors had published in the *Frankfurter Allgemeine Zeitung* and the *Financial Times* in February 1998. This letter called for a postponement of German entry into the Eurozone. Today, Stephen Frowen argues, Germany faces the difficulty of extracting itself from an accelerating decline. This problem, caused by structural barriers to economic growth, has been exacerbated by negative external shocks which include the high level of oil prices and the appreciation of the euro. Stephen Frowen asserts that, without the short-term interest rate tool, Germany had to find a new way out of its economic dilemma. Expansionary fiscal policy would be problematic if other European nations followed the German example, because it could prompt a monetary response from the European Central Bank that would make any actions by the government less effective. This scenario could create a crisis that would demand a break-up of the economic union or the formation of a political union. However, Stephen Frowen argues that a middle way to avoid this may be to strengthen the co-operation between fiscal and monetary authorities to overcome the inability of national governments to use interest rates to support economic activity. In Chapter 2, Norbert Kloten discusses Chapter 1 in detail and displays his insider knowledge of the currency union.

Iris Biefang-Frisancho Mariscal and Peter Howells address the issue of central bank transparency in Chapter 3, using a model that has been developed by Haldane and Read. This chapter looks in particular at the German Bundesbank and the European Central Bank (ECB), together with the Bank of England in the UK, and raises the question of whether the Bank of England really is more transparent than the German-based institutions. Popular opinion, as well as research on those (often statutory) characteristics that should give rise to the transparent conduct of policy, suggests that the Bank of England *is* more transparent. Attempts to measure transparency through the institutional characteristics of the central bank and surveys of money market traders' opinion have tended to indicate a relative lack of transparency for the Bundesbank and the European Central Bank. The institutional characteristics that are usually identified include things like publishing minutes and voting records, as well as providing public forecasts of inflation and economic growth. However, using the Haldane and Read model, and looking more closely at the behaviour of money market interest rates in the days leading up to a change in official interest rates, suggests that traders have no more difficulty reading the Bundesbank and the European Central Bank than they do reading the Bank of England. Estimation of an equation that includes a term for monetary policy 'surprises' finds that, for the period since 1992, between 8 per cent and 13 per cent of policy rate changes by the Bank of England are a revelation to traders on the day of the announcement. This compares with a policy surprise of between 6 per cent and 9 per cent for German interest rates over the whole period (January 1989 to July 2004).

The issue of whether money market traders feel more uncertain about Bundesbank and European Central Bank policy, while in fact being able to anticipate their actions correctly, was tested with the use of interest rate forecasts by private institutions, as reported in *Consensus Forecasts*. The results suggest that uncertainty regarding the 3-month euro–DM rate has risen since the ECB conducted monetary policy. However, the one-year-ahead forecasting range of the euro–DM interest rates produced more ambiguous results. For the UK there is no evidence that agents' unanimity over the money market rate has increased over time. Forecasting uncertainty, however, may not only be the result of transparency but also because it is easier to forecast the economy more generally. Results of a test for the uncertainty of forecasts for GDP and inflation in the UK and Germany over time show that there is a decline in forecasting uncertainty in the UK, but no underlying trend for Germany. Indeed, in the period since the creation of the euro, there has been some increase in the uncertainty of forecasting German GDP and inflation. This is not really surprising, given the great changes that took place at this time. This suggests that increased uncertainty over interest rate forecasts for Germany could be the result of increased uncertainty over forecasting macroeconomic variables rather than because of a lack of transparency of the European Central Bank.

Jörg Bibow's contribution entitled 'Bad for Euroland, Worse for Germany – the ECB's Record' asserts that the 'tough' monetary regime adopted by the Bundesbank and the European Central Bank resembled the action of a car driver obsessed with using the brake and being very cautious about using the accelerator: the central bank was swift to tighten policy but was reluctant to embark on monetary expansion. With the Growth and Stability Pact providing a constraint on fiscal policy, Bibow makes the case that a series of policy blunders have been responsible for the German economic slump, and that this is move a demand-related issue than the result of structural problems. Particular attention is paid to the inability of the European Central Bank to perceive that higher interest rates would not support the European single currency in the foreign exchange markets as interest parity theory would suggest. This, it was argued, was because of a time-inconsistency problem, with the market believing that higher interest rates would be unsustainable and merely increase the risk that interest rates in the Euro area would be lower in the future. The depreciation of the euro kept net export growth at the forefront of economic expansion in the Euro area and eventually, in conjunction with rising energy prices, caused some inflationary pressure. The Stability and Growth Pact did not allow automatic stabilizers to operate as the world economy slowed. Bibow says that this asymmetric type of monetary approach was successful in Germany before the introduction of the European single currency because other countries provided the economic stimulus to German growth. This allowed German exports to drive the economy forward in the face of this tight monetary stance. Now, however, with most of Europe having adopted the German position, with the European Central Bank modelled on its German predecessor, there is less scope for external stimulus. The author argues for a change in policy that would bring non-central bank and non-EU (European Union) nationals on to the Board of the European Central Bank, and would look at alternative policies, such as nominal GDP targeting in agreement with the national governments, as a means of avoiding budgetary constraints leading to high indirect taxes and tighter monetary policy.

Walter Heering's contribution, in Chapter 5, is 'Monetary Targeting by the German Bundesbank'. This contribution uses an IS–LM framework to highlight the importance of inflation expectations as a link between monetary targets and interest rate targets. Heering argues that, while the Bundesbank was successful in achieving price stability through its use of monetary targets, the relationship between money and prices is complex and depends crucially upon inflation expectations. The chapter suggests that the success of the Bundesbank, which the author discusses in some detail, was based on the fact that inflation expectations were anchored in Germany during the Bundesbank's reign. The author asserts that this stability of inflation expectations greatly facilitated the German central bank's ability to conduct monetary policy. The risk that variations in inflation expectations could cause problems for the European Central Bank's monetary policy highlights the importance of maintaining a two-tier policy system combining inflation targeting and monetary aggregates. Indeed, Heering states that the more difficult situation the European Central Bank finds itself in with divergent economies and traditions argues for a firm theoretical bridging of inflation and monetary targets, so that the European Central Bank will be more able to cope with any shocks to the system.

Khaled Soufani discusses the first part of the book by saying that while he liked the IS–LM framework presented by in Chapter 5, he questions the definition of transparency provided in Chapter 3. He argues that the uncertainty over the workings of the ECB could not be resolved by showing that they could drop hints to the market a few days before any change in policy.

Horst Feldmann's Chapter 7 is entitled From Initiating to Breaching to Diluting the Stability and Growth Pact. He outlines a comparative analysis of the German budgetary position with that of some of the other Euro area members. He argues that it was not the low rate of German economic growth that had caused Germany to undermine the pact that it had initiated. He argues that even in cyclically adjusted terms, there had been deterioration in the German budgetary position that required additional work by the German authorities. Feldmann contends that political economy can explain why the pact was breached: Germany, France and Italy each have ten votes in the Council of Ministers and have enough power to provide a blocking minority when questions of sanctions are raised. Feldmann also suggests that the regional fiscal autonomy in Germany is not sufficient to explain the breach because there is similar autonomy in Spain that has not been allowed to affect overall public finances. A comparison of the cyclically adjusted primary balance shows that fiscal loosening has tended to be pro-cyclical, which suggests that lack of political will has been the major cause of the breach.

Eckhard Hein and Achim Truger's Chapter 8 is entitled 'Macroeconomic policies, wages, developments and Germany's stagnation'. They say that there is little support for the consensus view in Germany that structural issues are responsible for the weakness of the German economy and the relatively high level of unemployment. He argued that matters often cited as being of concern, such as employment protection, benefit replacement rates, benefit duration, bargaining co-ordination and the tax wedge, have all declined in Germany in recent years, and that the difference between Germany and other nations has narrowed at a time when unemployment has risen sharply. Hein and Truger say that German macroeconomic problems are largely because policy is much tighter in Germany than in other countries. This was a result of low German inflation making the real level of interest rates relatively high, and a result of the constraints of the Growth and Stability Pact ensuring that fiscal policy could not be used in a countercyclical way. They argue that wage policy was the main domestic policy problem in Germany, with the weakness of unions and the breakdown of collective agreements preventing income growing at a pace sufficient to foster domestic demand.

Waltraud Schelkle takes issue in Chapter 9 with these two extreme views of the problems faced by Germany, arguing that the solutions they proposed were too radical. She questions the implication that policy-makers were to blame for German economic woes. She contends that there were no quick fixes, and says that Germany was adjusting gradually to its position in a new world where there was increased competition and where many other countries had learnt from German success. Rather than being the 'sick man of Europe', Germany was suffering a 'mid-life crisis' with the proposed actions of more fiscal tightening or higher wages being the equivalent of a rash Ferrari purchase or an extramarital affair.

Lothar Funk opens Part III with Chapter 10, entitled 'Current structural changes: Challenges for the German labour market and collective bargaining'. He highlights the need for the German economy to adjust to the changes wrought by globalization, ICT and demography. Funk stresses the need for a more flexible style of lifelong learning in an environment where risk for corporations had increased and demand for labour had become more diverse. He suggests that, while demand for skilled labour had increased in Germany, that for lower- skilled labour had fallen, as a result of the increased competition from abroad. The demand curve for low-skilled labour had become flatter and the level of real wages more important. This, he argues, could leave a large segment of the population without the skills necessary for many of the new jobs that were being created globally, but with a wage rate that was too high to be attractive for less-skilled activity. Funk presents figures showing that mining and quarrying employment had fallen 66 per cent in the 1991–2002 period, with agricultural employment down 38 per cent over the same timeframe. Jobs were being created in real estate and other more skilled service-sector areas. This increased flexibility required more flexible real wages and greater labour mobility. Some of these changes were already taking place, with a move towards individual wage contracts and with many more wage agreements now being effected at the plant level. The fact that wage drift had fallen sharply since the 1960s highlighted this phenomenon. Now national wage agreements were often seen as a maximum that would be negotiated downwards by individual firms.

While Eric Owen Smith agrees in general in Chapter 11 with all these observations, he contended that the German labour market was adapting to the megatrends more readily than some commentators had conceded. Examples of dampers on wage growth seem to be repeated: from the collapse of the East German engineering strike to the deals at Siemens, Daimler-Chrysler, Opel, VW and Karstadt. Flexibility in both hours worked and money wage rates, with a consequent fall in labour costs, were achieved. In addition, country-wide, part-time employment has almost doubled since 1991 to reach 30 per cent of employees. Whereas the total number of employees remained roughly stable, at 34 million, full-time employment fell to 24 million. In the west, the number of part-timers grew by 60 per cent, and in the east by 175 per cent. Mini jobs with maximum pay of 400 euro per month are, of course, included in this definition. Between April 2003 and April 2004 the number of such fringe workers increased by 1.3 million, to 6 million. Indeed, minimum wage protection was required. The capital market was much more inflexible, especially as state-owned banks were no longer permitted to give cheap loans to the small and medium-sized business sector. A market for corporate control is only just beginning to emerge. Finally, some macroeconomic policies have affected employment adversely. Unification was, of course, a political act with predictable and serious economic consequences. But it has also been suggested that French support for unification was gained at the expense of German entry into European Monetary Union (EMU), arguably at an overvalued nominal exchange rate. Moreover, the huge economic welfare burden of the Common Agricultural Policy (CAP) will continue to at least 2013 because of German support for the French policy stance.

Johannes Stephan's Chapter 12 looks at firm-specific reasons for different productivity levels among west and east German firms. He uses a unique database created through fieldwork in selected manufacturing industries. Though productivity levels have clearly converged since the initial shock of unification, productivity levels in the east remain below the level of the west and below the levels that would be accounted for by sectoral structures alone. The author takes survey evidence from manufacturing industries in both east and west and uses a matched pairs approach to reveal reasons for differences in productivity. The industries covered were machinery, furniture, cosmetics and electrotechnics. Stephan argues that management weakness, particularly lack of experience of strategic planning, was partly responsible for the lower level of productivity in the east of the country. Management factors that were designed to explain productivity differentials, such as strategic planning, marketing and communication techniques, were generally significant in most of the equations that are estimated.

Michael Kaser's Chapter 13 is entitled 'East Germany's economic transition in comparative perspective'. Kaser highlights the fact that, at a cumulative €1,200 billion, the unification of Germany represented the largest net transfer of resources ever seen from one region to another. This transfer, which accounted for a quarter of consumer demand in the Eastern *Länder* in 1998, could be assessed using the concept of 'psychic income'. This can be related to the benefit that a richer person receives in making a donation to someone poorer, whereby the richer weighs the benefit received by the poorer against the opportunity cost of surrendering resources. A survey of households in each part of the country for the period 1990 to 1997 suggest that both those in the west and those in the east consider they have lost 'psychic income'. Those in the west do not feel good about 'giving' and those in the east have a sense of second-class citizenship. Kaser went on to point out that the current western relativity in wealth and income was a comparatively recent characteristic of the German economy, but that the post-communist recession in the East had been steeper than in both the west and the neighbouring states of the Czech Republic, Hungary and Poland. Despite continuing west-to-east resource transfers, gross domestic product (GDP) growth in the east remained slower than in the west and in the three former communist states, just as transfers had failed to accelerate the Mezzogiorno in comparison with Northern Italy. Moreover, labour costs in the east were still higher with respect to relative labour productivities than in the west.

Norbert Walter's concluding (Chapter 14) is entitled 'Investment in Germany: flop or top?' He argues that despite broad short-term difficulties, Germany remained an attractive country for investment and this would start to become apparent after 2005. While German economic growth was weak and unemployment high, general scepticism was excessive. Market and cost attractions were limited in the short term, but structural reform of the economy was taking place. A new reform momentum would begin after the 2006 Federal elections. Small and medium sized enterprises had refocused business strategies to concentrate on core competences. Profits were growing strongly; P/E ratios were relatively low, while the earnings outlook was encouraging. Workers were more willing to accept lower wages and increased flexibility, and the enlargement of the European Union (EU) would maintain this pressure from abroad. None the less, the public remained very sceptical about Germany's future economic performance and this was limiting the growth of personal consumption.

Notes

1. These events are documented by S. F. Frowen and J. Hölscher (eds), *The German Currency Union of 1990 – A Critical Assessment* (London/New York: Macmillan/St Martin's Press, 1997) and J. Hölscher (ed.), *50 Years of the German Mark – Essays in Honour of Stephen F. Frowen* (London/New York: Palgrave, 2001).
2. See also J. Hölscher and A. Hochberg (eds), *East Germany's Economic Development: Domestic and Global Aspects* (London/New York: Macmillan/St Martin's Press, 1998).

1
The Post-Reunification Economy of Germany – Past, Present and Future

Stephen F. Frowen

Post-war recovery of the Federal Republic of Germany

Since the end of the Second World War, a period of six decades, Germany has experienced dramatic economic developments – not least in the monetary field. It is a period I have personally observed throughout. The first major event was, of course, a replacement of the broken down Reichsmark by the new D-Mark in terms of the currency reform of 20 June 1948. I vividly remember the moment I received my first instalment of the precious, newly issued D-Mark when a final-year student at the University of Bonn – forty, in fact, against forty of the discredited Reichsmark, the sole one-to-one exchange.

It is not a task of this conference to analyse events during the decades immediately following a currency reform that enabled Germany – or, more correctly, the Federal Republic of Germany, that is, West Germany – to start rebuilding its war-destroyed economy, vitally assisted by a new, decentralized and independent central bank, the Bank Deutscher Länder, later renamed Deutsche Bundesbank by the Bundesbank Act of 1957.

Once provided with a new and stable currency, the economic advance of the Federal Republic was startling. Problems arising over time had more to do with consequences of the increasing strength of the D-Mark requiring repeated revaluations.

By 1990, the time of the fall of the Berlin Wall and the reunification of Germany, the Federal Republic had re-emerged from the devastation of the 1939–45 War as one of the world's leading industrial countries next only to the USA, with its currency, the D-Mark, having become one of the world's strongest international transaction, reserve and investment currencies. In fact, West European countries, including the UK, later thought to benefit from the strong and stable German currency by shadowing the D-Mark in foreign exchange markets, in the hope of thereby achieving greater degree of monetary stability themselves. The Bundesbank became omnipotent, with its interest rate policy binding throughout West European markets, providing a de facto anchor currency for the European Monetary System (EMS). The EMS, set up in 1979, largely functioned through an acceptance of the Bundesbank's leading role in setting monetary policy.

The fall of the Berlin Wall and its consequences

This picture changed with the fall of the Berlin Wall and the reunification of the two parts of Germany, the economically flourishing Federal Republic of Germany in the west, and the economically ruined German Democratic Republic in the east, requiring a conversion of the GDR-Mark into the D-Mark through currency reform.[1] The next decade and a half – the period from 1990 until 2005 – witnessed the confrontation of the old *Bundesländer* in the west with the monumental task of rebuilding the new *Bundesländer* in the east. Prior to reunification, the old Federal Republic could pride itself on a per capita national debt that was the lowest among leading industrial countries, but now the national debt-to-GDP ratio began to rise astronomically, together with budget deficits of a size seldom previously experienced during the whole post-war period – all required to build up Germany's eastern territories.

A budget deficit of only 1.2 per cent of GDP for the old *Bundesländer* in 1990 jumped to 3.8 per cent in 1991 for a unified Germany; and it has remained around this level except for the five years from 1997 to 2001 when it was kept below 3 per cent. The debt quota itself stayed on average at slightly above the 60 per cent level, but jumped to 64.2 per cent in 2003 and further to 66 per cent in 2004.

Reunification, however, was, at least initially, not without short-term economic advantages. The East German population was starved of up-to-date and sophisticated Western consumer goods. This not only benefited West Germany, but also the balance of trade of other west European countries – and not least the UK's own trade figures with Germany.

The ERM crisis – a far-reaching effect

But these benefits were of short duration, and the price that had to be paid subsequently came at a time of crisis for the Exchange Rate Mechanism (ERM) in September 1992.[2] Maintaining the stability of the D-Mark required a restrictive monetary policy on the part of the Bundesbank so as to contain the inflationary pressures resulting from reunification. German interest rates eventually reached a level other member countries of the ERM felt unable to afford in view of the stagnant state of their own economies. Some in fact felt threatened enough to move into a serious recession. This applied in particular to the UK, though other major ERM members were equally affected.

This dilemma then led to the notorious meeting in Bath of the finance ministers and central bank governors in September 1992. It was handled in a most unfortunate and clumsy manner by the then UK Chancellor of Exchequer, Norman Lamont. Sterling and other major EU currencies came under considerable pressure to devalue, and the then Bundesbank president Helmut Schlesinger was subjected to unheard-of pressure from Chancellor Lamont to reduce German interest rates.[3] This attempt was resisted by Schlesinger and the Bundesbank Central Bank Council. Britain, faced with the choice of either devaluing sterling or leaving the ERM, opted for the latter, to the delight of Chancellor Lamont.

Without the sudden exit of Britain from the ERM, the UK might have remained within the system and joined the Eurozone from the very beginning, exercising its influence to introduce a greater degree of flexibility in setting ECB's monetary policy. As it is, it must be admitted that Gordon Brown, the UK's Chancellor of the Exchequer at the time of writing, has used the freedom from the restrictions imposed by the Maaastricht Treaty well and achieved substantially better economic results than the Eurozone in terms of economic growth, employment and consumer demand.

EMU, the euro and the SGP – problems for Germany[4]

The next event of fundamental importance for Germany's economic development was the establishment of the European Economic and Monetary Union (EMU) and the subsequent replacement of the D-Mark by the euro in 1999, with euro notes and coins being introduced in January 2002. In the conduct of monetary policy, now determined by the European Central Bank, the role of the once powerful Bundesbank was reduced to no more than that formerly played by the *Land* Central Banks within the Bundesbank system – just one voice and vote on the respective Central Bank Council.

The arrival of the euro, heralded as a great advance towards European unification, has not so far worked entirely to Germany's advantage. In retrospect, I am even more convinced that the open letter in the *Frankfurter Allgemeine Zeitung* and the *Financial Times* in February 1998, signed by 155 German-speaking economics professors, myself included, claiming that the euro was being brought in too soon and advocating a postponement of German entry was justified and the advice given correct. The economic differences between Germany's western and eastern territories have proved too great to be mastered within the restrictions imposed by the euro system. It deprived Germany of the power to set its own short-term interest rates, and left it subject instead to monetary policy decisions taken by the ECB, not in Germany's sole interest but, rather, in the interest of the entire Eurozone. The situation has been aggravated by the strict fiscal rules of the Maastricht

Stability and Growth Pact, stipulating a maximum 3 per cent deficit-to-GDP (gross domestic product) ratio, and a 60 per cent debt-to-GDP ratio. These rules, hard won by the German authorities themselves – especially the Bundesbank – at the time of the Maastricht negotiations, are based on the conviction that the stability of the value of money, in this case the euro, depends not least on the fiscal discipline of EMU member countries. Prior to EMU this fiscal discipline was enforced by changes in national exchange rates now excluded from within the Eurozone.

It could have been foreseen, I think, that many Eurozone countries, in particular Germany, with the financial impact of the reunification, would be unable to adhere to the Maastricht requirements on a sustained basis. This would have required restrictive measures far in excess of what would be tolerated politically. Neither could one see sanctions being imposed on other major EMU countries.

The Stability and Growth Pact effectively died in November 2003 when Germany and France blocked the European Commission's attempts to get tough on them for their excessive budget deficits. It therefore did not come as a surprise to see the Stability and Growth Pact substantially weakened by the relaxation of the enforcement procedures at the European finance ministers' meeting in Luxembourg in March 2005. All this did was to align the rules with the reality. The new 'get-out' clauses that can be cited if a country's budget deficit exceeds 3 per cent include an economic downturn, now defined as negative growth, and special factors, such as the German reunification. Furthermore, the time between a deficit exceeding the Pact's limit and the EU starting to talk about sanctions would be at least five years, and possibly longer in times of low growth. This makes it impossible to punish governments for fiscal profligacy.

Nevertheless, these changes sound quite sensible to me, provided we can be sure that countries of the enlarged Eurozone will not take undue advantage of these relaxations. Germany in any case requires sufficient fiscal flexibility at this stage, given that it is now deprived of the power to determine short-term interest rates. For the Eurozone as a whole, now left without a political sanction mechanism to prevent fiscally irresponsible behaviour, sufficient market pressure would be vital as an additional safeguard against fiscal profligacy.

Naturally, both the ECB and the Bundesbank are deeply concerned to see the Stability and Growth Pact substantially weakened.

The German economy today

Looking at Germany's economic situation at the time of writing, we see a country that has difficulty in extracting itself from an accelerating decline, marked by sluggish growth, fiscal chaos and rapidly rising unemployment. At the start of 2006 there were still over 5 million people registered as unemployed, the worst seen since the 1930s. Although statistical changes are partly responsible, these figures are truly alarming. Even the seasonally adjusted figure of registered unemployment has risen to 4.73 million in March 2006.

Nevertheless, we should remember that we have a situation where the unemployment ratio in March 2006 for west Germany alone was in fact 10.1 per cent, well above the Eurozone's average of 8.1 per cent. A disturbing unemployment ratio of 19.3 per cent in east Germany takes the rate for the whole of Germany to 12 per cent.

Germany's economic stagnation because of serious structural barriers to economic growth has been aggravated by negative external shocks. One of these is the persistently high level of oil prices and another is the strength of the euro, which in trade-weighted terms has surged against the US dollar by nearly 50 per cent since 2002.[5] Surprisingly, neither the underperformance of the Eurozone compared to the US economy nor the resulting widening of interest rate differentials have in any significant way slowed the surge of the euro.

In addition to the external shocks, Germany has also been affected by an asset price inflation of bonds and equities, partly because the ECB's expansionary monetary policy stance has created a novel form of stagflation. But this has remained without any significant effect on consumer demand.

The only positive and encouraging aspect of the German economy has been its excellent export performance, taking full advantage of favourable conditions in world markets. There have been sustained and significant increases since 1997, with exports in 2004 alone rising by 10 per cent. With a weaker rise in imports of only 7.5 per cent, the trade balance reached a new record of €156 billion rising further to €161 billion in 2005. But again, in contrast to earlier periods when German exports were the main motor towards the achievement of high growth rates, this positive effect on the German economy via an increase in domestic investment and consumer demand has so far been missing. The explanation lies, no doubt, in the fact that substantial parts of German export goods are now being produced in countries with lower wages, for assembly in Germany. This German foreign investment on a substantial scale has resulted in value added in the export sector being generated abroad rather than in Germany. However, this negative factor is to some extent counteracted by overall export growth having raised the *share* in aggregate value added in the export sector in recent years.

Future outlook

I have dealt briefly with the past and the present of the German economy. Predicting the future is problematic. I feel like Niels Bohr, the Danish physicist, who once said 'Predictions can be very difficult – especially about the future.' A similar thought, but in a more serious vein, was expressed by the celebrated but ultimately underestimated British economist G. L. S. Shackle in a letter to me in 1971, referring to the respectability economics has lost with the public 'by its over-ambition to become a mathematical exact science with absurd claims to predictive powers'.[6]

Being deprived of what used to be the Bundesbank's most powerful policy instrument virtually throughout the post-war period; that is, the setting of short-term interest rates, Germany now has to follow a new path. It faces two possible ways out of its economic dilemma: one is to take advantage of the relaxation of the Stability and Growth Pact and employ fiscal stimulation to revive its economy, accompanied by adequate measures to overcome its structural problems. The danger here is that, in response, other EU countries may follow the German example. Those who do so will further contribute to fiscal loosening. Of course, there will be others in favour of fiscal discipline in the hope of achieving growth through monetary stability – the ECB's and the Bundesbank's line of argument. The fiscal disciplinarians would then pay part of the price of the fiscal expansionists, a situation within a monetary union that would be bound to lead to discontent. If an overall fiscal expansion endangers price stability, the ECB would no doubt tighten monetary policy, thereby making the fiscal expansion less effective.

Disagreements of this kind might reach a crisis point where the solution lies in either the formation of a political union or a break-up of the monetary union. Both seem either too problematic or unrealistic. Regarding the issue of political union, the Bundesbank maintained as early as 1990 that past experiences have shown that, for a monetary union to function on a sustained basis, an all embracing political union is required.[7] The German Bundestag, too, welcomed the EMU as an important step towards closer integration, but stressed that the Economic Union should be transformed into a political union as soon as possible.[8] Furthermore, Otmar Issing, Board Member and Chief Economist of the ECB until his retirement in 2006, stated after the introduction of the euro in 1999 that 'a Europe that dares to step into a monetary union cannot shrink back from deciding on the form of its political union'.[9]

The second way for Germany to solve its economic problems would be to accept the ECB's and Bundesbank's view that higher growth rates and lower unemployment can in the long run and on a sustained basis be achieved only through monetary stability. In the best-case scenario this might have been true during a period when Germany still had its own policy-making central bank. We have to ask ourselves whether such a policy framework will also work for individual members of a monetary union where monetary policy cannot be applied in the interest of any one national government. I very much doubt that this is the case. What would help in this case would be a far closer co-operation between the ECB and the national fiscal authorities of the Eurozone than seems to exist at present, rather than one undoing the other. Such a policy does not necessarily conflict with the independent status of the ECB.

Notes

1. For a critical assessment of the Currency Reform of 1990, see S. F. Frowen and J. Hölscher (eds), *The German Currency Reform of 1990 – A Critical Assessment* (London/New York: Macmillan/St Martin's Press, in association with the Anglo-German Foundation for the Study of Industrial Society, 1997); see also H. Tietmeyer, 'Recollections of the German Treaty Negotiations of 1990' and N. Kloten, 'German Unification: A Personal View', both in S. F. Frowen and R. Pringle (eds), *Inside the Bundesbank* (London/New York: Macmillan/St Martin's Press, in association with *Central Banking*, 1998), pp. 68–109 and 110–19, respectively.
2. For a full account of the ERM crisis, see Hans Tietmeyer, *Herausforderung Euro. Wie es zum Euro kam und was er für Deutschlands Zukunft bedeutet* (Munich/Vienna: Carl Hanser Verlag, 2005).
3. See S. F. Frowen, 'Unjustified British Critique of the Bundesbank', *Central Banking*, vol. 10, no. 3, 1999–2000, pp. 40–45, reprinted in Deutsche Bundesbank, *Auszüge aus Presseartikeln*, no. 12, 8 March 2000, pp. 15–17.
4. Special attention is drawn to Norbert Kloten's views on these issues; see N. Kloten, 'European Monetary Union: Sovereignty and Hegemony', in S. F. Frowen and F. P. McHugh (eds), *Financial Decision-making and Moral Responsibility* (London/New York: Macmillan/St Martin's Press, 1995), pp. 197–205, with comments by Wim Kösters, pp. 207–212.
5. For a prediction of this sharp surge in the euro *vis-à-vis* the US dollar, see S. F. Frowen and E. Karakitsos, 'A Strategic Approach to the Euro Prospects', *Public Finance*, vol. 53, no. 1, 1998 (published 2002), pp. 1–18.
6. G. L. S. Shackle, 'Letter 196' (2.11.1971), in Stephen F. Frowen, *Economists in Discussion – The Correspondence between G. L. S. Shackle and Stephen F. Frowen, 1951–1992* (London/New York: Palgrave Macmillan, 2004), pp. 180–1.
7. Deutsche Bundesbank, 'Stellungnahme des Zentralbankrates', 6 September 1990.
8. Deutscher Bundestag, 'Entschluss des Deutschen Bundestages', 7 February 1992.
9. Issing, O., 'Staat-Markt-Währung, Elemente einer Wirtschaftsordnung in Europe', *FAZ* Lecture in Frankfurt, 20 September 1999.

2
Aftermath of the Reunification of Germany: Remarks on Stephen F. Frowen

Norbert Kloten

Comments on a Keynote Address certainly belong to a rare specimen of a contribution to an academic conference. Stephen F. Frowen provided the audience with an introduction to the Conference's topics. He and I first met in 1947, while studying economics at the University of Bonn. We have both been devoted to monetary affairs in Germany and Western Europe since the early 1970s, keeping in touch with each other regularly. Not surprisingly, we share many fundamental views, but that does not exclude a difference of opinion on a number of issues. The strong accents set by Frowen about German reunification give rise to some crucial remarks, intended primarily as amendments. His Address is focused primarily on the reunification's long-lasting effects, initiated first of all by central political measures producing long-term after-effects, especially with regard to German public finances and the labour market dilemma. I intend to show that what from today's point of view can justifiably be evaluated as the German disaster has to be judged principally as political lapses and ignorance, and not to be linked directly to reunification.

Impacts of the German Monetary, Economic and Social Union

The reunification of both parts of Germany started with the Monetary, Economic and Social Union, offered on 6 February 1990 by the Federal Republic of Germany (FRG) to the German Democratic Republic (GDR). The initiative came unexpectedly, interrupting the negotiations then taking place on *all* levels, discussing a transition of the GDR in stages, introducing step-by-step elements of a market economy, supported financially and otherwise by the FRG. Tying the East German Mark to the West German Deutsche Mark in the next phase should lead to a common currency area. The offered alternative – the creation of a union in one step – four days later was accepted reluctantly by the 'Modrow Administration' and finally legalized in the State Treaty of 18 March 1990 by a newly-elected GDR government under Lothar de Maizière.

Outstanding features consisted in the first place of points to underline that the offer and implementation of the union was at that time the only reasonable and feasible alternative. The GDR lacked a government with any authority and ability to administer the country. The population refused to obey any orders, pleaded for the Deutsche Mark and threatened to migrate to the West.

The monetary union replaced the GDR Mark by the Deutsche Mark, constituting from one day to the next a common currency area based entirely on the regulations of the West German monetary order.[1] The operation was not a monetary reform. On the contrary, such a reform would have aimed in its substance at capping the excess supply of the national currency and at the same time stabilizing the national monetary system.

The Economic and Social Union was simply *pari passu* realized by adopting West German regulations; in the case of social securities, connected with many quite often non-transparent transitory precautions. The Economic Union was never the object of any critical assessment. In contrast, the Social Union met many objections, and remained doubtful to the public. Nevertheless *nolens volens*, it was accepted by political circles as manifesting social justice in a reunified Germany. The Monetary Union was regarded as a great achievement of the Deutsche Bundesbank.

The strategic procedure of unification

Both sides of unification, the political and the economic (in a wider sense) have been contrasted fundamentally. The political procedures at all levels – national, European and international – constituted a formidable unity, simply a masterpiece of political craftsmanship. The economic performance, on the other hand, revealed severe shortcomings. But what has triggered these? To what extent were they unavoidable? How have their impacts been evaluated in the short and long run?

Most important is the fact that the sudden confrontation as the one in spring 1990 had never been experienced before. There was no clear information about the miserable state the GDR was in, despite numerous official annual reports and special studies. What prevailed were systems comparisons and excerpts of statistical data. What was not registered was that, for all practical purposes, the GDR was virtually bankrupt. The real capital stock was worn out and/or antiquated. An excessive surplus of uncompetitive industrial labour places nourished subsequent unemployment. West Germany believed in the virtues of market economy mechanisms as reliable dynamic forces of a rapid structural change and upswing in the East. The comparable model, advocated by politicians and even prominent economists, was the West German Monetary Reform of 20 June 1948, suggesting short time spans of restructuring and acceptable financial burdens.

The most fatal political decision was that reunification was financed solely by public indebtedness rather then an increase in taxation. This obviously pleased the German *Bundesländer* as well as commercial associations, which objected to anything that might jeopardize the planned reform of corporate taxes.

The entire focus on crediting at all involved levels led to public debt rising from about DM 930 Mrd (November 1989) to almost DM 2 billion five years later, while public expenditure increased from 47.3 per cent to 53.3 per cent. The Treuhandanstalt realized, instead of the privatization earnings calculated in 1991 at DM 600, a final deficit of DM 236 Mrd in December 1994. The *Fonds Deutsche Einheit*, agreed upon by the Federal Republic and the *Bundesländer* in May 1990 and regarded as a warranty for financing the reunification without tax amendments, turned out to be a fair-weather projection, even if the *Fonds* transferred up to 1994 were about 82 Mrd euro from West to East Germany. Stephen Frowen describes the financial disaster well in his Address.

Economists quite often regard a further shortcoming as even more important: the rapid rise of wages in East Germany. In their view, a lack of competitiveness in the labour market and unemployment were given a first decisive thrust as a result of the conversion rate of 1 GDR Mark to 1 DM for flow variables. The very negative impact of rising wages in the GDR is a fact. But another fact is that the government initially intended, advocated by the Deutsche Bundesbank, a conversion rate of 2:1 which would have afforded undisputed additional payments lifting net payments up to a final difference of about 10 per cent compared with a convergence rate of 1:1. Wages very soon got their main push from market forces, governed by the fact that in a common labour market borderlines cannot be drawn arbitrarily, and that labour unions as well as employers' associations were interested in agreeing to wage levels not much lower than the Western ones, consequently exceeding by far labour productivity. The situation today, heavily weighing shortcomings in the social security system, is to a certain extent a bandwagon effect, triggering the rise of wages in the East and regulations in the West.

First impacts

The fairly generous support of East Germany with central bank money became one of the sources for the rapid increase in demand supported by unaware big hidden savings of DM. Other sources were vast public transfers, rising wages and social security benefits.

The initial decisions and market reactions contributed to a commodity boom in West Germany which pushed prices up and stimulated exaggerated expectations. The Deutsche Bundesbank reacted as usual, tightening money supply, as described in Frowen's Address. Tension in relations with our partner countries in the EMS, especially with the UK, were unavoidable,[2] as was the recession of reunified Germany in 1992–4. The financial means to counteract this were blocked by transfers and so on. The private economy was hit severely, but what happened opened the eyes of many Germans to initially wrong estimates and doubtful decisions.

In 1991, both Parliament and the government ultimately introduced a special surtax, the *Solidaritätszuschlag* on income and corporation tax – known generally as 'Soli' – with a surcharge of 3.25 per cent levied in 1991–2, then abandoned by the Schröder Adminstration in 1993–4, but then reimposed in 1995 with a surcharge of 7.5 per cent. Since 1998, the Soli has been set at 5.5 per cent, collecting about 10 Mrd euro per annum. The *Solidaritätszuschlag* is a striking example of German vagueness to match financially the burden of reunification.

What became obvious in the first five years of the 1990s were the longer-lasting shortcomings of the German economic and social framework: labour market organization, the social security system and the public finance structure. What was at stake had already at the termination of the first Kohl mandate after reunification to a fairly large extent been made evident by scientific advisory boards. The recession, with its shocks, made the German population willing to accept a far-reaching reform programme, but instead politicians adhered in the main to the scheme in place in 1990. The new Kohl Administration travelled mainly along the old tracks. Even Solidarpakt I, which replaced the *Fonds Deutsche Einheit* and was in place from 1995, was implemented in order to integrate payments from West to East according to the traditional transfer mechanisms between Federal Republic, *Bundesländer* and local authorities manifested with regard to public debt instead of a principal change in financing the transfers. The Solidarpakt I provided, up to 2004, about 95 Mrd euro.

Blocked by internal disputes within the union parties were social reforms. Social rent payments were hailed as warranted. '*Die Rente ist sicher*' (pensions are secure) asserted a then very influential minister of the Kohl Administration. Even the only keen reform proposal, the Uldall tax system programme, was neutralized by the then social democratically dominated Bundesrat, but flanked by Union internal opposition. Kohl expected to win the 1998 elections by avoiding major conflicts on all fronts of domestic politics.

The main concern in this period were European affairs, especially the establishment of EMU, backed by the Growth and Stability Pact, put forward vigorously by Theo Waigel, the then Minister of Finance. But not seen – or at least disregarded – were the already virulent impacts of globalization and the common European market under the regime of a European currency area. In other words, proper initiatives were lacking to get overregulated, risk-adverse Germany into shape to match the new challenges.

A preliminary conclusion supports, in my view, the argument that the period between 1990 and 1998, not to mention 2005, cannot be regarded as a by a special causality interlocked time span, earmarked by the impacts, especially financial ones, of German reunification. At least between 1994 and 1998, the chances to readjust the main failures of the initial period were not made use of effectively. Not doing what the situation urgently required became a German habit.

Implications of the European Central Bank System

The establishment of EMU, pushed for not least by Germany – strangely enough, for some of Germany's Community partners – and heralded as a peacemaker of European political integration, weakened German influence on the European front substantially. Germany also sacrificed the DM as a previously omnipotent anchor currency in favour of the euro. Furthermore, the President of the Deutsche Bundesbank does not have a more powerful voice than his equally endowed colleagues in the European Central Bank Council whether representing a big or a small member country of the Eurozone. The former German Central Bank Council agreed – as did I – with the coming into being of the European Central Bank System when its statutes in the Maastricht Treaty reflected basic German requirements. But there were still sceptical second thoughts, as described by Stephen Frowen. The Growth and Stability Pact was regarded as an indispensable safeguard of independent fiscal policy pressure resisting stability orientated monetary policy, warranted by constitutional regulations, which guarantee the autonomy of the European Central Bank.

That Germany, together with France (who always disliked the Growth and Stability Pact) dismantled the Pact step by step is an historical mischief and a most depressing example of short-sighted opportunism. The abolishing of such a central, and in its core well-founded, political asset as the Pact was accomplished, in my view, by the fact that the former internal national stronghold of the Deutsche Bundesbank against the German government, especially the Minister of Finance, was weakened by the new organizational pattern of the Bundesbank, in particular the outstanding and powerful position of its president as its sole representative. No doubt, under the auspices of the former Bundesbank Central Bank Council with its impeccable reputation and its undisputed influence on public opinion building, the vital neglect of fiscal trustworthiness and its negative consequences for the Growth and Stability Pact would have been blocked.

Evaluating the German attitude on the European scene, I do not misjudge the extraordinary challenges of German fiscal policy. I have already shared some of the criticism of the Pact's expected performance, not trusting in particular the built-in mechanisms. Yet I also share the view of Otmar Issing, according to whom the Growth and Stability Pact, even in its new configuration, has to be applied thoroughly, still setting some limits to fiscal arbitrariness. In agreement with Issing, I am not prepared to see much virtue in a modelled co-operation between fiscal and monetary policy, specifically not a guarantee for any appropriate demand management. With regard to this issue I am certainly more conservative minded as well as more sceptically inclined than Stephen Frowen, although I too have in mind the very heavy weight of the financial burden still to be carried by West Germany.

The red–green disaster

What the Kohl Administration neglected under still comfortable conditions became a political dictate in the years of the Government of Gerhard Schröder. Schröder's Administration began under the ideological fixations of super-minister Oskar Lafontaine with back-dated measures, neutralizing the few reform initiatives of the previous government. The lop-sided German economy declined further, thereby intensifying the conflicts between employed and unemployed, between deficit-inclined public finances and the resulting rise of public debt – a burden ultimately to be carried by future German generations. Which will also have to bear the cost of eroded social security endangered by higher life expectancies, low birth rates and inadequate regulations?

Again, all this had not much to do with German reunification, even if the public and social transfers were going on and many severe structural problems in the new *Bundesländer* remained unsolved. Indeed, the main causes were political failures; specifically the inability to tackle macroeconomic problems properly. Appropriate scientific advice – as supported, for example, by the German Council of Economic Experts and the Scientific Advisory Boards of the Ministry of Economics and the Ministry of Finance, respectively – was voluntarily neglected by politicians. Other scientific advisory boards with high reputations were dissolved arbitrarily.

But the decline of the German economy, the unexpected rise in unemployment and the calamities of fiscal policy led at least to a ray of hope. The public felt increasingly that Germany was on the wrong track. Politically influential circles became aware of the fact that there was no choice but to make deep-rooted reforms. Germany, especially the public sector, has been driven by politicians, and to a certain extent by social groups, into a position where normative forces compel politics to react. With the famous dictum of Eugene von Böhm-Bawerk: economic laws outdo political power.

Chancellor Schröder with his fine sense what politically is at stake took the initiative in the new red–green coalition after he won the election with a wafer-thin margin in 1992. His new political credo vehemently pushed forward became Agenda 2010. This Agenda combined important reasonable reform elements, but lacked others and was never implemented. Vague compromises and initially hailed initiatives such as the so-called Hartz reform of the German *Bundesanstalt für Arbeit* paralyzed further the dynamic impacts generated by the first-rate performance of the German export industry on the domestic German economy. Germany remained the tail-light of Europe, with very low growth rates of GNP, decreasing real wages, labour market deficiencies and half-hearted deregulation here and elsewhere.

Germany in the mid-2000s is probably already in a situation of being a diminishing capital stock, certainly hidden by long-term structural incompatibilities which require far more than an upgraded Agenda 2010 or a similar reform programme. The 'sick man' of the German economy is apparently the public (including the social) sector. The private sector reacts remarkably well to globalization and the challenges of aggressive market performances within Europe, but even here the reactions are quite often more defensive than offensive. The latter would indeed require an adequate backing by a recovered and efficient public (and social) sector.

To sum up: the negative initial impacts of the Monetary, Economic and Social Union lie far back in the past. Admittedly, *Solidarpakt* II, since January 2005 the legal successor of *Pakt* I is still a crucial financial burden to be shouldered by the Federal Republic. The *Solidarpakt* II, guarantees the German East until 2019 total financial support of 156 billion euro. This is obviously not easy to channel into appropriate public activities as it is expressly prescribed for the *Korb* II of the Pact, according to which 51 billion euro are destined for the promotion of economic development. The experiences with former transfers are discussed controversially between those who pay and those who receive. Furthermore, the allocated financial means are, unfortunately, to a fairly large extent channelled into unsuitable public activities. Nevertheless, the paramount challenges of modern Germany reflect ongoing failures in politics in the years after the union came into being. The mismatch of the problems that had to be solved and political performance can only to a certain and limited extent be linked to the reunification of Germany.

Notes

1. See Norbert Kloten, 'German Unification: A Personal View', in Stephen F. Frowen and Robert Pringle (eds), *Inside the Bundesbank* (London/New York: Macmillan/St Martin's Press, 1998), pp. 110–19. A shortened version under the same title appeared in *Central Banking*, vol. 6, no. 2, Autumn 1995, pp. 53–8.
2. See S. F. Frowen, 'Unjustified British Critique of the Bundesbank', *Central Banking*, vol. 10, no. 3, 1999–2000, pp. 40–5 (reprinted in Deutsche Bundesbank, *Auszüge aus Presseartikeln*, no. 12, 8 March 2000, pp. 15–17).

Part I

Monetary Issues

3

Monetary Policy Transparency: Lessons from Germany and the Eurozone

Iris Biefang-Frisancho Mariscal and Peter Howells

Introduction

Since the late 1980s there has been a marked convergence in the conduct of monetary policy in developed economies. Broadly speaking, this has consisted of three phases. First, in the 1980s, a consensus emerged that the policy instrument should be a short-term rate of interest rather than any direct or quantititative control on the growth of money and credit. Second, in roughly the 1990s, governments came to accept the arguments for credibility based on the 'conservative central banker' and gave their central banks a considerable degree of independence in the conduct of monetary policy. More recently still, the argument that monetary policy outcomes are superior if policy-making is 'transparent' or 'open' has gained widespread support, though, as we shall see, what makes for a 'transparent' policy process is not universally agreed.

Given the alleged benefits of transparency, it is natural that we should want to measure and rank policy-making regimes. Much of this work has followed the independence literature by listing a number of characteristics which a priori should make policy-making clear to observers and then checking these against the actual features of individual policy regimes. Judged in this way, neither the Bundesbank, nor its successor the ECB, score very highly and yet, interestingly, judged by outcomes, the Bundesbank's conduct of monetary policy from 1948 to 1999 was the envy of all developed economies.

In the third section of this chapter we take a different, and we think more direct and relevant, approach to measuring the degree of transparency in monetary policy-making. With this test, the Bundesbank's decisions appear to have been widely understood and expected. This is consistent with the general view of the Bundesbank as a successful central bank, but undermines the argument that a specific set of institutional features is required as a pre-condition of transparency. Furthermore, we show that as far as German agents are concerned, nothing has changed significantly with the introduction of the ECB, in spite of its alleged shortcomings in communicating its policy deliberations. This leads us to question whether the popular view that policy-making is more confused or obscure under the ECB may be based on circumstances that have nothing directly to do with transparency itself.

In the fourth section we look at the possibility that agents have become more uncertain about monetary policy decisions in recent years. The logic of this is that although (in the third section) we see that agents are well able to anticipate interest rate decisions *on average*, this might conceal a widening dispersion of views about what the next move is likely to be. In the circumstances, agents will report themselves as being 'less certain' (and blame the ECB). We think that there is some evidence that agents have become more uncertain about monetary policy moves under the ECB.

Another possibility is that there has been an increase in the general level of macroeconomic uncertainty during the period. If agents find it harder to predict the course of variables that enter into what they take to be the central bank's decision rule, this will show in a widening dispersion of views about future interest rates and an increase in the proportion of agents reporting that uncertainty. In the fifth section we find that uncertainty about the future course of inflation does seem to have increased, while evidence for the other key variable, GDP, is mixed. We also find that there is some evidence that inflation uncertainty increases agents' uncertainty concerning money market rates. The implication is that it is not only the alleged opacity of ECB policy that has increased agents' uncertainty, but also short-term interest rate uncertainty is affected by uncertainty about future inflation.

But the first step, in the next section, is to look (as briefly as we can) at why transparency is expected to produce superior monetary policy outcomes. (These arguments will justify our approach to measuring transparency in the third section.) We shall also look at how the Bundesbank features in the existing transparency literature.

Transparency and the Bundesbank

One line of argument for the benefits of transparency, links it to credibility. In so far as being open about the inflation target and operating methods makes it easier for agents to hold the central bank to account, central banks have more incentive to deliver. With greater credibility, the sacrifice ratio is reduced. This is the basis of the paper by Chortareas *et al.*, 2003. A second argument is that transparency reduces noise and the possibility for error in private sector decision-making. Important here is that private sector agents understand the model of the economy with which the policy-makers are operating. This helps to anchor the public's expectations about future policy moves (Bean, 1998, p. 1796) and is the main argument behind the Bank of England's ambition to make monetary policy 'boring' (King, 1997, p. 440). If agents understand the central bank's thinking, then they can anticipate the next policy move, as though they were making policy for themselves. In these circumstances, the 'news' is in current economic developments and not in any subsequent interest rate change that the central bank might initiate in response. If this can be achieved, then monetary policy actions themselves no longer risk adding to the noise and general instability in the economy. A third argument follows from the breakdown of the policy ineffectiveness proposition. This is that monetary policy actions do have an effect on the real economy, but that the transmission mechanism often involves medium- or long-term interest rates, while the policy instrument is invariably a very short-term rate. What links the two is often said to be 'expectations', and from this it is argued that agents' expectations are more likely to be correct if they fully understand the thinking behind the authorities' actions. If all this is true, then policy transparency enhances the effectiveness of stabilization policy (Blinder *et al.*, 2001; Woodford, 2001; De Haan and Amtenbrink, 2002; Freedman, 2002).

Attempts to measure the degree of monetary policy transparency have taken three broad forms. The first, very reminiscent of the central bank independence literature (for example, Alesina and Summers, 1993), might be called the 'characteristics approach', since it lists the characteristics that seem necessary a priori for transparency (in all its dimensions) and then checks them against individual policy regimes. Such characteristics include:

- a fixed schedule of policy decision dates;
- the publication of the minutes of the meeting at which the decision is taken;
- publication of the voting record (where a committee is involved);
- a quantified inflation target;
- publication of the macroeconomic data underlying the decision; and
- an explanation of the macromodel used by the policy-makers.

A second approach is to use survey evidence. Since money-market traders have a powerful commercial incentive to anticipate central bank interest rate changes, it seems reasonable to assume that such agents will be particularly well-informed as to the principles guiding central bank decision-making, and will hold strong views on how easy it is to understand those principles.

Third, some studies have looked at the *behaviour* rather than the opinions of professional traders to see what this reveals about their ability to understand central bank thinking. Although there are many ways of doing the empirical tests, the central logic is to look at the extent to which market rates (determined by traders) anticipate the subsequent decision of central banks regarding the official rate. This is the ultimate and most direct test of the King (1997) ambition that the 'news' should be in the macroeconomic news and not in the central bank's decision.

It also addresses Daniel Thornton's (2003) reservations about the tendency to pursue transparency as an end in itself. Thornton issues a number of cautions. Prime among these is the argument that economists should view transparency as being beneficial only if it enhances monetary policy outcomes, and the possibilities for this are dependent on the objectives of policy. If, for example, stabilization was a major objective of monetary policy, then secrecy and surprise would be more likely to be outcome-enhancing than transparency. Transparency can only be relevant if price stability is the paramount objective. Even then, it is not clear that transparency is a *necessary* condition for success: 'For years, the Swiss National Bank and the Bundesbank had credibility for keeping inflation low and steady. This occurred despite the fact that neither central bank was a model of transparency' (Thornton, 2003, p. 485). If the principal objective of policy is price stability, then the ability of agents to understand and anticipate central bank decisions is one aspect of transparency that should be helpful.

Table 3.1 shows the rankings of a range of central banks as determined by a variety of the 'characteristics' studies and by two surveys. Some caution is needed in interpreting the results, since the studies vary considerably in size and range. But it is apparent that, *within each study* in which it appears, the Bundesbank comes low in the rankings (except for the Goldman Sachs survey), and the ECB ('Eurozone') also comes low in the rankings (except for the survey by Gros and Bini-Smaghi). The low ranking of the ECB is echoed,

Table 3.1 Central bank transparency – rankings by study

	Fry *et al.* (2000)	**Eijffinger and Geraats (2002)**	**De Haan and Amtenbrink (2002)**	**Bini-Smaghi and Gros (2000)**	**Goldman Sachs* (2000)**	**Waller and De Haan* (2004)**
Australia	15=	7=	–	–	–	–
Canada	13=	4	3	–	–	–
D Bundesbank	25=	–	6	5	2	5
Eurozone	–	5=	4	2	4	6
France	40=	–	–	–	–	4
Italy	12	–	–	–	–	1
Japan	5	7=	–	–	–	3
New Zealand	4	1	1	4	–	–
Sweden	1=	3	–	–	–	–
Switzerland	8=	9	–	–	–	–
UK	3	2	2	1	3	2
USA	1=	5=	5	3	1	7

Note: * = survey of market opinion.
Sources: See text.

of course, in the debate between Buiter (1999) and Issing (1999), where the former laments the ECB's decision not to publish minutes or voting records of meetings, or an inflation report.

As we said above, the third approach, focusing on the behaviour of short-term market interest rates, offers a more direct test of transparency, particularly if we see transparency as meaning the ability of agents to anticipate central bank decisions. Examples of this approach include Kuttner (2001) and Poole *et al.* (2002), who have all documented the ability of US money markets to anticipate monetary policy change; the latter showing that anticipation has improved since the Federal Reserve began announcing its target for the Federal Funds rate in 1994.

The remarkable feature of those studies that shed light on anticipation in the case of the Bundesbank and the ECB, however, bearing in mind variations in data, time periods and methodologies, is the extent of their agreement that agents understand the Bundesbank/ECB decision-making process at least as well as they do in regimes noted (in the other evidence) for their transparency. Typical is the paper by Perez-Quiros and Sicilia (2002), which makes explicit comparison between the ECB and the Federal Reserve and finds 'that markets do not fully predict the ECB decisions but the lack of perfect predictability is comparable with the results found for the United States Federal Reserve' (p. 4). In their study of Norway's central bank, Bernhardsen and Kloster (2002) found that market anticipation of policy was inferior to that of the Eurozone, but that the latter was higher than in the UK and USA. Coppell and Connolly (2003) looked at market anticipation in Australia using a methodology similar to that of Haldane and Read (2000) (see below) and compared it with other regimes including the USA, UK, Canada and Germany. The data covered the period 1996 to 2002, and thus for Germany covered a period of both Bundesbank and ECB policy-making. They found 'it [was] not possible to reject the hypothesis that the level of anticipation by the markets of a rate move in each country [was] equal'. Daniel Hardy's (1996) study for the IMF rather pre-dates the interest in transparency and is a rather oblique test of anticipation. It focused directly on the Bundesbank, without comparisons, but none the less shows evidence of German money markets having little difficulty in anticipating Bundesbank interest rate decisions. Ross (2002) is another IMF study, this time of the ECB after three years of operation. This too makes comparisons with the Federal Reserve and the Bank of England, and concludes 'That all three central banks are relatively predictable institutions with a high degree of credibility'. The study did, however, find that markets have had some difficulty in anticipating large changes, and in particular, cuts in ECB rates.

The study by Haldane and Read (2000) is particularly interesting, partly because it decomposes monetary 'surprises' into news about policy variables and policy preferences, but also because its approach has been taken up by other researchers such as Coppell and Connolly (2003) and is used in the empirical section of this chapter. Its immediate relevance here is that it compared the response to surprises of the yield curve in the UK, USA, Italy and Germany. News about policy variables shows up in movements at the short end of the yield curve, and is evidence of imperfect transparency. The sample period is March 1984 to January 1997 (so for Germany it covers only the Bundesbank regime). The results are worth quoting at some length:

> Looking first at surprises at the short end . . . these are significantly larger in the UK and Italy than in the United States and Germany. For example, in Italy the percentage surprise is between 40–80% at the short end, while in the UK it is between 30–60%. This compares with between 5–15% in the United States and Germany, pointing towards a much better defined reaction function in the latter two countries. *This seems intuitively plausible.* (Haldane and Read, 2000 p. 29; our emphasis).

In a three-way comparative study of the degree of anticipation and speed of adjustment of market rates to official rates using a GARCH model, we ourselves found that agents seemed best able to anticipate the decisions of the Bank of England, though the Bundesbank's also contained few surprises (Biefang and Howells, 2004a). Agents had more problems with the ECB. In particular, like Ross (2002), we found that they were often surprised by cuts in the ECB rate, a fact we attributed to the ECB being a relatively new institution and to very few instances of interest rate reductions from which markets could learn (see also *Financial Times*, 11 May 2001).

So, there is something strange here. On the basis of visible operating procedures, the Bundesbank and the ECB score relatively low on the transparency index. And yet the Bundesbank by reputation was the model of a successful central bank. Furthermore, tests of agents' ability to understand and anticipate central bank policy actions (the test that matters) both perform relatively well. In the rest of this chapter we go on to consider whether there may be other factors at work, giving the Bundesbank and the ECB an unwarranted reputation for opacity, when in reality agents have little difficulty in following the signals. The first step, in the next section, is to update agents' responses to Bundesbank/ECB decisions to check, first, the degree of anticipation, and second, to see whether this anticipation changes when policy is taken over by the ECB.

Policy anticipation

Agents do not have perfect knowledge of future central bank actions. There is uncertainty about the path of future macro variables and, in the absence of a published Taylor-rule or similar, uncertainty about the central bank's reaction function. Thus the conventional view is that, depending on the degree of central bank transparency, some amount of surprise will remain, which will cause a jump in the yield curve on the day of announcement. The size of the jump may be a measure of central bank opacity.

We use daily data for Germany from January 1989 until 21 July 2004. The market interest rates are the daily rates in Frankfurt for one, three, six and twelve months. This gave us about 3,890 observations on each maturity. During this period, the Bundesbank changed the discount rate twenty-two times over ten years, and the ECB changed its policy rate fifteen times in the last five and a half years. The median of the policy rate changes by the Bundesbank is 50 basis points, while the ECB median is 25 basis points. The Bundesbank only had one sign change, while the policy rate of the ECB changed sign twice.

In this section, we are interested in two questions, namely (i) what is the size of the average policy rate surprise over the whole sample period; and (ii) has policy surprise altered since the ECB took over the conduct of monetary policy from the Bundesbank. To extract some measure of policy surprise and its potential change along the yield curve, we estimate the change in the market interest rate as follows (Haldane and Read, 2000):

$$\Delta mar_{t,j} = c_j + \beta_j(L)\Delta mar_{t,j} + \lambda_j \Delta pol_t + \delta_j D99 \Delta pol_t + e_t \tag{3.1}$$

The subscript j stands for the term to maturity. The variable *mar* indicates the market rate, *pol* stands for the official rate, and *D99* is an impulse dummy with the value 1 from January 1999 onwards and zero otherwise.

Lags of the dependent variable were included to reduce serial correlation. The coefficient λ measures the average interest rate surprise over the full sample. If $\lambda = 0$, the market rate does not change in response to the change in the official rate, and policy was fully anticipated before the central bank changed the official rate. In other words, central bank policy itself is not news. Since the central bank is expected to change the policy rate in response to the change in the macroeconomic variables, market rates adjust in response to macroeconomic news, only and *before* the central bank changes the policy rate. Similarly, if $\lambda = 1$, market agents are completely taken by surprise by central bank policy, with all adjustment taking place on the day of announcement.

The coefficient δ measures the effect on mean interest rate surprises caused by the regime shift from Bundesbank to ECB. If $\delta = 0$, then there is no change in interest rate surprises as a result of the regime shift. If, as the financial press has suggested on various occasions, changes in the ECB policy rate are unexpected, then the sign of the coefficient δ should be positive. The sum of the coefficients λ and δ measures the size of the average interest rate surprise along the yield curve during the later period of ECB policy.

Table 3.2 below shows the results of Equation (3.1). The model was estimated with OLS. Since all equations have significant levels of serial correlation,

Table 3.2 The policy surprise in short-term interest rates in Germany

$Rate_j$	c	$\beta_{j,1}$	$\beta_{j,2}$	$\beta_{j,3}$	λ_j	δ_j	R^2
1 month	−0.001	0.123	0.045	−0.012	0.094	0.128	0.05
	(0.94)	(4.16)	(1.13)	(0.72)	(2.32)	(1.35)	
3 months	−0.001	0.185	0.062	0.027	0.077	0.103	0.08
	(1.17)	(6.46)	(2.45)	(1.02)	(2.10)	(1.25)	
6 months	−0.001	0.224	0.062	0.033	0.066	0.086	0.10
	(1.25)	(7.58)	(2.53)	(1.10)	(2.47)	(1.37)	
12 months	−0.001	0.207	0.030	0.029	0.058	0.089	0.07
	(1.13)	(8.64)	(1.45)	(1.07)	(2.24)	(1.46)	

Sources: European Central Bank and Deutsche Bundesbank.

the t-values in brackets in Table 3.2 are calculated on the basis of Newey – West adjusted standard errors to ensure consistency.[1] Turning first to R^2, we note that between 5 per cent and 10 per cent of the average variation in the market rate is explained by the model. The policy surprise coefficient λ is significant throughout the yield curve. Taking the sample period as a whole, between about 9 per cent and 6 per cent of a policy rate change comes as a surprise on the day of the announcement. These results indicate that the information advantage of the central bank on macroeconomic development over private agents is quite low.[2] The coefficient of the dummy variable is positive, though insignificant along the yield curve. Crucially, we do not find statistical evidence for the hypothesis that ECB interest rate decisions contain a greater surprise element than the former Bundesbank's.

Interest rate uncertainty

In the previous section we found that, on average, agents' ability to anticipate central bank monetary policy has not changed since the regime shift and that, again on average, anticipation is in fact quite high during both regimes. In this section, we look at central bank policy anticipation from a different angle. We now look at the degree of unanimity with which private agents anticipate interest rate changes by the central bank. In other words, we test whether the cross-sectional distribution of forecasting has changed. It may very well be that anticipation and implicit policy forecasting has not changed on average; however, the forecast spread of private forecasters may have altered. This effect would not show up in the estimations of the previous section.

If the distribution of cross-sectional dispersion has shifted since the ECB has conducted monetary policy, in that the range of forecasts has become wider, then this fall in private agents' unanimity indicates that private agents have become more uncertain about the conduct of monetary policy. Next, we turn to the measurement of consensus across agents' forecasts, and then we test whether there has been a change in this.

For measurement purposes, we looked at the range of forecasts of private institutions as reported in *Consensus Forecasts*. Every month, this publication shows the forecasts for, *inter alia,* the 3-month euro–DM interest rate for some twenty-five private sector institutions (although the number of institutions reporting forecasts varies somewhat during the year). The forecasts are for three and twelve months ahead. We calculated the range for the third-highest and third-lowest forecasts (which is about the 12th and 88th percentiles of the distribution) and compared it over time. Any changes in the cross-sectional distribution of forecasts are interpreted as a change in the conformity with which individual private agents forecast central bank policy. Figure 3.1 shows the annual (AnnualRange) and quarterly (Range) forecast range of the 3-month euro–DM rate.

The quarterly forecast range varies most of the time by between 0.2 and 0.6 percentage points. Between the two periods, 1994 and 1995, and 2001 and the beginning of 2002, the range is wider and falls thereafter. In 2000/1, the ECB was a new institution, which may be reflected in the initially widening and then declining forecasting spread of the money market rate. From the third quarter of 2002 onwards, the quarterly forecast range falls to, and below, its previous conventional level. The one-year-ahead forecast range has a more varied pattern. The forecast range peaked for the beginning of 1996 to 1.4 percentage points, indicating that agents' forecast uncertainty concerning interest rate predictions for 1996 was high. Agents' uncertainty fell steeply from then onwards, to about 0.6 percentage points between

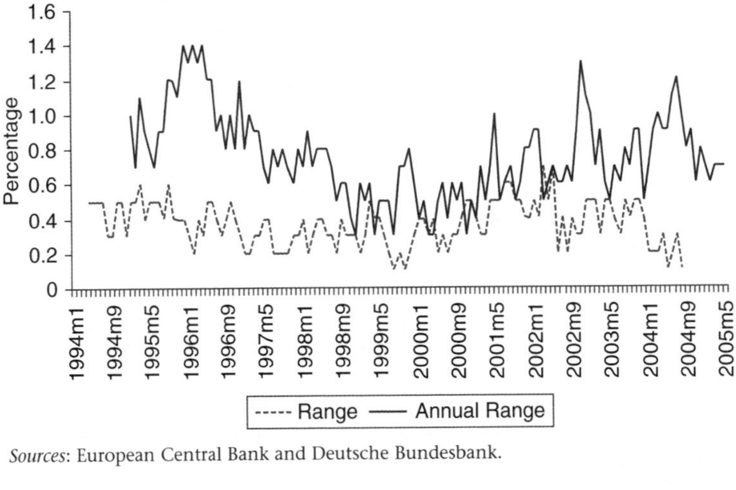

Sources: European Central Bank and Deutsche Bundesbank.

Figure 3.1 Range of quarterly and annual forecasts of 3-month euro–DM rates

mid-1998 and the end of 2000. This degree of consensus fell from 2001 onwards, where a positive trend seems to appear.

In order to test whether there was a significant change over time in agents' degree of uncertainty, and whether uncertainty changed significantly after the introduction of ECB policy, we estimated the following model:

$$Range_{t,i} = \alpha_i + \gamma_i D99 + \beta_i Trend + \delta_i D99Trend + e_t \qquad (3.2)$$

The subscript i distinguishes between the quarterly and one-year-ahead forecast range of the euro–DM rate. The dummy variable *D99* has the value 1 from January 1999 onwards and is zero otherwise. The variable *Trend* is a time trend. The coefficient γ measures the shift in the degree of uncertainty since 1999. If $\gamma = 0$, then the level of uncertainty has not changed since the regime change to ECB monetary policy. A positive coefficient γ indicates an increase in the forecasting range of private agents. The coefficient β measures the development of agents' uncertainty over time over the entire sample period. A negative β-coefficient indicates increasing forecasting consensus of the private institutions reported in *Consensus Forecasts*. The coefficient δ measures the change in degree of uncertainty over time since the institutional change. The sum of the coefficients β and δ measures the degree of agents' uncertainty over time during ECB policy. Table 3.3 shows the empirical results.

First, we turn to the results of the estimation of the quarterly forecast range (Range). We find that 12 per cent of the variation of the mean forecast range is explained by the model. Over the whole sample period, mean forecasting uncertainty declines by 0.004 percentage points per month. Since the ECB has taken over monetary policy, the downward trend in forecasting uncertainty has been reversed. For the later period alone, there is no (upward or downward) trend in the average forecasting range. The shift dummy is insignificant, so that for the ECB period, the average forecasting range (the difference between the third-highest and third-lowest euro–DM interest rate forecast) is not different from the overall sample range of 0.49 percentage points.

Table 3.3 Quarterly and annual forecasting range of the 3-month euro–DM rates

	α_i	γ_i	β_i	δ_i	R^2
Range	0.490 (17.54)	−0.171 (1.22)	−0.004 (5.11)	0.004 (2.63)	0.12
AnnualRange	1.161 (8.78)	−0.941 (5.69)	−0.012 (2.96)	0.017 (4.12)	0.45

Note: All equations are estimated by OLS and the *t*-values in brackets are calculated on the basis of Newey–West adjusted variances and covariances.
Sources: European Central Bank and Deutsche Bundesbank.

The R^2 in the second equation of Table 3.3 shows that 45 per cent of the average variation in the one-year-ahead forecast range of the 3-month euro–DM rate is explained by the model. All coefficients are significant. Over the sample period, the average forecasting range declines by 0.012 percentage points per year. This trend has been reversed since ECB policy was introduced. During the ECB regime, monetary uncertainty has been rising on average over time by 0.005 percentage points. As can be seen in Figure 3.1, the average forecasting range was high during the Bundesbank regime and declined thereafter. The average forecasting range has fallen significantly since the start of the ECB's monetary policy regime. During the later sample period, the average forecasting range has been about 0.3 percentage points, which compares with about 1.2 percentage points during the Bundesbank regime.

These results suggest that uncertainty regarding the 3-month euro–DM rate has risen since the ECB has conducted the monetary policy. However, the result is not so unambiguous for the one-year-ahead forecasting range of the euro–DM interest rate. There we found that the downward trend has become an upward trend in uncertainty since the start of ECB policy, but also that there has been a strong downward shift in the average forecasting range. Considering the results of the one-year-ahead forecasting range, we cannot generalize that ECB policy has increased agents' uncertainty. Also, it may not be ECB's *ad hoc* policy or lack of transparency that is responsible for the reported increase in uncertainty. We turn to this issue in the next section.

Macroeconomic uncertainty

In this section, we are concerned with the question of why agents have become more uncertain about forecasting the money market rate. The underlying hypothesis is, of course, that this is because the ECB conducts monetary policy relative to the former Bundesbank. However, since agents are assumed to 'guess' on the basis of a 'policy rule' which itself relates the official rate to macroeconomic indicators, uncertainty does not only arise about the coefficients in this relationship, but also about the terms relating to the coefficients. In other words, even if the central bank reaction function is well-known and well understood, it is possible that agents find it difficult to forecast relevant macroeconomic variables. If this is the case, then even for given and 'known' coefficients in the reaction function, the forecasting range of money market rates varies with the forecasting range of, say, the inflation rate. The uncertainty about future inflation (or economic growth), will then show up in a greater spread of the forecasts of money market rates.

Agents may become more uncertain about macroeconomic development, either because the economy moves away from a more stable state, or there is a turn in the business cycle, or the economy experiences shocks, to give just a few examples. Also, the establishment of new, major institutions may initially cause greater uncertainty for agents until these institutions have been established for some years.

EMU is a new phenomenon, and in this section we want to analyse whether agents found it more difficult in these circumstances to predict macroeconomic variables as inflation and GDP growth. Particularly at the beginning of the EMU, it may be more difficult for agents to predict the macroeconomy of individual countries in the 'new' area, given the uncertainty over the true degree of convergence of individual economies and how they would react to the 'one-size-fits-all' level of interest rates. Since the prediction of central bank policy moves depends to some extent on agents being able to forecast movements in the variables entering the bank's reaction function, then increasing difficulty in forecasting these variables would make agents less confident in their anticipation of policy moves.

The official interest rate is set by the central bank according to a monetary policy rule that describes how interest rate decisions link to the state of the economy, as inflation, output, employment and so on. Given this rule, agents will tend to make their guesses about future policy rates based not only on their knowledge and understanding of the central bank policy rule, but also on their ability to predict the terms in the policy rule, as inflation, output and so on. If the forecasting uncertainty of relevant macroeconomic variables has changed, this change must, via the central bank policy rule, affect agents' degree of monetary policy uncertainty.

First, we shall look at how agents' uncertainty regarding inflation and GDP growth in Germany has developed over time. Second, we shall test whether macroeconomic forecasting uncertainty has affected interest rate uncertainty.

We turn to the analysis of agents' degree of uncertainty with respect to inflation and real GDP growth. As before, we use the forecasting range, calculated as the difference between the third-highest and third-lowest forecasting value. We have monthly data for inflation and real GDP growth, each predicted one year ahead. The sample period for the inflation forecast range is from January 1995 to May 2005, and for the GDP growth range from June 1995 to May 2005. Forecasts for GDP growth refer to unified Germany throughout. Inflation forecasts are reported for West Germany until September 1997 only. Figures 3.2 and 3.3 below show the one-year-ahead inflation and GDP growth forecast range, respectively. Figure 3.2 shows that the forecasting range of the inflation rate varies between 0.4 and 0.8 percentage points until the end of 2000. After that period, an upward trend is discernible, with a generally higher level of the forecasting range.

Turning to Figure 3.3, uncertainty concerning forecasts of GDP growth is higher than inflation uncertainty. This is particularly so until mid-1998.

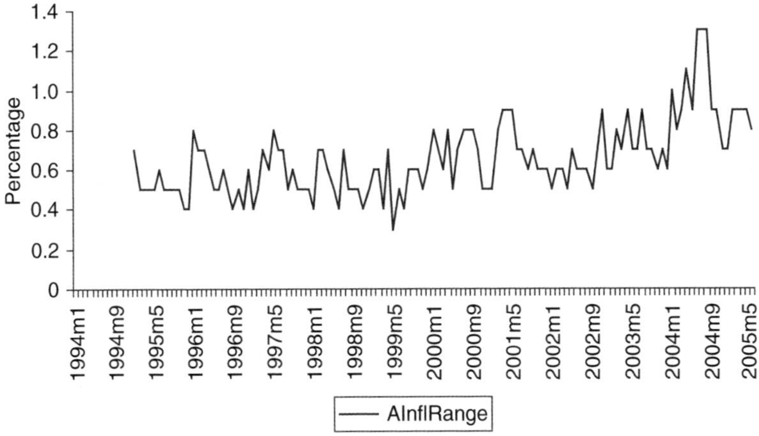

Source: *Consensus Forecast* (various issues).
Note: Calculated as the difference between the third-highest and third-lowest forecasts.

Figure 3.2 The one-year-ahead inflation forecast range

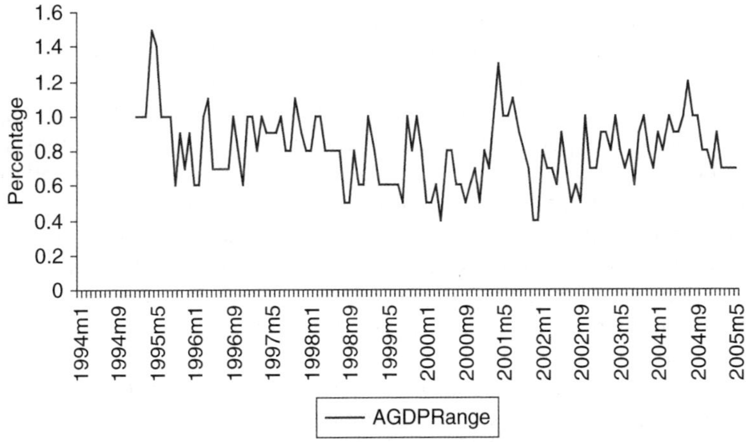

Sources: European Central Bank and Deutsche Bundesbank.
Note: Calculated as the difference between the fourth-highest and fourth-lowest forecast.

Figure 3.3 The one-year-ahead real GDP growth forecast range

From then onwards, there is a fall in the level of the forecasting range and later in the sample period, a slight upward trend.

The estimation results depicted in Table 3.4 confirm these observations. We used Equation (3.2) above, with the dependent variables changed to the one-year-ahead inflation and one-year-ahead real GDP growth forecasting ranges. Also, the dummy now has the value 1 from the year 2000 onwards,

Table 3.4 Annual forecasting range of the inflation rate and GDP growth

	α_i	γ_i	β_i	δ_i	R^2
InflationRange	0.553	−0.215	−0.0002	0.005	0.42
	(18.09)	(1.45)	(0.40)	(2.62)	
GDPRange	0.895	−0.435	−0.003	0.006	0.10
	(16.86)	(2.33)	(1.66)	(2.58)	

Note: All equations are estimated by OLS and the *t*-values in brackets are calculated on the basis of Newey–West adjusted variances and covariances.
Sources: European Central Bank and Deutsche Bundesbank.

and zero otherwise.[3] We included a further dummy to account for a change in the reporting of the inflation data from West Germany to Germany. It was insignificant and not reported here.

We turn first to the discussion of the inflation range. Over the entire sample period, the average inflation forecasting range was about 0.55 percentage points in Germany. Since the ECB regime began, there has been no change in the mean level of the forecasting range. However, we notice that while over the entire sample period there is no discernible trend in the mean forecasting range, the later period shows that average inflation uncertainty has risen steadily by 0.005 percentage points per month. The estimation results for GDP uncertainty confirm those of Figure 3.3. The average forecasting range for real GDP growth was rather high at the beginning of the sample period and fell dramatically after 2000. While there is no trend behaviour over the entire sample period, we find, as for the inflation range, that uncertainty has risen steadily since the ECB regime.

While the change in GDP uncertainty is not unambiguous from 2000 onwards, inflation uncertainty obviously has risen in the more recent period. As we discussed above, this rise in inflation uncertainty may account for some of the increase in money market rate uncertainty. In the following section, we want to test whether this is in fact the case.

We modified Equation (3.2) above and only added the one-year-ahead inflation range. We only estimated Equation (3.2) for the one-year-ahead forecast range of the euro–DM rate since we do not have inflation data that are forecast monthly or for three-months ahead. The estimation result is:

$$\begin{aligned} AnnualRange = {} & \underset{(7.20)}{1.025} - \underset{(5.45)}{0.877}D99 - \underset{(3.03)}{0.012}Trend + \underset{(3.94)}{0.016}D99Trend \\ & + \underset{(1.79)}{0.248}AInflRange \\ R^2 = 0.47 \quad & LM(10) = 36.05 \end{aligned}$$

The variables and diagnostics are defined as before, with *AInflRange* as the one-year-ahead inflation range. The values in brackets are *t*-statistics. We used OLS and the variances and covariances are Newey–West adjusted. The coefficients have not changed very much from those for the annual euro–DM interest rates as reported in Table 3.2. Inflation uncertainty increases the mean forecasting range of the euro–DM rates by 0.25 percentage points. However, this coefficient is only significant at the 8 per cent level and should therefore to be interpreted cautiously.

Conclusion

We addressed the question of Bundesbank and ECB policy anticipation from two angles. First, we estimated the average size of policy surprise during the Bundesbank and the ECB regimes, respectively. We found that during both regimes, money markets anticipated policy changes well. In comparison to other studies and our own, we found that the mean degree of anticipation for Bundesbank and ECB was as good as for the Bank of England during its inflation-targeting period (see also Biefang-Frisancho Mariscal and Howells, 2004b). Further, there was no break in the coefficients when the regime changed from Bundesbank to ECB. This part of the anticipation analysis has been concerned with the *average* degree of anticipation and implies that, on average, agents forecast well movements in the official rate.

Second, still concerned with the question of policy anticipation, we turn our attention to the cross-sectional spread of private sector policy anticipation. It is possible that mean anticipation has not changed during the two regimes, but that there has been a widening of the cross-sectional dispersion in policy anticipation. We interpret the widening of this spread as an increase in agents' uncertainty about the conduct of central bank policy. We measure the degree of cross-sectional dispersion by calculating the difference between the third-highest (about 90th percentile) and the third-lowest (about 10th percentile) private agent forecasts for the euro–DM money market rates. When we test formally, we find a clear indication that the 3-month-ahead forecasting dispersion for the 3-month euro–DM rate has risen since the ECB has conducted monetary policy. Is this rise solely a result of the ECB's opaque policy, or do other factors play a part?

In answer to this question, we find that private agents have become more uncertain about forecasting inflation. Inflation uncertainty has grown gradually since ECB has conducted monetary policy. The result of GDP growth uncertainty is more ambiguous.

In the last section of the empirical analysis, we tested whether the rise in private agents' inflation forecasting uncertainty has affected the dispersion of money market rates. We find some evidence that is so.

Notes

1. The results of the Lagrange Multiplier test are not reported here, but will be provided by the authors on request.
2. This compares with similar coefficients for the Bank of England since the introduction of inflation targeting (Biefang-Frisancho Mariscal and Howells, 2004b).
3. Agents forecast GDP growth and inflation in 1998 for 1999, in 1999 for 2000, and so on. In 1998, when the forecast was made for 1999, the ECB had not yet been established.

References

Alesina, A. and L. Summers (1993) 'Central Bank Independence and Macroeconomic Performance: Some Comparative Evidence', *Journal of Money, Credit and Banking*, vol. 25, pp. 151–62.

Biefang-Frisancho Mariscal, I. and P. G. A. Howells (2004a) 'Central Bank Transparency: A Market Indicator', *Revista Economica De Castilla La Mancha*, vol. 4, pp. 27–39.

Biefang-Frisancho Mariscal, I. and P. Howells (2004b) 'Monetary Transparency Policy: Too Good to Be True?', *UWE DP* (www.carecon.org.uk).

Bean, C. (1998) 'The New UK Monetary Arrangements: A View from the Literature', *Economic Journal*, vol. 108, no. 451, pp. 1795–809.

Bernhardsen, T. and A. Kloster (2002) 'Transparency and Predictability on Monetary Policy, *Economic Bulletin*, Norges Central Bank, p. 2.

Bini-Smaghi, L. and D. Gros (2000) *Open Issues in European Central Banking* (London: Macmillan).

Blinder, A. S., C. A. E. Goodhart, P. Hildebrand, D. Lipton and C. Wyplosz (2001) *How Do Central Banks Talk?* (Geneva: International Center for Monetary and Banking Studies).

Buiter, W. H. (1999) 'Alice in Euroland', *Journal of Common Market Studies*, vol. 37, no. 2, pp. 181–209.

Chortareas, G., D. Stasavage and G. Sterne (2003) 'Does Monetary Policy Transparency Reduce Disinflation Costs?', *Manchester School*, vol. 71, no. 5, September, pp. 521–40.

Coppell, J. and J. Connolly (2003), 'What Do Financial Market Data Tell Us About Monetary Policy Transparency?', Reserve Bank of Australia, Research Discussion Paper 2003/05.

De Haan, J. and F. Amtenbrink (2002) 'A Non-transparent European Central Bank? Who Is to Blame?' Paper presented at the Conference on Monetary Policy Transparency held at the Bank of England, 10 May.

Eijffinger, S. C. W. and P. M. Geraats (2002) 'How Transparent Are Central Banks'? Paper presented at the Conference on Monetary Policy Transparency held at the Bank of England, 10 May.

Freedman, C. (2002) 'The Value of Transparency in Conducting Monetary Policy', *Federal Reserve Bank of St. Louis Review*, July/August.

Fry, M., D. Julius, L. Mahadeva, S. Roger and G. Sterne (2000) 'Key Issues in the Choice of Monetary Policy Framework', in L. Mahadeva and G. Sterne, *Monetary Policy Frameworks in a Global Context* (London: Routledge).

Geraats, P. M. (2000) 'Why Adopt Transparency?', CEPR Discussion Paper, 2582.

Geraats, P. M. (2002) 'Central Bank Transparency', *Economic Journal*, vol. 112, no. 483, pp. 532–65.

Goldman Sachs (2000), quoted in D. Gros *et al.* (2000).

Gros, D. and L. Bini-Smaghi (2000) *Is the European Central Bank Sufficiently Accountable and Transparent* (Brussels: Centre for European Policy Studies).

Gros, D., O. Davanne, M. Emerson, T. Mayer, G. Tabellini and N. Thygesen (2000) *Quo Vadis Euro?* (Brussels: Centre for European Policy Studies).

Haldane, A. G. and V. Read (2000) 'Monetary Policy Surprises and the Yield Curve', Bank of England Working Paper No. 102.

Hardy, D. C. (1996) 'Market Reaction to Changes in German Official Interest Rates', Deutsche Bundesbank Discussion Paper No. 4/96.

Issing, O. (1999) 'The Eurosystem: Transparent and Accountable, or "Willem in Euroland"', *Journal of Common Market Studies*, vol. 37, no. 3, pp. 503–19.

King, M. (1997) 'The Inflation Target Five Years On', *Bank of England Quarterly Bulletin*, vol. 37, no. 4, pp. 431–42.

Kuttner, K. N. (2001) 'Monetary Policy Surprises and Interest Rates: Evidence from the Fed Funds Futures Market', *Journal of Monetary Economics*, vol. 47, no. 3, June, pp. 523–44.

Perez-Quiros, G. and J. Sicilia (2002) 'Is the European Central Bank (and the United States Federal Reserve) Predictable?', ECB Working Paper Series, No. 102.

Poole, W., R. H. Rasche and D. L. Thornton (2002) 'Market Anticipations of Monetary Policy Actions', *The Federal Reserve Bank of St. Louis Review*, vol. 84, no. 4, pp. 65–94.

Ross, K. (2002) 'Market Predictability of ECB Monetary Policy Decisions: A Comparative Examination', IMF Working Paper No. 02/233.

Thornton, D. L. (2003) 'Monetary Policy Transparency: Transparent for What?', *Manchester School*, vol. 71, no. 5.

Waller, S. and J. de Haan (2004) 'Credibility and Transparency of Central Banks: New Results Based on IFO's *World Economy Survey*', CESifo WP No. 1199.

Woodford, M. (2001) Monetary Policy in the Information Economy. Paper presented at the Federal Reserve Bank of Kansas City Conference, *Economic Policy for the Information Economy*, Jackson Hole, Wyoming, August 2001.

4

Bad for Euroland, Worse for Germany – the ECB's Record

*Jörg Bibow**

Overview

This chapter assesses the contribution of the ECB to Germany's ongoing economic crisis and reflects on the prospects for the euro's long-term survival in view of the experiences so far. The analysis begins with a reminder of the important fact that the Maastricht regime of EMU is essentially based on German (or Bundesbank) wisdom and policy traditions. From a German perspective, EMU was only acceptable to begin with if the country's institutions and traditions were expanded to Europe, thus safeguarding Germany's cherished 'stability culture'. The underlying presumption in all this was that, by exporting Germany's 'success story', this model would work even better, both for Europe and for Germany itself. It is argued that this premise was flawed, since it is based on a thorough misperception of why the German model worked in the past – for Germany, that is. Essentially, EMU created a huge economic area that forgoes proper demand management, instead relying on exports as its growth engine.

The chapter revisits the unification shock and supposed burden that arose from it, arguing that it was not unification but rather the chosen macroeconomic policy response to it that lastingly destabilized Western Germany and pushed the country into the vicious circle from which it has yet to emerge. Turning to the ECB's record, it is argued that the bank's policies may best be described as a series of policy blunders that pushed inflation up and GDP growth down, related to its adoption of the Bundesbank tradition of asymmetric policies.

The analysis then addresses the question of why the ECB's policies, which have been too restrictive for Euroland as a whole and are behind the prolonged domestic demand stagnation that characterizes the situation, have proved especially devastating for Germany. It is argued that the workings of some key adverse mechanisms, notably the Stability and Growth Pact (SGP), together with Germany's chosen response to the crisis – essentially;

wage deflation – are responsible for this outcome. The chapter concludes that because the ECB reneged on its stabilization mandate following Bundesbank traditions, serious deficiencies in the Maastricht regime design, with respect to fiscal policy in particular, and the irresponsible pursuit of beggar-thy-neighbour policies that run against the spirit of fifty years of European monetary integration, Euroland is today drifting apart in ways that jeopardize the long-term viability of the euro.

Of the grand idea of a German-style EMU, Bundesbank traditions, and what Maastricht really meant

The idea of establishing an economic and monetary union in Europe goes back a long way, almost to the beginning of the post-Second World War era, reaching its first peak with the famous 'Werner Plan' of 1970. It must be fair to say, though, that Germany was never at the forefront of this movement towards a single European currency. In the age-old dispute between the so-called 'economists' and 'monetarists', Germany's economics profession as well as its political authorities championed the 'coronation theory', according to which a common currency had to be the gracious final step in a drawn-out process that could only be risked if economic and political integration was firmly achieved beforehand. Germany's acclaimed guardian of monetary stability, the Deutsche Bundesbank, represented a stronghold of this view. And suspicions about the bank's fierce opposition to EMU were never far from the surface, both abroad and at home. For good reason, some would say, this influential institution was never too keen to lose its powerful grip on monetary affairs in Germany, and Europe too.

While the complacent view that what was good for Germany had to be good for the rest of Europe too may have been popular in Germany, much of the rest of Europe found Germany's monetary hegemony increasingly intolerable, and quite understandably so. In the second half of the 1980s, in the context of the 'Single Market Programme' and as the Basle–Nyborg agreement confirmed the Deutschmark's (DM's) status as the anchor currency within the 'hard EMS', the idea of replacing the unloved (outside Germany) hegemon attained new strength. Europe was lucky that not all German leaders were unsympathetic to the idea, as the Genscher memorandum of 1988 showed. Helmut Kohl's part in getting the Bundesbank aboard and the euro afloat cannot be overrated.

In any case, it was probably always clear to the German mind that, if Germany were ever to give up its beloved DM at all, the successor would have to be at least as hard, strong and sound as the DM itself ever was. From a German perspective, the prospect of a successful EMU always featured exporting the Bundesbank-cum-DM 'success story' to Europe as a *sine qua non*. The Delors Commission – with Bundesbank president Karl-Otto Poehl in charge – set the scene. And while a number of details may have been compromised on at the Maastricht negotiations of 1990–1, reflecting the fact that views and predispositions in the rest of Europe were in many cases fundamentally different, Germany got its way in the end. In a nutshell, if German monetary hegemony was to be overcome, Europe simply had to swallow Germany's conditions (or, the Bundesbank's, for its own abdication, that is).

Not only was the ECB modelled on the Bundesbank – Germany's acclaimed guardian of monetary stability provided the blueprint for the structure of monetary policy in EMU. The ECB's independence even surpasses the Bundesbank's, secured at the constitutional level rather than just by a simple law. In addition, under the Bundesbank's former chief economist, Otmar Issing, the pursuance of a 'stability-orientated' course was guaranteed too; as was the adoption of other Bundesbank traditions. The ECB's overall autocratic style and peculiar public relations is a case in point, featuring a passion for continuous public criticism of issues relating to other policy areas – paired with the standard dismissal of any criticism of its own policies and practices as an attack on its all-important independence.[1] To make the case really watertight, the ECB was to be further protected from fiscal policy by a 'Stability Pact' that would keep finance ministers' fingers firmly away from the printing press. Clearly, the presumption in all this was that, by exporting Germany's success model, this would work even better, for Europe as well as for Germany itself.

Alas, this is not the way things have played out since 1999 – which raises the question of why not. One answer stresses the role of allegedly all-pervasive 'structural problems' in Germany and across Euroland as the sole cause of all the troubles. This 'explanation' is particularly popular in Germany itself, where a tradition of 'supply-side-only' economics holds sway (for a critique, see Hein and Truger, 2005). While the emphasis on structural problems is popular among Anglo-Saxon mainstream economists too, the attitude is usually a more balanced one, with structural reform and demand management being seen as complements (Posen, 2003).

My own position is that while I would not deny the desirability of certain reforms, carrying through structural reform without proper demand management may be worse than useless. The fact is that, apart from the four-year interruption around unification, Germany has operated far below its potential ever since the early 1980s. And, for reasons to be investigated in what follows, the situation for much of the rest of Euroland is becoming increasingly similar to the German malaise. Arguably, under such conditions, structural reforms might in fact do more harm than good. Certainly, I consider assertions to the effect that structural reforms and/or fiscal consolidation *by themselves* – via alleged 'confidence effects' or whatever – would always and everywhere automatically look after sufficient domestic demand, as being no more than plain nonsense. (And, unfortunately, it is this kind of 'wisdom' that has dominated economic policy-making in Germany since the early

1980s; see Roloff, 2002). Thus the emphasis in what follows will be on the peculiar macroeconomic policies that Germany and Euroland have had to tolerate, especially the policies of the ECB.

In this regard, the key to 'stability-orientation' *à la* Bundesbank is the *asymmetry* in approach and mindset. Metaphorically speaking, the ECB acts like a driver who is quick at slamming on the brakes, but notoriously abstains from using the accelerator. While, quite obviously, this is not a recipe for smooth driving, it does beg the question of why it seems to have worked for the Bundesbank, and quite well for so long.

Essentially, it worked for the Bundesbank because – and as long as – everyone else behaved differently. In particular, the Bundesbank's peculiar driving style worked well when nominal exchange rates were stable, Germany's trading partners' inflation rates were generally higher than its own, and as the accelerator was applied skilfully 'elsewhere in the world economy' (to borrow one of those phrases the ECB coined to pass the buck). Things worked best under Bretton Woods. The situation was then almost replicated under the 'hard EMS' of the 1980s, with the rest of Europe bearing the economic and fiscal brunt of Bundesbank wisdom. In Germany's case, misconceptions about an – apparently – successful consolidation strategy of the 1980s that was to be replicated at the European level were important too.

In fact, and as an early warning of things to come, the Maastricht convergence process of disinflation-cum-coordinated fiscal consolidation saw Europe moving towards the brink of stagnation by the mid-1990s. Luckily, US 'new-era' growth and a soaring dollar provided a last-minute lifeline that allowed EMU to go ahead. Not quite so luckily, though, today's international imbalances are also partly rooted in these events.

The Maastricht Treaty meant the creation of an economic area comparable in size to the US economy, but without a proper demand management regime in place, and with certain key policy-makers' mindsets firmly predisposed against the use of stabilization policies. Ironically, exporting the Bundesbank 'success story' was doomed to failure because it had only worked in the past – and for Germany alone! – precisely because everyone else behaved differently. Hence a regime change requiring everyone else to behave just like Germany was surely asking for trouble. But Germany got itself into deep trouble even before EMU started – namely, by severe macroeconomic policy blunders in response to unification. A closer look at these mistakes offers some interesting lessons concerning events that have since been unfolding across Euroland.

Of Germany's pre-EMU history and the unification challenge: miracles and blunders, and a lasting burden

It cannot be denied that unification presented Germany with a huge economic challenge. With East Germany's capital stock in a pitiable shape, massive public and private investment for years and decades to come was the only way towards narrowing the gap in comparison to advanced economies. Luckily, West Germany was in a favourable economic position as the happy event drew near. After having grown rather sluggishly since the 1981–2 recession as a result of fiscal austerity and Bundesbank restraint, which led to weak demand, slack investment and underutilized capacity, growth of the former West German economy picked up markedly towards the end of the 1980s.

It so happened that, in 1989, when the Berlin Wall came down, there was non-inflationary and broad-based GDP growth because of strong domestic and foreign demand, which yielded high employment growth and a balanced budget, together with a trade surplus of 5 per cent of GDP. While exports, traditionally relied upon to ignite demand-led growth, performed strongly (and the oil price slump of 1986 brought a terms-of-trade boon), fiscal and monetary policies also contributed (although belatedly) to the recovery in domestic demand as a result of income tax cuts in 1986 and 1988 (and again in 1990), along with an accommodative monetary stance (in the aftermath of the 1987 stock market crash) that lasted until mid-1989.

In the years 1990–1, the former West Germany's economy coped impressively smoothly with the strains that unification put on its resources (see Bibow, 2003). Real GDP grew at a solid rate of 5 per cent in both years, and while producer-price inflation remained stable at around 2 per cent, and underlying CPI inflation was stable at around 2.5 per cent – perfectly in line with the inflation trend during the 1980s. Investment, potential output and labour productivity grew rapidly, with the result that supply-side growth was both strong and broad-based. Employment growth was evenly distributed and included people previously classified as structurally unemployed. Moreover, the influx of labour from the former East Germany provided important supply-side relief, so that general labour market pressures were abated. In addition, Germany drew on increasingly underutilized foreign resources, as reflected by the swift swing in the current account (from a 5 per cent of GDP surplus in 1989 to a small deficit in the early 1990s).

Germany's current account swing confirmed that unification also represented a great chance for Europe to remain clear of the slump that had hit, for example, the USA, the UK and Japan at that time. And Germany's stellar performance over the four-year period 1988–91, during which the alleged structural paralytic grew at a 4–5 per cent annual pace without any significant rise in *market-determined* inflation, produced the very evidence to put the structural ('eurosclerosis') myth to rest (which had been much in vogue during the 1980s too). Miraculously, it would have seemed that without any profound structural reforms, Germany was enjoying an employment boom just at a time when – for once – domestic demand was growing strongly too.

This lucky situation, which had come about by historical accident, was not to last, however. Clearly, the order of the day was to sustain growth and investment. But the Bundesbank was determined to slam on the brakes, and slam them on hard too. With Helmut Schlesinger at the helm, the Bundesbank pushed real interest rates up to 5–6 per cent in 1991, a level that was bound to crash Western Germany's economy. Subsequently, with Hans Tietmeyer at the helm, the Bundesbank even surpassed its own historical record when it eased interest rates in an extraordinarily slow fashion. From early on, though, the Bundesbank mounted pressure on the government to cut the budget deficit (Akerlof *et al.*, 1991; Smith Owen, 1994; von Hagen, 1994).

It is true that, from 1989 to 1991, the German government deliberately relied on borrowing to take up almost the whole of unification's fiscal brunt. By 1991, an overall budget deficit of €44 billion (a deficit ratio of 2.9 per cent) replaced a budget that had been balanced in 1989. Starting in 1992, the government began to introduce a series of new fiscal measures aimed at cutting its borrowing requirements. Between 1992 and 1995, a cumulative fiscal tightening occurred that was far in excess of initial borrowing requirements. According to Heilemann and Rappen (1997), by 1995, the total effect of expenditure savings and increases in taxes and social security contributions was sufficient to finance almost the whole of *gross* fiscal transfers amounting to €92 billion. Paradoxically, as it might have seemed, Germany's deficit ratio did not decline, but rose instead, reaching 3.4 per cent in 1996.

As we know today, Germany has yet to emerge from the debt trap it seems to fallen into in the aftermath of its unification. After a last-minute dash below the Maastricht 3 per cent hurdle in 1997 because of a US-sponsored export boom followed by a brief spurt of growth in 1999–2000, Germany has breached the 3 per cent limit of the Stability and Growth Pact in every year since 2002 – and is expected to continue doing so until 2007. Accordingly, for years to come, Germany is expected to cut its structural budget deficit by at least 0.5 per cent of GDP per year *no matter what*. This follows from the rules of the Stability and Growth Pact as currently interpreted, and abides by the wisdom that has guided fiscal policy in Germany and much of Euroland since the early 1990s. This wisdom asserts that one should never worry too much about possible negative demand effects of fiscal consolidation (so-called Keynesian effects), but trust that fiscal consolidation will instead stimulate domestic demand (so-called non-Keynesian effects).

From the beginning, the 'German view' (see Fels and Flöhlich, 1987; Hellwig and Neumann, 1987; Bibow, 2004d) has been at best a rather dubious story. Of course 'non-Keynesian effects' may arise in situations of financial crisis to the extent that the announcement of fiscal austerity leads to sufficiently sharp falls in interest rates. And, of course, dwarf economies such as Ireland's, for example, may be lucky enough to get away with a pro-cyclical fiscal squeeze while relying on net exports to keep the economy afloat. By contrast, in cases such as Germany's, sufficient interest rates falls can only be delivered by monetary policy to begin with, while freeloading on net exports is hazardous as it assumes that trade partners may be complacent enough to allow their trade positions to deteriorate correspondingly. Clearly, then, in Euroland's case, even more so than in Germany's, the latter is not a viable option at all, so that the whole burden to compensate public thrift campaigns clearly shifts to monetary policy alone.

In view of popular myths about the 'burden of unification' that allegedly still plagues Germany today it is important to set the record straight here. It is undeniable that unification destabilized the former East Germany's economy, even though the event may just have been the trigger for the ultimate wreckage of what was wrecked in any case. But large-scale public transfers were an *inevitable* consequence of this – the price to be paid for this historical responsibility. Transfers were needed both to cope with the resulting unemployment and to build up a First-World capital stock. The fact is that West Germany's economy coped smoothly with this challenge initially: through strong, non-inflationary growth. Another fact is that Germany could easily rely on foreign support too, since it started out from an intolerably large current-account surplus, and foreign resources were greatly underutilized. Finally, another key fact is that Germany's public finances remained on a sustainable course initially. There was thus no reason to panic: sustaining investment and growth was the order of the day.

In this context, it should always be remembered that even a permanent deficit of 3 per cent of GDP can be sustainable with a non-rising 60 per cent debt ratio, as long as nominal GDP grows at 5 per cent (Domar, 1944; Pasinetti, 1998; Bibow, 2003, 2004a). In fact, Germany was lucky enough to have a significant margin left *after* the fiscal brunt of unification had hit the budget. Figure 4.1 summarizes how Germany subsequently manoeuvred itself into a debt trap, namely by crushing GDP growth. To test whether or not the particular parameter constellation prevalent in any year would have implied a rising debt ratio, the 'stability financial balance' is defined here as the deficit ratio that is sustainable indefinitely, given the actual rate of nominal GDP growth and actual debt ratio for a particular period. As long as the actual financial balance does not exceed the stability financial balance this implies sustainable debt dynamics in the form of a non-rising debt ratio. Correspondingly, the concept of the 'sustainability gap' may be defined as the difference between actual and stability balances.

The point is that Germany's fiscal troubles were not a direct consequence of unification (that is, transfers to the East), but of plunging GDP growth in the West. Since 1993, a rising sustainability gap has opened up as Germany's consolidation efforts *no matter what* did not reduce the deficit ratio, but instead slashed the GDP growth rate.

Importantly, starting out from a balanced budget and a debt ratio of 40 per cent in 1989, there was no need for GDP growth to continue at 5 per cent and 9 per cent in real and nominal terms, respectively. My argument does not presume the perpetuation of the four-year miracle that had debunked the structural myth of the 1980s. Rather, the sad fact is that, over the course

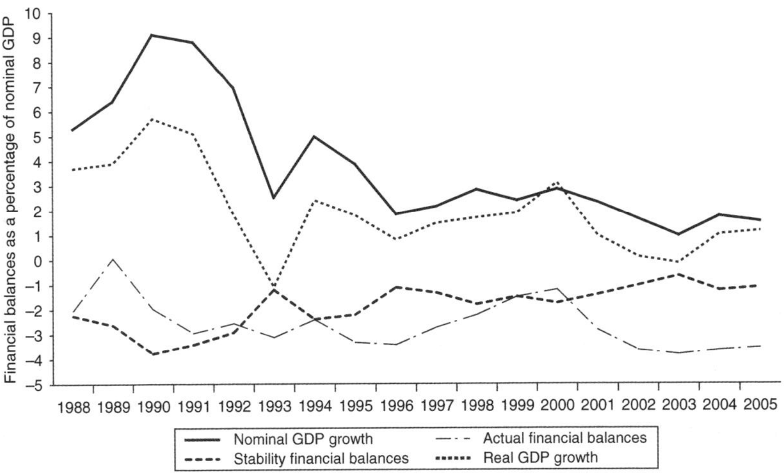

Notes: Financial balance for 2000 excludes one-off UMTS revenues. Deficit ratios not exceeding 'stability balances' (MSB) imply public debt sustainability (defined here as a non-rising debt ratio).
Source: OECD, *Economic Outlook*, No. 77.

Figure 4.1 No end to austerity, no end to crisis: Germany's vicious circle of thrift and stagnation

of the 1990s, GDP growth was in fact crushed to zero and below 2 per cent in real and nominal terms, respectively. This came about not because of sudden structural problems or external shocks, but as a consequence of remarkably inept macroeconomic policy-making. While the Bundesbank inflicted a long span of ultra-tight money that lasted from the early to the mid-1990s, Theo Waigel turned the fiscal rudder hard right in 1992, embarking on the fateful path of senseless public thrift campaigns from which Germany has never strayed since. Together, these macroeconomic policies massively and persistently destabilized *Western* Germany's economy.

Puzzlingly as it may have seemed, even as domestic demand was crushed and stagnation set in, inflation proved to be rather persistent: staying 'above 2 per cent' until 1995. This was the result of a phenomenon that I dubbed 'tax-push inflation' (Bibow, 1998), more of which will be heard in a moment. At this stage, the important point is that while wreckage in the east and a corresponding 'burden of unification' was quite inevitable, this second burden in the west was not. As a consequence, however, EMU began with united Germany in particularly poor shape.

Of Bundesbank legacies and ECB blunders with no end

No doubt the Bundesbank's legacies confronted the ECB with a formidable challenge. After the monetary overkill in response to German unification, followed by very sluggish interest-rate cuts, which had left Germany in the doldrums by the mid-1990s, the Bundesbank proved all too keen to raise interest rates in October 1997. By that time, Germany was just emerging from stagnation – thanks to US-sponsored export growth. When only a little later Germany was then hit by the Asian and Russian crises, the Bundesbank exemplified the peculiar tradition referred to above: it simply refused to cut interest rates, in contrast to central banks such as the US Fed and the Bank of England. And on top of its failure to ease, the Bundesbank's communications even invited DM appreciation – in time for the euro to start from what was soon seen as too high a level, and with Euroland's supposed economic powerhouse dubbed the 'sick man of the euro'.

Fragility at the core was not the only challenge, though. Another was divergence. The interest rate convergence process granted Euroland's periphery a nice boost to public finances, as the interest burden shrank. In addition, sharply-falling interest rates in traditional high-interest-rate countries boosted asset prices and domestic demand. Some parts of Euroland thus experienced robust domestic demand growth in the late 1990s, while Germany became ever more reliant on net exports (Bibow, 2001b). Both fragility and divergence have since become worse, as will be discussed further below. Before this, however, we need to address the ECB's role in bringing about the current EMU crisis.[2]

Indeed, the bank's performance since it took over its monetary reign from the Bundesbank can best be described as a series of policy blunders that pushed inflation up and GDP growth down. The first blunder consisted of a clash between the ECB and financial markets, which resulted in a marked depreciation of the euro. The second featured the bank's refusal to cut interest rates and boost growth, which resulted in a productivity slump that pushed up unit labour costs and core inflation. And the third blunder witnessed the ECB's continued refusal to cut interest rates to stimulate a recovery, which saw fiscal policy, constrained by the Stability and Growth Pact, shifting into reverse gear, prompting increases in indirect taxes and administered prices; quite apart from further destabilizing the Eurozone. This series of policy blunders pushed inflation up and left Euroland in a very fragile shape when the dollar's depreciation prevented the world's second largest economy from free-riding on external demand yet again.

As to the euro's plunge, the ECB's role was one of acting as a twofold propagation mechanism as the bank's words and deeds provoked market opposition. I can be brief on the bank's confusing words. Its first president was legendary for his gaffes. No less important was that Mr Issing's monotone 'price stability above all else' anthem was way out of tune with the climate in financial markets at the time: one of growth enthusiasm, with inflation risks not seen as presenting any serious threat. So when the ECB backed up its confusing words with all-too-clear actions, nearly doubling interest rates in less than a year, the markets simply took fright, preferring policy-makers that were perceived to be more growth-friendly.

Interestingly, the risks and foreseeable consequences of *euro-weakening interest rate hikes*[3] were clearly spelled out by no other than the European Commission, vigilantly observing in its 2000 review of the EU economy: 'To the extent that the depreciation in the euro is due to cyclical divergence between the euro area and the United States, a rise in interest rates in an attempt to support the currency could even backfire if it was perceived as stifling the euro-area recovery. The risk of creating an even more unbalanced growth pattern with weak domestic demand and higher export growth would be serious' (European Commission, 2000: 71). Similarly, the BIS's Annual Report (2001, p. 89) observed that: 'On balance, market participants may have considered the Eurosystem's monetary policy stance to be excessively tight inasmuch as it may have negatively influenced the outlook for euro area growth.' Meanwhile the OECD (2001, p. 106) referred to a 'countervailing impact of interest rates on exchange rates via growth expectations' and an 'unpleasant monetary policy dilemma' (p. 118). Notice that the ECB managed to push inflation up while choking domestic demand through its aggressive rises, as Figure 4.2 summarizes.[4]

Inflation *above* 2 per cent then seemed to excuse the ECB's subsequent refusal to cut rates as fast as it had raised them, nicely illustrating the Bundesbank tradition of 'quick to hike, slow to cut'. Between November 1999 and October 2000, the ECB raised rates by 225 basis points, nearly doubling policy rates within less than a year. It then stood by as domestic demand, quite predictably, plunged after mid-2000. The ECB's commentaries show that the bank was not just 'out of touch' with financial markets, but also with developments in the economy.[5] As the euro's plunge extended the

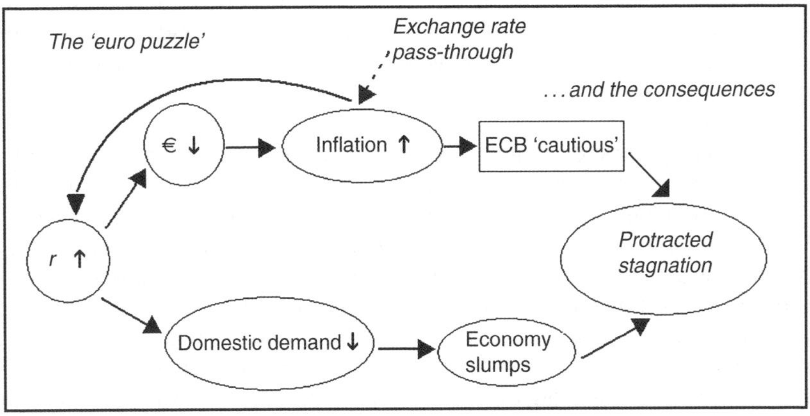

Source: Author's construction.

Figure 4.2 Slamming on the brakes, crashing the euro . . . and more

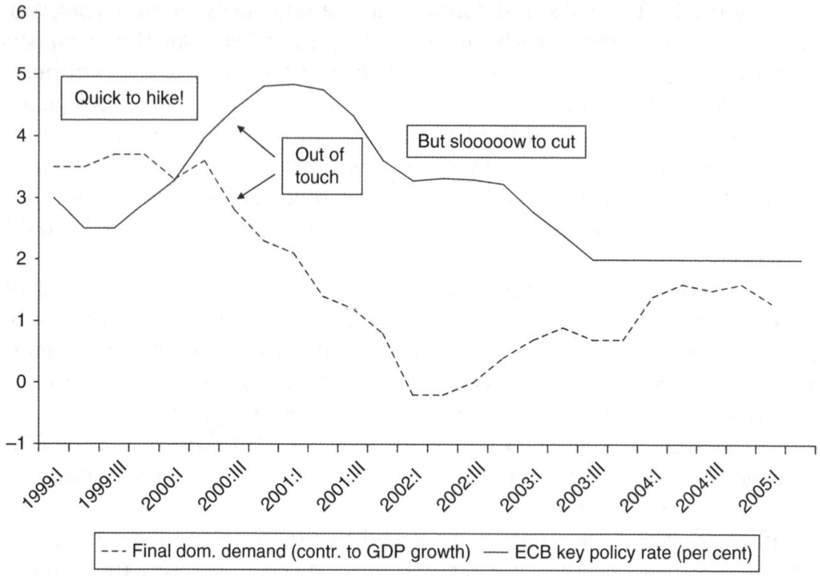

Source: Eurostat, ECB.

Figure 4.3 Asymmetric and out of touch with markets and the economy

export boom, domestic demand – seemingly unnoticed by the ECB – tanked (see Figure 4.3).

The trouble is that the ECB's 'wait and see' attitude (when it comes to easing) then provoked a severe productivity slowdown and a corresponding rise in unit-labour costs. Facing falling sales business was under pressure to keeping margins up. While the euro's plunge pushed up headline inflation through magnifying the price effects of high oil prices and rising import prices more generally, blunder No. 2 saw to it that core inflation followed suit in 2001.

Of course, protracted stagnation and rising unemployment are bound to cause budgetary troubles. And this is where the ECB's blunder No. 3 comes in. A sound monetary policy-maker internalizes fiscal policy. Given Euroland's fiscal regime, it was clear from the start that the ECB had to shoulder the bulk of the stabilization burden – or face the consequences of a destabilized economy. The IMF's head at that time, Horst Koehler, even reminded the ECB of this textbook wisdom when he explained that monetary policy would be 'the first line of defence'. Mr Duisenberg responded that he had never heard of that ('Duisenberg defends holding rates steady', *Wall Street Journal Europe*, 9 October 2002).

As refusing to listen to outside advice is held to be a virtue at the ECB – and as an always welcome opportunity to 'prove its independence' too – it should not be overlooked that it was the resulting protracted stagnation that has caused inflation to stay stubbornly above 2 per cent ever since. A conspicuous gap has opened up since 2001 between headline inflation and what may be seen as *market-determined* (as opposed to government-determined) inflation. Rises in indirect taxes and administered prices, reflecting finance ministers' desperate but vain attempts at keeping budget deficits below 3 per cent, led to an upward distortion in headline inflation of around 0.5 percentage points by 2004. While, individually, such measures only give rise to one-off price-level shifts, a continuous series of such measures can give rise to a continuous rise in general prices and significantly distort measured *inflation*. In fact, without 'tax-push inflation' the ECB would not have failed on its price stability mandate since 2001.

Figure 4.4 reminds us that a similar phenomenon could be witnessed in Germany in the first half of the 1990s (Bibow, 2005). At that time too, tax-push inflation was behind conspicuous inflation persistence in a stagnating economy. Meanwhile, however, the disease has spread across Euroland. In addition, Figure 4.4 also shows a measure of core inflation (core2) that excludes energy, food, alcohol and tobacco, apart from administered prices. After its recession-driven peak in 2002, underlying inflation in Euroland has declined sharply (reaching 1.2 per cent by mid-2005); reflecting 'historically low' wage inflation. No doubt this would make any properly cautious central bank's 'deflation alert' flash red.

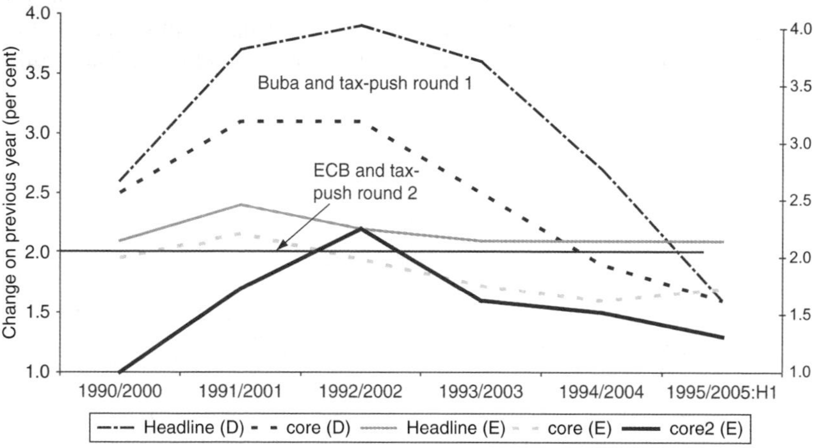

Notes: West Germany: 1990–4, core inflation measure by GCEE and Weeber (1998); Euroland: 2000–4, core inflation excludes proxy for tax-push inflation (ECB, 2004)
Sources: ECB (2004); Weeber (1998); SVR.

Figure 4.4 Déjà-vu: consumer prices and 'tax-push' inflation in Germany and Euroland

How the Maastricht regime has played out – spreading the 'German disease'

Figure 4.5 summarizes the actual play-out of the Maastricht regime over recent years. At the heart of the current EMU crisis is a counter-productive interaction between fiscal and monetary policies, featuring tax-push inflation as the key symptom in a macroeconomic policy blunder that has left the euro area stranded in stagnation. Courtesy of the ECB, Euroland has become stuck in a stability-orientated vicious circle, with headline inflation persistently *above* the set limit of 2 per cent because of tax-push inflation.[6] Notice how Euroland's two key 'stability-orientated' institutions, the SGP and the ECB, have thereby shot each other in the foot: as the ECB reneged on its growth mandate and failed to counter properly the symmetric shock of 2000–1, budget deficits of more and more member states began to exceed the 3 per cent threshold by 2002; finance ministers' desperate campaigns of frugality, in turn, have then not only further destabilized Euroland, but also kept inflation above the 2 per cent threshold ever since, too.

Much to its own surprise, Euroland is today finding out that emulating the Buba 'success story' of asymmetric 'management' of domestic demand, while fiscal policy is no longer allowed to take up the slack, in fact means the opposite of the promised land of stability and growth. With the exception of Ireland and Spain, domestic demand has plunged and seems set for subdued growth or protracted stagnation – the spreading of the 'German disease'. Accordingly, by mid-2005, there were few countries left that were not struggling with the 3 per cent limit of the SGP, excessive deficit procedures having been initiated against Germany, France, Italy, Portugal and Greece. Public frugality for years to come is in the pipeline across Euroland. And, according

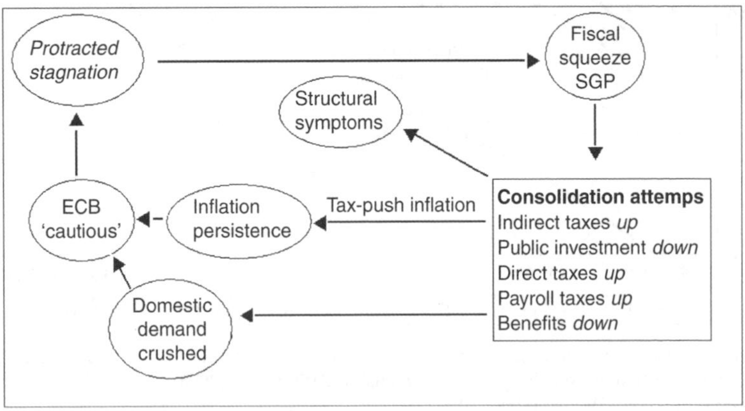

Figure 4.5 Getting stuck in a 'stability orientated' vicious cycle: play-out of Maastricht regime features tax-push inflation

to the 'German view' – but the German view only – this will continue to stimulate domestic demand growth.

While this may seem to contradict popular excitement about President Bush's 'irresponsible' tax cuts since 2001, in truth, Germany's and Euroland's fiscal positions are already in a worse state than that of the USA; despite – or because of? – frugality no matter what. Recall that the sustainability of public finances crucially hinges on GDP growth. As Figure 4.1 above shows, in Germany's case, public finances are on track for a continuous sharp rise in the debt ratio. In 2003, when Germany's nominal GDP growth crumbled to barely 1 per cent, the country's (close to) 4 per cent deficit ratio implied a steady-state debt ratio of 400 per cent! Even with slightly higher nominal GDP growth, courtesy the rest of the world, Germany's fiscal position remains in the doldrums; particularly as privatization revenues, which have helped to close many a hole en route so far, are set to dry up by next year.

In Euroland's case too, nominal GDP growth has meanwhile fallen far below the implicit Maastricht norm of 5 per cent. In 2005, the land of the euro saw nominal GDP grew a mere 3.2 per cent. With a deficit ratio of close to 3 per cent, Euroland was thus on course for a debt ratio of nearly 100 per cent! By contrast, while the USA may have a higher deficit ratio of around 4 per cent, its debt ratio is rising only slightly – thanks to nominal GDP growth of around 6 per cent. As Domar (1944) taught us more than half a century ago, growth is the key to public debt sustainability. Europe's taxpayers are paying a high price indeed for the ongoing fiscal folly.

But the real trouble is that signs of learning from mistakes have yet to emerge from Frankfurt's Eurotower, where confusion continues to reign as the ECB's top officials never seem to tire of congratulating themselves. It is noteworthy that back in 2001 the world's most independent central bank often excused its conspicuous refusal to cut interest rates by arguing that occurrences in the USA were of little importance, since 'the euro area is a large economy in which economic developments are determined mainly by domestic factors' (ECB, 2001a, p. 5). After years of domestic demand stagnation, Mr Trichet appeared to look for help elsewhere when he referred to the following 'normal sequence of events' in an interview: 'Growth starts with exports, then passes on to investment and then to consumption. That is the normal sequence for Europe in this phase of the cycle' (*Financial Times*, 22 April 2004).

And for a time Euroland even seemed lucky enough to freeload yet again on external stimuli in the first half of 2004. But this free ride was cut short by the euro's sharp appreciation. Beware, though, in blaming the strong euro (or external shocks) for Euroland's troubles. In truth, Euroland's GDP growth benefited significantly from net exports in the years 2000, 2001 and 2002. Only in 2003 did net exports leave a dent in Euroland's GDP growth. Over 2004 as a whole the strong euro then merely made sure that Euroland would be left behind by the global growth train pulled along by the USA and China, and harvest what it had sown itself.[7] For Euroland's problems are purely homemade: macroeconomic policy inflicted protracted domestic demand stagnation: the German disease, that is.

Once again exemplifying its peculiarly asymmetric driving style and habit for being out of touch with the economy, the ECB adopted what the markets perceived as a 'tightening bias' in September 2004 (*Financial Times Deutschland*, 8 September 2004). Just as the export boom was faltering and with domestic demand as sluggish as ever, the ECB was getting ready to slam on the brakes. This peculiar state of affairs continued until April 2005 (*International Herald Tribune*, 5 April 2005). Barely back to a neutral stance, the ECB was then not pleased when even the OECD (2005) advised that a 50 basis points cut would be appropriate in view of domestic demand stagnation.[8]

The ECB's position is based on its view that interest rates are 'historically low' already and *therefore* cannot be a hindrance to growth – as the bank repeats *ad nauseam*. It is all too obvious that this view ignores Knut Wicksell's fundamental insight that the absolute level of the market rate of interest is not an adequate indicator of monetary stance, because what matters is its level relative to the equilibrium rate. To really boost growth in a situation of stagnation and unemployment, the central bank has to push the market rate well below the level that would merely sustain the current situation. Deliberately kicking the accelerator down, however, is totally foreign to the ECB's mindset. In the ECB's view, 'cautiously' releasing the brakes (after slamming them hard, for whatever reason) is all it takes to move forward – as price stability *causes* growth (and if not, structural problems are surely to blame).

Curiously, in its efforts to resist outside pressures to ease policy, the ECB even argues that doing so would undermine confidence and push bond yields up. Effectively, the ECB thereby admits that Euroland may already be in a 'liquidity trap'. This is truly an embarrassing excuse, though, since manoeuvring the economy under its stewardship into a liquidity trap is generally seen as the ultimate blunder that a central bank can possibly commit.

Be that as it may, if it were really true that nominal interest rates cannot fall any further, Euroland would have to place its hopes for lower real interest rates on rising inflation (while wage trends and the possibility of more euro strength, if anything, point in the opposite direction). A closer look at Germany's situation today is in order here – the country that seems to suffer more than most under the Maastricht regime.

Why Germany suffers more

A key premise and expectation of a German-style EMU was that, by exporting Germany's success model, this would work even better, both for Europe and for Germany itself. It is clearly not working for Euroland, and it was shown above that this failure can largely be blamed on the ECB's reneging on its obligation to counter the symmetric shock to domestic demand that has left Euroland stranded in protracted stagnation. It also comes at no surprise that exporting the Buba 'success story' has undermined its working at home. But why are things even worse for Germany than for Euroland overall?

Even in Germany, some commentators have realized by now that Germany is today facing higher real interest rates than much of the rest of Euroland, when previously the country used to enjoy the (anchor currency) benefit of generally having the lowest rate. The German Council of Economic Experts also addressed this issue in its Annual Report of 2004/5. And, as Figure 4.6 shows, there is no denying the fact that Germany's traditional competitive advantage as to the relative levels of interest rates in Europe was turned on its head – *by EMU*, it seems.

Some commentators are then quick to jump to the conclusion that the ECB's excellent monetary policies are simply less good for Germany than the Bundesbank's used to be. This view misses the point on two counts. For one thing, the ECB's policies were clearly too restrictive not just for Germany, but also for Euroland as a whole (just as the Bundesbank's used to be inappropriate for EMS member countries as a group, one may add here). For another thing, if it really were just an incidence of the 'one-size-fits-all' problem, any excitement would be surprising as the issue was well

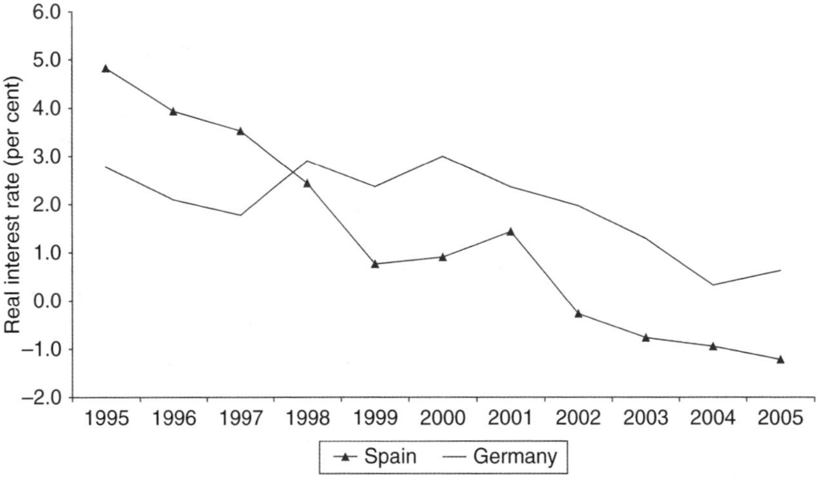

Note: Proxy used here for real short-term interest rates are the three-month money market rates deflated at national (headline) CPI.
Source: OECD, *Economic Outlook*, No.77, June 2005.

Figure 4.6 Germany's competitive advantage turned on its head

understood *ex ante*. It was agreed that, at any time, a common monetary policy is generally more suitable for some regions than for others. Hence the general question was, and remains, how this diversity in monetary policy impact might best be compensated for, so that it does not lead to divergence.

The *key fact* is that the workings of the Maastricht regime, together with Germany's chosen response to its troubles, have aggravated rather than alleviated those forces of divergence that were to be expected from the 'one-size-fits-all' problem.

To begin with, however, an important aspect in the turning on its head of Germany's traditional monetary competitive advantage during the 1990s is that it in fact originated from *two* sources. One was the convergence of nominal interest rates towards German levels that started in earnest in 1995. But no less important was another, which preceded it: the ERM crises of 1992–3, which saw a sharp appreciation of the DM against most European currencies, with Germany suffering a corresponding loss in competitiveness and slowdown in export growth. Arguably, this occurrence more than anything else prompted German 'supply-side-only' instincts that the proper response to the situation was to restore its competitiveness eroded by these events through a strategy of wage underbidding (euphemistically called 'wage restraint' (*Lohnzurueckhaltung*).

In this regard, it is common today to refer to the sharp rise in Germany's relative unit-labour costs in the aftermath of unification. And it is popular to then justify the decline in Germany's relative unit-labour costs since the mid-1990s as a reversal of this 'shock'. A number of points are relevant here. First, referring to all-German data overlooks that much of the rise in unit-labour costs over 1990–2 reflected developments in eastern Germany and does not explain massive job losses in the west during the 1990s. Second, as far as western Germany is concerned, much of the rise since 1992 was caused by the 1993 recession and protracted investment slump that ensued, depressing productivity growth accordingly. For neither workers nor unions are to blame when macroeconomic policies inflict such supply-side damages (repeated by the ECB for Euroland since 2001). In fact, wage inflation in the west exceeded the implicit Maastricht norm of 5 per cent nominal GDP growth only briefly and slightly (peaking at 6 per cent in 1991). This occurred in the context of high productivity growth and after a prolonged period of 'wage restraint' during the 1980s. Wage inflation quickly fell back to around 3 per cent during 1993–5, and to 'historically low' levels thereafter (to zero by 2004).

Third, as to the ERM crises of 1992–3, arguably, these – belatedly – merely compensated for the competitiveness gains Germany had accumulated during the 'hard EMS' era through its strategy of 'wage restraint', delivering relatively lower inflation and sizeable DM depreciation in real terms over the course of the 1980s. Explanations of the ERM crises feature the fact that real exchange rates no longer reflected fundamentals. And recall that, on the eve of unification, West Germany had a current-account surplus of 5 per cent of GDP, much of which had its counterpart in corresponding deficits among its European trading partners.

Arguably, then, there was never any basis for the idea that Germany should set out to restore the competitiveness loss that occurred during the first half of the 1990s. In order to balance West Germany's external position and prevent intra-European imbalances from escalating even further, the DM had to appreciate markedly; as it did, in fact, do in 1992–3. Unification did not change this need for readjustment. Rather, for all-Germany a current account deficit for years or decades to come was to be expected, simply reflecting a partial reliance on foreign resources in the rebuilding of the eastern German economy. (Witness the external positions of the new EU members today.) Obviously, however, this is not at all what has happened. Instead, all-Germany is today experiencing soaring trade and current-account surpluses. This implies that (hypothetical) west German surpluses have reached phenomenal dimensions, reflecting that (hypothetical) west Germany's competitiveness is probably the envy of China and the rest of Europe, not to mention the USA![9]

This has not helped Germany all that much, though, and relatively high real interest rates are certainly part of that story. Since 1995, wage inflation across Euroland has succumbed to a 2.5 per cent trend – as a tribute to German 'stability culture'. Hence 'wage restraint' 1980s-style does not work any more. So Germany goes for zero today! (And below zero tomorrow?) In addition, as the 'German view' on expansionary fiscal contraction has become the norm and pro-cyclical fiscal tightening is applied across Euroland today, Germany can no longer free-ride on fiscal laxity elsewhere in Europe to compensate for its own austerity. Hence the German economics profession with its fine memories of the 'successful' consolidation of the 1980s is at a loss. Alas, being at a loss does not seem to stop the country from administering itself ever more of the same medicine (Kromphardt, 2003).

It is this mixture of policies that lack any firm basis in theory or evidence, together with certain adverse mechanisms the EMU regime change has brought about, that are causing havoc in Germany's economy. Above all, the 'Instability and Stagnation Pact' (Bibow, 2001a) has turned out to be an amplifier of divergence. Recall: given the 'one-size-fits-all' problem, the issue was how to compensate those forces of divergence stemming from it. In fact, the 'stupid' pact means that those in deepest trouble already will face not less but more fiscal austerity to augment the wreckage incurred.

It is thus no surprise that the phenomenon of tax-push inflation is especially prominent in Germany's case; and bound to gain new impetus with the scheduled 2 percentage point rise in VAT in January 2007. A drastic decline in public investment is another. In recent years, Germany's net public investment has even turned negative. The country is quite literally letting its infrastructure rot! Given the notorious commonplace of 'today's deficits as tomorrow's taxes' that dominates Germany's economic policy debates and talk shows alike, it is ironic that Germany is proving that there is no better way to burden our children and grandchildren than to inflict senseless public thrift upon us. To describe this absurd situation I propose the following hypothesis: the more we refrain from spending on the right things (like infrastructure, education, research and development) in our desperate attempts at balancing the budget no matter what, the more we end up spending on the wrong things (for example, unemployment) – without actually borrowing any less, or even more. In fact, by lastingly depressing GDP growth the debt burden is becoming heavier!

To illustrate what is at issue for Euroland here, compare the cases of Germany and Spain (see Figure 4.7). Just as Germany started as the 'sick man of the euro' in 1999, thanks to the macroeconomic policies discussed further above, Spain experienced a domestic-demand-driven boom, courtesy of the interest rate convergence process. Germany's wage inflation has succumbed to its depressed economy and peculiar instincts, with income stagnation causing consumption stagnation, which is further aggravated as relatively high real interest rates depress asset prices and the ongoing fiscal squeeze crushes disposable incomes. Spain's wage inflation is holding up well, with income growth underpinning consumption and investment, which are further stimulated as relatively low real interest rates boost asset prices, and the budgetary boon of high growth keeps the 'stupid' pact as

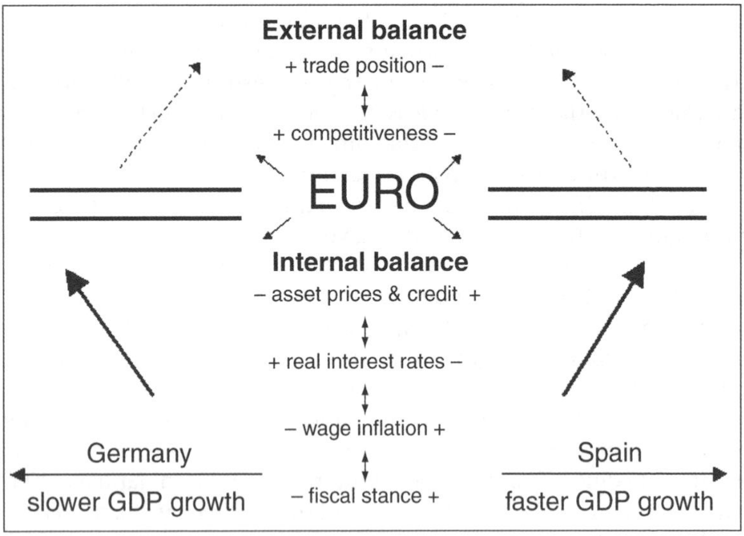

Figure 4.7 Partners drifting apart until...

the then EU commission president called it, at bay, and even provides room for tax cuts. Not surprisingly, intra-Euroland imbalances are soaring: as Germany's external position improves, Spain's deteriorates. This is alleviated to a small extent by the fact that Spain is a recipient of EU funds while Germany is a net payer, itself another aspect of the absurdity of the whole situation.

Beware: this comparative analysis is not meant to distract from the key fact that the 'German disease' has meanwhile spread across much of Euroland (with Spain as a rare exception), reflecting the fact that the ECB's policies were too restrictive not only for Germany, but for Euroland as a whole. What the analysis shows is that it is the inherent workings of the Maastricht regime together with Germany's chosen response to its troubles that are making the ECB's policies even worse for Germany. In fact, fragility and divergence are getting worse across Euroland – thanks to the peculiar design of German-style EMU and Germany's 'stability culture'. And in all this, Germany is still leading the pack, its economy having effectively been split: export champion abroad, but zombie economy at home. There are some important lessons for EMU here.

A vicious circle that has wrecked Germany and may sink the euro too

Watching the spreading of the 'German disease' with amazement, the rest of the world sees a rudderless economic giant drifting along, hoping for strong enough export currents to pull it along. Since its peak in March 2005, the euro has come back markedly against the US dollar, towards a level of 1.20. This easing of monetary conditions seems to have saved the ECB from cutting interest rates. Many observers currently place their bets, once again, on exports, as Euroland's rescue line and motor of growth. The rest of the world cannot be pleased about this, especially in view of soaring global imbalances. Nor can anyone who is really interested in the long-term survival of the euro project, for while external risks keep on growing along with global imbalances, recognizing the fact that Euroland's troubles so far have been purely home-made has been further postponed.

In fact, policy debates in Germany and Euroland remain trapped in the dogma of frugality and 'stability', which means that stagnation and decline stay on the cards, and the problems of fragility and divergence are set to get worse. Even international observers seem to have largely given up on any prospect of a belated use of macro stimuli, and place all their hopes on those easily invoked but rarely seen miracles that 'structural reform' allegedly unleashes. No doubt Germany's case offers clear evidence that structural reform combined with 'anti-demand policies', if anything, undermine confidence and weaken rather than boost growth.

Just as a prolonged fiscal tightening is in the pipeline across Euroland for years to come, pressures for 'wage restraint' seem to be boiling over. The Netherlands is learning the hard way that a repeat of the 'Dutch miracle' of the 1990s (Bibow, 2001a) is hard to come by when German wage inflation is zero. But the view prevails that Italy – recently dubbed the 'real sick man of the euro' – sinned in granting itself luscious wage inflation of around 3 per cent, for which it will have to endure chastisement in future years.

Truly, wage inflation of 3 per cent is anything but excessive. It corresponds to German-style 'wage restraint' of the 1980s, and it is also far below the implicit Maastricht norm of 5 per cent nominal GDP growth. It is only made excessive by the wage-underbidding practices of others – the true sinners in this sad game of passing the buck. Essentially, EMU is being undermined today by exactly those policies that fifty years of European integration had anxiously tried to prevent: competitive devaluations.

Yet, as Germany's example has shown, wage deflation drives up real interest rates and triggers other destabilizing forces. If others followed suit, divergence within Euroland might diminish, but fragility would increase. Moreover, if the ECB is right that 'historically low' nominal interest rates cannot fall further, across the board 'wage restraint' will primarily tend to drive up real interest rates across Euroland. As J. M. Keynes taught us a long time ago: nominal wages controlled by social partners are the wrong instrument – the wage unit merely anchors the price level; if it does.

What all this means is that euroization may still turn out to be a rather brief chapter in Europe's monetary history (which is often interpreted as a natural response to Germany's unification). Beware, though, of blaming the mess on the usual suspects – who were always lacking the right 'stability culture', as we (Germans) always knew. In Germany's case, a sharp appreciation of a new DM against, say, a new lira would merely wipe out the benefits of Germany's beggar-thy-neighbour policies of the recent past, just as the ERM crises of 1992/3 belatedly compensated for the wage-driven divergences of the 1980s. Behind all this lies a thorough misapprehension of why the German model worked in the past (for Germany, that is). The model cannot work for Euroland as a whole – no matter how deafening the structural waffle might yet become.

Notes

*This chapter was presented as a paper at the Conference 'Germany's Economic Performance: From Unification to Euroisation' in London on 29 April 2005. I thank the participants for their comments and RaeAnn Moore for computational assistance.

1. See Henning (1994), Kenen (1995) and Dyson and Featherstone (1999) on the route to Maastricht. See Bibow (2004b) on Bundesbank history and the intellectual origins of the Maastricht regime. In this context, it is quite extraordinary that Otmar Issing should try to paint this regime as having anything to do with the

views of Walter Eucken on sound 'Ordnungspolitik' (see Issing, 2004). Discretionary interest rate policies by uncontrolled central bank politicians are totally alien to Eucken's scheme. One might then just as well assert that Keynes's key insight was that fiscal policy is always and everywhere ineffective.

2. See Bibow (2004c) for a more detailed analysis of the ECB's record.
3. See Bibow (2001b, 2002) on the time-inconsistency hypothesis of the euro's plunge.
4. Note that I use interest rates here as shorthand for the whole transmission mechanism of monetary policy rather than the interest-rate channel alone. While some researchers seem to doubt the effectiveness of monetary policy, the ECB's (2002) research on the transmission mechanism has revealed a strong impact of interest rates on domestic demand, primarily investment.
5. For example, in February 2001, as global growth was clearly slowing and the US Federal Reserve had embarked on fast-track easing a month before, the ECB declared: 'While this deceleration will have some dampening effects on euro area net exports, the euro area is a large economy in which economic developments are determined mainly by domestic factors. Overall, the fundamentals in the euro area remain broadly favourable' (ECB March 2001a, ECB, 2001b, p. 5). Confirming this assessment in the ECB argued that 'at this juncture, there are no signs that the slowdown in the U.S. economy is having significant and lasting spillover effects on the euro area' (p. 5).
6. I focus here on the short-run aspect of stagnation-cum-inflation persistence. While this vicious circle itself can easily cause hysteresis, as another popular measure, Euroland's senseless thrift campaigns feature cuts in public investment, which cause even more clear-cut long-run damages.
7. While net exports' contribution to GDP growth was zero in 2004 overall, the enormous export boom during the first half was probably key to the temporary acceleration of domestic demand at the time.
8. The OECD made its position public at the press conference on the release of its *Economic Outlook*, No. 77, in which the organization is free to offer its independent view. It is of some interest that the OECD's explicit call for lower interest rates was not repeated in the annual survey on the euro area. This sparked some speculation that this was because of pressure from the ECB and European Commission, as those being assessed apparently have a say in what the verdict should be (FTD, 14 July 2005). We probably have to conclude, then, that the independence of tax-payer-funded central bank politicians has precedence over the independence of tax-payer-funded research.
9. Suffice here to mention a peculiar debate on Germany's supposed 'basar economy', which deserves the very comment that Keynes used to describe the so-called real balance effect: 'really too fantastic for words and scarcely worth discussing'.

References

Akerlof, G., A. Rose, J. Yellen and H. Hessenius (1991) 'East Germany in from the Cold: The Economic Aftermath of Currency Union', *Brookings Papers on Economic Activity*, vol. 1, pp. 1–87.

Bibow, J. (1998) 'Geldpolitik als Inflationsursache?', in A. Vilks and B. P. Priddat (eds), *Wirtschaftswissenschaft und Wirtschaftswirklichkeit* (Marburg: Metropolis), pp. 15–78.

Bibow, J. (2001a) 'Making EMU Work: Some Lessons from the 1990s', *International Review of Applied Economics*, vol. 15, no. 3, pp. 233–59.

Bibow, J. (2001b) 'Easy Money through the Back Door: The Markets Versus the ECB', Working Paper No. 323, Annandale-on-Hudson, NY: The Levy Economics Institute.

Bibow, J. (2002) 'The Markets Versus the ECB, and the Euro's Plunge', *Eastern Economic Journal*, vol. 28, no. 1, pp. 45–57.

Bibow, J. (2003) 'On the "Burden" of German Unification', *Banca Nazionale del Lavoro Quarterly Review*, vol. 61, no. 225, pp. 137–69.

Bibow, J. (2004a) 'Fiscal Consolidation: Contrasting Strategies and Lessons from International Experiences', Working Paper No. 400, Annandale-on-Hudson, NY: The Levy Economics Institute.

Bibow, J. (2004b) 'Investigating the Intellectual Origins of Euroland's Macroeconomic Policy Regime: Central Banking Institutions and Traditions in West Germany after the War', Working Paper No. 406, Annandale-on-Hudson, NY, The Levy Economics Institute.

Bibow, J. (2004c) 'Assessing the ECB's Performance since the Global Slowdown: A Structural Policy Bias Coming Home to Roost?' Working Paper No. 409, Annandale-on-Hudson, NY, The Levy Economics Institute.

Bibow, J. (2004d) 'Haushaltskonsolidierungsstrategien im Vergleich – Warum die deutsch-europäische Fiskalpolitik versagt', *Intervention*, vol. 1, no. 2, pp. 75–106.

Bibow, J. (2005) 'Germany in Crisis: The Unification Challenge, Macroeconomic Policy Shocks and Traditions, and EMU', *International Review of Applied Economics*, vol. 19, no. 1, pp. 29–50.

BIS (2001) *71st Annual Report* (Basle: BIS).

Domar, E. (1944) 'The burden of the Debt' and the National Income', *American Economic Review*, vol. 34, no. 4, pp. 798–827.

Dyson, K. and K. Featherstone (1999) *The Road to Maastricht: Negotiating EMU* (New York: Oxford University Press).

European Central Bank (ECB) (2001a) Editorial, *Monthly Bulletin*, February. European Central Bank (ECB) (2001b) Editorial, *Monthly Bulletin*, March.

European Central Bank (ECB) (2002) 'Recent Findings on Monetary Policy Transmission in the Euro Area', *Monthly Bulletin*, October, pp. 43–53.

European Central Bank (ECB) (2004) 'The Impact of Developments in Indirect Taxes and Administered Prices on Inflation', *Monthly Bulletin*, January, pp. 27–8.

European Commission (EC) (2000) 'The EU Economy: 2000 Review', *European Economy*, Brussels.

Fels, G. and H.-P. Fröhlich (1987) 'Germany and the World Economy: A German View', *Economic Policy*, vol. 2, no. 1, pp. 178–95.

Heilemann, U. and W. Rappen (1997) *The Seven Year Itch? German Unity from a Fiscal Viewpoint*, Research Report No.6 Economic Studies Program (Washington, DC: American Institute for Contemporary German Studies at Johns Hopkins University).

Hein, E. and Truger, A. (2005) 'Whatever Happened to Germany? Is the Decline of the former European Key Currency Caused by Structural Sclerosis or by Macroeconomic Mismanagement?, *International Review of Applied Economics*, vol. 19, no. 1, pp. 3–28.

Hellwig, M. and M. J. M. Neumann (1987) 'Economic Policy in 'Germany: Was There a Turnaround?', *Economic Policy*, vol. 2, no. 2, pp. 105–45.

Henning, C. R. (1994) *Currencies and Politics in the United States, Germany, and Japan* (Washington, DC: Institute for International Economics).

Issing, O. (2004) 'On the Primacy of Price Stability', ECB Press Release, Prager Frühlings-Vortrag, 10 June.

Kenen, P. B. (1995) *Economic and Monetary Union in Europe: Moving Beyond Maastricht* (Cambridge, Cambridge University Press).

Kromphardt, J. (2003) 'Lohnpolitik bei möglicher Deflation', *Wirtschaftsdienst*, vol. 8, pp. 501–8.

OECD (2001) *Economic Survey on the Euro Area* (Paris: OECD).

OECD (2005) *Economic Outlook, No. 77* (Paris: OECD).

Pasinetti, L. (1998) 'The Myth (or folly) of the 3% Deficit/GDP Maastricht "Parameter" ', *Cambridge Journal of Economics*, vol. 22,pp. 103–16.

Posen, A. (2003) 'Is Germany Turning Japanese?', Washington, DC: Institute of International Economics, Working Paper No. 03–2.

Roloff, O. (2002) 'Fiscal Policy in Germany from 1970 to 2001. The Unfulfilled Promises of Dogmatism', *Konjunkturpolitik*, vol. 48, no. 2, pp. 147–68.

Sachverständigenrat (SVR) (2004) *Jahresgutachten zur gesamtwirtschaftlichen Entwicklung 2004/05* (Annual Report) (Stuttgart: Metzler-Poeschel).

Smith Owen, E. (1994) *The German Economy* (London/New York: Routledge).

Von Hagen, J. (1994) 'Monetary Union and Monetary Policy: A Review of the German Monetary Union', in P. Siklos (ed.), *Varieties of Monetary Reforms: Lessons and Experiences on the Road to Monetary Union* (Dordrecht: Kluwer Academic Publishers), pp. 219–43.

Weeber, J. (1998) 'Der staatliche Einfluss auf die Verbraucherpreise', *WISU*, vol. 10, pp. 1066–74.

Media

Financial Times Deutschland (FTD) (2004) 'Zinswende ohne Anlass' (L. Zeise), 8 September.

FTD (2005) 'Notenbanker lobt deutsche Wettbewerbsfahigkeit' (M. Schieritz and R. Atkins), 12 July.

FTD (2005) 'Eichel gesteht desolate Finanzlage des Bundes ein' (B. Marschall), 13 July.

FTD (2005) 'OECD bestreitet Einknicken vor Brussel und EZB' (M. Schieritz), 14 July.

International Herold Tribune (2005) 'ECB Itches to Raise Rates, But Why?', (Carter Dougherty), 5 April 2005.

Wall Street Journal Europe (2002) 'Duisenberg Defends Holding Rates Steady', 9 October.

5

Monetary Targeting by the German Bundesbank: Some Reflections on Conceptual Issues

*Walter W. Heering**

> [T]he basic challenge of monetary policy is to anchor expectations
> (Adam S. Posen, 2000, p. 396)

> For a credible central bank [one which owns the public's belief of being able and willing to achieve price stability] in a large currency area, monetary policy becomes relatively easy
> (Peter Bofinger, 2001, p. 114)

Two aspects in the performance of the German Bundesbank stand out: first, its remarkable success when measured against its main goal – price stability. Second, that since 1974 up to the takeover of its mandate by the Eurosystem in 1999 it almost exclusively (apart from the Swiss National Bank – SNB) stuck to what has been labelled 'monetary targeting'. Do these two aspects bear any relationship to each other? This is the question I will try to answer in this chapter. To put it briefly: I think that such a relationship indeed exists, but it is far more complex than is usually perceived. In particular, there seems to be a mutual causality. While monetary targeting was probably one important reason for the Bundesbank's success, especially in the first ten years, it was this success in turn which allowed the Bank to retain its specific monetary targeting framework, even in periods when almost all central banks abandoned it. Monetary targeting by the Bundesbank survived not only two oil shocks and a period of high turbulence in the world economy and the international financial system, but also what appears to be the greatest shock for the German economy after the Second World War – reunification of East and West Germany.

---

* Data provision by the Deutscha bundasbank is gratefully acknowledged.

Some stylized facts

Let me first provide you with some details on the Bundesbank's performance. Its success in terms of price stability is, I sense, uncontroversial. Just look at Figures 5.1 and 5.2. The first one plots annual inflation rates in the German Federal Republic (after 1990, both parts of Germany together) and in Switzerland between 1948 and 1998. Both lines move very closely, although the Swiss data seem to be more volatile than the German.

For Germany, Figure 5.2 shows actual inflation and inflation targets (implicit in monetary targets) as well as the trend lines of both series. Remarkable is the closeness of the two trend lines, indicating the success of the Bundesbank to bring inflation rates gradually down to the normative value set by the Bank. Table 5.1 broadly confirms these results: both Bundesbank and SNB succeeded in maintaining medium-term inflation rates by monetary targeting at about the same level as during the low-inflation period in the 1950s and 1960s. Moreover, variability of inflation rates was reduced significantly in both cases; in that respect the Bundesbank seems to have been even more successful than its Swiss counterpart (see Georg Rich (1997) for an exploration).

Next I compare these findings with corresponding data from other countries, which also attempted monetary targeting for some time. Among others, these include Canada (1976–82), the UK (1976–96), the USA (1975–92) and (possibly) Japan (1978–2005). The respective targeting periods in these cases

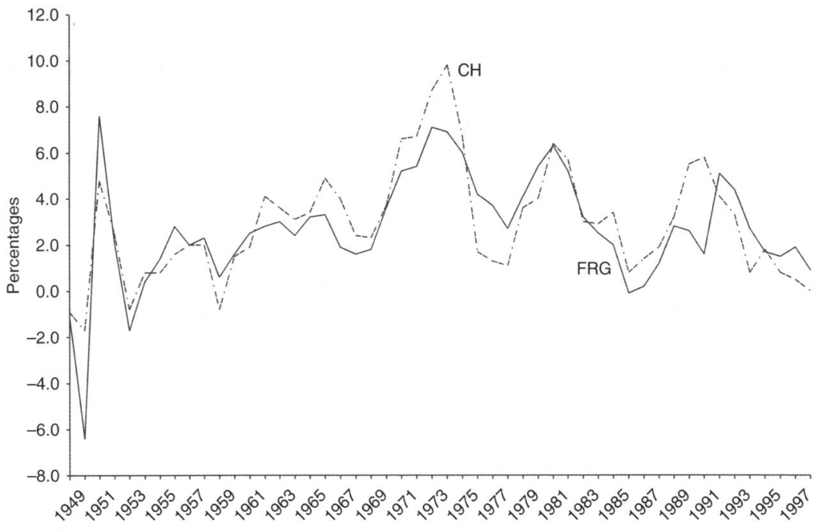

Sources: Statistisches Bundesamt (FRG); Schweizerische Nationalbank (CH).

Figure 5.1 Inflation in Germany and Switzerland, 1949–98 (annual changes of CPI, per cent)

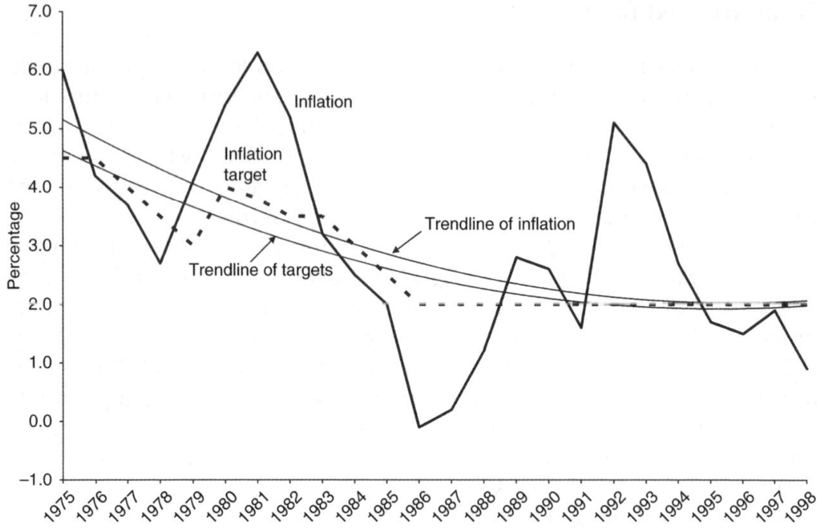

Sources: Statistisches Bundesamt; Deutsche Bundesbank; Bernanke and Mihov (1997).

Figure 5.2 Actual inflation and inflation targets in Germany 1975–98

are generally not well defined. The countries experimented with several approaches and switching to and from monetary targeting appeared gradually over time rather than at some specific date. Moreover, Japan is a special case altogether. Most of the time, the Bank of Japan operated with a variety of targets, for monetary aggregates among others (Kopcke, 2002; Rhodes and Yoshino, 2004). Accordingly, some authors have described the Bank of Japan (BoJ) as a monetary targeter (Bernanke and Mishkin, 1992), while others have not (Frey *et al.*, 2000; Higo, 2000).

Even so, the results documented in Table 5.1 are instructive. In all countries apart from Japan inflation rates during monetary targeting were on average much higher than during the whole post-war period; Canada's record in this respect is particularly bad. Japan, on the other hand, managed to bring its inflation rate over the monetary targeting period almost down to zero. With regard to the variability of inflation (measured either by the standard deviation or by the coefficient of variation) monetary targeting is also associated with mixed evidence, at best. From these observations we may conclude that something might have been wrong with the policy; at least with the way it was implemented.

Apart from measuring the success of the Bundesbank by realized inflation rates, we may consider its performance regarding monetary targets themselves. This kind of assessment usually leads to a negative judgement. For some authors, not even the Bundesbank was able to implement monetary targeting properly, while others maintain that the Bank acted in practice like an inflation targeter rather than a monetary targeter. Gerlach and Svensson

Table 5.1 Consumer prices inflation in selected monetary targeting countries

	Germany	Switzerland	UK	USA	Canada	Japan[b]
Annual percentage change of CPI: 1949–98[a]	2.7 (2.41) [0.90]	2.9 (2.44) [0.83]	6.2 (4.93) [0.78]	3.9 (3.14) [0.80]	4.2 (3.46) [0.81]	2.3 (4.78) [2.03]
	1975–98	**1975–98**	**1976–96**	**1975–92**	**1976–82**	**1978–98**
Annual percentage change of CPI: monetary targeting period[a,c,d]	3.0 (1.79) [0.60]	2.9 (2.00) [0.69]	7.4 (4.96) [0.66]	6.0 (3.20) [0.53]	9.7 (1.77) [0.18]	0.3 (2.19) [7.79]

Notes: [a] Geometric mean; standard deviation (...) and coefficient of variation [...] in brackets. [b] Japan's CPI jumped by 72 per cent from 1948 to 1949. Therefore the first year was dropped from the sample in this case. Including 1949 would alter the figures to 3.3 per cent (geometric mean), 10.95 (standard deviation) and 2.92 (coefficient of variation). [c] The definition of the monetary targeting period in the respective countries is somewhat arbitrary. All countries in the sample first had an introductory phase where monetary targeting was practised rather informally. Also the end date of the period is not always clear-cut. Here I take the period as the one for which the central bank (and/or the government) publicly announced monetary targets for whatever money aggregate. This period ends if monetary targets are no longer published or if the central bank officially declares it is abandoning monetary targeting, whichever of the two events comes first. The Fed, for example, is still legally obliged to publish monetary targets. However, Chairman Alan Greenspan declared publicly in February 1993 their de-emphasising (Blinder, 1998, p. 29). In view of this, monetary targeting in the USA is here taken to end in 1992. Still others consider the period 1979–82 as the Fed's active 'monetarist' experiment (Friedman, 1996). On the other hand, the British government adopted inflation targeting in 1992, but the Bank of England still proceeded to publish targets for the monetary base and M4 up to 1996 (Lewes and Mizen, 2000, p. 356). I therefore take the latter date as the end point of monetary targeting in the UK. This corresponds to the timing of Frey *et al.* (2000, p. 35), according to whom monetary targeting in the UK ended in 1997. [d] Note that, even if monetary targeting proceeded beyond 1998, to preserve comparability with the performance of the Bundesbank, the figures in the table refer to the respective monetary targeting period stopped by 1998. In particular, Switzerland retained monetary targeting through 1999; in December of that year the SNB announced the abandonment of monetary targeting in favour of a variant of inflation targeting similar to that followed by the ECB. In this concept, inflation forecasts will take the place of monetary targets as intermediary target, for which, however, the development of M3 will play a prominent role (Meyer, 2000). Interestingly, to date, the Bank of Japan seems to be the only central bank of a developed country which still practises some sort of monetary targeting (Bernanke and Mishkin, 1992; Rhodes and Yoshino, 2004).
Sources: Statistisches Bundesamt (Germany); Schweizerische Nationalbank (Switzerland); National Statistics (UK); Federal Reserve Bank of Minneapolis (USA); Bank of Canada (Canada); Bernanke and Mishkin, 1992; Bernanke *et al.* 1999; Frey *et al.* 2000; Lewis and Mizen 2000; own calculations.

(2003: 1650) remark that the Bundesbank's monetary strategy 'was best viewed as monetary targeting in words only, but inflation targeting in deeds'. Bernanke and Mishkin suggest that 'German and Swiss monetary policy is actually closer in practice to inflation targeting than it is to Friedman-like monetary targeting, and thus might best be thought of as "hybrid" inflation targeting' (Mishkin, 1999, p. 590). And Bernanke and Mihov (1997) spend considerable esprit and technical effort to show what, for careful observers of the Bundesbank, should have been clear in any case, namely that in the short run the Bundesbank did react more strongly to variables other than the money volume. They conclude 'that the Bundesbank is better characterized as an inflation targeter than as a money targeter' (1997; p. 1049). Brand (2001) provides a comprehensive and balanced discussion of these issues, in both theoretical and econometric terms.

However, even in a nominal sense, the record of the Bundesbank relative to its own targets appears not that bad. First, as Table 5.2 reveals, the

Table 5.2 German monetary targets and their achievement

Year[a]	Target[b]	Actual[c]	Achievement[d]
1975	CBM 8 (6½–9½)	10.1	No
1976	CBM 8 (6½–9½)	9.2	No (Yes)
1977	CBM 8 (6½–9½)	9.0	No (Yes)
1978	CBM 8 (6½–9½)	11.4	No
1979	CBM 6–9	6.1	Yes
1980	CBM 5–8	4.9	Yes
1981	CBM 4–7	3.5	No
1982	CBM 4–7	6.0	Yes
1983	CBM 4–7	7.0	Yes
1984	CBM 4–6	4.6	Yes
1985	CBM 3–5	4.5	Yes
1986	CBM 3½–5½	7.7	No
1987	CBM 3–6	8.1	No
1975–87[e]	CBM 5.3–7.1 (4.8–7.6)	7.1 [6.6]	Yes [Yes]
1988	M3 3–6	6.7	No
1989	M3 5 (4–6)	4.7	No (Yes)
1990	M3 4–6	5.6	Yes
1991	M3 3–5	5.2	No
1992	M3 3½–5½	9.4	No
1993	M3 4½–6½	7.4	No
1994	M3 4–6	5.7	Yes
1995	M3 4–6	2.1	No
1996	M3 4–7	8.1	No
1997	M3 3½–6½	4.8	Yes
1998	M3 3–6	5.6	Yes
1988–98[e]	M3 3.8–6.0 (3.7–6.0)	5.9 [6.1]	Yes [No]

Notes: [a] Since 1991 including East Germany. [b] Money growth targets in per cent per year. 1975–87 in terms of CBM = central bank money at reserve ratios of 1974; since 1988 in terms of M3. Figures in parentheses are imputed range targets on the assumption that the point targets announced for these years should rather be read as midpoints of a range the width of which equals those used in years before and/or after. [c] Actual money growth rates in per cent per year. Figures in square brackets are average annual growth rates on the basis of seasonally adjusted end-year stocks of the respective aggregate. [d] Statements in parentheses and square brackets refer to target achievement in terms of the definitions given before. [e] Average annual target and actual money growth in terms of geometric means.
Sources: Bernanke and Mihov (1997); Issing (1997); Deutsche Bundesbank; own calculations.

Bundesbank met its target in 54 per cent of the years (if we interpret the point targets of the years 1975–8 and 1989 as midpoints of ranges of three and two percentage points, respectively, which seems sensible in view of the overall practice of the Bank). The target was seriously missed (that is, one percentage point or more off the target zone) in seven years, namely, 1975, 1978, 1986, 1987, 1992, 1995 and 1996, and only in four years was the target missed by more than two percentage points (in 1992 by almost four percentage points). Only in two years (1981 and 1995) was the target undershot, indicating that the Bundesbank may have been more concerned about undershooting than about overshooting. Moreover, taking averages over the whole two periods, 1975–87, when the Bank targeted CBM (defined as central bank money at constant reserve ratios) and 1988–98, when the target was M3, actual money growth fell into the target range, although again, in both cases, the upper limit was reached.

The Bundesbank proclaimed persistently that it will treat its monetary targets as a medium-term guideline rather than a fixed goal to be achieved in any short-term period. With this perspective, the observations sum up to a remarkable success record, even in purely operational terms.

Misperceptions of the Bundesbank's policy conception

Let me next try to clear up some misinterpretations of the Bundesbank's monetary policy conception. Contrary to what is often contended, the Bundesbank has never been a monetarist fortress. In particular, its monetary targeting concept had little in common with the monetarists' vision, especially Milton Friedman's. Of course, the Bundesbankers were influenced by monetarist ideas and they have implemented some of them very early into practical policy.[1] But their relatively strong anti-inflation preference even predates the time, in which the influence of monetarism began to unfold,[2] and in the early 1970s they were not more monetarist than in the sense in which nowadays it may be said (with the same legitimacy and caveats that applied to Richard Nixon's famous statement in 1971) that 'we are all monetarists now'.[3] Academics and politicians alike have learnt (some of them earlier than others) that inflation is a very dangerous thing (a 'virus', as it has often been called) not only for the more technical reasons to which economists usually refer (Fischer, 1994), but more importantly because it undermines economic fairness and therefore destroys social cohesion in a complex market economy (Leijonhufvud, 1981; Tietmeyer, 1998; Heering, 2005a).

Moreover, the Bundesbank at no time paid exclusive attention to price stability. True, the Bank was in all phases of its operation vulnerable at its external flank. First, under Bretton Woods, mainly against the USA and later against the partners in the 'snake' and the European Monetary System (EMS) (König, 2001), but the evidence also suggests that the Bundesbank at all times kept its eyes on the overall performance of the domestic economy, especially, since the mid-1970s, on the unemployment figures (von Hagen,

1998; Baltensperger, 1998; Richter, 1999). No doubt the Bundesbank practised a degree of flexibility and discretion that would never been compatible with strict monetarism (Posen, 2000). Otmar Issing called this 'pragmatic monetarism' (1997, p. 72).

To avoid another misunderstanding, let me add that even strict monetarism cannot be portrayed by the statement that price stability is all that matters, if only for central banks. Suffice to point to the classical critique by Friedman and Schwartz (1963) of the Federal Reserve System (Fed) acting too tightly in the late 1920s having done everything to turn a stock market crash into the most severe worldwide depression in history. How can this position be reconciled with the above-mentioned caricature? Not at all, in my opinion. Note also that the monetary policy of the Fed at the time followed from an 'endogenous money' conception, that is, the 'real-bills doctrine', which Federal Reserve bankers then held (Humphrey, 2001). In a nutshell, the monetarist perspective rather implies that money matters, in the short as well as in the long run.[4] Add possible trade-offs between short-term and long-term effects of monetary policy, and considerable uncertainty about these effects in any case, and it follows rather straightforwardly that monetary policy should be handled with extreme caution, much more than Friedman and others thought politician could be trusted to do. Needless to say, I think that this extremely pessimistic view, born out of observing centuries of inflation in history and the fresh experience of the immediate post-war period, should probably be revised to some degree in the light of more recent and more promising experience, although Friedman's suspicion is to some degree still a productive one (Heering, 2006).

Anyway, the deep suspicion on the part of monetarists supports their advocacy for a strict mechanistic rule, and this in turn explains why they have proposed operating monetary policy by controlling the monetary base directly rather than by managing the base rate of interest (Friedman, 1984). Sensible interest rate policy must always be implemented by some sort of feedback rule, otherwise it tends to create Wicksellian cumulative processes (Woodford, 2003, pp. 46 ff; Howitt, 2004). Such a 'rule', Friedman apparently thought, would give politicians too much leeway. With a fixed monetary base rule this is different, because it displays a built-in stabilizing moment operating counter-cyclically while binding the monetary authority's hand to act in a discretionary manner.

The money growth rule as such also shows that monetarists were in fact worrying about output fluctuations as well as price movements. It is only that they did not want to give central bankers or others the freedom to act deliberately on those occasions. Moreover, the Bundesbank as well as Friedman were very well aware that the noblest task of a central bank is provision of 'adequate, and no more than adequate' liquidity, as Hawtrey (1932, p. 116) once put it, to support maximum inflation-free real economic activities. For this reason, monetary targets and Friedman's rule, respectively, are both based on a version of the equation of exchange that refers to *potential* rather than actual output.

There are, however, two clear differences between monetarism and the Bundesbank's approach, which follow from this discussion. First, money targets of the Bundesbank were never thought of as a mechanistic growth rule for money as in monetarism, but rather as a flexible guideline to monetary policy. These targets were therefore not announced once and for all, but annually, and were generally different from year to year. Second, monetary targeting was implemented by the Bundesbank via an interest rate policy; instead of controlling the monetary base directly as proposed by monetarists, the Bank pursued an 'indirect control of base money volume via the interest lever' (quoted by von Hagen, 1998, p. 453; my own translation). In the first months of its monetary targeting, the bank in fact experimented with a direct control of base money, but quickly abandoned this because of the induced high volatility of the base rate of interest and anticipated problems with the system of reserve requirements (von Hagen, 1998).

There is an additional factor, which made central bankers all over the world reluctant to switch to direct control of the monetary base.[5] Since the earliest days of central banking, monetary policy measures were implemented by using the respective base rate as main instrument. As central bankers are normally more conservative than other people, this element of historical continuity certainly mattered. In retrospect, Laidler (2003, p. 117) admits:

> This approach did have one great advantage, however, that I appreciate more now than I did then. It enabled the Bank [of Canada] to continue with its time-honored practice of implementing policy through interest rates rather than the monetary base ... If accurate and transparent communication between the central bank and financial markets is important to the smooth functioning of monetary policy, and if those communications in turn depend on a common understanding of what the Bank is doing and how markets will react, then to have shifted from interest rate to base control would have been a great deal more difficult than some of us outside of central banks appreciated at the time.

There is a third and final essential difference between the Bundesbank and monetarism. While the Bundesbank has often (for good or ill) been said to be the most independent central bank worldwide, Friedman has always been criticizing the independence of central banks (Friedman, 1962; 1987), both for reasons of democratic control and because he felt that separating power between government and monetary authority would dilute responsibilities. Curiously, he also meant that giving in to political pressure from the Congress would in most cases have improved performance of the Fed.

The problem of money demand stability

It is a commonplace that, in order to implement monetary targeting, one needs a stable money demand (Bernanke *et al.* 1999, p. 305). The main reason for most countries giving up monetary targeting is reported to be the sharp velocity shifts that occurred during the 1980s and 1990s (Blinder, 1998, p. 27 ff; Freedman, 1999; Clarida *et al.*, 1999). As the former Governor of the Bank of Canada, Gerald Bouey, stated before the Canadian House of Commons Standing Committee on Finance, Trade and Economic Affairs on 28 March 1983: 'We did not abandon M1, M1 abandoned us' (quoted is Pill, 2001, p. 11).

The discussion about money demand stability is frequently confused by mixing up different factors. In principle, there are two potential sources of instability of the money demand function: the velocity of circulation (v) and the money multiplier (m). Jointly, these two factors determine the demand for base money (b) relative to nominal income ($p \cdot y$). The equation of exchange can be written

$$b \cdot m = (1/v) \cdot p \cdot y$$

Financial innovations in the 1980s and 1990s were money supply shocks acting primarily on the money multiplier, while the great inflation of the 1960s and 1970s was a money demand shock, which had its main impact on money's velocity of circulation via inflation expectations. The Bundesbank was obviously very successful in anchoring inflation expectations rather quickly. Moreover, financial innovations in Germany spread more smoothly than elsewhere, and regulatory changes did not happen abruptly. The consequences can be inferred from Figures 5.3 and 5.4, showing the respective multipliers and velocities of M1, M2 and M3 for Germany from 1971 to 1998. As can be seen, they all remained remarkably stable compared to their linear trends. Deviation from trend was on average 18% for $m1$, 9% for $m2$, 12% for $m3$ and 11% for $v1$, 10% for $v2$, and 4% for $v3$.

Of course, things always look different *ex post* (Orphanides and Porter, 2001). But the behaviour of economic actors also depends crucially on the actions of the central bank, and with hindsight we can at least say that the policy choice of the Bundesbank was not a bad one. Moreover, as Orphanides and Porter (2001) argue, the dramatic changes in velocity in the early 1990s in the USA, for example, could have been accounted for by the FED in real time. From this perspective, the abandonment of monitoring monetary aggregates, announced by Alan Greenspan in February 1993, is possibly not grounded in facts. Nevertheless, several countries under similar circumstances have decided to adopt (direct) inflation targeting.

Source: Deutsche Bundesbank.

Figure 5.3 Multipliers of M1, M2 and M3 in Germany 1971–98

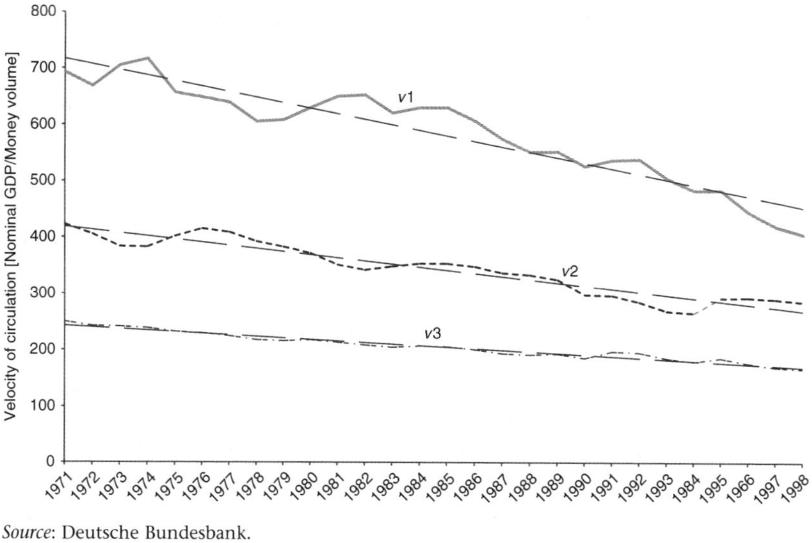

Source: Deutsche Bundesbank.

Figure 5.4 Velocities of M1, M2 and M3 in Germany, 1971–98

Inflation targeting – an alternative?

So, what about inflation targeting? Before briefly taking up this issue, let me insert a more general remark: if academic economists are any good at all, it is certainly with regard to two opposing, but none the less methodologically quite similar perspectives on the real world. On the one hand, they often criticize practical affairs as if their highly abstract models were a sufficiently accurate description of every facet of the outside world, so that the conclusions arrived at are immediately relevant for practical policy. The economics of central banking is no exception here, and academics who have worked, or are still working, inside central banks, such as Otmar Issing, Alan Blinder, Charles Goodhart and others, although not at all sharing similar opinions about substantial issues, all have often pointed out this methodological flaw in academic research. On the other hand, and following the same basic perception, we often find academic rationalizations of practices (and the history of central banking is rich with them) that have been invented by practitioners, quite often in rather desperate situations. If these practices seem to work, some academics tend to jump quickly on the band wagon of apparent success, explaining why and how these are exactly what fits into their theoretical framework. Many debates on independence and accountability of central banks in recent years fall into the first rubric. Inflation targeting, as adopted first by the government of New Zealand in 1990, falls into the second one. True, the young monetary policy regime seems to work reasonable well, as far as experience goes, and that is not that far. In particular, up to now inflation targeting has not been put to a serious test. In view of this we should always be aware of the following points.

First,

> inflation targets have most often been introduced at times when inflation was already low or falling, rather than (as one might expect) at times when inflation was on the rise and threatening to get out of control . . . Thus, while inflation targeting may not reduce the costs of the transition to low inflation, it may help central banks sustain price stability in the longer run (Bernanke *et al.*, 1999, pp. 36, 283)

Second, as a publication of the Bundesbank rightly observes,

> the transition to such a one-tier strategy of inflation targeting was not effected because such strategies are inherently superior – say, in terms of the theoretical approach. It was effected not by choice but rather of necessity, since (particularly in the wake of a radical change in the financial markets) the traditional monetary relationships had become unstable, and there was no longer a predictable correlation between the intermediate target variable and prices. (Deutsche Bundesbank, 1995, pp. 67 ff.)

> [I]nflation targeting was developed mainly as an *ad hoc* solution ... [A] new strategy had to be found almost overnight. This explains the quite pragmatic approach of inflation targeting, for which a theoretical framework was developed only many years after its first application. (Bofinger, 2001, p. 258)

Third, even proponents of the approach frankly admit 'that the economic performance of the non-targeters over the period considered is not appreciably different from that of the inflation targeters' (Bernanke *et al.*, 1999, p. 283).

Inflation targeting is usually defined as a monetary policy strategy by which a central bank aims at controlling inflation 'directly'; that is, without using an intermediary target. In theory, it is possible to introduce inflation forecasts as a formal analogue for the latter (Svensson, 1997). In practice, however, this is highly problematic, because, among other things, serious inflation forecasts must account for the public's inflation expectations, which are not easily observable and are in any case not controllable at will by the central bank (Bofinger, 2001, p. 267). In practice, inflation targeting therefore uses all sort of indicators and information, which makes it 'very much a "look at everything" strategy' (Bernanke *et al.*, 1999, p. 22). A central element of the strategy is a publicly announced inflation target, and usually a high degree of transparency for central bank's internal decision procedures and its implementation is also requested, both as a matter of democratic accountability and professional communication with market participants.

While these requirements sound reasonable, it remains rather unclear where hard differences to other policy conceptions can be found. With regard to the concept used by Bernanke *et al.* (1999) in their famous book, Peter Bofinger notes that '[t]his definition [of inflation targeting] more or less circumscribes what in Germany, above all, has long since been understood as a "stability-oriented monetary policy"' (Bofinger, 2001, p. 258). Moreover,

> inflation targeting ... comes relatively close to pure discretion ... [I]n spite of its seeming transparency, inflation targeting is a rather intransparent approach, as far as the realization of the ultimate targets of monetary policy is concerned. It can be compared to a cookery book that, instead of providing concrete recipes, only contains pictures of the prepared dishes and the advice to buy the best ingredients and prepare them as skilfully as possible. (Bofinger, 2001, p. 265)

Hardliners nevertheless emphasize that inflation targeting is, after all, not monetary targeting (Svensson, 1999). If pressed, though, they would possibly subscribe to the following formula:

Inflation targeting = monetary targeting – monetary targets

But this can be written equivalently as:

$$\textit{Monetary targeting} = \textit{Inflation targeting} + \textit{Monetary targets}$$

On the other hand, King (1997, p. 435) has claimed that 'monetary targeting is simply a limiting case of inflation targeting in which the policy-maker assigns a weight of unity to money and of zero to all other variables'. Being (for trivial reason) a suitable characterization of Friedman-type monetary targeting (which in any case has seldom been applied), this description is certainly not accurate for the type of monetary policy pursued by the Bundesbank and other central banks. While having no problem at all with subsuming monetary targeting (properly understood) under the broad roof of inflation targeting, I would prefer to add that monetary targeting is 'inflation targeting *plus*'. It is a small but very important '*plus*', as I am going to argue.

The Bundesbank's success again

The Bundesbank used monetary aggregates (first a modified concept of monetary base and then M3 since 1988) in a threefold role (Deutsche Bundesbank, 1995):

1. As an *indicator* variable.
2. As an *intermediary* target.
3. As a *signalling* (and communication) *device*.

The first two are standard notions in the literature on monetary policy strategy (Neumann, 2000). In the case of the Bundesbank there is, however, a slight irritation with respect to the second notion: in accordance with the ultimate goal of medium- to long-term price stability, monetary targets have to be interpreted as applying to a longer time period too. This seems to conflict with the fact that the Bundesbank not only announced its targets annually but also successively lower targets.[6] The reason for this, of course, was that the Bank gradually slid down the inflation rate, leading also to shifting monetary targets. Yet this was a necessary interim stage, because the Bundesbank was well aware that it would be very hurtful (if possible at all) to disinflate the German economy at a stroke. On the other hand, whilst the SNB in 1990 switched to a five-year target for the monetary base (Rich, 1997), the Bundesbank stuck to its announcement of annual targets. It was only at the end of 1996 that the Bundesbank, for the first time, announced a two-year target for 1997/98 in order to facilitate transition into the Eurosystem (Deutsche Bundesbank, 1998).

Probably the most important and most successful function of monetary targets for the Bundesbank was the third one, their role as a medium to signal the Bank's intention to the public. This implies an essential strategic role of monetary targets, which transcends their tactical role in the short run. As von Hagen (1999, 2004) has argued convincingly, this strategy was masterfully (and successfully) applied by the Bundesbank. Obviously, economic and political actors took the corresponding announcements of the Bundesbank seriously (Honohan, 2004, p. 430), despite the fact that the yearly targets were missed in almost half of the cases (Posen, 2000). There can be little doubt that this contributed significantly to the Bank's success. But this is only part of the story.

What, then, are the sources of success for the Bundesbank? It appears that there was no single element but rather a whole complex of mutually supporting factors:

1. The abandonment of Bretton Woods released the Bundesbank from the commitment of foreign exchange intervention, at least to a large extent. Although the external flank remained a weak link over the whole period, the fact that the DM rather quickly became the leading currency within Europe gave the Bundesbank considerable room for manoeuvre.
2. Inflation rates in Germany rose quite late compared to other countries, namely in the very late 1960s and early 1970s. Therefore inflation expectations had just begun to creep into the minds and attitudes of economic actors and did not prove to be very resistant. This was central to stabilizing the demand for money function.
3. Financial innovation and regulation in Germany developed more smoothly over time compared to the partly shock-wise introduction during the 1980s and 1990s in other countries, especially the USA and the UK. This fact had stabilizing consequences for money multipliers as well as for money demand functions (Issing, 1997).
4. Germany and Switzerland are often quoted as being countries where the populations are particularly inflation averse. Helmut Schlesinger coined the term 'stability culture' (Neumann, 1998, p. 343) to describe this attitude.
5. The Bundesbank had a very strong position *vis-à-vis* the government which was enforced originally by the Western Allied (Buchheim, 2000). Equally, or even more important, was that the Bundesbank on several occasions used its formal powers to resist successfully governmental pressure; through this, it was able to establish its independent position

in public opinion (Neumann, 1998). Its announcement (including its monetary targets), which were always publicly explained and defended, have therefore been taken seriously by economic actors.

6. The Bundesbank was certainly more determined than other central banks at the time to pursue what it understood as its main goal – namely, middle-term to long-term domestic price stability. And it interpreted this objective as being backed by the law.

In sum, while the Bundesbank's monetary targets were certainly more than just an 'empty ritual', as was claimed by Pohl (1987), or a 'phantom', as Bofinger (1994) put it, the overall success of this monetary policy must still be attributed to a set of more or less lucky circumstances. And the real question, of course, is not whether the Bundesbank (or the SNB) was, for some reason or other in a lucky position, but whether this sort of policy can be applied more systematically, and, in particular, whether it might fit the European Central Bank (ECB)?

Saying that the Bundesbank was just lucky is, to be sure, not an entirely fair account of the excellent job it did in these more or less turbulent years. My critique is directed towards the monetary policy framework of the Bank rather than its actual policy.[7] Indeed, in my opinion there is a potential deficiency related to the operational procedure by which the Bundesbank implemented its strategy – indirect control of the money volume via the nominal interest rate. Remember that this is contrary to what monetarists would suggest. Obviously, in this case, the money volume is an endogenous variable, determined by the money demand of individual actors. This, of course, also holds for inflation targeting regimes. In this respect, there is nothing inflation targeting can do that monetary targeting cannot. I should, however, also emphasize that there is nothing wrong with an interest rate policy *per se*. The crux is rather the conventional doctrine that requires central banks to choose between a price-orientated (interest rate) and a quantity-orientated (monetary base) strategy. In what follows I argue that this alternative is misconceived, because it does not pay due attention to private inflation expectations. Let me get this straight: the problem is the choice as such rather than the way it is resolved. In this sense, the argument applies as well to a pure quantity-orientated monetary policy, as the Swiss experience may indicate.

The Bundesbank was lucky, because it was very successful in pinning down private inflation expectations very quickly. Given this anchoring, and by maintaining it, together with relative stable money multipliers and velocities over the whole time horizon, the Bundesbank's monetary strategy was never seriously at risk, not even in the first years of Germany's reunification. But other central banks did have a less positive experience with essentially the same approach. Consider the Bank of Canada, which also explicitly, and unsuccessfully, tried for some time in the 1970s and early 1980s to control money growth by manipulating its interest rate. Laidler (2003, pp. 116 ff) provides the following instructive record:

> [T]he Bank implemented its policy by: settling on its target for money growth, forecasting the values of output and prices, substituting these into an estimated demand for money function, solving for the value of the interest rate, and then setting the latter. This procedure was based either on theoretically incomplete foundations . . . or, at the least, rendered money growth a variable that responded passively to, among other things, the very inflation rate that it was supposed to be influencing.

More generally, Goodfriend (1999, p. 414) has observed:

> It is important to remember that interest rate policy models that ignore money presume that a central bank has established in the public's mind the credibility that gives it the power to pin down and expected future price level or the expected rate of inflation at each point in time. When a central bank has credibility to anchor the path of the price level, it can allow the stock of money to be demand-determined each period at the chosen setting for its interest rate policy instrument. Money needn't play a causal role in the transmission of policy in this case.
>
> *Money plays a critical role, nevertheless, because credibility for a price-path stems from a central bank's power to manage the stock of money, if need be, to enforce that objective. Models that ignore the role of money in the policy-making process can do so only because the central bank has somehow already established credibility for its control over the price level.*
>
> Practically speaking, interest rate policy works well when it is easy for a central bank to judge the effect of its interest rate policy actions on expected inflation. With inflation and inflation expectations anchored near zero, nominal interest rate policy actions translate clearly into real interest rate actions.
>
> This is the case today for many central banks around the world. However, an inflationary shock could create a problem for interest rate policy. It was the collapse of its credibility for low inflation that caused the Federal Reserve to move temporarily from interest rate targeting to non-borrowed-reserve targeting in 1979. (Emphasis added)

A modified IS/LM model

To illustrate this and some other points of interest, consider the following version of the IS/LM model. The reason for choosing IS/LM is not that I particularly fancy this type of model. It is just the easiest way to make my point analytically clearer. Nor am I interested here in the highest possible degree of generality or rigour. Moreover, the nowadays fashionable 'consensus' macro models are congruent to IS/LM in their conceptual basis and logical structure. The standard IS/LM model has, however, many theoretically debatable aspects, and so have most of its more recent successors. Some of the problematic features are responsible for the redundancy of money in most of those models. In light of this, I use an extended and modified IS/LM model. As this is not the place to explain the design in detail, I shall just briefly introduce its main features:[8]

$$\begin{aligned}
\textit{IS-curve}: &\ y_t = \phi(i_t - \pi_t^e, m_t^a),\ \phi_1(..) < 0,\ \phi_2(..) > 0 \text{ for } m_t^a < \mu \cdot y_t \\
&\ \phi_2(i_t - \pi_t^e, \mu \cdot y_t) = 0,\ \phi_2(..) < 0 \text{ for } m_t^a > \mu \cdot y_t \\
&\ \text{and } y^* = \phi(r, m^*) \\
&\ \text{where } m^* = \mu \cdot y^* \qquad (5.1)
\end{aligned}$$

$$\begin{aligned}
\textit{LM-curve}: &\ m_t = \ell(i_t, y^*, \pi_t^e) \cdot \varsigma_t,\ E(\varsigma_t) = 1,\ \ell_1(...) < 0 \\
&\ \ell_2(...) > 0,\ \ell_3(...) < 0 \\
&\ m_t^a = \ell(i_t, y^*, \pi_t^e),\ m^* = \ell(r + \pi^*, y^*, \pi^*) \qquad (5.2)
\end{aligned}$$

$$\textit{Phillips curve}: \pi_t = \pi_t^e + \Pi(y_t - y^*),\ \Pi(0) = 0,\ \Pi'(.) > 0 \qquad (5.3)$$

$$\textit{Nominal money}: M_t = m_t \cdot p_t \text{ and } M_t^a = m_t^a \cdot p_t \qquad (5.4)$$

$$\textit{Price level}: p_{t+1} = p_t \cdot (1 + \pi_t) \qquad (5.5)$$

$$\textit{Policy rule}: i_t = r + \pi^* + R(\pi_t^e - \pi^*) \geq 0,\ R(0) = 0 \text{ and } R'(.) > 1 \qquad (5.6)$$

$$\begin{aligned}
\textit{Expectations}: &\ \pi_{t+1}^e = \pi^* + \alpha(\pi_t - \pi_t^e) + \beta(i_t, \omega_{t+1}),\ \alpha(0) = 0,\ \alpha'(.) > 0 \\
&\ \beta_1(..) < 0,\ \beta_2(..) > 0 \text{ and } \beta(r + \pi^*, 0) = 0 \qquad (5.7)
\end{aligned}$$

t indicates the time period, y is current aggregate output and y^* its long-run equilibrium level (alias 'potential output'); the latter is taken as exogenous. i is the nominal interest rate, π is actual inflation, π^e the expected inflation rate, and π^* the inflation target of the monetary authority. m and m^a denote different concepts of aggregate real balances to be explained below, m^* is their (joint) equilibrium level. r is Wicksell's 'natural rate of interest', the real interest rate which would hold in a long-run equilibrium with inflation at its target. M and M^a are the nominal counterparts to m and m^a, respectively, and p is the price level. ς and ω are stochastic disturbances, and μ is a positive constant.

Equation (5.1) is a modified IS curve linking aggregate output (demand) y to the real interest rate $i - \pi^e$ and the aggregate real money stock m^a, abstracting from output shocks. m^a reflects a variant of the 'shopping-time' concept (Heering, 2005b; 2006), which captures money's role as a mean of reducing transaction costs. However, the idea is not that individual money balances are what is relevant in this respect, but the total money volume (and possibly its allocation) because of the network property of money. μ is a positive constant and $\mu \cdot y$ is Friedman's (1969) 'optimum quantity of money', which equals m^* if output is at its potential y^*. Equation (5.2) is a modified LM curve linking real money demand to nominal interest rate i, potential output and expected inflation π^e. This conceptualization follows Friedman (1956) and is consistent with the transaction role of money embedded in Equation (5.1).[9] Hereby, I assume that money holdings are the result of portfolio choices, which depend on individual wealth rather than current income. The conventional assumption that individuals have to hold money in order to be able to do shopping is certainly outdated, to say the least.

Furthermore, I assume that liquidity preference shifts erratically because of money demand shocks. ς denotes a stochastic money demand shock, such that money demand monotonically increases with ς. These shocks, however, mainly affect precautionary motives; people hold more or less money balances than normal because of increased or decreased uncertainty. These balances are not available for transaction purposes and therefore have no influence on overall transaction costs; they are held as buffer stock against future contingencies. For lack of a better term, I adopt Keynes' (1937) notion of 'active' and 'inactive' balances, where the latter stands for the 'hoards' just described. m^a then denotes 'active' real balances; if the monetary system accommodates any idiosyncratic shock to money demand, m^a will remain unaffected.

Equation (5.3) is an expectations-augmented Phillips curve, more accurately described as an expectations-augmented aggregate supply curve. It links actual inflation to inflation expectations and the output gap. Equations (5.4) define real money demand and Equation (5.5) provides the definition of the inflation rate in terms of the price level. Equation (5.6) is a simple forward-looking Taylor rule, where $R'(.) > 1$ captures the so-called 'Taylor principle', which is necessary in order to counter effectively an increase in expected inflation by an increase in the real rate of interest. For convenience, I here adopt a pure inflation targeting rule; short-run output stabilization is of no concern to the monetary authority. Note that $i \geq 0$ reflects the lower zero bound for nominal interest rates. It implies a restriction on $R(.)$ or, alternatively, on π^e, as $\pi^e \geq \pi^* + R^{-1}(-r - \pi^*)$.

Finally, Equation (5.7) describes how (inflation) expectations are formed. It states that the public starts with the inflation target π^* of the central bank, being aware that inflation in the short run must, and will, generally not coincide with the target. Therefore, an up- or downgrading is done, taking into account two factors: first, the deviation of actual inflation from past expectations. Second, current information from the central bank as signalled by its short-term nominal interest rate. If i is increased, then inflation expectations are downgraded; if i is reduced then inflation expectations are upgraded (Bofinger, 2001, pp. 267 ff; Geraats, 2001). ω is a noise variable indicating other potential influences on inflation expectations. If the nominal interest rate equals the equilibrium rate $r + \pi^*$, and no noise is present, then inflation expectation equals the inflation target in equilibrium (where $\pi = \pi^e$).

Let Z be a set of information potentially relevant for inflation expectations. I assume that an element of Z is made available to the representative member of the public at random. For convenience, I suppose that elements of Z can be transformed into an ordinal measure by a function $\omega : Z \rightarrow [0, 1]$ with $\omega(\emptyset) = 0$. However, not all bits of information contained in Z may be used by market participants. Let us assume that this depends on a filter $F(.)$, such that $F(Z) \subset Z$, which narrows the scope of activated information. Given $F(Z)$, a bit of information $z \in Z$ is used for expectation formation if and only if $z \in F(Z)$. The public's inflation expectation then is given by:

$$\pi^e_{t+1} = \pi^* + \alpha(\pi_t - \pi^e_t) + \beta(i_t, \omega[F(Z_{t+1})]), \tag{5.6}$$

which, generally, is a random variable. I assume that the central bank knows the function (5.7), but it does generally not know which $z \in Z$ the public has access to at the moment, and what the filter $F(.)$ looks like.

What private inflation expectations are and how volatile they are depends a good deal on the credibility of the central bank. Adopting the notion of game theory, a person (or a group of people) may be said to be (perfectly) *credible*, if acting according to his her promises (or to what he/she is otherwise generally supposed to do) is in his/her own interest at the time the respective deed comes due – that is, to act according to the commitment is her best response given any feasible actions of other parties, and other parties are aware of this (Kreps, 1990, p. 52). Note that this implies that living up to one's word must be a dominant strategy in order to translate into credibility. If someone has credibility, others will act on his/her word, even if there is 'noisy' information suggesting that he is lying. One way to conceptualize credibility in the context of the present model is by thinking of it as a filter, which selects the active subset $F(Z)$ from Z. 'Full' credibility then amounts to a situation where $F(Z) = \emptyset$; that is, whatever information is out there, only that coming directly from the monetary authority (plus an adaptive moment) will be used. Complete incredibility would amount to $F(Z) = Z$.

The system in Equations (5.1) to (5.7) displays eight equations [note that (5.4) contains two equations] with nine endogenous variables, namely, y, i, π, π^e, m, m^a, M, M^a and p; hence it seems to be underdetermined.[10] We may, however, note that p_t is determined by π_{t-1} via (5), given p_{t-1}, and so on. The system therefore determines the time path of the price level, given some historical level. Analytically, the rates of change of the price level are determined, while the latter itself is not. This is a common feature of all models in this class. However, for the moment, we can treat p_t as being predetermined in the current period.

There is a second and even more important problem, though. The policy rule in Equation (5.6) can only be implemented if π^e is an observable variable, or is at least a function of observable variables. This indeed is usually assumed, either in a backward-looking (adaptive expectations) or forward-looking (rational expectations) variant. Via Equation (5.7), however, π^e also depends on a random element which is, by assumption, not observable. But even if ω (and thus π^e) is not directly observable, the central bank may infer the value of π^e, provided it can observe monetary demand shocks ς and allows a perfectly elastic money supply. By observing M_t, i_t, p_t and ς_t, the bank can then use Equations (5.2) and (5.4) to gain knowledge about the inflation expectations of the public. Let us see what this means.

Define:

$$\pi_t^e = \varphi(i_t, m_t^a) \tag{5.8}$$

such as

$$m_t^a \equiv \ell[i_t, y^*, \varphi(i_t, m_t^a)], \text{ where } m_t^a = \frac{m_t}{\varsigma_t} = \frac{M_t}{p_t \cdot \varsigma_t} \text{ and } \varphi(r + \pi^*, m^*) = \pi^*$$

Then

$$\varphi_1(i_t, m_t^a) \equiv -\frac{\ell_1[i_t, y^*, \varphi(i_t, m_t^a)]}{\ell_3[i_t, y^*, \varphi(i_t, m_t^a)]} < 0$$

$$\varphi_2(i_t, m_t^a) \equiv \frac{1}{\ell_3[i_t, y^*, \varphi(i_t, m_t^a)]} < 0$$

Note also that $\varphi(\ldots)$ is *not* an expectation-forming function. Inserting Equation (5.8) into (5.6), we get

$$i_t = r + \pi^* + R[\varphi(i_t, m_t^a) - \pi^*] = r + \pi^* + R[\varphi(i_t, m_t^a) - \varphi(r + \pi^*, m^*)] \tag{5.9}$$

and by taking a linear approximation around $(r + \pi^*, m^*)$

$$i_t = r + \pi^* + \theta \cdot (m_t^a - m^*), \text{ where } \theta = \frac{R'(0) \cdot \varphi_2(r + \pi^*, m^*)}{1 - R'(0) \cdot \varphi_1(r + \pi^*, m^*)} < 0$$

$\theta < 0$ implies that the central bank acts inversely to a positive 'money gap'. The rationale is straightforward: if the public's inflation expectations rise, the central bank should increase the rate of interest. But an increase in inflation expectation is here equivalent to a decrease in money demand. This is how it should be: an increase in the money demand (that is, a decrease in money's velocity), is no direct threat to price stability. Only an increase in velocity would be.

Moreover, by inserting Equation (5.8) into Equations (5.1) and (5.3), we obtain:

$$y_t = \phi[i_t - \varphi(i_t, m_t^a), m_t^a] \tag{5.10}$$

$$\pi_t = \varphi(i_t, m_t^a) + \Pi(y_t - y^*) \tag{5.11}$$

We thus end up with three equations – (5.9) to (5.11) – and four endogenous variables – i_t, m_t^a, y_t and π_t; again, the model is one equation short. This under-determinacy, which results from non-observableness of private inflation expectations, is the crux of the matter. It implies that, in general, an interest rate policy is not sufficient to pin down a unique equilibrium of the system.

Pitfalls of the Taylor rule

This problem obviously does not exist if the central bank owns full credibility, so that $F(Z_{t+1}) = \emptyset$ and thus $\omega_{t+1} = 0$. In this case, the system is closed. However, there may be another problem. To see this, define $x_t = \pi_t^e - \pi^*$. Then, using Equations (5.1) to (5.3), (5.6) and (5.7):

$$\begin{aligned} x_{t+1} = \pi_{t+1}^e - \pi^* = \alpha[\Pi(\phi[r + R(x_t) - x_t, \ell(r + \pi^* + R(x_t), y^*, \pi^* + x_t)] - y^*])] \\ + \beta[r + \pi^* + R(x_t), 0] \equiv G(x_t) \end{aligned} \tag{5.12}$$

where

$$\begin{aligned} G'(.) \equiv \alpha'(.) \cdot \Pi'(.) \cdot (\phi_1(..) \cdot [R'(.) - 1] + \phi_2(..) \cdot [\ell_1(\ldots) \cdot R'(.) + \ell_3(\ldots)]) \\ + \beta_1(..) \cdot R'(.) < 0 \end{aligned}$$

Note that the path of x_t will be oscillating. Moreover, the stability of the process requires

$$|x_{t+1}| \leq |x_t|$$

where strict inequality should hold whenever $|x_t| > 0$.

With full credibility of the central bank and taking a linear approximation around the stationary solution and we get:

$$x_{t+1} = G'(0) \cdot x_t \text{ or } |x_{t+1}| = |G'(0)| \cdot |x_t|$$

A necessary and sufficient condition for stability of inflation expectations then is

$$|G'(0)| < 1 \text{ or } G'(0) > -1 \tag{5.13}$$

It is obvious that Equation (5.13) cannot be met under all circumstances. In particular, with a very aggressive monetary policy rule – that is, $R'(.)$ rather large – stability is at risk. On the other hand, it may be possible to design monetary policy in a way to assure stability. Whether or not this is feasible cannot be decided in general on theoretical grounds alone. In any case, the result may help to explain the success of inflation targeting via an interest rate feedback rule in developed countries with highly credible central banks. But it also warns that a pure interest rate policy may be destabilizing in other environments.

Next, let us assume an inflation expectations shock $\omega_t > 0$, starting from a position of long-run equilibrium. As has been explained, it suffices to assume $\pi_t^e > \pi^*$. By inserting Equations (5.2) and (5.7) into (5.1) we obtain:

$$\begin{aligned} y_t &= \phi[r + \pi^* + R(\pi_t^e - \pi^*) - \pi_t^e, \ell(r + \pi^* + R(\pi_t^e - \pi^*), y^*, \pi_t^e)] \\ &\equiv \hat{\phi}(\pi_t^e) \end{aligned} \tag{5.14}$$

where

$$\hat{\phi}'(.) \equiv \phi_1(..) \cdot [R'(.) - 1] + \phi_2(..) \cdot [\ell_1(\ldots)R'(.) + \ell_3(\ldots)] < 0 \tag{5.14a}$$

We can distinguish three effects:
The *real interest effect*: $R'(.) - 1 = \frac{dr^e}{d\pi^e} > 0$,
the *nominal interest rate effect*: $\ell_1(\ldots) \cdot R'(.) + \ell_3(\ldots) = \frac{dm^a}{di^e} \cdot \frac{di^e}{d\pi^e} < 0$,
and the (direct) *inflation expectations effect*: $\ell_3(\ldots) = \frac{dm^a}{d\pi^e} < 0$.
Therefore

$$\frac{dy_t}{d\pi_t^e} = \phi_1(..) \cdot \frac{dr_t^e}{d\pi_t^e} + \phi_2(..) \cdot \frac{dm_t^a}{d_t^e} \cdot \frac{di_t^e}{d\pi_t^e} + \phi_2(..) \cdot \frac{dm_t^a}{d\pi_t^e} \tag{5.14b}$$

Note, in particular, that all three effects work in the same direction. Thus, given the model as specified, a Taylor rule policy may lead to very sharp counter-reactions of output in case inflation expectations deviate from the target. In particular, a positive innovation on inflation expectations provokes a threefold negative reaction in output, which (*ceteris paribus*) is larger the larger the shock. Of course, if the central bank also cared for output as well as price stability, as in the original Taylor rule and many of its variants, then this consequence could be mitigated. Even so, this demonstrates that the Taylor principle $R'(.) > 1$ may be too aggressive upon which to base a sensible monetary policy, and in any case may be unnecessarily tough. It is true that such a policy will bring actual inflation down by depressing the economy. The impact on expected inflation is, however, far from certain and will take some time.

Even worse, for any given inflation expectation there exists a nominal interest rate, which stabilizes output around its potential. To see this, consider the interest rate rule $i_t = \lambda(\pi_t^e)$ defined by the condition

$$\phi[\lambda(\pi_t^e) - \pi_t^e, \ell(\lambda(\pi_t^e), y^*, \pi_t^e)] \equiv y^* \tag{5.15}$$

which gives $\lambda(\pi^*) = r + \pi^*$ and

$$\lambda'(.) \equiv \frac{\phi_1(..) - \phi_2(..) \cdot \ell_3(\ldots)}{\phi_1(..) + \phi_2(..) \cdot \ell_1(\ldots)} \tag{5.15a}$$

Note that this rule is well-defined as long as the denominator in Equation (5.15a) does not vanish, which will be the case as long as $m_t^a \leq m^*$. Note further that by Equation (5.3) it then follows that $\pi_t = \pi_t^e$ for any π_t^e.

Note also that, in terms of the policy rule in Equation (5.6), to keep output at its potential requires $R'(.) < 1$, maybe even $R'(.) \leq 0$, given the specification of the model, as can be seen from Equation (5.14a). To follow rule (5.15) therefore implies a violation of the Taylor principle, which means that the central bank does not care much, or even at all, about inflation. This result is compatible with the 'expectations trap hypothesis' brought forward by Lawrence Christiano in collaboration with several co-authors, who apply the idea to the 'great inflation' of the 1970s (Chari *et al.*, 1998; Christiano and Gust, 1999, 2000; Albanesi *et al.*, 2003; Christiano and Fitzgerald, 2003).

Thus, the central bank can stabilize output if it is ready to compromise on price stability. If the public is aware of this potential, then the inflation target announced by the central bank may not have credibility; that is, the filter $F(Z)$ is supposed to be wide. Therefore inflation expectations may be very volatile, worsening the bank's position further by making it even more costly to pursue an anti-inflationary policy. With inflation expectations unanchored; that is to say, the central bank faces a dilemma, similar to the traditional trade-off along a given short-run Phillips curve. Here, in contrast, the bank has to choose between either depressing the economy with uncertain prospects on expectations or accommodating inflation expectations, thus stabilizing output but boosting inflation.

A two-pillar approach to monetary policy

But now suppose that the monetary authority implements the following strategy: first, it sets its nominal interest rate in such a way that real active balances are always equal to the level m^* (where I abstract from any trend in active balances); that is, it follows an interest rate rule $i = f(\pi^e)$, defined by the condition

$$\ell[f(\pi_t^e), y^*, \pi_t^e] \equiv m^* \tag{5.16}$$

where

$$f'(\pi_t^e) \equiv -\frac{\ell_3[f(\pi_t^e), y^*, \pi_t^e]}{\ell_1[f(\pi_t^e), y^*, \pi_t^e]} < 0 \text{ and } f(\pi^*) = r + \pi^* \tag{5.16a}$$

Note, in particular, that this implies that, at the given interest rate, the authority always accommodates any demand for inactive balances – that is, it accommodates any stochastic (temporary) money demand shock.

Second, the authority announces a monetary targeting of letting the nominal money volume grow by and only by a rate of π^*, and it backs this commitment by the announcement of switching to a direct money control in case the market demand for money deviates from this target.

The policy can be implemented as follows, where we only have to consider two consecutive periods. In period t the central bank fixes a nominal stock of active money

$$M_t^a = p^* \cdot m^* \tag{5.17}$$

so that the total nominal stock of money fluctuates around this level; that is,

$$M_t = p^* \cdot m^* \cdot s_t$$

In equilibrium we then have

$$p^* \cdot m^* = p_t \cdot \ell(i_t, y^*, \pi_t^e)$$

Now, if the market reveals $p_t > p^*$ and therefore $\ell(i_t, y^*, \pi_t^e) < m^*$, then the central bank chooses the interest rate $i_t = f(\pi_t^e)$. In practice, the central bank would reduce the interest rate in successive small steps until $p_t \leq p^*$. In the case that $p_t < p^*$, and hence $\ell(i_t, y^*, \pi_t^e) > m^*$, the opposite action will be taken.

$$\text{In this way } p_t = p^* \text{ and } \ell[f(\pi_t^e), y^*, \pi_t^e] \equiv m^* \text{ will be established.} \tag{5.18}$$

For period $t+1$ the central bank fixes a nominal stock of active money

$$M_{t+1}^a = p^* \cdot m^* \cdot (1 + \pi^*) \tag{5.19}$$

so that the total nominal stock of money again fluctuates around this level; that is,

$$M_{t+1} = p^* \cdot m^* \cdot (1 + \pi^*) \cdot s_{t+1}$$

In equilibrium we then have

$$p^* \cdot m^* \cdot (1 + \pi^*) = p_{t+1} \cdot \ell(i_{t+1}, y^*, \pi_{t+1}^e)$$

By the same sort of argument as above we then arrive at

$$p_{t+1} = p^* \cdot (1 + \pi^*) \text{ and } \ell[f(\pi_{t+1}^e), y^*, \pi_{t+1}^e] \equiv m^*. \tag{5.20}$$

Suppose now $\pi_t^e > \pi^*$. Then by Equations (5.1) and (5.16a):

$$y_t = \phi[f(\pi_t^e) - \pi_t^e, m^*] > \phi[f(\pi^*) - \pi^*, m^*] = \phi(r, m^*) = y^*,$$

which implies $\pi^* = \pi_t = \pi_t^e + \Pi(y_t - y^*) > \pi_t^e$ by Equations (5.3), (5.18) and (5.20), in contradiction to the hypothesis. Hence $\pi^* \geq \pi_t^e$. In an analogous way we also show that $\pi^* \leq \pi_t^e$. It follows that $\pi_t^e = \pi^*$.

There are three levels of credibility of a central bank that can be distinguished here, which give rise to three different interpretation of the foregoing scenario: first, the highest level of credibility pertains if the central bank's inflation targeting as such is taken seriously by the public. That is, the public believes that the central bank is willing and has the power to stabilize inflation within a narrow band around π^*. This is the case discussed above, when assuming $F(Z_t) = \emptyset$. In the foregoing scenario it amounts to $\pi_t^e = \pi_{t+1}^e = \pi^*$. Everything else then follows straightforwardly.

Second, a middle level of credibility pertains if the public does not in fact believe in the inflation target set by the bank; it may even not know the target explicitly. However, it believes that the central bank is willing (and able) to pursue the announced policy. In this case, it would be foolish not to expect an inflation of π^*, because that will be realized, whatever the public is expecting.

Third, if the bank has no credibility in either of the two senses mentioned, but is determined, regardless of this, to follow its announced policy, it should eventually be able to lock-in inflation expectations at π^*, because this value is the only one compatible with equilibrium. If the central bank consequently follows the described policy, then sooner or later the public's inflation expectations will settle down around the inflation target.

Of course, matters are more complicated in reality than in this simple model. Central banks have neither all the information necessary to select the exact appropriate money–interest rate combination (in particular, the monetary authority is normally not in a position to observe directly shocks in money demand) nor have they full control over money volume, at least not in the short run. Note that, under given institutional conditions of modern banking systems, this even holds for the monetary base in the very short term (Goodhart, 1994; Gebauer, 1996). A central bank trying to implement the above idea in its pure form would probably create more irritation for market participants than contribute to stabilizing expectations. Furthermore, the scenario sketched here is (at present) certainly not relevant for most of the developed world. From a practical point of view, central bankers may well be satisfied with their well-functioning monetary policy approach, which, irrespective of whether it is inflation targeting or monetary targeting, relies solely on interest rate control. But these obvious caveats do not undermine the logical validity of my point. At least, the latter illustrates how dangerous it can be to advise countries, where the rules of the game are not that clear, where appropriate enforcement mechanisms are lacking and where the central bank has not the same standing, simply to mimic the practice of central banks based in much more mature environments.[11]

Moreover, to render the idea of a 'two-pillars strategy' fruitful for practical matters, it is not at all necessary to interpret the model presented here in strict terms. The monetary target a central bank wants to realize, by and large, can be formulated as a target range much in the same way as the Bundesbank (and other central banks) did. But more important, and this is the missing link in the traditional monetary targeting approach, it can and should be complemented by an explicit 'escape clause' along the lines recently suggested by Christiano and Rostagno (2001). These authors study models of monetary policy, where a Taylor rule is supplemented by monitoring money growth and by an 'escape clause', committing the monetary authority to switch from the Taylor-rule regime to a money-growth rule in case the money growth rate exceeds a predetermined range around some sort of equilibrium level. In their models, the threat implied by such an escape clause suffices to keep money growth within the range of tolerance.

In this perspective, monetary targets can serve as a safety-belt for monetary policy. If the central bank has sufficient knowledge about the range of money demand shocks, it is able to formulate a range of money demand fluctuations within which it would commit to following a simple Taylor rule. But it would also commit to the fact that, if the money demand falls outside this range, it will shift to the policy described above. With such a strategy, the central bank should be able to lock-in inflation expectations within a suitable channel. This analysis gives rise to four tentative conclusions.

First, in principle there is no inconsistency involved in a central bank choosing a 'two-pillar' approach to monetary policy, which combines the simultaneous operation of the nominal interest rate with the operation of the monetary base (Baltensberger, 2000). In a soft variant, this may imply an escape clause that accounts for real-life complications. As mentioned above, I call such an approach 'inflation targeting *plus*'.

Second, by choosing a suitable model, an inflation targeting *plus* strategy can be shown to be appropriate when inflation expectations are not settled. Essentially, it enables the central bank to force inflation expectations into a narrow range around its target, even if the target as such lacks credibility. In contrast, a pure interest rate policy in accordance with the Taylor approach may lead to disaster.

Third, if the central bank's inflation target has full credibility, it appears to be unnecessary to complement inflation targeting with a safety-belt of a monetary target. Logically, however, this is just a special case which cannot provide a general guideline. Experiences of different types of countries with pure inflation targeting are relevant here.

Fourth, in case the money velocity becomes unreliable, because of financial innovation or the like, inflation targeting *plus* may not be possible. While in this case (direct) inflation targeting may be the only sensible option for a central bank, this does not prove that it is superior to inflation targeting *plus*. Quite the contrary, in fact, as the latter should be adopted whenever possible. If uncertainty about the money demand function increases, however, then the required monetary target range might become too broad to provide any sensible guide to inflation expectations. Monetary targets then become useless. Whether this has really been the case in the near past is an unsettled issue. For Germany (and probably for most of Europe at the time) there seems to be little evidence for that.

Conclusions

We are now in a position to clarify the notion that the Bundesbank was in a lucky position. In fact, the chosen monetary aggregate never happened to be that far from its target as to jeopardize the whole approach. True, there were some years when the target was seriously missed, and we know from the minutes of the Central Bank Council's meeting that those events often led to debates about whether to abandon the strategy (Baltensperger, 1998; von Hagen, 1998; Richter, 1999). In the end, the majority of the council held on to it, if only to avoid creating an impression of surrender that might have induced adverse expectations. But nothing within the monetary policy strategy of the Bundesbank indicated what should be done in the worst case. Other central banks, finding themselves just in a worst case scenario, simply dismissed the strategy. An escape clause along the lines sketched here might have been an alternative.

The issue has got special importance in view of the fact that the newly founded ECB has obviously tried to establish itself as the legitimate successor of the Bundesbank. As Honohan (2004, p. 430) has noted: 'By evoking slogans that justified and underpinned the Bundesbank's credibility in the past, the inclusion of the monetary pillar in the ECB's stated strategy should probably best be seen as an attempt to sing a lullaby as the German public are gently moved from one bed to another.'[12] But this is certainly not the only possible interpretation. One that is more in favour of the ECB is that it, quite rightly, feels that there is a good rationale behind keeping a close eye on the development of monetary aggregates, but is not yet able to give this intuition a proper and convincing formulation. As a consequence, the 'reference value' for M3 is somewhat hanging in the air, with nobody, including the ECB itself, really taking it seriously.

In view of the foregoing analysis, I would argue that the 'two-pillars' strategy of the ECB is conceptually very sensible. It is obviously a heritage from the German Bundesbank, the most successful European central bank during the post-war period, and to me there is nothing wrong with that. Moreover, the ECB has obviously realized that it has to make its strategy more explicit and more sophisticated than the Bundesbank ever felt the need to do. That is the good news. But the ECB has also inherited the strategic flaw within the design of the German monetary policy framework of not having an escape clause when monetary aggregates get out of hand. What is the ECB supposed to do in this case? We simply do not know!

Overall, while remaining sympathetic to the general approach of the ECB, I do agree with the critics in two respects:[13] first, I am not quite sure whether the ECB thus far has made the most sensible use of the framework. Contrary to what some populists argue, namely that the ECB is bound too rigidly to the aim of price stability (which in any case is its main legal objective according to the Treatise), serious empirical research suggests that the truth may rather lie at the other end (Hayo and Hofmann, 2003; von Hagen and Brückner, 2001).[14] Inflation (even medium-term inflation) in the Eurozone has been rising continuously and is now clearly above the ECB's mark of 2 per cent (Galí *et al.*, 2004; pp. 49 ff). The real crux of the matter is, however, that what the ECB is in fact doing is not clear: in spite of the high degree of transparency that ECB officials pretend permanently to practice, the strategy of the ECB is still to a large degree opaque.

Second, and this is strongly related to the first point, a clear and convincing conceptual and analytical integration of the two pillars is still missing. In view of this, I am prepared to interpret the opaqueness of the ECB strategy as the inevitable consequence of a lack of knowledge and understanding (true, though this does not only apply to members of the ECB). To point to the close, long-run correlation between nominal money growth and inflation may have been sufficient in Germany for some time, but it is questionable that it will be enough for an extended European public. Equally important, it clearly seems not to be sufficient to convince academics, who have gained significant influence over monetary policy matters recently.

Certainly, in recent years there has been much research on the topic, not the last from the ECB itself.[15] However, most of this work is empirical and partly of a highly technical nature. Although certainly important, I am afraid this sort of research will not be able to settle the issue at the end of the day. Moreover, almost all these studies refer to monetary aggregates as information variables. While there is now plenty of evidence available indicating that such a role in fact exists for long-run inflation prospects (Nicoletti-Altimari, 2001; Jaeger, 2003; Gerlach, 2004; Neumann and Greiber, 2004; von Hagen, 2004), this evidence proves neither that a monetary aggregate is the only, nor the most effective, variable to gather the relevant information. After all, the studies do not show that monetary aggregates should have a prominent place in this regard. That monetary aggregates could also be used as an *additional* policy instrument is rarely considered. The main impediment here is conceptual in nature: the doctrine of the instrument choice central banks have to make between a price-orientated and a quantity-orientated monetary policy. However, while true under some circumstances, the doctrine seems not to apply in general.

What we need, I sense, is more theoretical work on this matter, and much more innovative conceptual approaches. And let me add one final point, not least because it is my favourite research interest: contrary to what some prominent researchers suggest nowadays (for example, Woodford, 1998,

2003), I believe that without a clear understanding of the role of money in society, we shall not be able to design an appropriate monetary policy strategy. As long as politicians and academics continue to toy with the idea of money being just an additional instrument for short-run macroeconomic stabilization, Friedman's basic suspicion will have to remain with us.

Notes

1. At a meeting in 1970, the Central Bank Council learnt about Friedman's ideas from a scholarly dispute between two members of the Directorate, Rolf Gocht (pro) and Leonard Gleske (contra). Interestingly, Gleske noted: 'The task of Mr Gocht, who had to act as Friedman's advocate, was psychologically certainly more difficult than mine; for Friedman's doctrines appear to suggest that, at the end of the day, we at this table are redundant' (quoted in Neumann, 1998, p. 340; my own translation).
2. This is confirmed by a rather strange accusation raised recently by German economic historian Alfred Ritschl (2004) in a review of Issing *et al.* (2001). He claims that the Bundesbank cheated on the rules of the Bretton Woods System by sterilizing massive capital inflows during the Vietnam War. Specifically, he argues: 'In a fixed exchange rate system with capital mobility such as the EPU [European Payments Union] and the Bretton Woods standard of the 1950s, there is little scope for central bank policy on a national level. Unless a country is the dominant player, such as the United States in the Bretton Woods standard, monetary policy is rather passive, and consists in following the interest rate movements of the system leader step by step. The quantity of money and the national price level both are endogenous to the international flows of goods and funds; there is just precious little an individual member bank can do about it. Not so the Bundesbank in the 1960s. Defying theory [?], it sought to exert domestic anti-inflationary policy in spite of its international commitments [?] Bundesbank orthodoxy against inflation thus contributed to the breakdown of the Bretton Woods standard, just as French and American orthodoxy in the late 1920s contributed to the breakdown of the gold standard in 1931. The various fixed exchange rate systems of Europe after the collapse of Bretton Woods in 1973 all grouped around the Bundesbank. Playing non-cooperatively and forcing the breakdown of Bretton Woods had thus paid off; the new system honoured the proven anti-inflationary stance of the Bundesbank. It was during this time that the Bundesbank adopted monetarism and, specially, monetary targeting. The Bundesbank policy maintained its monetary orthodoxy to the very end, and stuck to its monetarist principles up to the establishment of the ECB.' According to Ritschl, the infamous story does not end here: 'ECB policy has faced a dilemma since its inception in 1999. On the one hand, the ECB felt the need to define a modern, widely accepted approach to monetary policy. The only obvious candidate for this nowadays is inflation targeting [?]. On the other hand, the ECB could not distance itself from the Bundesbank doctrine if it was to inherit its rock-solid credibility. This in turn would call for an adherence to monetary targeting Bundesbank-style. The two are hardly compatible, and the resulting problem is not an easy one to sort out.' Having heard such a convincing plea from the prosecutor, the verdict of the jury can only be: guilty on all charges! Not only has the Bundesbank unscrupulously murdered Bretton Woods, its stubborn, selfish and dogmatic attitude,

supported by its infant but even more reckless offspring the ECB, has also put the Eurosystem's life at risk.

3. See Bernanke (2004) for a recent appraisal of Friedman's approach in this spirit.
4. Recently, Friedman (2002) has been criticising Gaspar and Issing, who argue that '[s]tandard long run monetary neutrality propositions are among the few results a prudent central banker can get comfort from' (2002, p. 355). Somewhat perplexingly, Friedman even coquets with a famous quote from his great opponent: 'I find this proposition baffling. Taken seriously, monetary neutrality means that central bankers are irrelevant; real magnitudes – which are what ultimately matter to people – go their own way, independently of what the central banker does. Central bankers are important insofar as money is not neutral and does have real effects. Neutrality propositions give little if any guide to effective central bank behaviour under such circumstances. *Perhaps they offer comfort to central bankers by implying that all mistakes will average out in that mythical long run in which Keynes assured us "we are all dead"*' (2002, p. 366; italics added). The last sentence makes Friedman's intention clear: to rely on long-run neutrality proposition may serve as a cheap alibi for central bankers to act carelessly in the short-run.
5. As far as I am aware, the SNB (before 2000) was the only central bank (at least in the developed world) that directly controlled the monetary basis, in terms of 'bank reserves' (Bernanke and Mishkin, 1992, p. 203; Bernanke *et al.*, 1999, p. 65; Meyer, 2000, p. 43; Jordan *et al.*, 2001, p. 48).
6. Note that it is this long-term orientation that led the ECB to announce in May 2003 that it will no longer assess its monetary reference value on an annual basis (ECB, 2003).
7. Just recently, Gary Stern and Preston Miller have raised a similar point with regards to the FOMC (Federal Open Market Committee): 'We emphasize that the criticisms voiced here are directed at the policy framework and not at policy decisions. We recognize that the framework could be flawed, but the policy could have been fine' (2004, p. 3).
8. These ideas will be dealt with in more detail in a forthcoming paper.
9. Note that the potential output-based money demand function also answers to one of the criticisms raised against the strategy of the ECB: 'What is genuinely difficult to measure in real time ... is the output gap, owing to the absence of any direct observation of potential output. There is, however, no obvious reason that monetary aggregates should provide information about this, as money demand should depend on aggregate output (the volume of transactions), rather than on output relative to current potential output' (Galí *et al.*, 2004, p. 20).
10. Note that Equations (5.2) and (5.4) each contain two equations, while Equation (5.5) must be neglected since it introduces a further endogenous variable.
11. Note, in particular, that inflation targeting 'has become a popular recommendation by the IMF to countries in need of advice' (King, 1997, p. 435).
12. 'In its policy choices, the ECB has not given much attention to monetary growth rates. Rather, this has been a rhetorical means to borrow the reputation of the Bundesbank as the guarantor of a stable European monetary policy' (Galí *et al.*, 2004, p. 33).
13. An authoritative summary of recent critiques of the ECB is provided by a recent report of the MECB network (Galí *et al.*, 2004).
14. '[The] data ... suggest that the ECB attaches greater weight to movements in activity than to movements in inflation. The sometimes-heard claim that the

ECB ignores the real economy due to an exclusive focus on price stability thus seems ill founded' (Galí *et al.*, 2004, p. 58).

15. For detailed references see Heering (2005c).

References

Albanesi, S., V. V. Chari and L. J. Christiano (2003) 'Expectation Traps and Monetary Policy', *Review of Economic Studies*, vol. 70, pp. 715–41.

Baltensberger, E. (2000) 'Die Europäische Zentralbank und ihre Geldpolitik', *SNB Quartalsheft*, vol. 1, pp. 48–73.

Baltensperger, E. (1998) 'Geldpolitik bei wachsender Integration (1979–1996)', in Deutsche Bundesbank (eds), *Fünfzig Jahre Deutsche Mark. Notenbank und Währung in Deutschland seit 1948* (Munich: C. H. Beck), pp. 475–559.

Bernanke, B. S. (2004) 'Friedman's Monetary Framework: Some Lessons', in M. A. Wynne, H. Rosenblum and R. L. Formaini (eds), *The Legacy of Milton and Rose Friedman's 'Free to Choose'. Economic Liberalism at the Turn of the 21st Century*, Proceedings of a Conference Sponsored by the Federal Reserve Bank of Dallas, Dallas, pp. 207–14.

Bernanke, B. S. and I. Mihov (1997), 'What Does the Bundesbank Target?', *European Economic Review*, vol. 41, pp. 1025–53.

Bernanke, B. S. and F. S. Mishkin (1992) 'Central Bank Behavior and the Strategy of Monetary Policy: Observations from Six Industrialized Countries', in O. J. Blanchard and S. Fischer (eds), *NBER Macroeconomic Annual* (Cambridge, Mass./London: MIT Press), pp. 183–228.

Bernanke, B. S., T. Laubach, F. S. Mishkin and A. S. Posen (1999) *Inflation Targeting. Lessons from the International Experience* (Princeton, NJ: Princeton University Press).

Blinder A. S. (1998) *Central Banking in Theory and Practice* (Cambridge, Mass./London: MIT Press).

Bofinger, P. (1994) 'Die Bundesbank jagt ein Phantom', *Frankfurter Allgemeine Zeitung*, 19 May.

Bofinger, P. (2001) *Monetary Policy. Goals, Institutions, Strategies, and Instruments*, (Oxford University Press).

Brand, C. (2001) *Money Stock Control and Inflation Targeting in Germany. A State Space Modelling Approach to the Bundesbank's Operating Procedures and Intermediate Strategy* (Heidelberg: Physica-Verlag).

Buchheim, Ch. (2000) 'Die Unabhängigkeit der Bundesbank. Folge eines amerikanischen Oktrois?', *Vierteljahreshefte für Zeitgeschichte*, vol. 49, pp. 1–30.

Chari, V. V., L. J. Christiano and M. Eichenbaum (1998) 'Expectation Traps and Discretion', *Journal of Economic Theory*, vol. 81, pp. 462–92.

Christiano, L. J. and C. Gust (1999) 'The Expectations Trap Hypothesis', in, *Money, Monetary Policy, and Transmission Mechanisms*, Proceedings of a Conference held by the Bank of Canada, November, pp. 347–83.

Christiano, L. J. and C. Gust (2000) 'The Expectations Trap Hypothesis', *Economic Perspectives*, Federal Reserve Bank of Chicago, vol. 24, 2nd quarter, pp. 21–39.

Christiano, L. J. and M. Rostagno (2001) 'Money Growth Monitoring and the Taylor Rule', *NBER Working Paper* No. 8539, October.

Christiano, L. J. and T. J. Fitzgerald (2003) 'Inflation and Monetary Policy in the Twentieth Century', *Economic Perspectives*, Federal Reserve Bank of Chicago, vol. 27, 1st quarter, pp. 22–45.

Clarida, R., J. Galí and M. Gertler (1999) 'The Science of Monetary Policy: A New Keynesian Perspective', *Journal of Economic Literature*, vol. 37, pp. 1661–707.

Deutsche Bundesbank (1995) *The Monetary Policy of the Bundesbank* (Frankfurt am Main: Deutsche Bundesbank), October.

Deutsche Bundesbank (1998) 'Review of Monetary Targeting in 1997–8 and more detailed Definition of the Monetary Target for 1998', *Monthly Report*, January, pp. 17–23.

European Central Bank (2003) 'The Outcome of the ECB's Evaluation of its Monetary Policy Strategy', *ECB Monthly Bulletin*, June, pp. 79–92.

Fischer, S. (1994) 'Modern Central Banking', in F. Capie, C. Goodhart, S. Fischer and N. Schnadt, *The Future of Central Banking*, The Tercentenary Symposium of the Bank of England (Cambridge University Press) pp. 262–308.

Freedman, C. (1999) 'Panel Discussion', in *Money, Monetary Policy, and Transmission Mechanism*, Proceedings of a Conference held by the Bank of Canada, November, pp. 407–12.

Frey, M., D. Julius, L. Mahadeva, S. Roger and G. Sterne (2000) 'Key Issues in the Choice of Monetary Framework', in L. Mahadeva and G. Sterne (eds), *Monetary Policy Frameworks in a Global Context* (London/New York: Routledge), pp. 1–216.

Friedman, B. M. (1996) 'The Rise and Fall of Money Growth Targets as Guidelines for U.S. Monetary Policy', NBER Working Paper No. 5465, February.

Friedman, M. (1956) 'The Quantity Theory of Money – A Restatement', in M. Friedman (ed.), *Studies in the Quantity Theory of Money* (Chicago/London: University of Chicago Press), pp. 3–21.

Friedman, M. (1962) 'Should There Be an Independent Monetary Authority?', in L. B. Yeager (ed.), *In Search of a Monetary Constitution* (Cambridge, Mass.: Harvard University Press), pp. 219–43.

Friedman, M. (1969) 'The Optimum Quantity of Money', in M. Friedman, *The Optimum Quantity of Money and Other Essays* (Chicago: Aldine), pp. 1–50.

Friedman, M. (1987) 'Monetary Policy: Tactics versus Strategy', reprinted in J. A. Dorn and A. J. Schwartz (eds), *The Search for Stable Money. Essays on Monetary Reform* (Chicago/London: University of Chicago Press), pp. 361–82.

Friedman, M. (2002) 'Comment on Gaspar and Issing', *Australian Economic Papers*, vol. 41, pp. 366–8.

Friedman, M. and A. J. Schwartz (1963) *A Monetary History of the United States, 1867–1960*, Princeton University Press.

Galí, J., S. Gerlach, J. Rotemberg, H. Uhlig and M. Woodford (2004) *The Monetary Policy Strategy of the ECB Reconsidered: Monitoring the European Central Bank 5* (London: CEPR).

Gaspar, V. and Otmar Issing (2001) 'Exchange Rates and Monetary Policy', *Australian Economic Papers*, vol. 41, pp. 342–65.

Geraats, P. M. (2001) *Why Adopt Transparency? The Publication of Central Bank Forecasts*, ECB Working Paper No. 41, January.

Gebauer, W. (1996) 'Geld: Angebot versus Nachfrage' in P. Bofinger and K.-H. Ketterer (eds), *Neuere Entwicklungen in der Geld theoutril und Geld politik. Implikaltionen für die Europäische Währungsunion*, Tübingen: Mohr Siebeck, pp. 243–62.

Gerlach, S. (2004) 'The Two Pillars of the European Central Bank', *Economic Policy*, vol. 40, pp. 389–439.

Gerlach, S. and L. E. O. Svensson (2003) 'Money and Inflation in the Euro Area: A Case for Monetary Indicators?' *Journal of Monetary Economics*, vol. 50, pp. 1649–72.

Goodfriend, M. (1994) 'Panel Discussion', in *Money, Monetary Policy, and Transmission Mechanisms*, Proceedings of a Conference held by the Bank of Canada, November, pp. 413–20.

Goodhart, C. A. E. (1994) 'What Should Central Banks Do? What Should Be Their Macroeconomic Objectives and Operations?', *Economic Journal*, vol. 104, pp. 1424–36.

Hawtrey, R. G. (1962) *The Art of Central Banking*; 2nd edn (1st edn 1932). (London: Frank Cass).

Hayo, B. and Boris Hofmann (2003) 'Monetary Policy Reaction Functions: ECB versus Bundesbank', ZEI Working Paper B24-2003, December.

Heering, W. W. (2005a) 'Money and Reciprocity in the Extended Order. An Essay on the Evolution and Cultural Function of Money', in Jürgen Backhaus (ed.), *Entrepreneurship, Money and Coordination* (Cheltenham Northampton Mass.: Edward Elgar), pp. 156–89.

Heering, W. W. (2005b) 'On the Theoretical Foundation of Monetary Policy', in J. Hölscher and H. Tomann (eds), *Globalization of Capital Markets and Monetary Policy* (Basingstoke New York: Palgrave) 2005 pp. 93–112.

Heering, W. W. (2005c) 'Monetary Policy Without Money? Reflections on Hamlet Without Prince or Ghost', Paper presented at the 59th IAES Conference, 11 March, Revised draft 31 March.

Heering, W. W. (2006) 'Monetary Efficiency, Financial Intermediation and Interest Rate Policy. Solving Some Puzzles with the Optimum Quantity of Money', *Brighton Business School Occasional Paper* (forthcoming).

Higo, M. (2000) 'What Can Inflation Expectations and Core Inflation Tell Us About Monetary Policy in Japan?', in L. Mahadeva and G. Sterne (eds), *Monetary Policy Frameworks in a Global Context*; (London/New York: Routledge), pp. 421–40.

Honohan, P. (2004) 'Discussion', *Economic Policy*, vol. 40, pp. 429–33.

Howitt, P. (2004) 'Monetary Policy and the Limitations of Economic Knowledge', Mimeo, Providence, RI: Brown University. 8 November.

Humphrey, T. M. (2001) 'The Choice of a Monetary Policy Framework: Lessons from the 1920s', *Cato Journal*, vol. 21, no. 2, pp. 285–313.

Issing, I. (1997) 'Monetary Targeting in Germany: The Stability of Monetary Policy and of the Monetary System', *Journal of Monetary Economics*, vol. 39, pp. 67–79.

Issing, I., Vítor Gaspar, Ignazio Angeloni and Oreste Tristani (2001) *Monetary Policy in the Euro Area. Strategy and Decision-Making at the European Central Bank* (Cambridge University Press).

Jaeger, A. (2003) 'The ECB's Money Pillar: An Assessment', IMF Working Paper No. 03/82, April.

Jordan, T. J., M. Peytrignet and G. Rich (2001) 'The Role of M3 in the Policy Analysis of the Swiss National Bank', in H.-J. Klöckers and C. Willeke (eds), *Monetary Analysis: Tools and Applications* (Frankfurt am Main: ECB), August, pp. 47–62.

Keynes, J. M. (1973) 'The General Theory of Employment', Originally published 1937, reprinted in D. Moggridge (ed.), *The General Theory and After. Part II: Defence and Development. The Collected Writings of John Maynard Keynes, Vol. XIV* (London: Macmillan), pp. 109–23.

King, M. (1997) 'The Inflation Target Five Years On', *Bank of England Quarterly Bulletin*, November, pp. 434–42.

König, R. (2001) 'Paradigm Changes of German Monetary Policy', in J. Hölscher (ed.), *50 Years of the German Mark. Essays in Honour of Stephen F. Frowen* (Basingstoke/New York: Palgrave), pp. 56–69.

Kopcke, R. W. (2002) 'The Practice of Central Banking in Other Industrialized Countries', *New England Economic Review*, 2nd quarter, pp. 3–9.

Kreps, D. M. (1990) *Game Theory and Economic Modelling* (Oxford: Clarendon Press).

Laidler, D. (2003) 'Monetary Policy Without Money: *Hamlet* Without the Ghost', in *Macroeconomics, Monetary Policy, and Financial Stability. A Festschrift in Honour of Charles Freedman*, Proceedings of a Conference held by the Bank of Canada, June, pp. 111–34.

Leijonhufvud, A. (1981) 'Costs and Consequences of Inflation', in Axel Leijonhufvud, *Information and Coordination. Essays in Macroeconomic Theory* (New York/Oxford: Oxford University Press), pp. 227–89.

Lewis, M. K. and Paul D. Mizen (2000) *Monetary Economics* (Oxford University Press).

Meyer, H. (2000) 'Zur Geldpolitik im neuen Jahr', *SNB Quartalsheft*, vol. 1, pp. 38–46.

Mishkin, F. S. (1999) 'International Experiences with Different Monetary Policy Regimes', *Journal of Monetary Economics*, vol. 43, pp. 579–605.

Neumann, M. J. M. (1998) 'Geldwertstabilität: Bedrohung und Bewährung', in Deutsche Bundesbank (ed.), *Fünfzig Jahre Deutsche Mark. Notenbank und Währung in Deutschland seit 1948* (Munich: C. H. Beck), pp. 309–46.

Neumann, M. J. M. (2000) 'Strategien der Geldpolitik', in J. v. Hagen and J. H. V. Stein (eds), *Obst/Hintner: Geld-, Bank- und Börsenwesen. Handbuch des Finanzsystems*, 40th edn (Stuttgart: Schäfer-Poeschel), pp. 1594–1604.

Neumann, M. J. M. and C. Greiber (2004) 'Inflation and Core Money Growth in the Euro Area', Discussion Paper No. 36 Studies of the Economic Research Centre, Deutsche Bundesbank.

Nicoletti-Altimari, S. (2001) 'Does Money Lead Inflation in the Euro Area?', ECB Working Paper No. 63, May.

Orphanides, A. and R. D. Porter (2001) 'Money and Inflation: The Role of Information Regarding the Determinants of M2 Behavior', in H.-J. Kloeckers and C. Willeke (eds), *Monetary Analysis: Tools and Applications* (Frankfurt am Main: ECB), August, pp. 77–95.

Pill, H. (2001) 'Summary "Monetary Analysis: Tools and Applications"', in H.-J. Klöckers and C. Willeke (eds), *Monetary Analysis: Tools and Applications* (Frankfurt am Main: ECB), August, pp. 11–30.

Pohl, R. (1987) 'Brauchen wir eine neue geldpolitische Konzeption?', *Wirtschaftsdienst*, VII, pp. 339–45.

Posen, A. S. (2000) 'Lessons from the Bundesbank on the Occasion of Its Early Retirement', in L. Mahadeva and G. Sterne (eds), *Monetary Policy Frameworks in a Global Context*; (London/New York: Routledge), pp. 393–420.

Rhodes, J. R. and Naoyuki Yoshino (2004) 'Japan's Monetary Policy Transition, 1955–2004', Paper prepared for the Econometric Society 2004 for Eastern meeting, February.

Rich, G. (1997) 'Monetary Targets as a Policy Rule: Lessons from the Swiss Experience', *Journal of Monetary Economics*, vol. 39, pp. 114–41.

Richter, R. (1998) 'Die Geldpolitik im Spiegel der wissenschaftlichen Diskussion', in Deutsche Bundesbank (ed.), *Fünfzig Jahre Deutsche Mark. Notenbank und Währung in Deutschland seit 1948* (Munich: C. H. Beck), pp. 561–606.

Richter, R. (1999) *Deutsche Geldpolitik 1948–1998 im Spiegel der zeitgenössischen wissenschaftlichen Diskussion* (Tübingen: Mohr Siebeck).

Ritschl, A. (2004) 'Review of Otmar Issing, Vítor Gaspar, Ignazio Angeloni and Oreste Tristani', *Monetary Policy in the Euro Area. Strategy and Decision-Making at the European Central Bank*, H-German, H-Net Reviews, July (http://www.h-net.msu.edu/reviews/showrev.cgi? path=11481093889116).

Stern, G. and P. Miller (2004) 'Avoiding Significant Monetary Policy Mistakes', *Federal Reserve Bank of Minneapolis Quarterly Review*, vol. 28, no. 2, pp. 2–9.

Svensson, L. E. O. (1997) 'Inflation Forecast Targeting: Implementing and Monitoring Inflation Targets', *European Economic Review*, vol. 41, pp. 1111–46.

Svensson, L. E. O. (1999) 'Inflation Targeting as a Monetary Policy Rule', *Journal of Monetary Economics*, vol. 43, pp. 607–54.

Tietmeyer, H. (2001) 'Fifty Years of the Deutsche Mark – A Currency and its Consequences', Address delivered on 20 June 1998 in the Paulskirche, Frankfurt am Main, English translation in J. Hölscher (ed.), *50 Years of the German Mark. Essays in Honour of Stephen F. Frowen* (Basingstoke/New York: Palgrave), pp. 7–14.

von Hagen, J. (1998) 'Geldpolitik auf neuen Wegen (1971–1978)', in Deutsche Bundesbank (ed.), *Fünfzig Jahre Deutsche Mark. Notenbank und Währung in Deutschland seit 1948* (Munich: C. H. Beck), pp. 439–73.

von Hagen, J. (1999) 'Money Growth Targeting by the Bundesbank', *Journal of Monetary Economics*, vol. 43, pp. 681–701.

von Hagen, J. (2004) 'Hat die Geldmenge ausgedient? Plenumsvortarg zur Jahrestagung des Vereins für Socialpolitik', *Perpektiven der Wirtschaftspolitik*, vol. 5, pp. 423–453.

von Hagen, J. and M. Brückner (2001) 'Monetary Policy in Unknown Territory: The European Central Bank in the Early Years', Centre for European Integration Studies, University of Bonn, Working Paper B18-2001, August.

Woodford, M. (1998) 'Doing Without Money: Controlling Inflation in a Post-Monetary World', *Review of Economic Dynamics*, vol. 1, pp. 173–219.

Woodford, M. (2003) *Interest and Prices. Foundations of a Theory of Monetary Policy* (Princeton, NJ/Oxford: Princeton University Press).

6
Comment on Part I

Khaled Soufani

Monetary targeting adopted by central banks has the objective of anchoring the expectation of economic agents. Central banks usually announce a growth rule for what they consider to be a sustainable and proper monetary aggregate with the ultimate goal of controlling inflation in the long run and possibly influencing the level of output and employment in the short run. Central banks have these ultimate goals, but they only have direct control over a set of tools that will influence some operating and intermediate targets, and then have an impact on the economic goals. It is important to note that emphasizing the transparency and communication of the economic agents are important elements contributing to the success of monetary targeting. It is argued by Mishkin (2001) that transparency can help to improve the time-inconsistency trap in which central bankers try to expand output and employment in the short run by pursuing overly expansionary monetary policy, and to achieve price stability in the long term. It was argued by Friedman (1968) that economic agents have to decide whether to rely on these official projections, or whether to form their own expectations. Economic agents usually consider the credibility of the central bank and the accuracy of the stated targets compared to the alternative monetary information available when they depend on the monetary target announcement to meet their expectations. However, the monetary targeting approach depends to a large extent on the choice of the monetary target, where this operating or intermediate target has to have a direct impact on the goal and that it should be highly correlated with it; furthermore the intermediate target has to be easier to control than the goal.

Monetary targeting seems to have been successful in both Germany and Switzerland. Walter Heering's chapter on monetary targeting by the German Bundesbank highlights the aspects that contributed to the successful performance of the German central bank. The main question addressed in the chapter pertains to whether there is a strong and consistent relationship between the success of the Bundesbank in achieving price stability on the one hand, and monetary targeting on the other. The author believes that such a relationship does exist, but this causality is more complex than was originally perceived. The argument states that the success in controlling inflation was largely a result of monetary targeting, but also that the credibility of the Bundesbank in achieving price stability was probably a cause for retaining the monetary targeting framework. The German Bundesbank retained monetary targeting at a time when all other central banks had abandoned it, and furthermore survived the economic shocks resulting from oil prices, turbulences in the world economy and the international financial system, and the reunification of East and West Germany.

Chapter 5 is divided into nine sections, where the first section presents details on the Bundesbank's performance and the success of the bank in achieving its goal of price stability as depicted by the comparison of actual inflation with the inflation target; the section accentuates this point by graphically showing the changes in the CPI in Germany. The Bundesbank succeeded in keeping medium-term inflation rates by monetary targeting consistent with the low inflation period in the 1950s and 1960s. Dr Heering also looked at the performance of the monetary targets, and argued that the Bundesbank met its target in 54 per cent of the years. The second section addresses the misconception of the German central bank's stance on policy issues; the author argues that the Bundesbank 'has never been a monetarist fortress . . . had little in common with the monetarists' vision'. The author argues that although the bank was influenced by monetarist ideas, the strong anti-inflationary stance pre-dates the time of modern monetarists. This section gives a brief insight into monetarist thinking and the similarities with and differences from the ideas of the Bundesbank. The third section deals with the problem of money demand stability, where the distinction between the two sources of instability of the money demand function – namely, the velocity of circulation and the money multiplier – are addressed. The fourth section deals with inflation targeting and whether it should be seen as an alternative approach to monetary targeting. This section emphasizes the point that inflation targeting is not the same as monetary targeting where the latter is composed of inflation targeting *plus* monetary targets. In the fifth section, Dr Heering looks at the reasons for the success of the Bundesbank in achieving its objectives by using monetary targeting, and indicates that the central bank used monetary aggregates in three different roles: as an indicator variable, as an intermediary target, and as a signalling device. The author emphasizes the part of 'lucky circumstances' but also recognizes the systematic nature of conducting monetary policy. The sixth section presents the modified IS/LM model where he introduces the main features relating to the IS curve, the LM curve, the Phillips curve, nominal money function, price level, policy rule and expectation. The author identifies an interesting result relating to the state of equilibrium, namely the presence of three equations and four endogenous variables indicating, as he argues, that 'an interest rate policy is not sufficient to pin down a unique equilibrium of the system'. The seventh section discusses the pitfalls of the Taylor rule, while the eighth section introduces a two-pillar approach to monetary policy, where the author discusses the uncertainty about the money demand function and the implications for the required monetary target range, and thus the consequent perception of the broadness of monetary targeting and its usage as a reasonable guide for inflation expectation. The ninth section concludes the chapter with a statement relating to the need to have a clearer understanding of the role of money in our economy.

The chapter is well written and provides very interesting and important observations about the philosophical workings of the Bundesbank in general, and the notion of monetary targeting in particular. The arguments of the author are well reasoned and in my opinion he not only introduces an important dimension to the economic rational of the utilization of monetary targeting, and consequently the potential reasons of their success in the case of the German Bundesbank, but also accentuates (theoretically) the shortcomings that might possibly exist if the framework and context of monetary targeting were not applied efficiently, and if the targeting were to be misinterpreted by the economic agents. The use of the modified IS/LM model is, in my opinion, appropriate to simplify the relationships that exist in the economy, assuming that we recognize hypothetically that there is potentially a simultaneous equilibrium in both the goods and money market; however, in reality this might not be the case. But the author does recognize the existence of some 'debatable aspects' in the model; nevertheless he makes interesting assumptions about the endogenous as well as the exogenous variables and their role in the model, and then describes how inflation expectations are formed. In addition, the author recognizes the pitfalls of the Taylor rule, and argues that a Taylor rule policy might affect domestic output in the event that there is a deviation in the inflation expectation from the announced target. The concluding remarks pertaining to the 'two-pillar' strategy of the European Central Bank (ECB) is understandable from a conceptual point of view, and that the possible desire of the ECB to conduct a more sophisticated approach than the one followed by the Bundesbank in terms of monetary targeting would be interesting to observe over the coming years. It is certainly the case that some more years have to pass before we can observe accurately the performance of the ECB in managing monetary policy in Europe, especially in that the conditions that govern the workings of the ECB are not identical to those faced by the Bundesbank. The economic agents in the different European countries will certainly have different sets of economic conditions relating to output, employment, prices and so on, and therefore possibly different monetary expectations. In addition to this, the author's reflection about a more detailed understanding of the role of money in our economy in order to assess the success or failure of monetary targeting is reasonable.

It would be useful to include in the chapter a brief, simplified conceptual discussion to support the mathematical presentation about the operational mechanism and conditions that have to be attained in order to evaluate more efficiently the effectiveness and relevance of a monetary targeting approach. Generally speaking, a number of conditions have to exist for the successful conduct of monetary targeting – namely the controllability of the operating monetary target aggregates, and the stability and predictability of the money multiplier, as well as the stability of the demand for money function. In addition, there is a need for the existence of a viable linkage between the target and the final objective of the central bank and, something very important from a monetarist point of view – the potential and actual success of the central bank in generating the correct expectation from the economic agents, and the lack of fiscal dominance signalling the absence of fiscal interference in the conduct of monetary policy. Some of the above conditions were mentioned specifically in the chapter, and others were not, but a brief reminder for the reader about the importance of these conditions would be useful.

Overall, this part of the book makes a very important contribution to the debate and discussions that exist about the notion of potential success or failure of monetary targeting and the working of central banks.

References

Friedman M, (1968) 'The Role of Monetary Policy', *American Economic Review*, vol. LVIII, (1), March.

Mishkin, Fredric S. (2001) 'From Monetary Targeting to Inflation Targeting: Lessons from Industrialized Countries', Policy Research Working Paper Series 2684, *The World Bank*.

Part II

Macroeconomic Performance

7

From Initiating to Breaching to Diluting the Stability and Growth Pact

Horst Feldmann

Introduction

In European Monetary Union (EMU) with its decentralized fiscal policies there is a strong bias towards large chronic budget deficits. Having a common currency implies that a member country running high fiscal deficits does not have to bear the full cost of doing so. In particular, high deficits in an individual member country are unlikely to cause a rise in that country's interest rates. If interest rates rise, they rise in the whole currency area. Thus each individual member state can shift part of the cost of its own fiscal profligacy on to other member countries. However, large chronic budget deficits and the ensuing rising debt-to-GDP ratios are harmful. They crowd out private investment and thus lower long-term economic growth. Furthermore, sooner or later they may induce governments to put pressure on the European Central Bank (ECB) to permit higher inflation in order to erode the real value of the debt. These adverse effects of national fiscal policies make it necessary to effectively limit budgetary deficits of EMU member states. They are the fundamental justification for the Stability and Growth Pact ('Stability Pact' for short).

Germany always played a pivotal role with respect to the Stability Pact. It initiated the Pact, it breached it several years in a row, and it was the major driving force behind the 2005 reform that considerably diluted the Pact. This chapter analyses Germany's role and performance under the Stability Pact. The second section briefly looks at Germany's 1995 proposal for a Stability Pact. The third section points out how Germany prepared its public finances for the 1998 convergence test. The fourth section analyses, first, why Germany's government deficits got out of hand, and whether this can be justified. Second, it analyses what effects this had on the level of debt, and whether Germany, compared to those countries that consistently consolidated their public budgets, was able to achieve higher rates of economic growth and to avoid cutbacks in public investment. The fifth section briefly illuminates Germany's role in the 2005 reform, and the sixth section concludes.

Initiating the Stability and Growth Pact

After the Maastricht Treaty came into force on 1 November 1993, it became obvious that many German economists and a large part of the German population regarded the Treaty's stipulations intending to ensure that member states 'avoid excessive government deficits' (Article 104c (1)) as being too lax. Indeed, the Maastricht Treaty leaves a wide scope for political discretion, ranging from the decision on whether an excessive deficit exists, to the decision on whether to impose sanctions. In Germany, the so-called 'excessive deficit procedure' of the Maastricht Treaty was also regarded as time-consuming; it was estimated to need three to four years. Many Germans were anxious that some countries, after being admitted to participate in monetary union, might thus fall back into their old habits of running high government deficits, eventually undermining the stability of the new currency. In order to address this concern, and thus to strengthen the rather weak support for EMU among the German population, in autumn 1995 the German government proposed that countries participating in EMU should be required to sign a 'Stability Pact for Europe' (Stark, 2001).

The German government's proposal had two intentions (see Table 7.1). The first aim was to tighten the reference values of the Maastricht Treaty. According to the proposal, the treaty's 3 per cent deficit ceiling was not to be exceeded, not even during economically less prosperous times. During 'normal' economic periods, deficits should not exceed a medium-term ceiling of 1 per cent of GDP. Countries with a debt ratio of more than 50 per cent of GDP were committed to undershooting the 1 per cent ceiling, 'if possible.' Overshooting the 3 per cent ceiling was to be allowed only in 'extreme cases' and only with the approval of a qualified majority.

The second intention of Germany's proposal was to speed up the excessive deficit procedure and to limit the Council's and the Commission's scope for discretion. To this end, Germany proposed that sanctions should be imposed automatically as soon as it emerged that a member state had exceeded the 3 per cent limit, even if this was only the case according to budgetary planning. The member state concerned was then to be required to make a non-interest bearing deposit equal to 0.25 per cent of GDP for each whole percentage point in excess of the 3 per cent limit. If, after two years, the 3 per cent limit was still being exceeded, the deposit was to be converted into a fine.

Although most governments of the other European Union (EU) member states publicly approved Germany's proposal, in reality many of them rejected its basic ideas. During the negotiations that followed, Germany's proposal was substantially watered down. While Germany wanted to tolerate

Table 7.1 Main provisions of different versions of the Stability and Growth Pact

	Germany's 1995 proposal	**Version adopted in 1997**	**Revised version adopted in 2005**
Medium-term budgetary objective	A deficit ceiling of 1% of GDP during 'normal' economic periods. Countries entering monetary union with a debt ratio of more than 50% of GDP are committed to undershooting this deficit ceiling, 'if possible.' The 3% deficit ceiling set by the Maastricht Treaty is not to be exceeded, not even during economically less prosperous times. The debt ratio is to be consistently reduced, even if it falls below the 60% reference value set by the Maastricht Treaty.	Budgetary position close to balance or in surplus (a deficit of no more than 0.5% of GDP)	Country-specific objectives ranging between −1% of GDP (given high growth rates and low levels of debt) and a budgetary position close to balance or in surplus. Member states are permitted to diverge temporarily from their medium-term budgetary objective in the case of certain structural reforms.
Adjustment path towards medium-term objective	No specific provision	No specific provision	Annual consolidation of 0.5% of GDP if the medium-term objective is not achieved. More consolidation in 'good times' and less consolidation in 'bad times.' Deviations in the case of certain structural reforms allowed.

Table 7.1 (Continued)

	Germany's 1995 proposal	Version adopted in 1997	Revised version adopted in 2005
Justification for overshooting the 3% deficit ceiling set by the Maastricht Treaty	Only in 'extreme cases' and only with approval of a qualified majority of the states participating in monetary union	• Natural disasters • GDP decline of at least 2% p.a. • GDP decline between 0.75% and 2% p.a. at the Council's discretion	• Natural disasters • Negative growth rates • Growth rates below potential growth with considerable accumulated loss of output • Development of potential growth • Prevailing cyclical conditions • Implementation of the Lisbon strategy • Expenditure on research, development and innovation • Earlier fiscal consolidation in 'good times' • Sustainability of debt level • Public investment • 'Quality' of public finances • Burdens resulting from 'financial contributions to fostering international solidarity'

			• Burdens arising from 'achieving of European policy objectives, notably the unification of Europe' • Pension reform
Deadline for correcting an excessive deficit	None	The year after the deficit is identified unless 'special circumstances' exist. (After giving notice, the Council is free to decide on the deadline for deficit correction.)	Generally, the year after the deficit is identified. Given 'special circumstances', two years after the deficit is identified. In case of unexpected adverse economic events during the correction phase, the first recommendations for correcting the deficit and the recommendations when giving notice may be repeated and reformulated, and the deadline may be extended. (After giving notice, the Council is free to decide on the deadline for deficit correction.)
Deadlines under the excessive deficit procedure	No provision		
• Identification of an excessive deficit		3 months after semi-annual budgetary report	4 months after semi-annual budgetary report

Table 7.1 (Continued)

	Germany's 1995 proposal	Version adopted in 1997	Revised version adopted in 2005
• Taking effective measures		4 months	6 months
• Giving notice after identifying insufficient measures		1 month	2 month
• Taking effective measures after being given notice		2 months	4 months
Imposition and type of sanctions	Automatic imposition of sanctions. If it emerges that a country participating in monetary union has, either in its budgetary planning or in the implementation of its budget, exceeded the 3% deficit ceiling, the member state concerned is required to make a non-interest-bearing deposit. The size of the deposit is equivalent to 0.25% of GDP for each whole percentage point in excess of the deficit ceiling. The deposit will be repaid as soon as the deficit ceases to exceed the reference value. If, after two years, the deficit ceiling is still being exceeded, the deposit is converted into a fine.	Council decision to impose sanctions. As a rule, a non-interest-bearing deposit. The amount of the deposit shall comprise a fixed component equal to 0.2% of GDP, and a variable component equal to one tenth of the difference between the deficit ratio in the preceding year and the 3% reference value. Upper limit of 0.5% of GDP. As a rule, the deposit shall be converted into a fine if the excessive deficit has not been corrected after two years.	Same as in 1997 version

Sources: Deutsche Bundesbank (2005a); European Commission (2005a); Konow (2002); Stark (2001).

a breach of the 3 per cent ceiling only in case of a natural disaster or a severe recession, the Stability Pact adopted in 1997 permitted such a breach also in the case of a mild recession (see Table 7.1). More importantly, while Germany's proposal was intended to replace political discretion with an automatic mechanism, the 1997 version ensured that the Council of Ministers was allowed to vote at each stage of an excessive deficit procedure. In making these decisions, it had wide scope for discretion. For example, at the sanction stage, the 1997 version stipulated that a non-interest bearing deposit was only to be required 'as a rule', and that the deposit was only to be converted into a fine after two years 'as a rule'.

It is true that there were several vague phrases allowing for political discretion in Germany's proposal as well ('normal' economic periods; undershooting the 1 per cent limit, 'if possible'; 'extreme cases'). Still, the scope for discretion in that proposal was much smaller. Furthermore, although the 1997 version limited the period between the communication of budgetary figures and the decision on the imposition of sanctions to ten months in the normal case (see Table 7.1), this was much longer than according to Germany's proposal (which stipulated that sanctions were to be imposed immediately). Also, contrary to Germany's proposal, there was a cap on the amount of the fine (see Table 7.1).

While none of the basic elements of Germany's proposal was adopted in its original form, and the 1997 version that eventually took effect in 1999 was full of escape clauses, the German government still regarded this version as a successful outcome of its initiative. In 1998, the German Minister of Finance stated before the German Parliament that it represented 'the final and fundamental rejection of unsound fiscal policies' (Steuer, 2001, p. 108).

Preparing for the convergence test

In the mid-1990s, Germany, like all other EU member states, substantially reduced its government deficit. The main motive was to fulfil the deficit criterion of the Maastricht Treaty by 1997, which was the reference year for the convergence criteria compliance test that took place in spring 1998. Indeed, Germany succeeded in cutting its deficit from 3.4 per cent of GDP in 1996 to 2.7 per cent of GDP in 1997 (see Table 7.2). However, Germany, like several other countries (France and Italy, in particular), implemented various creative accounting methods that lowered its public deficit only temporarily and only at first sight.

In spring 1997, the German Minister of Finance proposed that the Bundesbank's gold and foreign exchange reserves should be revalued according to market prices and that the valuation gains, estimated at around DEM 60 billion, should mostly be distributed to the federal government to reduce the debt incurred for German unification. The Bundesbank was firmly opposed to this proposal. It pointed out that the proposal neither accorded

Table 7.2 General government financial balances[a], percentage of GDP

	1974–85	1986–90	1991–95	1996	1997	1998	1999	2000	2001	2002	2003	2004
Austria	−2.3	−3.5	−3.9	−3.9	−1.7	−2.3	−2.2	−1.9	0.1	−0.4	−1.2	−1.0
Belgium	−9.0	−8.0	−6.4	−3.8	−2.1	−0.8	−0.5	0.1	0.4	0.0	0.1	0.0
Finland	3.7	4.5	−4.7	−2.9	−1.3	1.6	2.2	7.1	5.2	4.3	2.5	2.1
France	−1.6	−2.3	−4.7	−4.1	−3.0	−2.7	−1.7	−1.4	−1.6	−3.2	−4.1	−3.7
Germany	−2.8	−1.5	−2.9	−3.4	−2.7	−2.2	−1.5	−1.2	−2.9	−3.8	−4.1	−3.7
Greece	−5.0	−12.0	−11.6	−7.4	−6.6	−4.3	−3.4	−4.1	−6.6	−4.9	−5.7	−6.6
Ireland	−10.0	−5.3	−2.5	−0.1	1.1	2.4	2.5	4.4	0.8	−0.6	0.2	1.4
Italy	−9.6	−11.8	−9.9	−7.1	−2.7	−2.8	−1.7	−2.0	−3.2	−2.7	−3.2	−3.2
Luxembourg	1.8	*n.a.*	1.7	2.2	3.0	3.3	3.5	6.1	6.5	2.1	0.2	−1.2
Netherlands	−3.4	−4.9	−3.5	−1.8	−1.1	−0.7	0.6	1.4	−0.2	−2.0	−3.2	−2.1
Portugal	−6.8	−4.3	−5.2	−4.6	−3.4	−3.0	−2.7	−3.2	−4.2	−2.8	−2.9	−3.0
Spain	−2.6	−4.1	−5.6	−4.9	−3.2	−3.0	−1.2	−1.0	−0.5	−0.3	0.0	−0.1
Euro area	−3.9	−4.2	−5.0	−4.3	−2.7	−2.2	−1.3	−1.0	−1.8	−2.5	−3.0	−2.7

Note: [a]Excluding one-off revenues from the sale of mobile telephone licenses (UMTS) in 2000–2.
Sources: European Commission (2003a), p. 113; European Commission (2005b), table 7.

with current accounting law nor with the arrangements envisaged for the European System of Central Banks (ESCB), that it was an infringement of the Bundesbank's independence, and that there was the danger that the proposed measure would undermine people's confidence in the stability of the future European currency (Deutsche Bundesbank, 1997). The Minister of Finance was forced to negotiate a compromise with the Bundesbank that postponed the proceeds from a much more moderate revaluation until 1998 (Bundesminister der Finanzen, Präsident der Deutschen Bundesbank, 1997).

While the government's attempt to lower its 1997 deficit with the help of the Bundesbank's reserves eventually failed, it applied several other dubious measures that did lower its deficit figure for that year (and some for earlier years as well). For example, in 1995, after the dissolution of the Treuhandanstalt (the privatization agency for East Germany), the debt of this agency, amounting to DEM 204 billion, was transferred to the government. Consequently, the German Federal Statistical Office recorded it as an increase in government debt, and the service on this debt as an increase in the government deficit. However, the government held the opinion that this debt should be excluded from the statistics as it resulted from an 'extraordinary transaction' (Münster, 1997, p. 4). Eurostat, the statistical office of the European Commission, agreed. It allowed the German government to exclude the debt and the debt service transferred from the Treuhandanstalt.

Eurostat also assisted the German government in lowering its debt and deficit figures by another pure accounting measure. In Germany, the debt of public hospitals used to be part of general government debt. However, in 1997 Eurostat ruled that the debt of public hospitals should be excluded. This accounting fudge alone lowered Germany's 1997 deficit by 0.2 per cent of GDP (Münster, 1997).

Germany also lowered its 1997 deficit figure by privatizing state-owned enterprises on a large scale. In particular, it simply sold shares in Deutsche Telekom to the state-owned bank Kreditanstalt für Wiederaufbau. Additionally, it sold real estate owned by the public railway company and induced Airbus Industries to repay the discounted value of subsidies that were due to be repaid only over a period stretching to the year 2013 (Sachverständigenrat zur Begutachtung der gesamtwirtschaftlichen Entwicklung, 1997, pp. 191–2; Sachverständigenrat zur Begutachtung der gesamtwirtschaftlichen Entwicklung, 1998, pp. 127–31). Furthermore, the government substantially lowered its deficit by massively resorting to short-term rather than long-term loans. Since the beginning of the 1990s, the share of loans with a period of less than two years in the total gross loans raised by the federal government increased from 9 per cent to 36 per cent in 1997 (Sachverständigenrat zur Begutachtung der gesamtwirtschaftlichen Entwicklung, 1998, p. 130). This lowered the deficit, because at that time short-term interest rates were below the long-term rates.

All these creative accounting methods were used with the sole intention of pushing the 1997 deficit figure below the 3 per cent reference value. They were either purely cosmetic or implied lower receipts and/or higher expenditure in the following years. The shortening of the term structure of loans implied the risk of substantially higher expenditure in the future once interest rates started to rise. Thus, contrary to the German government's stated policy of ensuring sound public finances in EMU, Germany itself actually was far from truly consolidating its public finances even during the run-up to monetary union. Instead, it cooked its public sector books in order to pass the convergence test.

Breaching the Stability and Growth Pact

Causes

The Cyclical Downturn

In 2002, Germany exceeded the deficit ceiling for the first time, and its public deficit has remained substantially above this ceiling ever since (see Table 7.2). The main excuse used by the government was the cyclical downturn that started in 2000. Figure 7.1 shows the change in the output gaps in the euro countries, indicating that the economy decelerated substantially between 2000 and 2003 in all countries except Greece. As the change in the cyclical components of the general government financial balances shows, this had a negative impact on public budgets. Cyclical revenues decreased while cyclical expenditure increased. Germany's output gap diminished from +1.1 per cent to −1.1 per cent of potential GDP and the cyclical component of its budget balance deteriorated by 1.5 percentage points of GDP.

However, the cyclical downturn was stronger in all other euro countries except Spain and Italy. In Luxembourg, Finland, Ireland and Austria, the economy declined substantially more than in Germany (see Figure 7.1). Still, none of these countries incurred high budget deficits during the recession (see Table 7.2). This is all the more remarkable, since the negative impact of the business cycle on the budget balance was much stronger in most of these countries than in Germany. Specifically, the government budget balance deteriorated by 3.4 percentage points of GDP in Luxembourg, 2.7 in Finland and 1.8 in Ireland because of the economic slump (see Figure 7.1). In the Netherlands, the adverse impact of the recession on the public budget was almost three times as high as in Germany (see Figure 7.1). Still, the Netherlands only exceeded the deficit ceiling in 2003, and then only by a slight margin, and managed to undershoot it again in the following year (see Table 7.2).

This illustrates that, while the cyclical downturn did contribute to Germany's higher government deficits, this explanation is not sufficient on its own and is by no means an acceptable excuse. As a matter of fact,

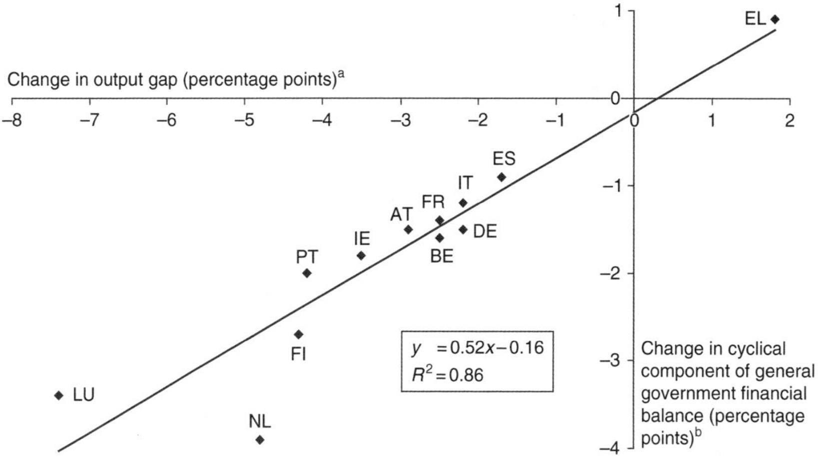

Notes: [a] Change from 2000 to 2003 in percentage points of potential GDP; *x*-axis.
[b] Change from 2000 to 2003 in percentage points of GDP; *y*-axis.
Sources: European Commission (2005b), table 8A; European Commission (2005c), pp. 184–95.

Figure 7.1 Cyclical downturn and general government financial balances

Germany's cyclically adjusted government balance had already exceeded the 3 per cent ceiling in 2001 (that is one year before the nominal budget) and has stayed markedly above that ceiling ever since (Table 7.3). The deterioration of a government's budget balances in the course of the downturn is only the consequence of the working of the automatic stabilizers. However, the Stability Pact allows enough leeway for these to act. As empirical studies have uniformly shown, all euro countries would be able to stay within the 3 per cent mark during a normal recession without any problem, provided their budgets are balanced or slightly in surplus during a normal cyclical situation as set out in the Stability Pact.[1] Germany not even managed to balance its budget in the boom year 2000 (see Table 7.2). A cyclical downturn like the one seen in the years 2000 to 2003 does not justify breaching the deficit ceiling. The exception clause of the Stability Pact in the event of severe recessions – according to which a breach of the reference value may be acceptable if real GDP declines by at least 0.75 per cent year on year (see Table 7.1) – was not applicable either, because Germany's GDP growth rates during the cyclical downswing were positive in all years apart from 2003, when GDP declined by a mere 0.2 per cent.

Structural unemployment

Can Germany's high government deficits be explained by its high structural unemployment? Mass unemployment not only entails high levels of expenditure for unemployment benefits and active labour market policy

Table 7.3 General government cyclically adjusted balances,[a] percentage of GDP

	1974–85	1986–90	1991–95	1996	1997	1998	1999	2000	2001	2002	2003	2004
Austria	−2.3	−3.2	−4.1	−3.6	−1.2	−2.4	−2.8	−3.0	−0.3	−0.3	−0.8	−0.9
Belgium	−9.0	−7.9	−6.4	−2.8	−1.8	−0.4	−0.7	−1.0	0.0	−0.2	0.5	0.1
Finland	3.9	1.6	−1.2	−1.5	−1.8	0.2	0.9	4.9	4.7	4.4	3.0	2.3
France	−1.5	−2.5	−4.7	−2.9	−2.1	−2.5	−2.2	−2.7	−2.7	−3.9	−4.0	−3.6
Germany	−2.6	−0.9	−3.8	−2.5	−1.9	−1.6	−1.1	−2.0	−3.6	−3.8	−3.3	−3.3
Greece	−4.9	−11.8	−11.4	−6.1	−5.5	−3.3	−2.5	−3.5	−6.5	−5.0	−6.0	−7.5
Ireland	−10.3	−4.9	−1.2	1.0	0.5	1.7	0.6	1.9	−1.1	−2.1	−0.5	1.4
Italy	−9.5	−12.1	−9.8	−7.1	−3.0	−3.2	−2.1	−2.9	−4.1	−3.1	−3.0	−3.0
Luxembourg	2.6	*n.a.*	1.0	4.5	3.7	3.4	2.7	3.8	5.9	2.6	1.3	−0.3
Netherlands	−3.4	−4.8	−3.2	−0.9	−1.0	−1.8	−1.4	−1.2	−2.0	−2.2	−1.9	−1.0
Portugal	−6.7	−4.4	−5.2	−3.7	−3.2	−3.5	−3.6	−4.6	−5.5	−3.4	−2.3	−2.4
Spain	−2.5	−4.5	−5.6	−3.4	−2.2	−2.8	−1.7	−2.3	−1.8	−1.1	−0.4	−0.3
Euro area	−3.8	−4.3	−5.3	−3.4	−2.1	−2.2	−1.6	−2.1	−2.8	−2.9	−2.6	−2.5

Note: [a]Excluding one-off revenues from the sale of mobile telephone licences (UMTS) in 2000–2.
Sources: European Commission (2003b), pp. 205–18; European Commission (2005b), table 9A.

programmes (especially further education and public employment schemes) but also causes the revenues from taxes and social insurance contributions to be far lower than would otherwise be the case.

On average over the years 1999 to 2004, Germany's unemployment rate amounted to 8.2 per cent. Yet Germany has been suffering from high structural unemployment for many years. In comparison to the six-year period before 1999, unemployment did not increase but rather decreased slightly (see Table 7.4). Moreover, in Finland and Spain, unemployment between 1999 and 2004 was higher than in Germany. None the less, Finland's public budget had been in surplus in every single year from 1998 (see Table 7.2). Spain has substantially improved its public finances since the mid-1990s, resulting in a balanced budget between 2002 and 2004. Therefore, Germany's high level of structural unemployment can neither explain nor justify its poor fiscal performance.

Optimistic forecasts

Germany's poor performance under the Stability Pact can be explained in part by the fact that the government based its stability programmes on overly optimistic assumptions with respect to future economic growth and future fiscal balances. The governments of the euro countries usually submit their annual stability programmes between the end of November and mid-December. To arrive at the average overestimation of the real GDP growth rate presented in Table 7.4, the stability programmes of the years 1999 to 2003 have been used to calculate the divergence of the GDP growth rate forecasted for the respective subsequent year from the actual GDP growth rate.

As the figures arrived at show, Germany overestimated future economic growth with a larger margin than most other euro countries. Only Italy, Portugal and the Netherlands overestimated their GDP growth rates to a similar or larger extent. The difference in the average overestimation of economic growth between Germany and most countries that successfully consolidated their budgets is noticeable. For example, Austria overestimated its GDP growth rate only by an average of 0.2 percentage points. Belgium's estimates exactly matched its actual outcomes, on average. Ireland, Luxembourg, Spain and Finland even underestimated their GDP growth rates (see Table 7.4). Obviously, the German government based its budgetary projections on much more optimistic assumptions with respect to future growth than the governments of most other countries. Consequently, its projections implied a lesser need to consolidate its budget.

As a matter of fact, Germany's projections of future fiscal balances were also over-optimistic (see Figure 7.2). The discrepancies between the projected figures and the actual outcomes are huge. At the end of 2001 – the year when the nominal and the structural deficit reached 2.9 per cent and 3.6 per cent of GDP, respectively – the government projected that it would balance its budget within three years. At the end of 2002 – the year when both the

Table 7.4 Possible reasons for exceeding the reference value

	Average unemployment rate (%)[a]		Real GDP growth rate overestimated by . . . percentage points 1999–2004[b]	Cyclical safety margin (percentage points)[c]	Number of votes in the Council of Ministers[d]	Local and regional government financial balance 2000–04 (%)[e]
	1993–98	1999–2004				
Austria	4.2	4.1	0.2	0.9	4	0.5
Belgium	9.4	7.6	0.0	2.3	5	0.3
Finland	14.5	9.3	−0.0	3.8	3	−0.2
France	11.4	9.3	0.4	1.3	10	0.2
Germany	8.4	8.2	0.8	1.4	10	−1.2
Greece	9.5	10.8	−0.3	1.3	5	0.1
Ireland	11.9	4.5	−0.9	1.7	3	0.0
Italy	11.0	9.2	1.1	1.5	10	0.1
Luxembourg	2.8	3.0	−0.6	3.1	2	0.1
Netherlands	5.7	3.2	0.7	2.3	5	−0.4
Portugal	6.5	5.1	0.9	1.8	5	−0.1
Spain	18.0	11.5	−0.3	1.5	8	−0.3
Euro area	10.5	8.6	–	1.6	70	n.a.

Notes: [a] Unemployed as a percentage of labour force – Eurostat definition.

[b] Deviation of the GDP growth rate forecasted for the respective subsequent year from the actual GDP growth rate (percentage points). Forecasts for the years 2000–04 in the 1999–2003 national stability programmes. A minus sign indicates that the growth rate of real GDP was underestimated.

[c] Difference between the maximum value for the general government cyclically adjusted balance and the 3% reference value (percentage points of GDP); European Commission estimates.

[d] Until October 2004. Total number of votes in the Council of Ministers until October 2004: 87.

[e] As a percentage of GDP.

Sources: Belgian Ministry of Finance (various issues); Bundesministerium der Finanzen (various issues); Department of Finance (various issues); European Commission (1999); European Commission (2001); European Commission (2002a); European Commission (2003b); European Commission (2003c); European Commission (2004a); European Commission (2005c); Finnish Ministry of Finance (various issues); Government of Portugal (various issues); Government of the French Republic (various issues); Government of the Netherlands (various issues); Grand Duchy of Luxembourg Ministry of Finance (various issues); Hellenic Republic Ministry of Economy and Finance (various issues); Kingdom of Spain (various issues); Ministro dell'Economia (various issues); Österreichisches Bundesministerium der Finanzen (various issues).

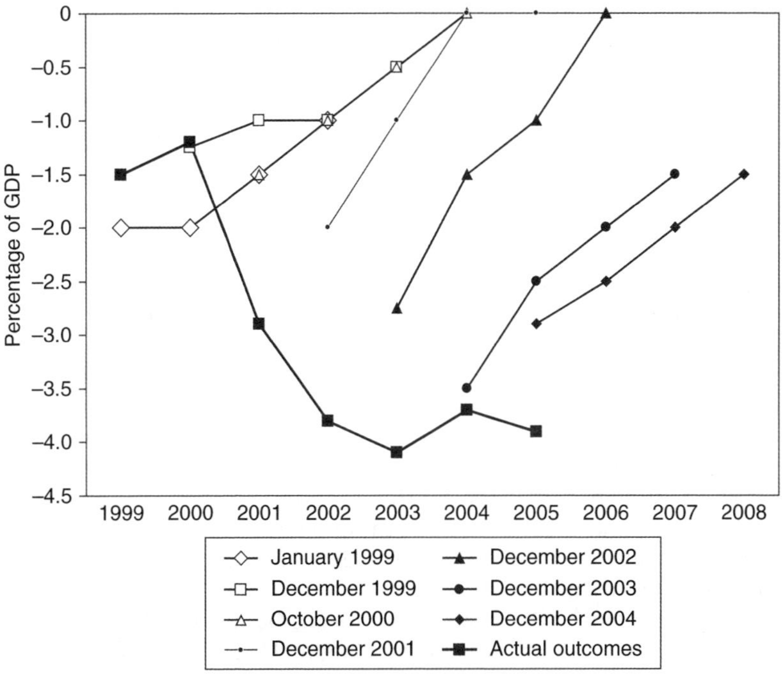

Note: [a]Excluding UMTS proceeds (2.5% of GDP in 2000).
Sources: Bundesministerium der Finanzen (various issues); European Commission (2003a), p. 113; European Commission (2005b), table 7.

Figure 7.2 Projections of general government financial balances from the German stability programmes[a]

nominal and the structural deficit reached 3.8 per cent of GDP – the government still stated it would eliminate its fiscal deficits by 2006. Obviously, for as long as possible it tried to give the impression that it was in a process of balancing its budget. At the same time, it was unwilling to undertake the policy measures necessary to achieve this goal. Since 2003, the government has become more realistic in its fiscal projections. Neither the 2003 nor the 2004 stability programme indicate that the government is willing or able to balance its budget (Figure 7.2).

Low cyclical safety margin

Germany's poor fiscal performance could also be caused by a low cyclical safety margin. The European Commission, among others, estimates cyclical safety margins. They indicate the distance a state's cyclically adjusted budget balance should have *vis-à-vis* the 3 per cent reference value in order for the nominal deficit not to exceed this value during a recession. The cyclical safety margins vary from country to country: the more the business cycle fluctuates and the stronger the reaction of the government budget balance to cyclical swings, the higher is the required cyclical safety margin. If only a small margin is necessary, the government of the country concerned might be tempted to postpone the consolidation of the state budget and tolerate relatively high deficits.

A comparison of the euro countries' cyclical safety margins reveals that Germany does indeed need a much lower one than Finland, Luxembourg, Belgium or the Netherlands (see Table 7.4). It also needs a smaller safety margin than Euroland as a whole. The difference between Germany's safety margin and the average value for the entire monetary union is only slight, though. Moreover, Austria, Ireland and Spain require similarly low cyclical safety margins as Germany's; none the less, they have pursued a much stricter budgetary consolidation policy (see Tables 7.2 and 7.3).

Overall, this leads us to conclude that the consolidation pressure exerted on Germany could in fact have been ameliorated by the relatively smaller cyclical safety margin required by this country. However, the example of Austria, Ireland and Spain shows that the differences in consolidation policy can only partially be explained by the potential disincentive effect of a small cyclical safety margin.

High government deficits can by no means be justified by the requirement of only a small cyclical safety margin. First of all, this margin is only for information purposes. On no account does it suspend or diminish the obligation laid down in the Stability Pact to attain close to balance or surplus budgets in the medium term. Second, the European Commission (2000, pp. 53–4; 2002a, p. 59) has always stressed that, in addition to the cyclical safety margin, a further safety margin is necessary for unforeseen non-cyclical additional spending or lower revenues such as, for example, in the case of a sharp rise in interest rates or in the case of a natural disaster. According to estimates by the Commission, this additional margin should be around 0.5 per cent to 1.0 per cent of GDP.

Number of votes in the Council of Ministers

It is remarkable that all three countries with the largest number of votes in the Council of Ministers (France, Germany, Italy) exceeded the deficit ceiling (see Tables 7.2 and 7.4). The greatest obstacle in the way of imposing sanctions against a member state is the fact that, according to Article 104 (6) EC Treaty, the Council has to take a decision on the existence of an excessive deficit by a qualified majority. Until October 2004, this meant that at least 62 (out of 87) votes by at least 10 (out of 15) members of the Council were required. A minimum of 26 votes or 6 member states constituted a blocking minority. Therefore, France, Germany and Italy could always jointly block a decision on the existence of an excessive deficit and thus also the imposition of sanctions. Furthermore, it was relatively easy for one or two of the large countries to obtain the required votes for a blocking minority by engaging in political barter deals. Evidently, its voting power also tempted Germany to pursue a lax consolidation policy.[2]

It is also remarkable that the countries with the smallest number of votes (Luxembourg, Finland, Ireland, Austria) have all largely consolidated their government budgets (see Tables 7.2 and 7.3). These countries have the least certainty of being able to organise a blocking minority in the event that they exceed the deficit ceiling. The fact that Greece and Portugal also exceeded the deficit ceiling despite the fact that neither of those countries has a large number of votes suggests that there were other factors responsible for the performance of public finances since the start of EMU apart from the number of voting rights in the Council of Ministers.

Although the relatively large number of votes that Germany has in the Council of Ministers can partly explain its poor deficit performance, it does not, of course, justify this performance. The decision on the existence of an excessive deficit and on the imposition of sanctions should be taken solely on the basis of objective criteria. The criteria should be applied to all countries equally. Power politics should not play a role.

The role of local and regional governments

Under the Stability Pact, every central government has committed itself to limit the deficit of the entire state. However, the amount of this deficit is not influenced by the central government alone, but also by local and regional governments. In fact, in all member states of monetary union local and regional governments play a significant role in fiscal policy. A major share of government spending is carried out at these levels. This is particularly true for Germany, where the *Länder* (the regional authorities) and the municipalities carried out 41 per cent of total government expenditure between 2000 and 2003. However, in Finland and Spain the share of local and regional governments' expenditure is also high. In both of these countries, as well as in Austria and Belgium, local and regional governments enjoy a higher degree of financial autonomy than in Germany (European Commission, 2001, p. 55), but each of these four countries still managed to successfully consolidate its general government budget (Tables 7.2 and 7.3).

Over the past few years, most EMU member states have either tightened existing regulations that control local and regional government financial performance (for example, Belgium, Finland) or have introduced new regulations (for example, Austria, Spain). These new regulations are often referred to as national stability pacts. They are intended to ensure that the local and regional governments also contribute to the country's compliance with the European Stability Pact.[3] Germany adopted a national stability pact as well. However, while Austria concluded its national stability pact as early as 1998, in Germany, the federal government, the *Länder* and the municipalities only managed to reach an agreement as late as March 2002. More importantly, while Austria's national stability pact – as the one adopted by Spain – is legally binding, Germany's national stability pact is non-binding. It also lacks any sanction mechanism. As a result, Germany's national stability pact is largely ineffective.

The results of these deficient regulations can be seen in Table 7.4. Between 2000 and 2004, the combined deficits of German local and regional authorities amounted to 1.2 per cent of GDP. During this period, these authorities accounted for 37 per cent of the overall deficit. They were thus indeed responsible for a substantial share of Germany's overall fiscal deficit. By contrast, in Austria, Belgium, France, Greece, Ireland, Italy and Luxembourg, the budgets of the local and regional governments were in surplus between 2000 and 2004 (see Table 7.4). In Finland, the Netherlands, Portugal and Spain, the deficits of these authorities were moderate. Thus all other euro countries managed to keep the public finances of the local and regional governments under control – despite the often large proportion in overall public expenditure and the often extensive financial autonomy of these authorities.

Of course, the high share of the *Länder* and municipalities in Germany's overall deficit does not justify the breach of the deficit ceiling. The federal government has committed itself *vis-à-vis* its partners in the European Union and the Union's bodies to respect the European Stability Pact. It was the responsibility of the federal government to ensure that it can fulfil its obligation. For this purpose, the federal government should have assured itself of the co-responsibility of the *Länder* and municipalities at an early stage.

Preference for government deficits

A country's long-term average government deficit strongly depends on the preferences of its people and its politicians. If high deficits are generally tolerated or even considered positive, this will be reflected in a corresponding magnitude of the actual government deficits, at least in the long term. At the same time, such preferences probably change only slowly. If the politicians and the citizens of a country have been convinced for a long time that high government deficits are unproblematic or even desirable, it will be hard to make them change their minds – even with a Stability Pact concluded at the European level.

In principle, Germany's poor fiscal performance could be attributable to such an attitude. Perhaps Germany has reduced its deficit only in the short term to pass the convergence test and thus gain admission to EMU. Now that it is a member of monetary union, its government deficit tends back towards the range preferred by the German people and politicians.

However, Germany has long been famous for its so-called 'stability culture'. In the past, this term primarily referred to its low rates of inflation, but to some extent to its comparatively low fiscal deficits as well. Indeed, Germany does not have a tradition of high government deficits.

Between 1974 and 1995, both its nominal and its structural deficit averaged 2.5 per cent of GDP (see Tables 7.2 and 7.3). Thus the high deficits Germany incurred since 2001 are a new experience for this country.

Remarkably, there are several euro countries – Belgium and Ireland, in particular, but to some extent the Netherlands and Spain as well – that do have a long tradition of high nominal and structural deficits and yet have reduced these substantially since the mid-1990s – not only in anticipation of the convergence test, but afterwards too (see Tables 7.2 and 7.3). Once again, these examples illustrate that Germany's high fiscal deficits since 2001 were by no means inevitable. Given this country's long tradition of moderate government deficits, the German people probably would have preferred much lower deficits.

Discretionary fiscal policy

Germany's poor fiscal performance was partly caused by the fact that, during the last boom, the government engaged in an expansive discretionary fiscal policy. The stance of discretionary fiscal policy can most easily be discerned in the changes in the cyclically adjusted primary balance. The automatic stabilizers as well as the effects of changes in interest rates on public budgets are excluded in the computation of this indicator.

As the positive values for the output gap in Figure 7.3 indicate, capacity utilization in Euroland as a whole was above average between 1999 and 2002. The year 2000, in particular, was a boom year. None the less, in the euro area as a whole, discretionary fiscal policy was expansionary in 2000, 2001 and 2002. Despite above-average capacity utilization rates, the euro area's cyclically adjusted primary balance worsened by an average of 0.6 percentage points of GDP against each previous year.

In 2000 and 2002, Germany's discretionary fiscal policy was just as expansionary as the EMU average although Germany's capacity utilization was also above average in both years. In 2001, Germany's discretionary fiscal policy was much more expansionary than the EMU average. In that year alone, Germany's cyclically adjusted primary balance deteriorated by 2.2 percentage points of GDP although capacity utilization was above average in this year as well (Figure 7.3). Because of the apparently favourable development of public finances in the previous years, the government markedly cut direct taxes while reducing expenditure only marginally. Also, tax evasion accelerated as the level of taxes remained high, particularly in comparison to other countries.[4] As a consequence, the nominal and structural deficits increased sharply as capacity utilization fell (see Tables 7.2 and 7.3). Because of the high deficits, the German government even pursued a contractive discretionary fiscal policy in 2003 despite the slump in the economy, that is, it acted pro-cyclically once again (see Figure 7.3).

To a certain degree, the poor performance of Germany's fiscal balance was thus caused by the government's failure to consolidate its budget during the

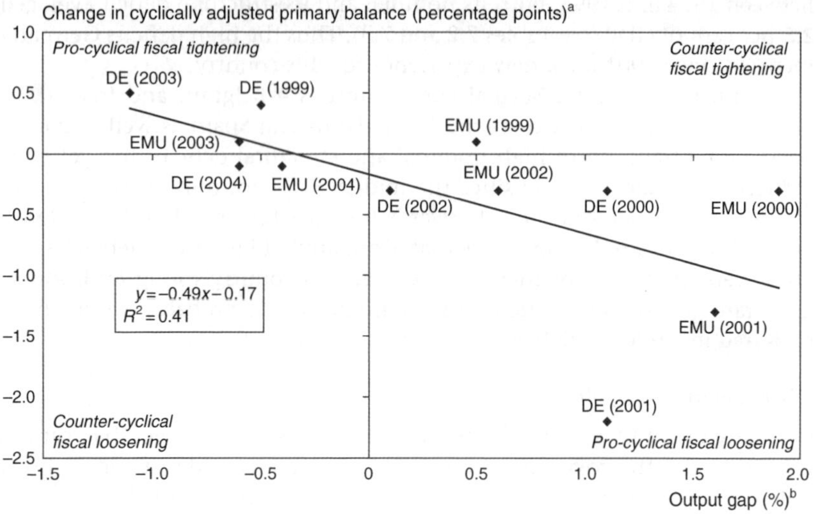

Notes: [a]Change from previous year in percentages points of GDP; *y*-axis.
[b]As a percentage of potential GDP; *x*-axis.
Sources: European Commission (2003a), p. 114; European Commission (2005c), pp. 185, 196; European Commission (2005d), p. 137; European Commission (2005e), p. 141.

Figure 7.3 Discretionary fiscal policy and cyclical conditions

boom, and by the fact that it pursued an expansive discretionary fiscal policy instead. Since Germany's expansionary orientation was extremely strong in 2001, this partly explains the disproportionately poor deficit performance.

Of course, the fact that discretionary fiscal policy was expansionary during the boom does not justify Germany's excessively high deficits – not even the fact that such a policy was pursued in most other EMU countries as well. First, discretionary fiscal policy in Germany was excessively expansionary. Second, every member state is responsible for consolidating its own budget. Third, the expansionary fiscal policies of the neighbouring countries would have made it even easier for Germany to consolidate its public budget as its neighbours' expansionary fiscal policies boosted Germany's exports and thus its tax revenues.

Insufficient limitation of expenditure

Numerous empirical studies have shown that a consolidation of public budgets will only be successful in the long term if it is based essentially on the limitation and reduction of government spending (especially government consumption).[5] Consolidations that were primarily based on tax increases have largely proved to be short-lived. As Figure 7.4 illustrates, Germany actually reduced its government expenditure ratio between 1998 and 2004.

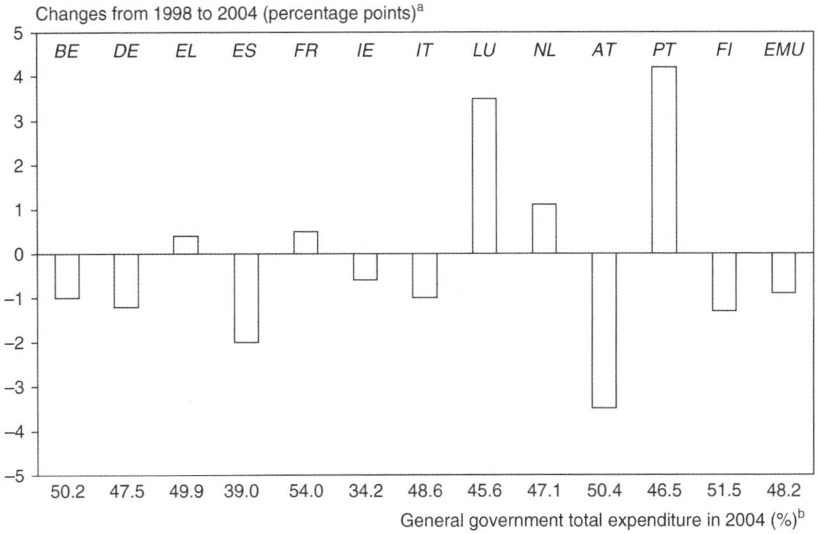

Notes: [a]Percentage points of GDP.
[b]As a percentage of GDP.
Source: European Commission (2005c), p. 176.

Figure 7.4 General government total expenditure

However, the size of the reduction – 1.2 percentage points of GDP – was comparatively modest. In Austria and Spain, the value dropped much more sharply. Unsurprisingly, both countries thus managed to balance their budgets, in both nominal and structural terms (see Tables 7.2 and 7.3).

Tax increases in order to cut the budget deficit would not have been advisable in the case of Germany. First, revenue-based consolidations have largely proved to be unsuccessful in the long term. Second, although the German government cut income tax rates in several stages, starting in 2000, the tax burden is still high, particularly in comparison to other countries. For example, in 2003 labour taxes amounted to 51.9 per cent of total labour cost for a production worker who earned the average wage, was single and had no children. This was far more than in all other countries listed in Table 7.5, apart from Belgium. In case of a one-earner family with two children, labour taxes for an average production worker were much lower. They were at a level comparable to many other European countries (see Table 7.5). However, even this tax wedge by far exceeded the levels of Ireland, Luxembourg, Switzerland, the United Kingdom and the USA.

In today's globalized economy, countries compete for mobile resources. The most mobile resources, and the ones that are particularly important to long-term economic growth, are highly skilled employees and capital. As Table 7.5 illustrates, in 2003 the tax burden for highly skilled employees

Table 7.5 Taxation and the shadow economy

	Tax wedge (%)[a], average production worker 2003		Tax wedge (%)[c], highly skilled employee 2003		Company taxation (%)[d] 2003		Shadow economy (%)[e] 2002/03
	Single person, no children	Married with two children[b]	Single person, no children	Married with two children	Effective average tax rate	Effective marginal tax rate	
Austria	45.0	29.5	41.7	38.2	30.4	22.9	10.9
Belgium	54.6	39.1	54.0	50.3	28.7	16.3	21.0
Czech Republic	43.2	27.1	43.6	43.2	23.5	17.4	20.1
Finland	44.4	37.6	56.6	55.4	26.5	21.2	17.4
France	48.3	39.9	47.3	39.4	32.1	25.5	14.5
Germany	51.9	33.4	47.6	35.2	37.3	28.4	16.8
Hungary	45.6	30.3	45.2	44.9	19.4	18.9	26.2
Ireland	24.2	6.4	40.3	35.8	14.0	11.9	15.3
Italy	45.4	35.7	49.8	49.2	31.8	18.9	25.7
Luxembourg	31.5	9.2	39.2	26.0	25.8	14.7	*n.a.*

Netherlands	35.2	24.5	42.9	40.2	30.2	21.1	12.6
Poland	42.9	37.9	38.6	36.8	23.7	16.1	28.9
Slovakia	41.4	32.3	40.7	40.4	21.3	12.0	20.2
Sweden	47.9	40.8	51.8	51.1	22.5	15.1	18.3
Switzerland	29.0	17.5	32.6	26.7	21.0	13.6	9.4
UK	31.0	17.4	39.2	37.4	28.1	24.2	12.2
USA	29.5	15.6	38.2	31.3	36.0	25.8	8.4

Notes: [a]Income tax plus employee's and employer's social security contributions less cash benefits as a percentage of gross labour costs.
[b]One-earner family. Takes account of family allowances and/or tax relief.
[c]Effective tax rates for an employee demanding a disposable income of €100,000. Taxes in this context are all income taxes including surcharges and state and municipality taxes, as well as payroll taxes paid by the employer. Social security contributions are part of the tax burden inasmuch as the employee does not earn a specific, individual benefit by paying them.
[d]Taxes on profits and capital levied at the national, the state and the municipal level. The figures are based on a model considering an incremental, hypothetical corporate investment. The investment consists of five different types of assets (intangibles, industrial buildings, machinery, financial assets, and inventories) and takes into account three different sources of finance (retained earnings, new equity, and debt). The calculations consider the statutory tax rates as well as the interaction of different kinds of taxes, and the most important rules determining the tax base, e.g., differences in depreciation allowances and inventory valuation.
[e]As a percentage of official GDP. The shadow economy includes all market-based legal production of goods and services that are deliberately concealed from public authorities to avoid payment of taxes and social security contributions, to avoid having to meet legal labour standards, or to avoid complying with administrative procedures. The estimates are based on the DYMIMIC approach (latent estimation approach) and on the currency demand method.
Sources: Elschner *et al.* (2005), pp. 14–15; OECD (2005), p. 61; Schneider (2005), pp. 44–7.

living in Germany was much higher than in many countries competing with Germany for these workers – for example, Ireland, Switzerland, the UK and the USA. This is true both in case of a single worker with no children and, except for Ireland and the UK, in case of a married worker with two children.

Germany's level of company taxation even ranks the highest among all the countries listed in Table 7.5. In many major industrial countries, competing for corporate investment, the level of company taxation was much lower. Prime examples include not only Ireland, Switzerland and the UK but also Belgium, Finland and Sweden. After reforming their tax systems, many transition countries have become strong competitors for internationally mobile capital as well. As can be seen from Table 7.5, in 2003 all transition countries included in this table had lower levels of company taxation than Germany.

To raise indirect instead of direct taxes would not have been advisable either because this would have increased the shadow economy.[6] In Germany the shadow economy is already much larger than in many other industrial countries (see Table 7.5). Thus, raising direct or indirect taxes in order to consolidate its public budget would not have been an adequate strategy for Germany. Instead, expenditure cuts should have been much larger. Germany's insufficient limitation of public expenditure is a major reason why this country continuously breached the 3 per cent ceiling since 2002. The examples of Austria and Spain prove that the government expenditure ratio can be cut back substantially. They also prove that Germany's insufficient limitation of public expenditure is not justified.

Effects

Government debt

As a result of Germany's continuously high fiscal deficits, the country's public debt ratio increased substantially. From 1998 to 2004, it rose by 5.8 percentage points of GDP (see Figure 7.5). In 2004, Germany was far above the second Maastricht threshold for public finances, namely the 60 per cent limit on the debt-to-GDP ratio. Germany's poor performance with respect to the debt ratio is all the more remarkable because this country obtained by far the highest revenues of all euro countries (2.5 per cent of GDP) from the sale of mobile telephone licences (UMTS) and used these revenues to redeem debts. In fact, there were only two other euro countries that also experienced a substantial increase in their debt ratios between 1998 and 2004: France and Portugal. Most euro countries lowered their debt ratios. Ireland and Belgium reduced their debt ratios by no less than 23.9 and 23.1 percentage points of GDP, respectively. Spain and the Netherlands also substantially reduced their debt ratios. Even Italy managed to lower its debt ratio by 10.2 percentage points of GDP, even though its nominal deficit averaged 2.7 per cent of GDP between 1999 and 2004 (see Table 7.2). This indicates that Germany during that period was characterized not only by high government deficits but also by comparatively modest economic growth. Germany could have avoided

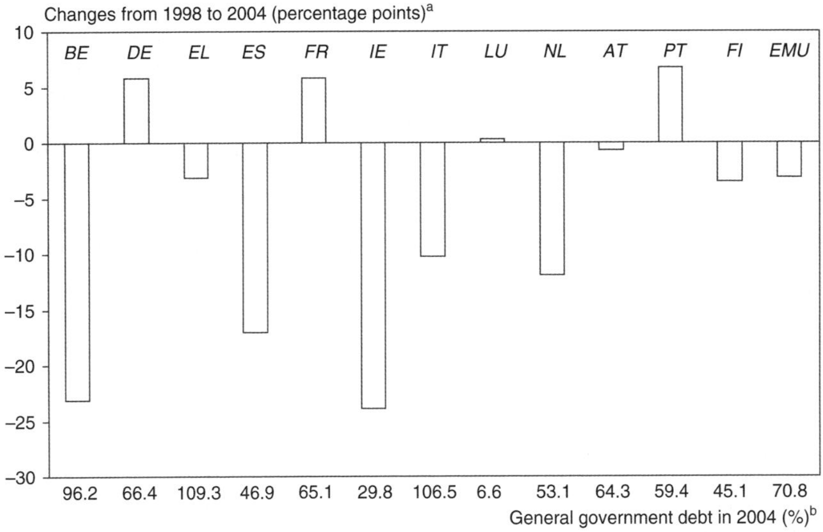

Notes: [a]Percentage points of GDP.
[b]As a percentage of GDP.
Source: European Commission (2005c), p. 182.

Figure 7.5 General government debt

continuously breaching the 60 per cent rule not only by lowering its deficits but also by boosting the growth momentum of its economy – particularly by deregulating product and labour markets – in order to 'outgrow' its government debt. Belgium, Ireland, Spain and the Netherlands have pursued this type of policy with great success.

Economic growth

Between 1999 and 2004, Germany's economic growth rate was far below the EMU average. In fact, it was the lowest in the whole euro area (see Table 7.6). By contrast, countries whose cyclically adjusted budgets were either balanced or in surplus (Belgium, Finland, Ireland, Luxembourg) achieved growth rates that exceeded the EMU average. Austria and Spain not only almost completely eliminated their structural deficits by 2001 and 2003, respectively (see Table 7.3), but they also attained above average rates of economic growth between 1999 and 2004.

In the four countries whose cyclically adjusted budgets were either balanced or in surplus, the consistently pursued policy of budgetary consolidation obviously did not retard economic growth. Rather, between 1999 and 2004 these countries achieved higher growth rates than during the previous twenty-five years (see Table 7.6). Neither did Spain have to pay

Table 7.6 Structural balances, economic growth and public investment

	General government cyclically adjusted balance 1999–2004 (% of GDP)[a]	Average annual percentage change in real GDP		Gross fixed capital formation of general government (as a percentage of general government total expenditure)	
		1974–98	1999–2004	1974–98	1999–2004
Austria	−1.4	2.4	2.1	7.0	2.6
Belgium	−0.2	2.1	2.2	5.4	3.5
Finland	3.4	2.5	2.9	7.2	5.6
France	−3.2	2.2	2.3	6.7	5.9
Germany	−2.9	2.1	1.3	5.9	3.5
Greece	−5.2	1.7	4.3	7.5	7.7
Ireland	0.0	4.8	6.9	7.8	11.3
Italy	−3.0	2.3	1.4	6.1	4.9
Luxembourg	2.7	3.9	4.7	11.0	11.0
Netherlands	−1.6	2.4	1.8	5.5	7.0
Portugal	−3.6	3.0	1.7	9.2	8.1
Spain	−1.3	2.5	3.7	8.5	8.8
Euro area	−2.4	2.2	2.0	6.4	5.3

Note: [a]Excluding one-off revenues from the sale of mobile telephone licences (UMTS) in 2000–02.
Source: European Commission (2003b), pp. 184–7, 190–3, 205–18; European Commission (2005b), table 9A; European Commission (2005c), pp. 172, 176, 184–96.

the price for the consolidation of its government budget in the form of a slowdown of economic growth. Its growth rates for the years 1999 to 2004 substantially exceeded those of the years 1974 to 1998. In Austria, which also consistently reduced its structural deficit, economic growth was slightly slower than during the preceding twenty-five years (see Table 7.6).

The picture is very different for those five countries that exceeded the 3 per cent deficit ceiling (France, Germany, Greece, Italy, Portugal). In three of those countries (Germany, Italy, Portugal), economic growth was much slower between 1999 and 2004 than between 1974 and 1998 (see Table 7.6). The high government deficits apparently did not boost their economies, but rather dampened growth. France's growth rate between 1999 and 2004 was only marginally above its average over the preceding twenty-five years. Greece is the only high-deficit country that managed to substantially increase its growth rate.

On the whole, those countries that consistently consolidated their government budgets had a better economic growth performance than Germany and most other high-deficit countries. How can this be explained? By sustainably reducing structural fiscal deficits, a government can substantially reduce its borrowing or even completely abstain from borrowing. This lowers interest rates on capital markets, in turn leading to a higher level of private investment, which strengthens economic growth. At the same time, a sustainable reduction of structural deficits signals to the private economic agents of a country – to private enterprises as well as to individual households – that, in the future, fewer taxes will be required to service government debt. Since they can thus expect to have higher levels of disposable income in the future, spending on consumption and capital goods increases. This also stimulates economic growth.[7]

The effects of sustained high or even growing government deficits are the exact opposite of this. Capital market interest rates remain at high levels, thus crowding out private investment.[8] People moreover anticipate that they will have to pay higher taxes sooner or later to service the growing public debt, and that their disposable income will thus decrease. They are already reacting to this perspective today by reducing their current spending on consumption and investment. Both the crowding-out and the expectation effects lead to slower economic growth.

Public investment

Not only private investment, but also many forms of public investment are of great significance for the long-term development of an economy, such as investments in the transportation and communication infrastructure. How did Germany perform in this respect compared to those countries that consolidated their public budgets?

Between 1999 and 2004, Germany's public investment ratio (the share of public gross fixed capital formation in total public expenditure) was far lower than the EMU average (see Table 7.6). By contrast, three out of four countries whose structural budgets were either balanced or in surplus on average between 1999 and 2004 (Finland, Ireland, Luxembourg) had an above-average public investment ratio. In Ireland and Luxembourg, this ratio was more than twice as high as in Euroland as a whole. Spain also spent a much larger share on public capital formation than the average of the euro area countries, although it consistently pursued a policy of budgetary consolidation. Austria and Belgium are the only countries that were relatively consistent in consolidating their budgets and had a public investment ratio that was below the EMU average between 1999 and 2004. Apart from these exceptions, this example illustrates that a policy of consistent budgetary consolidation does not necessarily entail a low level of public investment.

A comparison of the first six years the Stability Pact was in force with the years before also reveals some interesting facts. Among the most successful budgetary consolidation countries (Austria, Belgium, Finland, Ireland, Luxembourg, Spain) only Austria, Belgium and Finland had a lower public investment ratio between 1999 and 2004 than in the preceding twenty-five years (see Table 7.6). The ratio remained stable in Luxembourg, while in Spain and Ireland it was even higher. By contrast, Germany's public investment ratio was no higher between 1999 and 2004 than during the period 1974 to 1998, but rather lower. In fact Germany cut its public investment ratio by no less than 41 per cent. France, Italy and Portugal also substantially reduced their public investment ratios. In Greece, the public investment ratio increased only marginally, despite record deficits. Clearly, neither Germany nor the other high-deficit countries used their high levels of borrowing to increase their public investment ratio. On the contrary, they incurred high structural deficits although most of them lowered public investment. Conversely, the example of the most successful budgetary consolidation countries illustrates that the Stability Pact by no means necessarily imposes a cutback of public investment. All in all, Germany performed much worse than those countries that have consistently consolidated their budgets, not only with regard to public investment but also with regard to public debt and economic growth.

Diluting the Stability and Growth Pact

In 2005, the Council of Ministers and the European Council agreed to fundamental changes to the Stability Pact that crucially weakened its rules. In the preceding months, Germany (together with France) had strongly demanded such a revision. During the preceding years, the European Commission and the Council of Ministers had already bent and breached the rules of the Stability Pact in order to avoid sanctioning Germany, often under severe political pressure from the German government.

The first time such an incident occurred was in 2002. When it began to be apparent at the beginning of that year that Germany was likely to exceed the deficit ceiling, the European Commission (2002b), in accordance with the provisions of the Stability Pact, recommended that the Council of Ministers send an early warning to Germany together with recommendations for necessary adjustment measures. However, because of pressure exerted by the German government, the Council refrained from doing so. The recommendation of the Commission was not even put to the vote at the Council's meeting in February 2002. The Council simply declared the procedure closed. In return, Germany agreed to ensure that the 3 per cent reference value would not be breached; to reach a close to balance budget position by 2004 (as already promised in 2000); and to decrease the debt ratio continuously over this period (Council of the European Union, 2002).

By not sending an early warning to Germany, the Council of Ministers circumvented a central provision of the Stability Pact. According to Article 6 (2) of Regulation EC 1466/97, it shall give an early warning and a recommendation for adjustment measures if the budgetary position of a member state diverges significantly 'from the medium-term budgetary objective, or the adjustment path towards it'. As the Commission stated in its recommendation, this is exactly what had happened in Germany. As it turned out, the Council's decision not to send an early warning to Germany was the first serious blow to the credibility of the Stability Pact.

In January 2003, after it had long become obvious that Germany had exceeded the deficit limit the year before, the Council of Ministers acknowledged that Germany had run up an excessive deficit (Council of the European Union, 2003a). On this occasion, it adopted a recommendation urging Germany to bring the deficit back below the reference value by 2004 at the latest (Council of the European Union, 2003b).

In autumn 2003, the Commission considered that the actions implemented by the German government were inadequate. It thus recommended that the Council of Ministers initiate the next step of the excessive deficit procedure. At the same time, however, it suggested that the deadline for correcting the deficit should be extended by one year, to 2005 (European Commission, 2003d). The extension of the deadline was inconsistent with the spirit of the Stability Pact, which was aimed at achieving a rapid correction of an excessive deficit.

Worse still, in November 2003 the Council of Ministers did not follow the Commission's recommendation to give Germany (and France that also had an excessive deficit) a warning as the last step before the imposition of sanctions. Instead it decided to hold both excessive deficit procedures in abeyance (Council of the European Union, 2003c). Simultaneously, Germany promised to lower its deficit below 3 per cent of GDP by 2005 – but only on the condition that the Commission's growth forecasts turned out to be correct.

Obviously, the Council's decision was a severe breach of the Stability Pact. Therefore, the Commission brought the case before the European Court of Justice (European Commission, 2004b). In July 2004, the Court annulled the Council's conclusions in so far as they aimed at formally suspending the procedure and modifying the existing recommendations. In its judgment, the Court clarified that 'the Council cannot break free from the rules laid down by Article 104 EC and those which it set for itself in Regulation No 1467/97' (Court of Justice of the European Communities, 2004).

After the ruling of the European Court of Justice, the logical course of action, according to the rules of the Pact, would have been to give notice to Germany (and France) to take measures to remedy their excessive deficits. Instead, at the end of 2004 (the third year in which both Germany and France exceeded the 3 per cent ceiling), the Commission decided that it deemed the measures announced by both countries to be adequate (European Commission, 2004c). It concluded that no further steps were necessary at that point under the excessive deficit procedure. In January 2005, the Council declared that it also considered no further steps within the excessive deficit procedure to be necessary at that time (Council of the European Union, 2005a). Obviously, the sole intention of the Commission and the Council – and of the German government that was pressuring both – was to avoid the imposition of sanctions for as long as possible. By that time, public trust in the fiscal framework of monetary union had already been severely damaged, particularly in Germany.

In the meantime, Germany and France had lobbied among the other member states for a substantial loosening of the Pact's rules. In March 2005, they succeeded. Both the Council of Ministers and the Heads of State and Government of the EU decided to adopt a new version of the Stability Pact that almost completely abandoned its fiscal rules (Council of the European Union, 2005b; European Council, 2005). Although the basic goals of a maximum deficit ratio of 3 per cent and a maximum debt ratio of 60 per cent were retained, the medium term objective of a budgetary position close to balance or in surplus was replaced by country-specific objectives ranging from −1 per cent of GDP for countries with high growth rates and low debt ratios to budgetary positions close to balance or in surplus (see Table 7.1). In case of certain structural reforms, member states are now permitted to diverge temporarily from their medium-term objectives. Although member states that fail to achieve their medium-term objectives are required, in principle, to reduce their structural deficits by 0.5 per cent of GDP per year, the rate of consolidation may be lower in economically 'bad times'. Deviations in case of certain structural reforms are also allowed.

Furthermore, the 2005 version includes a long list of factors justifying an overshooting of the 3 per cent ceiling (see Table 7.1). Now a country can legitimately exceed the deficit ratio if the spending that causes the violation results from, *inter alia*, measures to achieve 'European policy objectives, notably the unification of Europe,' 'financial contributions to fostering international solidarity', the implementation of the EU's Lisbon strategy, expenditure on research, development and innovation, public investment and pension reforms. Negative or below-average growth rates or 'prevailing cyclical conditions' are also specified as exemptions.

Furthermore, the deadlines under the excessive deficit procedure were extended (see Table 7.1). Specifically, the period between the communication of budgetary figures and the decision on the imposition of sanctions was extended from ten to sixteen months in the normal case. More importantly, in 'special circumstances', the deadline for correcting an excessive deficit may be extended from one to two years. Should there be unexpected adverse economic events during the correction phase, the first recommendations for correcting the deficit and the recommendations when giving notice may be repeated and reformulated, and the deadline may also be extended. According to the new rules, a country now has up to five years from the time it breaches the deficit ceiling to get back below it.

Obviously, the 2005 version of the Stability Pact does not effectively restrict fiscal deficits. In particular, the long list of factors justifying an overshooting of the 3 per cent ceiling and the long deadlines for correcting deficits hardly exert adjustment pressure on deficit countries and don't foster member states' readiness to conduct sound fiscal policies in the first place. The list leaves open-ended scope for justifying deficits above the reference value. For example, in the case of Germany, the net payments to the EU budget and the cost of unification are now eligible for consideration when assessing the deficit. As the treaty provision that a deficit must be 'close to the reference value' when permitting deficit overruns was not quantified as part of the revision, an excessive deficit procedure is likely to be initiated by the Commission and the Council only in cases where the limit has been overshot by a very large margin.

All in all, after several years of negative publicity during the application of the 'old' Stability Pact, Germany succeeded in de facto abolishing binding fiscal rules for European Monetary Union altogether. It is unlikely that the German government, or the government of any other euro country, needs to worry about the EU sanctioning their budgetary deficits in the future. It is a sad irony that the very country that initiated the Stability Pact was key in bringing it down.

Conclusion

Restricting member countries' budgetary deficits effectively is of major importance for the functioning of European Monetary Union in the long term. The set of fiscal rules proposed by Germany in 1995 would have gone a long way towards achieving this goal. However, Germany's proposal was watered down substantially. The version of the Stability Pact that was adopted in 1997 was full of escape clauses. Ironically, Germany, from the very start, made use of these loopholes and thus actively contributed to undermining the Pact. As early as in 1997, it used various creative accounting methods to push its budgetary deficit below the 3 per cent ceiling. From 2002 onwards, it breached the deficit ceiling year after year, without any reason that could justify this poor performance. Although the high deficits did not have any noticeable benefits for the German economy, the German government never seriously attempted to consolidate its budget. Worse still, it pressured the European Commission and the governments of the other member states to apply the rules of the Pact as loosely as possible. When the imposition of sanctions could not be delayed for much longer, it pressured them to adopt a new version of the Pact that seriously weakened EMU's fiscal framework. As a result, budget deficits and debt ratios of many euro states are likely to increase in the medium to long term. It is unlikely that this will not have adverse economic effects, in general, and that it will not hamper the working of monetary union, in particular.

Notes

1. Buti *et al.* (1997); International Monetary Fund (1998); Dalsgaard and de Serres (2000); Barrell and Dury (2001); European Commission (2002a).
2. Since November 2004, the total number of votes in the Council of Ministers has been 321. Germany, France and Italy each have 29 votes. As 90 votes constitute a blocking minority, it is now slightly harder for them to block a decision on the existence of an excessive deficit.
3. For more information on the national stability pacts, see Deutsche Bundesbank (2005b); European Commission (2001), pp. 55–6; European Commission (2002a), pp. 168–213; European Commission (2003c), pp. 167–203; Fischer and Giudice (2001), pp. 175–9; von Hagen *et al.* (2002a), pp. 106–9; Hausner (2004); Sachverständigenrat zur Begutachtung der gesamtwirtschaftlichen Entwicklung (2002), para. 541.
4. For more on the structural developments of Germany's public finances, see Kremer and Wendorff (2004).
5. Perotti (1996); Alesina and Perotti (1997); Perotti *et al.* (1997); Alesina and Ardagna (1998); Perotti (1999); von Hagen *et al.* (2002b).
6. A rise in direct taxes would have been likely to have increased the shadow economy as well.
7. Such so-called non-Keynesian effects of budgetary consolidation have already been detected in a number of empirical studies. See, for example, Alesina and Perotti (1995); Alesina *et al.* (1998); Giavazzi *et al.* (2000); Alesina *et al.* (2002); Giudice *et al.* (2003); Ardagna (2004); Schuknecht and Tanzi (2005).
8. Numerous empirical studies have shown that government deficits reduce economic growth in the long term, because they drive up real interest rates and thus crowd out private investment. See Miller (1983); Boskin (1988); Saunders (1989); Cebula and Scott (1992); Allvine and Belton (1993); Easterly and Rebelo (1993); Sarantis (1993); Cebula (1995); Gong *et al.* (2001).

References

Alesina, A. and S. Ardagna (1998) 'Tales of Fiscal Adjustment', *Economic Policy*, no. 27, pp. 487–545.

Alesina, A. and R. Perotti (1995) 'Fiscal Expansions and Adjustments in OECD Countries', *Economic Policy*, no. 21, pp. 205–48.

Alesina, A. and R. Perotti (1997) 'Fiscal Adjustments in OECD Countries: Composition and Macroeconomic Effects', *IMF Staff Papers*, vol. 44, pp. 210–48.

Alesina, A., R. Perotti and J. Tavares (1998) 'The Political Economy of Fiscal Adjustments', *Brookings Papers on Economic Activity*, no. 1, pp. 197–266.

Alesina, A., S. Ardagna, R. Perotti and F. Schiantarelli (2002) 'Fiscal Policy, Profits, and Investment', *American Economic Review*, vol. 92, pp. 571–89.

Allvine, F. C. and W. Belton (1993) 'Government Borrowing, Fiscal Policy, Interest Rates, and Growth: The United States Experience, 1952–1991', *Rivista Internazionale di Scienze Economiche e Commerciali*, vol. 40, pp. 953–8.

Ardagna, S. (2004) 'Fiscal Stabilizations: When Do They Work and Why', *European Economic Review*, vol. 48, pp. 1047–74.

Barrell, R. and K. Dury (2001) 'Will the SGP Ever Be Breached?', in A. Brunila, M. Buti and D. Franco (eds), *The Stability and Growth Pact: The Architecture of Fiscal Policy in EMU* (Basingstoke: Palgrave), pp. 235–55.

Belgian Ministry of Finance (various issues) *Belgium's Stability Programme* (Brussels: Ministry of Finance).

Boskin, M. J. (1988) 'Concepts and Measures of Federal Deficits and Debt and Their Impact on Economic Activity', in K. J. Arrow and M. J. Boskin (eds), *The Economics of Public Debt* (New York: St Martin's Press), pp. 77–112.

Bundesminister der Finanzen, Präsident der Deutschen Bundesbank (1997) 'Erklärung des Bundesministers der Finanzen und des Präsidenten der Deutschen Bundesbank vom 19. Juni 1997', in Deutsche Bundesbank, *Auszüge aus Presseartikeln*, no. 36 (23 June), p. 4.

Bundesministerium der Finanzen (various issues) *Deutsches Stabilitätsprogramm* (Berlin: Bundesministerium der Finanzen).

Buti, M., D. Franco and H. Ongena (1997) 'Budgetary Policies during Recessions: Retrospective Application of the "Stability and Growth Pact" to the Post-War Period', *Recherches Economique de Louvain*, vol. 63, pp. 321–66.

Cebula, R. J. (1995) 'The Impact of Federal Government Budget Deficits on Economic Growth in the United States: An Empirical Investigation, 1955–1992', *International Review of Economics and Finance*, vol. 4, pp. 245–52.

Cebula, R. J. and G. E. Scott (1992) 'Fiscal Policies and Growth: An Extension', *Rivista Internazionale di Scienze Economiche e Commerciali*, vol. 39, pp. 91–4.

Council of the European Union (2002) *Statement of the Council (ECOFIN) on the Budgetary Situation of Germany*, SN 1382/1/02 REV 1 (12 February) (Brussels: Council of the European Union).

Council of the European Union (2003a) 'Council Decision of 21 January 2003 on the Existence of an Excessive Deficit in Germany', *Official Journal of the European Union*, L 34 (11 February), pp. 16–17.

Council of the European Union (2003b) *2480th Council Meeting – Economic and Financial Affairs*, 5506/03 (Presse 15) (21 January) (Brussels: Council of the European Union).

Council of the European Union (2003c) *2546th Council Meeting – Economic and Financial Affairs*, 14492/1/03 REV 1 (en) (Presse 320) (25 November) (Brussels: Council of the European Union).

Council of the European Union (2005a) *2634th Council Meeting – Economic and Financial Affairs*, 5283/05 (Presse 6) (18 January) (Brussels: Council of the European Union).

Council of the European Union (2005b) *Improving the Implementation of the Stability and Growth Pact*, 7423/05 (21 March) (Brussels: Council of the European Union).

Court of Justice of the European Communities (2004) *Judgement of the Court (Full Court) of 13 July 2004 in Case C-27/04: Commission of the European Communities v Council of the European Union* at: http://curia.eu.int/jurisp/cgi-bin/form.pl?lang=en.

Dalsgaard, Th. and A. de Serres (2000) 'Estimating Prudent Budgetary Margins for EU Countries: A Simulated SVAR Model Approach', *OECD Economic Studies*, no. 30, pp. 115–47.

Department of Finance (various issues) *Ireland – Stability Programme* (Dublin: Department of Finance).

Deutsche Bundesbank (1997) 'Revaluation of Gold and Foreign Exchange Reserves', *Monthly Report*, vol. 49, no. 6, pp. 5–7.

Deutsche Bundesbank (2005a) 'The Changes to the Stability and Growth Pact', *Monthly Report*, vol. 57, no. 4, pp. 15–21.

Deutsche Bundesbank (2005b) 'Deficit-Limiting Budgetary Rules and a National Stability Pact in Germany', *Monthly Report*, vol. 57, no. 4, pp. 23–37.

Easterly, W. and S. Rebelo (1993) 'Fiscal Policy and Economic Growth: An Empirical Investigation', *Journal of Monetary Economics*, vol. 32, pp. 417–58.

Elschner, Ch., L. Lammersen, M. Overesch and R. Schwager (2005) 'The Effective Tax Burden of Companies and on Highly Skilled Manpower: Tax Policy Strategies in a Globalized Economy', Discussion Paper no. 05–31 (Mannheim: ZEW).

European Commission (1999) Budgetary Surveillance in EMU: The New Stability and Convergence Programmes, *European Economy*, Supplement A, no. 3 (Brussels: European Commission).

European Commission (2000) 'Public Finances in EMU – 2000', *European Economy*, no. 3, (Brussels: European Commission).

European Commission (2001) 'Public Finances in EMU – 2001', *European Economy*, no. 3, (Brussels: European Commission).

European Commission (2002a) 'Public Finances in EMU – 2002', *European Economy*, no. 3, (Brussels: European Commission).

European Commission (2002b) *Commission Assesses the German Stability Programme (2001 – 2005)*, DN: IP/02/164 (30 January) (Brussels: European Commission).

European Commission (2003a) 'Economic Forecasts Spring 2003', *European Economy*, no. 2, (Brussels: European Commission).

European Commission (2003b) *Statistical Annex of European Economy. Spring 2003* (Brussels: European Commission).

European Commission (2003c) 'Public Finances in EMU – 2003', *European Economy*, no. 3, (Brussels: European Commission).

European Commission (2003d) *Commission Proceeds with Excessive Deficit Procedure for Germany*, IP/03/1560 (18 November) (Brussels: European Commission).

European Commission (2004a) 'Public Finances in EMU – 2004', *European Economy*, no. 3, (Brussels: European Commission).

European Commission (2004b) 'Action Brought on 28 January 2004 by the Commission of the European Communities Against the Council of the European Union (Case C-27/04)', *Official Journal of the European Union*, C 35 (7 February), pp. 5–6.

European Commission (2004c) *Communication from the Commission to the Council: The Situation of Germany and France in Relation to Their Obligations Under the Excessive Deficit Procedure Following the Judgement of the Court of Justice*, COM (2004) 813 (14 December) (Brussels: European Commission).

European Commission (2005a) 'Public Finances in EMU – 2005', *European Economy*, no. 3 (Brussels: European Commission).

European Commission (2005b) *Cyclical Adjustment of Budget Balances. Autumn 2005* (Brussels: European Commission).

European Commission (2005c) *Statistical Annex of European Economy. Autumn 2005* (Brussels: European Commission).

European Commission (2005d) 'Economic Forecasts Spring 2005', *European Economy*, no. 2, (Brussels: European Commission).

European Commission (2005e) *Economic Forecasts Autumn 2005* (Brussels: European Commission).

European Council (2005) *European Council Brussels 22 and 23 March 2005 – Presidency Conclusions*, 7619/1/05 REV 1 (23 March) (Brussels: Council of the European Union).

Finnish Ministry of Finance (various issues) *Stability Programme for Finland* (Helsinki: Ministry of Finance).

Fischer, J. and G. Giudice (2001) 'The Stability and Convergence Programmes', in A. Brunila, M. Buti and D. Franco (eds), *The Stability and Growth Pact: The Architecture of Fiscal Policy in EMU* (Basingstoke: Palgrave), pp. 158–82.

Giavazzi, F., T. Jappelli and M. Pagano (2000) 'Searching for Non-Linear Effects of Fiscal Policy: Evidence from Industrial and Developing Countries', *European Economic Review*, vol. 44 pp. 1259–89.

Giudice, G., A. Turrini and J. in 't Veld (2003) *Can Fiscal Consolidations be Expansionary in the EU? Ex-Post Evidence and Ex-Ante Analysis*, Economic Papers, no. 195 (Brussels: European Commission).

Gong, G., A. Greiner and W. Semmler (2001) 'Growth Effects of Fiscal Policy and Debt Sustainability in the EU', *Empirica*, vol. 28, pp. 3–19.

Government of Portugal (various issues) *Stability and Growth Programme* (Lisbon: Government of Portugal).

Government of the French Republic (various issues) *French Multiyear Public Finance Programme* (Paris: Government of the French Republic).

Government of the Netherlands (various issues) *Stability Programme – The Netherlands* (The Hague: Government of the Netherlands).

Grand Duchy of Luxembourg Ministry of Finance (various issues) *The Luxembourg Stability and Growth Programme* (Luxembourg: Ministry of Finance).

von Hagen, J., A. Hughes Hallett and R. Strauch (2002a) 'Budgetary Institutions for Sustainable Public Finances', in M. Buti, J. von Hagen and C. Martinez-Mongay (eds), *The Behaviour of Fiscal Authorities: Stabilization, Growth and Institutions* (Basingstoke: Palgrave), pp. 94–112.

von Hagen, J., A. Hughes Hallett and R. Strauch (2002b) 'Quality and Success of Budgetary Consolidations', in M. Buti, J. von Hagen and C. Martinez-Mongay (eds), *The Behaviour of Fiscal Authorities: Stabilization, Growth and Institutions* (Basingstoke: Palgrave), pp. 17–38.

Hausner, K. H. (2004) 'Die innerstaatliche Umsetzung des Stabilitäts- und Wachstumspaktes in Deutschland und Österreich', *Vierteljahrshefte zur Wirtschaftsforschung*, vol. 73, pp. 371–80.

Hellenic Republic Ministry of Economy and Finance (various issues) *The Hellenic Stability and Growth Programme* (Athens: Ministry of Economy and Finance).

International Monetary Fund (1998) *World Economic Outlook*, October (Washington, DC: International Monetary Fund).

Kingdom of Spain (various issues) *Stability Programme* (Madrid: Kingdom of Spain).

Konow, Ch. (2002) *Der Stabilitäts- und Wachstumspakt: Ein Rechtsrahmen für die Stabilität in der Wirtschafts- und Währungsunion* (Baden-Baden: Nomos).

Kremer, J. and K. Wendorff (2004) 'Germany after Qualification for EMU: A Disaggregated Approach to the Analysis of Structural Public Finance Developments', *Vierteljahrshefte zur Wirtschaftsforschung*, vol. 73, pp. 358–70.

Miller, P. J. (1983) 'Examining the Proposition that Federal Budget Deficits Matter', in L. H. Meyer (ed.), *The Economic Consequences of Government Deficits* (The Hague: Kluwer-Nijhoff Publishing), pp. 3–24.

Ministro dell'Economia (various issues) *Programma di Stabilità dell'Italia* (Rome: Ministro dell'Economia).

Münster, W. (1997) 'Das Spiel mit den Defiziten', in: Deutsche Bundesbank, *Auszüge aus Presseartikeln*, no. 48 (27 August), p. 4.

OECD (2005) *Taxing Wages 2003/2004* (Paris: OECD).

Österreichisches Bundesministerium der Finanzen (various issues) *Österreichisches Stabilitätsprogramm* (Vienna: Bundesministerium der Finanzen).

Perotti, R. (1996) 'Fiscal Consolidation in Europe: Composition Matters', *American Economic Review*, vol. 86, pp. 105–10.

Perotti, R. (1999) 'Fiscal Policy in Good Times and Bad', *Quarterly Journal of Economics*, vol. 114, pp. 1399–436.

Perotti, R., R. Strauch and J. von Hagen (1997) *Sustainability of Public Finances* (London: Centre for Economic Policy Research).

Sachverständigenrat zur Begutachtung der gesamtwirtschaftlichen Entwicklung (1997) *Wachstum, Beschäftigung, Währungsunion – Orientierungen für die Zukunft*, Jahresgutachten 1997/98 (Stuttgart: Metzler-Poeschel).

Sachverständigenrat zur Begutachtung der gesamtwirtschaftlichen Entwicklung (1998) *Vor weitreichenden Entscheidungen*, Jahresgutachten 1998/99 (Stuttgart: Metzler-Poeschel).

Sachverständigenrat zur Begutachtung der gesamtwirtschaftlichen Entwicklung (2002) *Zwanzig Punkte für Beschäftigung und Wachstum*, Jahresgutachten 2002/03 (Stuttgart: Metzler-Poeschel).

Sarantis, N. (1993) 'Fiscal Deficits and Capital Investment in OECD Countries: A Cross-Section Analysis', *British Review of Economic Issues*, vol. 15, pp. 43–62.

Saunders, P. J. (1989) 'Federal Budget Deficits, Interest Rates, and Inflation: Their Implications for Growth', *Eastern Economic Journal*, vol. 15, pp. 213–9.

Schneider, F. (2005) Shadow Economies of 145 Countries all over the World: What Do We Really Know?, Mimeo (University of Linz).

Schuknecht, L. and V. Tanzi (2005) *Reforming Public Expenditure in Industrialised Countries: Are There Trade-Offs?*, Working Paper Series No. 435 (Frankfurt am Main: European Central Bank).

Stark, J. (2001) 'Genesis of a Pact', in A. Brunila, M. Buti and D. Franco (eds), *The Stability and Growth Pact: The Architecture of Fiscal Policy in EMU* (Basingstoke: Palgrave), pp. 77–105.

Steuer, W. (2001) 'European Stability and Growth Pact', in R. Caesar and H.-E. Scharrer (eds), *European Economic and Monetary Union: Regional and Global Challenges* (Baden-Baden: Nomos), pp. 99–113.

8

Macroeconomic Policies, Wage Developments and Germany's Stagnation

Eckhard Hein and Achim Truger

Introduction

Since 2001 the German economy has been facing its most serious stagnation in post-war history: after the upswing in 1999/2000 real GDP growth more or less stagnated between 2001 and 2003; 2004 saw a weak recovery with a growth rate of 1.6 per cent, but in 2005 growth has decelerated again.[1] Unemployment has been rising again and reached its post-war maximum. The budget deficit, though not excessively high in international terms, has been rising despite strong consolidation efforts since 2001. In 2005, it exceeded the 3 per cent (of GDP) deficit limit of the Maastricht Treaty and the Stability and Growth Pact for the fourth time in four consecutive years.

Of course, other European countries are also currently facing economic problems, and the European Monetary Union (EMU) as a whole has been doing worse than the USA,[2] but in comparison with the other EMU countries Germany has been hit much harder by the recent economic slowdown (see Table 8.1). During the period 2001–4 average annual GDP growth in Germany amounted to only half of the meagre growth in the EMU (including Germany). In contrast to the EMU as a whole, Germany's growth is completely driven by export surpluses; the contribution of domestic demand to GDP growth has been negative on average over this period. Unemployment has climbed to the EMU average and inflation is considerably below the EMU average. The former key currency country of the European Monetary System (EMS) has indeed become 'Europe's sick man'.

There has been lively discussion about the reasons for the German crisis and about how to overcome it. With few exceptions, however, mainstream researchers seem to agree that institutional sclerosis – that is, rigid and over-regulated labour markets and too-generous welfare state institutions, have driven Germany into crisis. Consequently, there are many

Table 8.1 Real GDP growth, unemployment and inflation rate in Germany and the EMU, 2001–04, annual average, per cent

	Germany	EMU
Real GDP growth	0.6	1.3
Growth contribution of domestic demand	–0.4	1.1
Growth contribution of net foreign balances	1.0	0.2
Rate of unemployment	8.5	8.5
Inflation rate (HCPI)	1.5	2.2

Sources: European Commission (2005a); OECD (2004).

who have called, and still call, for far-reaching structural reforms, radical deregulation of the labour market and a radical dismantling of the welfare state.[3] Alternative macroeconomic explanations and policy advice are hardly ever considered seriously and are often dismissed purely as attempts to prevent the (perceived) urgently necessary process of structural reform. The proponents of radical deregulation have been politically successful: after some reluctance during the first term of the red–green administration (1998–2002), Chancellor Schroeder's 'Agenda 2010' presented in March 2003 was the turning point towards the implementation of far-reaching structural reforms to overcome the (perceived) institutional sclerosis (Schroeder, 2003).

In this chapter we fundamentally challenge the institutional sclerosis explanation for the German crisis. Instead, we shall present a macroeconomic explanation for Germany's falling behind which is indeed not a short-term phenomenon but in fact began almost ten years ago. Our macroeconomic story will focus on the combined effects of too-restrictive monetary policies, too-restrictive and sometimes counter-cyclical fiscal policies, and too-moderate wage policies in Germany since the mid-1990s. This view is broadly consistent with modern macroeconomics and with empirical data. From this perspective we shall finally argue that, instead of further 'structural reforms', Germany urgently needs more expansive fiscal and monetary policies in the short term. In the medium term, the economic and institutional conditions for nominal wage growth in Germany according to the sum of long-run national productivity growth and the ECB's inflation target have to be improved. Further pursuing a policy of structural reforms with respect to the labour market and the social benefit system in combination with a restrictive macroeconomic policy mix, however, will prolong Germany's economic stagnation and will considerably increase the risk of deflation.

In this chapter we shall not address explicitly the problem of German unification and its effects on German stagnation,[4] but it should be noted that there is a substantial discrepancy in macroeconomic performance between

West and East Germany in terms of GDP growth and unemployment. West Germany's growth rates have exceeded those of East Germany since the mid-1990s (that is, the catch-up process of East Germany has virtually come to a stop since then), and East Germany's unemployment rates are roughly three times higher than those in West Germany. This situation causes eminent fiscal transfers from West to East in the dimension of 3–4 per cent of German GDP.

The chapter is organized as follows. The second section describes briefly Germany's long-term economic problems with respect to growth, unemployment and inflation. The third section deals briefly with the institutional sclerosis view. The fourth section presents the alternative macroeconomic policy explanation of German stagnation. The fifth section deals with the development of wage bargaining in particular, and the sixth section concludes with the fundamental problems that economic policies in Germany and Europe will have to solve in order to escape stagnation and deflation.

Macroeconomic performance since the mid-1990s

A closer look at the annual German GDP growth rates from 1985 to 2004 in comparison with the EMU average growth rates (including Germany) reveals that there is not only a short-term growth problem starting with the recent recession, but also that Germany has faced a long-term absolute and relative growth problem since the mid-1990s (Figure 8.1).

Since 1995, the German GDP growth rate has been systematically lower than the EMU average. In what follows we shall therefore compare macroeconomic development and its determinants in Germany and in the EMU as a whole for two different time periods: the ten-year period starting in 1995, and the ten-year period before 1995 (see Table 8.2). Both periods include a recession and cover a full business cycle. Average values can therefore be compared without being affected too much by cyclical fluctuations.

Comparing the 1995–2004 period with the 1985–94 period, Germany's average real GDP growth rate has decreased remarkably. Whereas it exceeded the EMU average in the former period it was considerably below this average – which has also fallen slightly – in the latter period. EMU GDP growth has been driven almost exclusively by domestic demand in both periods. In Germany, however, the growth contribution of net foreign demand has increased significantly, whereas the growth contribution of domestic demand has decreased dramatically. Germany's economy has performed very well on international markets and gained considerable export surpluses in the period 1995–2004, but suffered from weak domestic demand during this period.

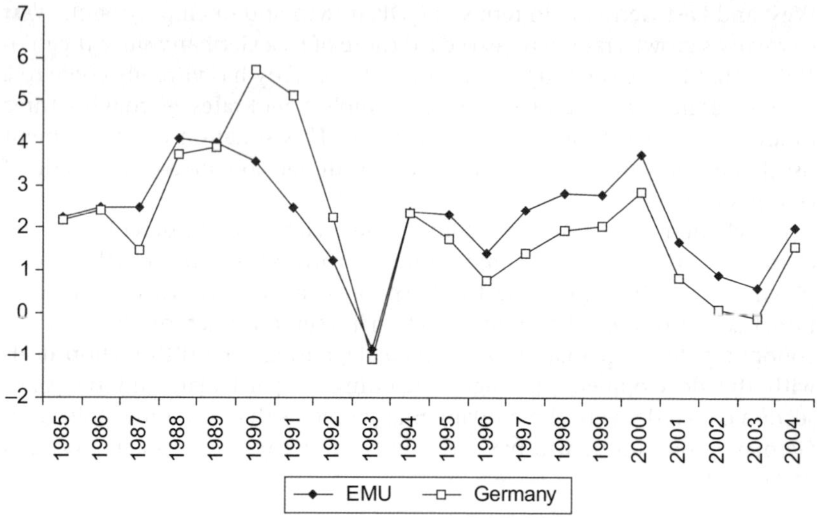

Sources: European Commission (2005a); OCED (2004).

Figure 8.1 Real GDP growth rate in Germany and in the EMU, 1985–2004, per cent

Germany's growth problems have caused rising unemployment. Although average unemployment in the period 1995–2004 is still below the EMU average, the increase in Germany's unemployment rate from the first to the second period exceeds the increase in the EMU rate. Since 2003, Germany's unemployment rate has been even higher than the EMU rate. With the exception of 1992 and 1993, Germany's inflation rate has been consistently

Table 8.2 Real GDP growth, unemployment and inflation in Germany and the EMU, 1985–94 and 1995–2004, annual average, per cent

	1985–94[1]		1995–2004	
	Germany	**EMU**	**Germany**	**EMU**
Real GDP growth	2.8	2.4	1.3	2.1
Growth contribution of domestic demand	2.6	2.4	0.8	1.9
Growth contribution of net foreign balances	0.2	0.0	0.5	0.1
Rate of unemployment	6.1	8.8	8.3	9.4
Inflation rate (HCPI)	2.5	4.1	1.3	2.0

Notes: 1. 1985 to 1991: West Germany and EMU, including only West Germany.
Sources: European Commission (2005a); OECD (2004).

below the EMU rate. The rate of inflation has halved when one compares the second period with the first period in Germany as well as in the EMU as a whole.

Institutional sclerosis as the cause of Germany's stagnation?

For most of the German economics profession, the answer to the German growth and employment problems is clear and simple: institutional sclerosis – that is, rigid and over-regulated labour markets and too-generous welfare state institutions – have driven Germany into crisis. This institutional sclerosis view is based on simple neoclassical labour market theory. With a complete and perfect neoclassical labour market as a standard of reference, unemployment can only arise because market imperfections prevent a market clearing real wage at full employment (Siebert, 1997).[5] Institutions of collective wage bargaining (unions and employers' associations at the regional, sectoral or national level), labour market regulation (for example, employment protection legislation, minimum wages) and the welfare state (unemployment benefits, social benefits and the 'tax wedge') are seen as market imperfections and therefore creators of unemployment.

But can the institutional sclerosis view really explain the systematic lagging behind of Germany by comparison with the EMU average since the mid-1990s? In order to render a good explanation for the German crisis, the institutional sclerosis view would have to obey to three conditions. First, it would have to be based on a consistent and realistic economic theory. Second, the derived theoretical relationship between labour market regulation and welfare state institutions, on the one hand, and unemployment, on the other, should have been confirmed by empirical studies. Third, in order to be applicable to the German case it would have to be shown that German labour market and welfare state institutions are in fact as sclerotic as to fit to the German economic performance since the mid-1990s. However, the institutional sclerosis view does not meet any of the three conditions convincingly.[6]

First, with respect to theory, the institutional sclerosis view runs into serious problems, as soon as the traditional model of a complete neoclassical labour market as a standard of reference is abandoned and replaced by the models of modern labour market theory. With modern theoretical foundations it becomes difficult to derive unambiguous implications concerning the employment effects of labour market regulation and welfare state institutions. As soon as asymmetric information between employers and employees, incomplete contracts and active price-setting are taken into account, there are good reasons to question the institutional sclerosis view and its economic policy implications.[7]

Second, with respect to empirical research, the results from the literature are rather mixed and far from being as clear as the proponents of deregulation like to claim. Since the fundamental work by Layard *et al.* (1991) there have been many complex econometric studies examining the influence of institutional rigidities on economic performance and the unemployment rate.[8] Among the standard institutional variables usually covered are indices of employment protection, the benefit replacement rate, benefit duration, union density, bargaining co-ordination and the tax wedge. All in all, the empirical work does not provide clear and unambiguous results in favour of the institutional sclerosis view concerning 'rigid' labour markets, welfare state institutions and unemployment. A considerable part of the unemployment differences over time and between countries cannot be explained by differences in the institutional structures of the labour market. Rather, time and country specific factors and macroeconomic variables have to be taken into account. Finally, some of the results found to favour the institutional sclerosis view do not seem to be particularly robust.

Third, the development of Germany's labour market and welfare state institutions in international comparison simply does not correspond to Germany's economic development over time. In order to show this, we use the set of indicators compiled by Baker *et al.* (2004). Table 8.3 lists the six institutional indicators (index of employment protection, benefit replacement rate, benefit duration, union density, bargaining co-ordination and tax wedge) for Germany for eight five-year periods from 1960 to 1999. It

Table 8.3 Indicators of labour market institutions and the welfare state: Germany in international comparison, 1960–99[1]

Period	Employment protection[2]	Benefit replacement rate[3]	Benefit duration[4]	Union density[5]	Bargaining coordination[6]	Tax wedge[7]
Indicators for Germany[8]						
1960–4	0.45	42.7	0.57	33.8	2.5	42.9
1965–9	0.80	41.9	0.57	32.4	2.5	42.8
1970–4	1.54	39.7	0.58	32.5	2.5	46.7
1975–9	1.65	39.6	0.62	35.1	2.5	48.3
1980–4	1.65	38.8	0.62	34.9	2.5	49.7
1985–9	1.63	37.8	0.60	33.4	2.5	50.5
1990–4	1.50	37.4	0.61	31.0	2.5	52.2
1995–9	1.30	36.3	0.60	27.4	2.5	53.9
German indicators minus average indicators for 20 OECD countries[9]						
1960–4[11]	−0.34	17.1	0.22	−4.9	0.29	6.3[12]
1965–9[11]	−0.05	13.0	0.22	−6.7	0.29	1.7[13]
1970–4[11]	0.55	7.0	0.19	−8.9	0.26	1.5[13]
1975–9	0.53	−0.1	0.21	−10.4	0.20	3.2
1980–4	0.50	−5.0	0.18	−10.5	0.37	1.8
1985–9	0.48	−8.9	0.15	−8.9	0.49	−0.3
1990–4	0.41	−10.1	0.12	−9.7	0.49	0.2[14]
1995–9	0.34	−11.1	0.09	−12.0	0.58	1.8[14]

Table 8.3 (Continued)

Period	Employment protection[2]	Benefit replacement rate[3]	Benefit duration[4]	Union density[5]	Bargaining coordination[6]	Tax wedge[7]
German indicators minus average indicators for 13 EU countries[9]						
1960–4[11]	−0.31	17.3	0.20	−5.9	0.23	4.0
1965–9[11]	−0.08	12.2	0.22	−8.5	0.21	−0.8
1970–4[11]	0.43	5.6	0.19	−12.9	0.11	−1.1
1975–9	0.33	−2.4	0.23	−15.9	0.10	0.6
1980–4	0.27	−6.7	0.19	−16.5	0.30	−1.5
1985–9	0.26	−10.1	0.15	−14.6	0.50	−4.8
1990–4	0.21	−11.7	0.09	−15.4	0.37	−3.4
1995–9	0.21	−12.5	0.05	−18.5	0.42	−2.3

	Germany	Average of 20 OECD countries	Average of 13 EU countries
Total indicator of institutional sclerosis[15]			
1995–9	**52**	**47**	**52**

Notes:

1. An exact definition and a documentation of the origin of the data is given by Nickell *et al.* (2002) and Baker *et al.* (2004).
2. Index of employment protection legislation (0–2): 0 = low, 2 = high.
3. Benefit replacement rate before taxes as percentage of previous income before taxes. Average values for two income levels (100% and 67% of average income) and three family types (single, family with one earner, family with two earners), based on OECD data.
4. Index of benefit duration: weighed arithmetic mean of benefit replacement ratios after 2 to 5 years in proportion to first year benefit replacement ratio (see Nt.3). Based on OECD data.
5. Index of trade union density: employed union members as percentage of total employed.
6. Index of wage bargaining co-ordination (1–3): 1 = low, 3 = high. Based on OECD data.
7. Total average labour tax burden (payroll taxes, social security contributions, labour income tax, consumption taxes).
8. Except for benefit duration: West Germany.
9. Australia, Austria, Belgium, Canada, Denmark, Finland, France, Germany, Ireland, Italy, Japan, Netherlands, New Zealand, Norway, Portugal, Spain, Sweden, Switzerland, UK, USA.
10. Austria, Belgium, Denmark, Finland, France, Germany, Ireland, Italy, Netherlands, Portugal, Spain, Sweden, UK.
11. Without Portugal.
12. Without Portugal, New Zealand and Norway.
13. Without Portugal and New Zealand.
14. Without Australia and New Zealand.
15. Arithmetic mean of the six single indicators previously scaled to the interval [0; 100].

Sources: Baker *et al.* (2004); Nickell *et al.* (2002).

also shows the differences between the values for Germany and the average values for twenty OECD and thirteen EU countries.

Quite obviously, the evolution of the indicators for Germany is not consistent with Germany's economic development and is therefore in striking contrast to the institutional sclerosis view. If the latter were true, one would expect the values for Germany to be very high in international comparison, and increasing both absolutely and in international comparison over time, in particular during the 1990s when Germany entered its period of absolutely and comparatively unsatisfactory economic performance. However, only one indicator, the tax wedge, has grown consistently over time, with considerable increases during the 1990s. Two indicators (bargaining co-ordination and benefit duration) have remained essentially constant since the mid-1970s. And three indicators have even decreased: employment protection, the benefit replacement rate and union density have been decreasing since the mid-1970s and so considerably during the second half of the 1990s.

The contradictions to the institutional sclerosis view become even more apparent when the indicators for Germany are compared with the average indicator values for the twenty OECD and thirteen EU countries: in the second half of the 1990s, two indicators for Germany (benefit replacement rate and union density) are lower than the 'OECD 20' average. In comparison to the 'EU 13' average, the former two indicators plus the tax wedge are below the average, though the values for the tax wedge are moving closer to the average. With respect to the German indicators above the average, the difference has increased only for bargaining co-ordination since 1990. For employment protection and benefit duration, the difference from the OECD 20 and EU 13 averages has been decreasing continually since the early (employment protection) or the late (benefit duration) 1970s. In order to capture the sum of all relevant indicators and their changes over time, we have calculated an aggregate indicator for total institutional sclerosis from the individual indicators for Germany, the EU 13 and OECD 20. As was to be expected from the individual indicators, Germany's total indicator in the second half of the 1990s is a little above the OECD 20 average and exactly equal to the EU 13 average. To sum up: on the basis of the data presented for Germany, hardly any institutional change can be detected that could, according to the institutional sclerosis view, be made responsible for Germany's poor economic performance since the mid-1990s.

A macroeconomic policy story of Germany's poor economic performance

Macroeconomic policy co-ordination as the key to growth and employment

A macroeconomic policy story of Germany's slump can rely on both post-Keynesian and New Keynesian approaches.[9] In the two modern Keynesian views, monetary, fiscal and wage policies have a common responsibility for employment and price stability. In order to attain these goals the three policies have to be co-ordinated at least at the national level,[10] and better even at the international level, in particular in currency areas with a common monetary policy. In the post-Keynesian approach the development of aggregate demand determines growth and employment in the short term as well as in the long term.[11] Monetary policies' interest rate setting and firms' profit expectations essentially affect private investment, which in turn is an essential determinant of effective demand and macroeconomic growth. Fiscal policy is also a central short- and long-run determinant of aggregate demand, working through both the tax and the expenditure channel, in particular through public investment. And it is effective demand which, via the level of aggregate output, determines the level of employment realized in the labour market. The labour market, in this view, is a derived market because wage setting has no direct influence on employment. Instead, employment is determined by the interaction of the financial market where the interest rate is set – mainly by the policies of the central bank – and the goods market where total output is determined. Nominal wages set by labour unions and employers' associations, however, are the crucial determinant of the price level and inflation: with labour productivity given or following an exogenous trend and mark-up pricing in incomplete goods markets, the nominal wage rate determines the price level when the mark-ups are constant. Whereas monetary and fiscal policies are capable of affecting effective demand, and hence employment, wage policies are in charge of preventing cumulative inflation as well as deflation. Therefore, rigid wages have to provide the nominal anchor for the whole system of a monetary production economy.

In New Keynesian economics, effective demand, and hence monetary and fiscal policies, have at least a short-run impact on production and employment, because prices and wages are assumed to adjust rather slowly to their long-run equilibrium values.[12] In the long-run equilibrium, however, unemployment is determined by the NAIRU (Non-Accelerating Inflation Rate of Unemployment), which may depend on those structural factors discussed in the previous section. In the short run, however, the exact duration of which is not clear, but which may be assumed to last at least a few years (Blanchard, 2003, p. 34), effective demand determines production and employment. From this it follows that mainstream New Keynesian implications for monetary and fiscal policies in the short run are rather similar to the post-Keynesian approach: monetary and fiscal policies are capable of stimulating demand and employment when the economy is in a slump and unemployment exceeds the NAIRU. Utmost importance is also assigned to the co-ordination of the two policies (Blanchard, 2003, pp. 101–4, 431–2).[13]

With respect to wage policies, however, the New Keynesian analysis differs substantially from the post-Keynesian approach. In the short run, wage policy is, strictly speaking, not even a policy variable, because the short run is defined by exogenous and/or sticky nominal wages. And in the long run, wage policy is completely endogenous because mainstream models assume nominal wages adapting to the level consistent with the NAIRU (Blanchard, 2003, pp. 113–33). In contrast to the post-Keynesian view, nominal wage moderation can be an effective way of accelerating the reduction of actual unemployment to the NAIRU level. In New Keynesian models, however, it is not clear how effective demand determining unemployment in the short run can adjust to the level of production associated with the NAIRU in the long run.[14] In order to have increasing effective demand when nominal wages and prices are falling in the face of unemployment above the NAIRU, a real-balance effect may be assumed. This requires the dominance of exogenous or outside money, which is not the case in modern monetary production economies. Or, if we assume the dominance of endogenous money coming into existence via credit creation, symmetric monetary policy interventions are required (Allsopp and Vines, 1998). These may, however, not be sufficient to increase demand and employment when profit expectations are depressed and debt deflation works its way through the private sector. Because of these considerations, we prefer the post-Keynesian view of rigid nominal wages as a macroeconomic stabilizer rather than the New Keynesian view of nominal wages as an adjustment variable to the long-run equilibrium.

Restrictive and ill-coordinated macroeconomic policies in Germany

In order to provide a macroeconomic policy explanation for German stagnation, it must be shown that monetary, fiscal and wage policies for Germany have indeed been less favourable than for the EMU average since the mid-1990s as compared to the ten-year period from 1985–94 (see Table 8.4).[15]

Monetary policies

Monetary policy will be assessed by the development of the short-term real interest rate. Of course, modern central banks use the short-term nominal interest rate as an economic policy instrument. But if central banks target inflation they will set nominal interest rates with an eye to the ensuing real rate. In order to take into account the underlying economic situation, we also consult the difference between the short-term real interest rate and real GDP growth. We expect a negative influence of real interest rates on economic growth working through different transmission channels (money, credit, asset prices, exchange rates) (Bernanke and Gertler, 1995; Cecchetti, 1995).

With respect to monetary policies, Germany has lost its former status as the key currency country within the EMS at the start of EMU in 1999. Since then it has no longer been in a position to reap the advantages of the lower interest rates it used to have compared to the other EMS countries. During the process of convergence, these countries gained from a considerable decrease of short- and long-term nominal interest rates towards the lower German level. This convergence and decrease in nominal interest rates was associated

Table 8.4 Macroeconomic policy indicators for Germany and the EMU, 1985–94 and 1995–2004, annual average values

	1985–94[1]		1995–2004	
	Germany	EMU	Germany	EMU
Monetary policy				
Short-term real interest rate (per cent)	4.0	5.1	2.1	1.9
Short-term real interest rate minus real GDP growth rate (percentage points)	1.2	2.7	0.8	−0.1
Fiscal policy				
Number of years with pro-cyclical fiscal policy	7	8	6	5
of which during economic slowdown	3	3	4	2
Real total government expenditure, growth rate (per cent)	3.5	3.1	0.7	1.3
Real government investment, growth rate (per cent)	1.2	2.1	−3.7	1.1
Ratio of real government investment to real GDP (per cent)	2.7	3.0	2.0	2.6
Wage policy				
Compensation per employee, growth rate (per cent)	4.6	4.7	1.3	2.3
Unit labour cost, growth rate (per cent)	2.4	3.4	0.5	1.4
Labour income share (per cent of GDP at factor cost)	68.6	70.3	67.1	67.4
Change in labour income share to previous year (percentage points)	−0.1	−0.4	−0.3	−0.3

Notes: 1. 1985–91: West Germany and EMU, including West Germany.
Sources: OECD (2004); European Commission (2005a).

with a stronger decrease in real interest rates for the EMU average than for Germany over the 1990s. Since the German inflation rate has been lower than the EMU average, and the nominal interest rates have converged almost completely since 1999, Germany's real interest rates have been even higher than the EMU average since then. Whereas Germany had an average short-term real interest rate advantage of 1.1 percentage points relative to the EMU average in the period 1985–94, this completely reversed in the period 1995–2004, when the EMU gained an average short-term real interest rate advantage of 0.2 percentage points. The relation between the short-term real interest rate and the real GDP growth rate in Germany decreased only slightly from 1.2 percentage points in the first period to 0.8 percentage points in the second, whereas in the EMU as a whole this relation decreased considerably, from 2.7 to –0.1 percentage points. From this it follows that Germany in particular has suffered from European monetary integration and the ECB's 'anti-growth bias' whereas the other countries have gained from monetary integration. The ECB's 'anti-growth' bias consists of a too-restrictive definition of price stability for the heterogeneous currency area – as an annual increase of the harmonized consumer price index of below but close to 2 per cent (ECB, 2003, p. 79) – and an asymmetric response to the expected deviation of actual from target inflation.[16] Germany's weak performance, however, is only partly a result of the ECB's monetary strategy. It is also because, within the monetary union, the ECB can only address average inflation and cannot take into account Germany's special economic situation with both a higher output gap and lower inflation than the EMU average. This is where the role of fiscal and wage policies also have to be considered.

Fiscal policies

In order to capture the effects of fiscal policies on macroeconomic performance we focus on two measures. First, the extent to which fiscal policy exerts a stabilizing or destabilizing influence on the business cycle can be assessed by comparing changes in the output gap and the primary budget balance potential GDP ratio (PBR). The output gap serves as an indicator of the current state of economic activity. If it is positive, then capacity is outstripped; and if it is negative, this means that capacity is not fully utilized. Consequently a positive change in the output gap indicates a cyclical upturn, whereas a negative change points to a cyclical downturn. While the overall budget balance is the result of the macroeconomic process and cannot be controlled by fiscal policy, the cyclically adjusted primary budget balance the PBR, can be seen as a fiscal policy instrument.[17] If there is a negative change in the PBR, then structural deficits rise or structural surpluses fall, and fiscal policy provides an expansive stimulus to aggregate demand. If there is a positive change in the PBR, then structural deficits fall or structural surpluses rise, and fiscal policy provides a restrictive stimulus to demand. If the PBR remains constant when there is a change in the output gap, then fiscal policy is neither expansive nor restrictive and the automatic stabilizers are simply left to take effect.

Second, we take a look at the development of real government expenditure, in particular at real government investment. In the short run, government investment is an essential component of aggregate demand. Moreover, it provides public infrastructure, making it a key condition for growth in the long run. We assume a positive relationship between its growth rate and GDP growth.[18]

Considering fiscal policies, the Maastricht Treaty, and especially the Stability and Growth Pact (SGP), have enforced budget consolidation and restrictive policies on (potential) EMU member countries at least since the mid-1990s. Since then, German fiscal policies have been restrictive in four years (positive change in the PBR) in the face of a slowdown in economic activity (negative change in the output gap), pro-cyclically worsening the crisis. For the EMU average, this has happened only twice. The restrictive stance of German fiscal policies becomes even more obvious if one considers the growth rates of real public expenditure and of real public investment, in particular. The growth rate of real total public expenditures has decreased dramatically from an annual average of 3.5 per cent in the first period to only 0.7 per cent in the second period.[19] There has been a substantial decrease in the EMU rate as well; however, with an annual 1.3 per cent, it is still almost twice as high as its German equivalent. Even more dramatic is the development of German public investment since the mid-1990s. Real public investment expenditure declined, with an annual rate of −3.7 per cent, whereas the EMU as a whole had an average annual increase of 1.1 per cent. The German decline in public investment has led to a share of real public investment in real GDP that is very low, both in absolute terms and in comparison with the EMU average: after almost reaching the EMU level of about 3.0 per cent of GDP during the first period it has decreased continually to only about 2.0 per cent, compared to 2.6 per cent in the EMU as a whole in the second period.

Wage policies

Wage policies can be assessed by nominal wage growth (compensation per employee), unit labour cost growth and the labour income share. Nominal wage-setting affects unit labour cost growth and inflation. If nominal wages increase at a faster pace than does productivity plus the price level, unit labour cost growth and inflation will speed up.[20] This will cause real interest rates to fall, and may make the central bank increase nominal interest rates in order to reach its inflation target. If nominal wages increase at a rate below the sum of productivity growth and inflation, unit labour cost growth will slow down and cause disinflation. Finally, deflation may be the consequence. Deflation causes increasing real interest rates and rising real debts with negative effects on investment and growth. If deflationary processes have started, monetary policies lowering interest rates may be ineffective.

Wage policies, however, may not only affect prices, but may also change distribution if firms do not pass unit labour cost variations completely to prices. Under these conditions, nominal wage moderation causes the labour income share to fall. Empirical analysis for Germany and the EMU since the 1960s has shown that the development of unit labour costs affects the development of output prices (Hein *et al.*, 2006). The adjustment of the inflation rate to nominal unit labour cost growth, however, is incomplete. Therefore, nominal wage moderation is also associated with a tendency of labour income shares to fall. Hypothetically, the effects of income shares on GDP growth are ambiguous (Bhaduri and Marglin, 1990). With the propensity to save out of wages falling short of the savings propensity out of profits, a falling labour income share means a cut-back in consumption with directly contractive effects on investment and GDP growth. A fall in labour income shares that is associated with nominal wage restraint would, on the other hand, improve international competitiveness and, therefore, stimulate demand for exports, investment and growth. With a slowdown in inflation, the central bank may also cut interest rates and stimulate investment and growth. Finally, a falling labour income share is associated with rising unit profits, which may also improve investment and growth. Since the stimulating effects of wage moderation and declining labour income shares for investment and growth are rather indirect and uncertain, the direct and contractive effects may dominate in medium-sized and large economies mainly relying on domestic demand. Therefore, nominal wage growth according to the sum of productivity growth and inflation, and hence constant labour income shares, should be generally favourable conditions for growth.

Germany's too moderate nominal wage increases are the major cause for the below average inflation rate (see Table 8.4): nominal wage moderation has been more pronounced in Germany than in the EMU on average during the second period, and has also forced unit labour cost growth and inflation considerably below the EMU average. However, slower unit labour cost growth and lower inflation can also be observed in the first period from 1985–94 when Germany's absolute and relative economic performance had been much better. But during the first period low unit labour cost growth and the resulting low inflation rates were the basis for the DM's status as the regional key currency within the EMS, allowing the Deutsche Bundesbank to set substantially lower nominal and actual real interest rates than in the other EMS countries. Since the beginning of the interest rate convergence process in the mid-1990s and with the completion of EMU in 1999, however, lower inflation rates for Germany no longer pay off in terms of lower interest rates.

The overly moderate wage setting in Germany did not only cause below-average inflation rates. This wage policy also contributed to the acceleration of a tendency of declining labour income shares which had already started in the first period (see Table 8.4). This decline, however, can also be witnessed in the EMU as a whole. Redistribution at the expense of labour can therefore not add to the explanation of Germany's *relative* performance compared with the EMU. However, this redistribution has contributed to the weak development of domestic demand and hence to Germany's weak *absolute* performance since the mid-1990s.

On the other hand, moderate wage policies have improved price competitiveness and profitability of German firms which made German export surpluses almost triple between 2000 and 2003. Germany's share of international trade improved, making Germany the 'world champion' in exports in 2003 and 2004. But this extraordinary export performance was insufficient to compensate for the associated deficiencies in domestic demand, as has been shown above.

A restrictive macroeconomic policy mix in Germany

In sum, macroeconomic policy variables have indeed been less favourable in Germany than in the EMU since the mid-1990s. Macroeconomic mismanagement, therefore, can be considered to be the main cause of Germany's slump. This is partly a result of the integration of a former key currency country into a monetary union, and the associated loss of the interest rate advantage, and is thus inevitable. But it is also caused by the restrictive macroeconomic policy mix implemented at the EMU level, which is particularly affecting a slowly growing, low-inflation country like Germany: the too-restrictive ECB monetary policy strategy and the Stability and Growth Pact enforcing a restrictive stance on the member countries' fiscal policies. And a major contribution to macroeconomic mismanagement has come from German wage developments. We shall take a closer look at the reasons for this in the following section.

Why has wage policy in Germany been so moderate?

One of the key problems identified in the previous section is Germany's below-EMU average inflation rate, in particular since 1999. Below-EMU average inflation has been caused by below-EMU average unit labour cost growth which was not (and could not be) directly rewarded by the ECB's monetary policy. Therefore, the German economy has been particularly hit by the too-restrictive ECB monetary policy strategy, has suffered from above average real interest rates, and has recently faced an increasing risk of deflation.

Also, the EMU as a whole has seen a downward trend in inflation and unit labour cost growth since the mid-1990s, based on wage moderation (see Table 8.4). Against a background of sustained mass unemployment, the collective bargaining power of trade unions was weakened substantially. The most visible indicators of this were falling trade union membership and a significantly lower number of strikes and industrial disputes (Boeri *et al.*, 2001, Schulten, 2004). In addition, the 1990s saw the emergence in many European countries of new corporatist competitive structures which, as a result of national social pacts and 'alliances for jobs' led to the trade unions becoming firmly tied into the political agenda and committed to a competitive wages policy (Fajertag and Pochet, 2000).

It should be pointed out, however, that wage trends in the individual EMU countries were by no means uniform during the 1990s, and in fact occasionally reflected major differences in economic growth and employment trends between countries. Wage increases have been distinctly higher than the EMU average in some of the smaller EMU countries that achieved especially dynamic economic growth, such as Ireland, the Netherlands and recently also Spain. This has contributed to higher-than-average inflation as a result of these countries exceeding the national scope for distribution (productivity growth plus inflation), in some cases by a considerable margin (Schulten, 2002).

The situation was somewhat different in the larger EMU countries – that is, in France, Italy and Germany. While overall wage increases in Italy were slightly higher than the EMU average and slightly lower than the EMU average in France, in Germany they have remained consistently below the EMU average since 1996. Germany has been pursuing the most moderate wage policy in the EMU since then, and given that it is the largest economy in the EMU, this has also exerted a downward pressure on EMU average wage increases (see Table 8.4). In 2004, wage moderation in Germany has caused a fall in nominal unit labour cost growth, which means increasing deflation risks in this country.[21]

The particularly low wage increases in Germany can be attributed to different causes (Hein *et al.*, 2006):

(i) First, there has been a lessening of the trade unions' bargaining power. At the start of the 1990s, the trade unions were still able to achieve (too) high collectively agreed wage settlements on the back of the boom following German reunification, contributing to high inflation and to overly restrictive monetary policies by the Bundesbank. But since 1996 trade unions' collective bargaining policy has been plunged into a major crisis and they have been forced to accept collectively agreed wage increases of less than 3 per cent and on occasion even less than 2 per cent (see Table 8.5).
(ii) The crisis of trade unions' collective bargaining policy is shown even more clearly by actual earnings trends. In contrast to most other EMU countries, wage trends in Germany since the mid-1990s have mainly been characterized by a negative wage drift, with actual earnings growing even more slowly than collectively agreed wages. This is also a consequence of fundamental changes in the structure and operation of the German collective bargaining system. One clear indicator of this is the decline in the number of companies and employees covered by collective agreements that has been observed since the mid-1990s (Schnabel, 2003).[22] The negative wage drift seems to suggest that wage increases in companies not bound by collective agreements were significantly lower.
(iii) Furthermore, even within the German collective bargaining system there are numerous indicators which suggest that the binding nature of collective agreements is being eroded, making negotiated collective wage increases harder to implement in practice and consequently favouring a negative wage drift. There is now a significant number of companies that are formally bound by collective agreements but which in practice do not comply with them.[23]
(iv) In addition to the above, 'hardship' and 'opening' clauses were introduced into virtually all of the major sectoral collective agreements in

Table 8.5 Wages, productivity and prices in Germany, 1995–2004, annual growth rates, per cent

	(1) Collectively agreed hourly wages	(2) Actual earnings per employee hour	(3) Wage drift[1]	(4) Employee compensation per hour	(5) Labour productivity per hour	(6) Unit labour costs	(7) Prices (HCPI)
1995	4.9	4.5	−0.4	4.9	2.5	2.4	1.7
1996	2.6	3.0	0.4	2.8	2.3	0.5	1.2
1997	1.5	1.0	−0.5	1.6	2.0	−0.4	1.5
1998	1.9	1.4	−0.5	1.5	1.3	0.2	0.6
1999	2.9	2.3	−0.6	2.0	1.5	0.5	0.7
2000	2.0	2.8	0.8	3.3	2.2	1.1	1.4
2001	1.9	2.7	0.8	2.5	1.4	1.1	1.9
2002	2.7	2.1	−0.6	2.1	1.5	0.6	1.3
2003	1.9	1.2	−0.7	1.6	0.7	0.9	1.1
2004	1.3	0.2	−1.1	0.2	1.1	−0.9	1.7

Notes: 1. 1(2) minus (*n*) in percentage points.
Sources: Deutsche Bundesbank (2005); Federal Statistical Office (2005).

the 1990s, allowing companies to deviate from the terms contained in collective agreements under certain circumstances.[24]

(v) One final significant cause of the negative wage drift is the reduction of payments that are above the collectively agreed rate. A large number of companies in Germany continue to pay wages that are higher than those established in their collective agreement. Nevertheless, during the course of the 1990s, several companies began to use 'company alliances for jobs' to 'compensate for' the wage increases negotiated in collective agreements by cutting back on payments above the collectively agreed rate. This has led to the emergence of a new form of concession bargaining, in which employees agree to give up established benefits in exchange for limited job security, thereby contributing to a substantial reduction in labour costs.

The fundamental problems for German (and European) economic policies and wage bargaining

We have argued that the main causes for Germany's stagnation and its below-EMU average economic performance can be found in a restrictive macroeconomic policy-mix enforced on the German economy, causing serious problems of domestic demand. This is partly a result of the integration of the former key currency country into a monetary union, and it is thus inevitable.

But it is also caused by the restrictive macroeconomic policy mix implemented at the EMU level, which is particularly affecting a slowly growing, low-inflation country: the too restrictive ECB monetary policy strategy and the SGP which enforces a restrictive stance on fiscal policies.

The stagnation caused by monetary and fiscal policies is aggravated by Germany's excessive wage restraint. Nominal wage growth and unit labour cost growth since the mid-1990s have been significantly lower than the EMU averages, and this is to a large extent responsible for the below-EMU average inflation rate and has recently caused serious deflation risks. Consequently, even a monetary policy that might be suitable for the EMU as a whole is too restrictive for a country where growth and inflation are as low as in Germany. Furthermore, the fact that nominal interest rates have converged across the EMU and inflation in Germany is below average means that German consumers and investors are faced with real interest rates that are higher than the EMU average. On top of this, excessive wage restraint has also led to an acceleration in the tendency of the German labour income share to fall, which has in turn further weakened domestic demand.

The combination of a pronounced trend towards stagnation and significant deflation risks in the largest EMU country, together with the ECB's overly ambitious inflation target for the EMU as a whole, represents a major challenge for macroeconomic policies and in particular for wage policies in Germany and in the EMU:[25]

First, if Germany is to achieve an economic recovery with wage policies providing the nominal anchor, nominal wage growth will have to rise in order to achieve the sum of long-term productivity growth plus the ECB's target inflation rate. However, given the deterioration of the German wage bargaining system and the weak bargaining position of the trade unions, an increase in nominal wage and unit labour cost growth requires improved employment and higher GDP growth as a pre-condition. But more expansive macroeconomic policies at the national level generating more employment are difficult to achieve, given the restrictions by the EMU policy mix.

Second, even if German trade unions managed to increase nominal wage and unit labour cost growth, and if inflation in Germany rose, such a rise would lead to an EMU inflation rate above the ECB's target as long as other EMU countries have inflation rates considerably above that target rate. Restrictive monetary policies will then be unavoidable as long as the ECB is not prepared to increase its inflation target substantially in order to allow the slowly-growing larger economies more room to achieve a recovery.

Third, if the ECB is not prepared to raise its inflation target, it will be necessary to reduce inflation in the other EMU countries in order to allow Germany more inflation. It is therefore important for the bargaining parties, and in particular the trade unions, to intensify their efforts towards European-level effective co-ordination of wage policy. The aim of this process should be for each country to increase wages on the basis of its long-term domestic productivity growth rates plus the ECB's target inflation rate.[26] There are, however, major obstacles for wage bargaining co-ordination across Europe arising from the different degrees of co-ordination within the national bargaining systems, from the overall weakness of trade unions in Europe, from the tendency towards decentralization of bargaining imposed by labour market policies and so on. In addition, reducing inflation in the rapidly-growing high inflation EMU countries would mean higher real interest rates and lower growth for these countries.

From these considerations it follows, first, that wage policies in Germany – although they have contributed significantly to German stagnation – in the short run are rather impotent when it comes to improving German growth and employment. Wage policies in Germany urgently need to be supported by more expansive fiscal policies, and particularly monetary policies. Second, in the medium-term the conditions for the achievement of nominal wage growth in Germany according to the sum of long-run domestic productivity growth and the ECB's inflation target have to be improved. Third, if it proves impossible either to convince the ECB to raise its inflation target or to co-ordinate wage policies across the EMU countries in the way described above, then in the medium to long term Germany's stagnation and deflation risks are likely to spread increasingly to the other EMU countries. Excessive wage restraint in Germany will not only fuel national economic stagnation but will also put pressure on wage policies in the other EMU countries in the medium term if they lose competitiveness and their current account deteriorates. If wage policies start to be widely used to protect or improve price competitiveness, then further redistribution at the expense of labour, rising effective demand problems and the threat of deflation will spread accordingly. If this happens, then even a more growth-friendly monetary policy by the ECB might be ineffective and in the next cyclical downturn the deflation risks may become actual deflation – not only in Germany but also in the EMU as a whole.

Notes

1. Germany's growth rate has been below 1 per cent in 2005.
2. See Hein and Niechoj (2005) for a comparison of economic performance of the EMU with the USA since the mid-1980s.
3. See, for example, the annual reports of the German council of economic experts (SVR, 2003, 2004), the majority view in the semi-annual joint reports of the leading economic research institutes in Germany (Institute, 2003, 2004) and, in particular, an economic policy paper by the German central bank (Deutsche Bundesbank, 2003).
4. See Bibow (2003, 2005) for an extensive discussion of the effects of German unification and the macroeconomic reactions by the Bundesbank and by German fiscal policies in the course of the 1990s.

5. Note that in this approach it is unemployment that lowers the growth rate and not low growth that is responsible for rising unemployment.
6. For a more detailed discussion, see Hein and Truger (2005).
7. See, for example, Nickell (1997), Nickell and Layard (1999) and, in particular, Schettkat (2003a, 2003b).
8. Baker *et al.* (2004) provide an excellent overview of the more recent econometric studies and demonstrate the lack of robustness of their results. See Hein and Truger (2005) for more details.
9. See Snowdon *et al.* (1994, pp. 286–330, 367–80) for textbook reviews of the two approaches.
10. Many papers have shown that a favourable co-ordination between monetary and fiscal policies rather than deregulated labour markets can be considered responsible for the superior development of the US economy during the 1990s compared to Germany or the European economies (Palley, 1998; Solow, 2000; Fritsche *et al.*, 2005; Hein and Niechoj, 2005).
11. See Davidson (1994), Heine and Herr (1999) and Lavoie (1992) for textbook presentations of the post-Keynesian approach, and Arestis (1996) for a survey.
12. See Stiglitz (1997), Auerbach and Kotlikoff (1998), Mankiw (2002) and Blanchard (2003) for textbook presentations in the New Keynesian vein, and Truger (2003) for a survey of macroeconomic policy implications.
13. The requirement of co-ordinated monetary and fiscal policy intervention increases considerably if hysteresis is taken into account. With hysteresis, the NAIRU is not stable but rather depends on the past development of the actual unemployment rate, which can be affected by macro-policies (Ball, 1999; Blanchard, 2003; p. 283).
14. For a critique of the New Keynesian NAIRU approach from a post-Keynesian perspective see Sawyer (2001, 2002) and Hein (2004).
15. It should be noted that using the EMU average as a standard of reference by no means implies that macroeconomic policies for the EMU have been optimal or adequate. On the contrary, EMU macroeconomic policies have in general suffered from the same problems as Germany: macroeconomic mismanagement and a lack of co-ordination (Hein and Truger, 2005a; 2005b; Hein and Niechoj, 2005). Unfortunately, German macroeconomic policies have been even worse.
16. The ECB has tended to tighten whenever inflation increased above the target without relaxing when inflation expectations came down. For a general critique of the ECB's 'anti-growth bias', see Bibow (2002) and Hein (2002).
17. Using primary deficits puts into focus those components of public debt directly connected to effective demand.
18. At least for Germany, long-term positive growth effects of public infrastructure investment should be uncontroversial. See Kitterer (1998) and Pfähler *et al.* (1996).
19. The growth rates of primary government expenditure have also been below the EMU average since 1997. The same is true for the growth rates of real social benefits.
20. See Arestis and Sawyer (2003) and Hein (2002, 2004) for models of distribution conflict and inflation.
21. See the IMF (2003) on deflation risks in Germany. For a more extensive discussion of deflation risks in Germany and the EMU see Hein *et al.* (2005).
22. According to the IAB (Institut für Arbeitsmarkt- und Berufsforschung) figures for 2001, only 48 per cent of all companies in western Germany and 71 per cent of all employees were bound by collective agreements, while in eastern Germany

the figures were as low as 28 per cent of companies and 56 per cent of employees (Bispinck, 2003, p. 395).

23. According to the results of the 2002 WSI Works Council Survey, which probably covers only part of the problem, 10 per cent of companies occasionally failed to comply with the terms of current collective agreements, and a further 5 per cent did so frequently. In the majority of these cases, the non-compliance involved failure to pay the collectively agreed wages (Bispinck and Schulten, 2003, p. 159).
24. Opening clauses are now used by more than a third of all companies, although it is true that in the majority of cases these relate to the divergence of working time organization from the collective agreement, and the use of opening clauses with regard to remuneration is for the time being still not very widespread (Bispinck and Schulten, 2003, p. 160).
25. On the interaction of the ECB's monetary policy with wage bargaining in Europe, see Hein (2002).
26. For more detailed information on the current status and future prospects of the various trade union co-ordination initiatives, see Schulten (2003, 2004) and Traxler and Mehrmet (2003).

References

Allsopp, C. and D. Vines (1998) 'The Assessment: Macroeconomic Policy after EMU', *Oxford Review of Economic Policy*, vol. 14, no. 3, pp. 1–23.

Arestis, P. (1996) 'Post-Keynesian Economics: Towards Coherence', *Cambridge Journal of Economics*, vol. 20, pp. 111–35.

Arestis, P. and M. Sawyer (2003) 'Aggregate Demand, Conflict, and Capacity in the Inflationary Process', Working Paper No. 391, The Levy Economics Institute, Annandale-on-Hudson.

Auerbach, A. J. and L. J. Kotlikoff (1998) *Macroeconomics. An Integrated Approach*, 2nd edn (Cambridge, Mass.: MIT Press).

Baker, D. A. Glyn, D. R. Howell and J. Schmitt (2004) 'Labor Market Institutions and Unemployment: A critical Assessment of the Cross-country Evidence', in D. R. Howell (ed.), *Fighting Unemployment. The Limits of the Free Market Orthodoxy* (Oxford: Oxford University Press), pp. 72–118.

Ball, L. (1999) 'Aggregate Demand and Long-run Unemployment', *Brooking Papers on Economic Activity*, vol. 2, pp. 189–251.

Bernanke, B. and M. Gertler (1995) 'Inside the Black Box: The Credit Channel of Monetary Policy Transmission', *Journal of Economic Perspectives*, vol. 9, pp. 27–48.

Bhaduri, A. and S. Marglin (1990) 'Unemployment and the Real Wage: The Economic Basis for Contesting Political Ideologies', *Cambridge Journal of Economics*, vol. 14, pp. 375–93.

Bibow, J. (2002) 'The Monetary Policies of the European Central Bank and Euro's (Mal)Performance: A Stability-oriented Assessment', *International Review of Applied Economics*, vol. 16, pp. 31–50.

Bibow, J. (2003) 'On the "burden" of German unification', *Banca Nazionale del Lavoro Quarterly Review*, vol. 56, pp. 137–69.

Bibow, J. (2005) 'Germany in Crisis: The Unification Challenge, Macroeconomic Policy Shocks and Traditions, and EMU', *International Review of Applied Economics*, vol. 19, pp. 29–50.

Bispinck, R. (2003) 'Das deutsche Tarifsystem in Zeiten der Krise – Streit um Flächentarif, Differenzierung und Mindeststandards', *WSI-Mitteilungen*, vol. 56, pp. 395–404.

Bispinck, R. and Schulten, T. (2003) 'Decentralization of German Collective Bargaining – Current Trends and Assessments from a Works and Staff Council Perspective', *WSI-Mitteilungen*, Special English Issue, vol. 56, pp. 24–33.

Blanchard, O. (2003) *Macroeconomics*, 3rd edn (London: Prentice-Hall).

Boeri, T., A. Brugiavini and L. Calmfors (eds) (2001) *The Role of Unions in the Twenty-First Century: A Report for the Fondazione Rodolfo Debenedetti* (Oxford: Oxford University Press).

Cecchetti, S. G. (1995) 'Distinguishing Theories of the Monetary Transmission Mechanism', *Federal Reserve Bank of St Louis Review*, vol. 77, no. 3, pp. 83–97.

Davidson, P. (1994) *Post-Keynesian Macroeconomic Theory* (Aldershot: Edward Elgar).

Deutsche Bundesbank (2003) *Wege aus der Krise – Wirtschaftspolitische Denkanstöße für Deutschland* (Frankfurt: Deutsche Bundesbank).

Deutsche Bundesbank (2005) *Monatsbericht*, March, vol. 57, no. 3.

ECB (2003) 'The Outcome of the ECB's Evaluation of its Monetary Policy Strategy', *Monthly Bulletin*, June, pp. 79–92.

European Commission (2005a) 'Annual Macroeconomic Database (AMECO)'; available at: http://europa.eu.int/comm/economy_finance/indicators/annual_macro_economic_database/ameco_en.htm.

European Commission (2005b) *Economic Forecast*, Spring, Brussels.

Fajertag, G. and P. Pochet (eds) (2000) *Social Pacts in Europe – New Dynamics* (Brussels: ETUI).

Federal Statistical Office, Statistisches Bundesamt (2005): Volkswirtschaftslehre Gesamtrechuungen, Fachseric 18, Reihe 1.4 (Wiesbaden: Statistisches Bundesamt.)

Fritsche, U., M. Heine, H. Heri, G. Horn and C. Kaiser (2005) 'Macroeconomic Regime and Economic Development: The Case of the USA', in E. Hein *et al.* (eds), *Macroeconomic Policy Coordination in Europe and the Role of the Trade Unions* (Brussels: ETUI), pp. 69–107.

Hein, E. (2002) 'Monetary Policy and Wage Bargaining in the EMU: Restrictive ECB Policies, High Unemployment, Nominal Wage Restraint and Inflation above the Target', *Banca Nazionale del Lavoro Quarterly Review*, vol. 55, pp. 299–337.

Hein, E. (2004) 'Die NAIRU – eine post-keynesianische Interpretation, Intervention, *Journal of Economics*, vol. 1, pp. 43–66.

Hein, E. and E. Niechoj (2005) 'Guidelines for Sustained Growth in the EU? The Concept and Consequences of the Broad Economic Policy Guidelines', Paper prepared for the conference 'Development in Economic Theory and Policy', Bilbao, 7–8 July.

Hein, E. and A. Truger (2005a) 'Whatever Happened to Germany? Is the Decline of the Former European Key Currency Country Caused by Structural Sclerosis or by Macroeconomic Mismanagement?', *International Review of Applied Economics*, vol. 19, pp. 3–28.

Hein, E. and A. Truger (2005b) 'European Monetary Union: Nominal Convergence, Real Divergence, and Slow Growth?', *Structural Change and Economic Dynamics*, vol. 16, pp. 7–33.

Hein, E. and A. Truger (2005c) 'Macroeconomic Coordination as an Economic Policy Concept – Opportunities and Obstacles in the EMU', in E. Hein *et al.* (eds), *Macroeconomic Policy Coordination in Europe and the Role of the Trade Unions* (Brussels: ETUI), pp. 19–67.

Hein, E., T. Schulten and A. Truger (2005) 'Deflation Risks in Germany and the EMU: The Role of Wages and Wage Bargaining', in E. Hein, A. Heise and A. Truger (eds), *Wages, Employment, Distribution and Growth. International Perspectives* (Basingstoke: Palgrave), pp. 67–92.

Heine, M. and H. Herr (1999) *Volkswirtschaftslehre* (Munich: Oldenbourg).

IMF (International Monetary Fund) (2003) *Deflation: Determinants, Risks and Policy Options – Findings of an Interdepartmental Task Force* (Washington, DC: IMF).

Institute, Arbeitsgemeinschaft deutscher wirtschaftswissenschaftlicher Forschungsinstitute (2003), Die Lage der Weltwirtschaft und der deutschen Wirtschaft im Herbst 2003, DIW Wochenberichte, vol. 43, pp. 643–86.

Institute, Arbeitsgemeinschaft deutscher wirtschaftswissenschaftlicher Forschungsinstitute (2004), Die Lage der Weltwirtschaft und der deutschen Wirtschaft im Herbst 2004, DIW Wochenbericht, vol. 43, pp. 629–82.

Kitterer, W. (1998) 'Langfristige Wirkungen öffentlicher Investitionen – Theoretische und empirische Aspekte', *Zeitschrift für Wirtschaftspolitik*, vol. 47, pp. 289–316.

Lavoie, M. (1992) *Foundations of Post-Keynesian Economic Analysis* (Aldershot: Edward Elgar).

Layard, R., S. Nickell and R. Jackman (1991) *Unemployment. Macroeconomic Performance and the Labour Market* (Oxford: Oxford University Press).

Mankiw, N. G. (2002) *Macroeconomics*, 5th edn (London: Worth).

Nickell, S. (1997) 'Unemployment and Labor Market Rigidities: Europe versus North America', *Journal of Economic Perspectives*, vol. 11, pp. 55–74.

Nickell, S. and R. Layard (1999) 'Labour Market Institutions and Economic Performance', in O. Ashenfelter and H. Card (eds), *Handbook of Labour Economics* (Amsterdam: Elsevier), pp. 3029–84.

Nickell, S., L. Nanziata, W. Ochel and G. Quintini (2002) 'The Beveridge Curve, Unemployment and Wages in the OECD from the 1960s to the 1990s', Discussion Paper 502, Centre for Economic Performance (Version May 2002) (London School of Economics and Political Science).

OECD (2004) *Economic Outlook*, vol. 76 (data on CD-ROM).

Palley, T. (1998) 'Restoring Prosperity: Why the U.S. Model is Not the Answer for the United States or Europe', *Journal of Post Keynesian Economics*, vol. 20, pp. 337–52.

Pfähler, W., U. Hofmann and W. Bönte (1996) 'Does Extra Public Infrastructure Capital Matter? An Appraisal of Empirical Literature', *Finanzarchiv N.F.*, vol. 53, pp. 68–112.

Sawyer, M. (2001) 'The NAIRU: A Critical Appraisal', in P. Arestis and M. Sawyer (eds), *Money, Finance and Capitalist Development* (Cheltenham: Edward Elgar), pp. 220–54.

Sawyer, M. (2002) 'The NAIRU, Aggregate Demand and Investment', *Metroeconomica*, vol. 53, pp. 66–94.

Schettkat, R. (2003a) 'Institutions and the Economic Fitness Landscape: What Impact Do Welfare State Institutions Have on Economic Performance?', IZA Discussion Paper No. 696, Bonn, Forschungsinstitut zur Zukunft der Arbeit.

Schettkat, R. (2003b) 'Are Institutional Rigidities at the Root of European Unemployment?', *Cambridge Journal of Economics*, vol. 27, pp. 771–87.

Schnabel, C. (2003) *Tarifpolitik unter Reformdruck, Benchmarking Deutschland Aktuell* (Gütersloh: Bertelsmann Foundation).

Schroeder, G. (2003) 'Niemand darf sich künftig zu Lasten der Gemeinschaft zurücklehnen', *Frankfurter Rundschau*, March 15, p. 7.

Schulten, T. (2002) *Tarifpolitik in Europa 2001/2002 – 2. Europäischer Tarifbericht des WSI, Reihe WSI Informationen zur Tarifpolitik* (Dusseldorf: Hans Boeckler Foundation).

Schulten, T. (2003) Europeanization of Collective Bargaining: Trade Union Initiatives for the Transnational Coordination of Collective Bargaining', in H.-W. Platzer and B. Keller (eds), *Industrial Relations and European Integration. Trans- and Supranational Developments and Prospects* (Aldershot: Ashgate), pp. 112–36.

Schulten, T. (2004) *Solidarische Lohnpolitik in Europa. Zur Politischen Oekonomie der Gewerkschaften* (Hamburg: VSA).

Siebert, H. (1997) 'Labor Market Rigidities: At the Root of Unemployment in Europe', *Journal of Economic Perspectives*, vol. 11, pp. 37–54.

Snowdon, B., H. Vane and P. Wynarczyk (1994) *A Modern Guide to Macroeconomics* (Cheltenham: Edward Elgar).

Solow, R. M. (2000) 'Unemployment in the United States and in Europe: A Contrast and the Reasons', *Ifo-Studien*, vol. 46, pp. 1–12.

Stiglitz, J. E. (1997) *Principles of Macroeconomics*, 2nd edn (New York: W. W. Norton).

SVR, Sachverständigenrat zur Begutachtung der gesamtwirtschaftlichen Entwicklung (2003), Jahresgutachten 2003, Staatsfinanzen konsolidieren – Steuersystem reformieren, Berlin (Deutscher Bundestag, Drucksache 15/2000).

SVR, Sachverständigenrat zur Begutachtung der gesamtwirtschaftlichen Entwicklung (2004), Jahresgutachten 2004, Erfolge im Ausland – Herausforderungen im Inland, http://www.sachverstaendigenrat-wirtschaft.de/.

Traxler, F. and E. Mehrmet (2003) 'Coordination of Collective Bargaining: The Case of Europe', *Transfer: European Review of Labour and Research*, vol. 9, pp. 229–46.

Truger, A. (2003) 'Der missachtete Mainstream – die deutsche wirtschaftspolitische Debatte leidet weniger unter dem Neu-Keynesianismus als unter seiner fast völligen Missachtung', in E. Hein, A. Heise and A. Truger (eds), *Neu-Keynesianismus – der neue wirtschaftspolitische Mainstream?* (Marburg: Metropolis), pp. 254–78.

9

'Sick Man of Europe' or 'Midlife Crisis in Europe'? Germany's Woes since the Mid-1980s – A Comment

Waltraud Schelkle

My aim here is to survey the previous contributors' analysis and comment on the entire spectrum of diagnoses why Germany has become the sick man of Europe.

Horst Feldmann, in Chapter 7, (HF) presents an analysis of the mainstream view of German economists towards the situation in Germany. According to this view, the government's breach of the Stability and Growth Pact (SGP) contains in a nutshell what is wrong with the country's economy: the economic policy-makers do not try hard enough to overcome resistance to sensible policies – in this case, the consolidation of public finances. The mainstream view usually extends this verdict to structural reforms of labour markets and the welfare state more generally. The recommendation to policy-makers, then, is a resolute 'Try harder!': that is, to consolidate so as to reap the non-Keynesian effects of budget consolidation, effects that promise to achieve economic expansion through fiscal contraction.

Eckhard Hein and Achim Truger (EH/AT) present in Chapter 8 a (post-) Keynesian interpretation, (largely compatible with what has become a mainstream view in the rest of the world, namely the New Keynesian macroeconomics; within the German establishment, European Central Bank (ECB) economists seem to be the only ones who have heard of it, but then they are mainly foreigners![1] According to this interpretation, it is the mismanagement of monetary, fiscal and wage policies since the mid-1990s that account for Germany's stagnation. The recommendation to policy-makers is to allow for wage-induced inflation, accommodated by monetary policy and supported by deficit spending, that is, to go for what its enemies would call Keynesian pump-priming.

Yet, while the assessments and recommendations of HF and EH/AT could not be more opposite to one other, they fundamentally agree on one point: that bad policies are to blame. Even though the authors make a number of good points in arguing their cases, I remain unconvinced. Rather, I pity for once the policy-makers who are offered such contradictory policy advice from respectable German economists. The policy-makers' excuse for not taking any of this advice seriously is obviously that the recommendations are too radical – neither Feldmann's heroic 'Per aspera ad astra; embrace more hardship' nor Hein's youthful 'Forget about the mainstream and history, try Mitterrand's 1982 trick again' are pragmatic enough to be politically attractive. My own doubts are related more to the underlying diagnosis that it is nothing but bad policy-making that caused the breach of the Pact or Germany's stagnation. A corollary of this verdict is that economists and enlightened policy-making could fix Germany's woes rapidly enough if only politics didn't hold them back, be it politics in the disguise of special interests or misguided neo-liberal ideologies. In contrast, it seems to me that there are no quick fixes for Germany's woes.

The country is undergoing a secular process of economic change. The change required, and already under way, is from an economy that engaged successfully in catching up, but was structurally still geared to behaving like an emerging market dependent on demand stimuli from exports and an external nominal anchor of a stable exchange rate to the dollar. This is no longer an option, largely because others copied that model successfully, which in macroeconomic terms boils down to the maxim: 'undervalue the real exchange rate'; that is, combine mercantilism in trade with a hard currency policy that pays off in a low equilibrium interest rate and rising real income.[2] Enlightened Keynesian demand management tried to shift market equilibria, not to upset them.

In this perspective, Germany resembles a middle-aged person grappling with the fact that he/she is ageing but would still like to behave like an adolescent – doing all the things that adults do (that is, behaving like an economic and political power to be reckoned with) – but at the same time refusing to accept the responsibilities of a grown-up (for domestic stimulation, not exporting its unemployment). This period is coming to an end, with the German economy no longer succeeding in behaving like an emerging market. Such an interpretation concedes that German unification and the European monetary union have not made this transition any easier, but sees these two unifications more as aggravating circumstances than as major causes. The process of painful restructuring that has been going on since the mid-1980s does not make it the 'sick man of Europe' but rather a case of a 'mid-life crisis in Europe'. I agree with all three authors that it would be useful if policy-makers could see that and make the necessary adjustments. Yet, in a moment of academic modesty, we should admit that none of us know what the necessary adjustments are exactly; Chapters 7 and 8 together illustrate that there is considerable uncertainty about the way to go. It seems to me that Germany needs time to adjust, as do all people in a midlife crisis who start running marathons or have extramarital affairs, only to find that it is not all that healthy for their ageing bones and hearts.

This hypothesis that Germany's problems are caused by a secular process of change in its economy rather than bad policy or the exogenous shocks of two unifications is so far only an idea. It warrants more research than I have found time to do. Instead, I take only the first step to substantiate my hypothesis by pointing out why I find the two policy-centred explanations not really convincing. That still leaves open many other explanations – for example, those blaming EMU or German unification – but this is beyond me at this stage.

In each case, I shall first indicate the main problem I see in the underlying theory, then question the empirical evidence, and finally the economic policy advice. First, on Horst Feldmann's contribution: An Achilles heel for explanations of the SGP's failure that heaps all the blame on policy-makers for want of trying is the fact that the list of delinquents gets longer by the day. Among them are not only the usual suspects, such as Greece, but also the Netherlands and the UK, which even as a European Monetary Union (EMU) outsider is still subject to the stipulations of the Pact, just not to the Excessive Deficit Procedure – but then no country seem to be subject to the Excessive Deficit Procedure. Non-compliance is an Achilles heel for the proponents of the Pact. After all, the conceptual framework underlying the SPG was justified by economists of the New Classical tradition, supposedly so superior to mechanical Keynesian macroeconomics, since it is built on sound microfoundations ('get incentives right!') and hard-nosed political economy ('never trust politicians!'). Yet, how is it that we eventually had a Pact with so little self-enforcement and incentive compatibility that even finance ministers who are very concerned to keep their reputation and popularity as hardliners and 'iron chancellors' do not manage to play by the self-imposed rules? The truth is that one should not bind governments' hands just when one has taken away the option to set country-specific interest rates. This is what sensible macroeconomists such as Charles Goodhart or Willem Buiter said all along.

A piece of empirical evidence that questions the economic rationale of the Pact is in fact a lack of evidence, namely that for negative spillovers. I readily admit that I am rather surprised that there is not the slightest sign of a rise in the long-term interest rate, as a glance at the *Monthly Reports* of the ECB to date will reveal. On the contrary, the euro has appreciated against the dollar ever since Germany and Portugal were let off the hook. The softening of the Pact has not changed any of that. Only political events, namely the rejection of the draft constitution in the Dutch and French referenda, sent the euro into a nose-dive. European government bonds are obviously seen as safe havens at a time when there is a scarcity of profitable investment opportunities and a lot of liquidity around. This exposes the fiscal rule enshrined in the Pact as being motivated by a legalistic, disciplinarian logic rather than based on an understanding of financial markets.

The proponents of the Pact understood eventually that there must be some positive incentives if governments are expected to comply, not only a threat of pro-cyclical fiscal sanctions. The academic designers of the Pact should have acknowledged that fact from the beginning – after all, if governments are crooks that need to be handcuffed, then it must be made worthwhile for them to keep their self-imposed chains. Yet, it is rather questionable that the non-Keynesian effects of fiscal consolidation are in general the promised carrots now. The evidence on these effects is very mixed, and for good reason: only if fiscal contraction is seen as an indicator of long-term regime change will households and firms start spending more, despite the fact that they receive fewer transfers and subsidies or pay higher taxes. I do not deny that this may happen but it is unlikely to work for a country like Germany that does not have the reputation of a fiscal rogue; moreover, the government cannot pretend that. It could cut expenditure drastically in the near future – say, for pensions, health care and East Germany's lack of a viable source of self-sustaining growth. Thus, a fundamental regime change seems neither necessary nor credible, and non-Keynesian effects are therefore unlikely to materialize.

I move on now to Eckhard Hein and Achim Truger's explanation – again, the comment will be, first, about the main problem I see in theoretical terms, then about the empirical evidence and finally the economic policy advice: The weakness of an explanation that blames an overly restrictive or deflationary macroeconomic stance for Germany's stagnation is the underlying investment theory. Chapter 8 does not talk a great deal about it, but mainly refutes the view that labour market regulations are responsible for low growth and high unemployment. I share that latter view; but what about the missing link of what determines income and employment? Where EH/AT talk explicitly, if cautiously, about it: 'a falling labour income share is associated with rising unit profits which may also improve investment and growth' – they give the impression that this is *current* profits. Now EH/AT, being good Keynesian scholars, hardly need reminding that investment in a post-Keynesian economy relies on *expected* profits or 'animal spirits', the latter expression to emphasize that there is no reliable market mechanism that could stimulate business. Even worse, the modern theory of investment under uncertainty conceptualizes investments as depending on the 'option value of waiting' and can thus explain the low interest elasticity we find empirically.[3] This puts a question-mark on a diagnosis that depends heavily on an overly restrictive macroeconomic, in this case monetary policy. Even if it had been this restrictive, there is little in modern post-Keynesian theory that would support the verdict that it is above all monetary policy and excessively high interest rates that depressed investment in Germany.

The other part of the explanation – namely, that it was the restrictive fiscal stance – is hardly borne out by the empirical evidence. I can be brief about that, since Horst Feldmann presented the evidence. EH/AT's figures in Table 8.4 show us growth rates but not levels of government expenditure and no evidence on deficits or the growth of public debt. There was no such a thing as a restrictive fiscal stance, although I agree that deficit spending was caused less by active intervention than by the working of automatic stabilizers, thus more passive compensation than pre-emptive stimulation. If EH/AT was less broadbrush in their assessment of the fiscal stance, they could even argue against the mainstream that the one instance of active stimulation we observed does not fit the prediction that this can only lead to higher inflation. Even the pro-cyclical stance in the mini-boom of 2000/1 did nothing of the sort, inflation remained low, and arguably stimulated growth, even if only briefly and at the wrong time, when fiscal consolidation could have been achieved less painfully.

So where should we go from here, according to EH/AT? While I congratulate them for their boldness in asking for a rise in inflation, I still think that is unfortunate advice. It is unfortunate in that it gives the wrong impression that Keynesian economic policy depends crucially on nominal illusion of the wage bargaining parties. First, every academic economist should resist the Bundesbank terminology that calls every rise in the price level 'inflation'. There is a fundamental difference between inflation in the sense of a process of rising profits and wages and one-off rises in the price level, even if it is hard to distinguish between them in statistical terms – but then it is the job of central bankers to distinguish them. To accommodate one-off price rises allows firms to realize the equilibrium mark-up. In a situation of booming investment it can provide for windfall gains that over-fulfil investment expecations and can thus stimulate further investment. But that is not inflation. In such a situation of booming investment – and only then – wage moderation is crucial to maintain the growth in employment. But an active inflationary policy through monetary and fiscal accommodation cannot but lead to higher long-term interest rates that will ultimately spell the end of an investment dynamic, since rising interest rates eliminate windfall gains by increasing the equilibrium mark-up. Too bad, but we cannot simply go back to the recipes of pump-priming that American Keynesians such as Alvin Hansen invented. They got away with such advice because the USA was the unchallenged key currency area and everybody else shadowed the US inflation rate. Even that did not last for long, though, because economies like that of Germany undercut it, and thus won the competitive advantage that enabled it to catch up.

To sum up: unfortunately, I think that it is neither all bad policies that made Germany break the Pact, nor the stagnating economy. Nor do I expect a switch to what the authors consider to be good policy – fiscal contraction or inflationary expansion – to be a recipe for revival. Yet policy-makers cannot take much comfort from my comments either. We shall have to watch the secular process of restructuring to play itself out. And while there are more or less sensible policies to help it along the way, such as making the welfare state more service- and employment-intensive, I do not see salvation in the radical policy shifts that these two chapters advocate. My policy advice will not come as a surprise to readers of this comment: in middle age, you had better take it easy and enjoy the fact that the race to stay young is over.

Notes

1. Several authors of ECB Working Papers have adopted this approach, specifically O. Arratibel, D. Rodriguez-Palenzuela and C. Thimann, *Inflation Dynamics and Dual Inflation in Accession Countries: A 'New Keynesian' Perspective*, No. 132 (Frankfurt: ECB), March 2002; or P. McAdam and A. Willman, *New Keynesian Phillips Curves: A Reassessment Using Euro-area Data*, No. 165 (Frankfurt: ECB), September 2003. For an excellent discussion as to whether New Keynesianism captures the key concerns of Keynes' economic theory, see R. van der Ploeg, 'Back to Keynes?', *CESifo Economic Studies*, vol. 51, no. 4, 2005, pp. 1–46.
2. See H. Riese, 'Strukturwandel und unterbewertete Währung in der Bundesrepublik Deutschland. Bemerkungen zur theoretischen Position des Instituts für Weltwirtschaft Kiel', *Konjunkturpolitik*, vol. 24, 1978, pp. 143–69.
3. The standard reference is A. K. Dixit and R. S. Pindyck, *Investment under Uncertainty* (Princeton, NJ: Princeton University Press, 1994).

Part III

Structural Developments

10
Current Structural Changes: Challenges for the German Labour Market and Collective Bargaining

Lothar Funk

Introduction

High unemployment is, as it has been for so long, the number one political and economic problem in Germany. Germany is one of the very few Organization for Economic Co-operation and Development (OECD) countries where structural unemployment appears to have increased significantly since the early 1990s (Brandt *et al.*, 2005, p. 6). If effective solutions can be found to overcome these abject circumstances, then not only will the economic situation improve, but Germany will, in all probability, in the medium term, also achieve higher trend-rate growth. Even though the measures adopted as part of Agenda 2010, which have partly reduced the generosity of German social benefits, are steps in the right direction,[1] they are by no means enough to solve the problem of persistently high unemployment in Germany. In the words of the Swedish economist, Lars Calmfors: 'If reductions in benefit generosity are to make a maximum contribution to employment generation, they must be translated into lower real wage costs as efficiently as possible. It is, therefore, a step in the right direction that the unemployed may now have to accept jobs that pay less than the jobs they had before' (Calmfors, 2004, p. 40). The German pay-setting system does not, however, appear to be responsive enough in reducing real wage levels to make welfare state and labour market reforms successful over a relatively short period. Therefore, further reforms are necessary if labour-market outcomes in Germany are to improve considerably, and lastingly. This is especially true of the system of collective bargaining, which, unlike unemployment benefits, has not in recent years been subject to major employment-enhancing legal reforms.

The German labour market has been characterized for a long time now by persistently high unemployment. Until the middle of the 1990s, the number of unemployed people rose from one business cycle to the next.In each recession, roughly a million people were added to the unemployed in western Germany, and the high unemployment rate was not significantly reduced during the intervening years. Therefore, each recession started from a higher level of unemployment than the one before. Moreover, German unification added the structural problems of eastern Germany, and the labour market adjusted badly to these challenges. Persistently high unemployment cannot be explained by structural changes in the world economy and the shock of unification alone (even if such factors would lead to temporary increases in unemployment in a properly functioning labour market). Institutional factors that interact with these changes must play a prominent role in explaining Germany's current problems (Funk, 2000; Deutsche Bundesbank, 2004; Siebert, 2005, pp. 69–113). In particular, the stepwise ratcheting-up of unemployment and the continuously high level of unemployment – in 2004, the German unemployment rate was just below 10 per cent – have remained high by OECD standards (OECD, 2005, p. 237); this signals that Germany's labour-market-related institutions are not functioning properly.

Indeed, many studies demonstrate that labour-market-related institutions are at the heart of explanations of Germany's unemployment problems (for example, Deutsche Bundesbank, 2001; Sinn, 2003, pp. 14–19; Nickell *et al.*, 2005; Siebert, 2005, pp. 69–113). Three major aspects can be considered in this respect:[2]

1. The role of the welfare state in fixing reservation wages: on the one hand, Germany's welfare state traditionally tends to fix the reservation wage at a relatively high level, which either allows unemployed people to remain in a state of (inefficient) search over long periods of time or allows a late entry and an early exit from the labour market because of ineffective education systems and generous early retirement pathways (Funk, 2004, pp. 22–3; Streeck and Trampusch, 2005, pp. 174–5). On the other hand, the welfare state, if it is the root cause of high payroll taxes, as it is in Germany (Boss and Elender, 2005), also contributes to a systematic weakening of the demand for labour.
2. Directly or indirectly, labour-market-related regulations that are within the purview of legislators prevent innovation and flexible forms of employment from emerging. It is well known that Germany, according to a range of different indicators, has a comparatively highly regulated labour market. Other regulations imposed by the state that hamper employment creation need to be considered here as well (Matthes and Schroeder, 2005, pp. 42–3; Funk, 2005b). For example, 'the German product market is still comparatively highly regulated. Inducing competition in the product market is one way of curbing excess union power. Price-taking firms offer fewer opportunities for rent-seeking unions' (Heckman, 2003, pp. 375–9). All these factors can suppress outsider competition and support employment-reducing wage agreements.

3. A collective bargaining system where trade unions and employers' associations still conclude wage agreements that do not give sufficient importance to the re-employment chances of (unemployed) outsiders. This is because the union side negotiates on behalf of employed insiders and the employers' representatives do not resist too strongly when employment becomes more expensive than is justified by labour-market outcomes (Albeck and Roth 2004, 88).

This chapter will focus on wage-bargaining aspects. It argues that the insufficient adjustment of wage-bargaining practices and institutions to two major challenges – unification and new structural changes – can partly explain why the unemployment problem in Germany has persisted and has indeed become worse since the 1990s. After a brief overview of the basic features of the current German wage-bargaining system in the second section, the third section will highlight, first, the challenges faced by Germany since the early 1990s, and, second, the effects that the current structural changes are having on the wage-bargaining system. The fourth section will set out both the need for, and the chances of, reforms. The fifth section concludes.

Basic features of the German wage-bargaining system

Traditionally, conditions of work in Germany have been settled to a large extent collectively. About 70 per cent of all employees are employed in production units that are covered either by an industry-wide agreement or by an agreement specific to the enterprise. There are more than 60,000 industry-wide (between a trade union and an employers' association) or company agreements (between a trade union and an individual employee) currently in force. These regulate both general working conditions – such as working hours, bonuses and holiday entitlements – in the form of 'master labour agreements', and the level of wages and salaries in the form of wage agreements.[3]

The prominence of such agreements is because German law guarantees freedom of collective bargaining: trade unions, on the one hand, and employers' associations or individual enterprises, on the other, negotiate and agree on binding contracts that regulate labour remuneration and other conditions of employment. The relevant law on collective bargaining also establishes a hierarchy in which collective agreements take precedence over agreements at the level of the production unit or over individual employment contracts. The Works Constitution Act rules out agreements on remuneration or on working conditions in general at the production unit level, if these have been settled in a collective agreement, or if they would normally be settled by such an agreement. In principle, the generally binding nature of collective agreements obliges employers and employees who are subject to such agreements to apply the provisions of these agreements. Moreover, the so-called favourability principle restricts individual contractual freedom by a narrow definition of what is in the interests of the employee. This, in general, means that, all other things being equal, higher wages or shorter working hours (for the same pay) are deemed to be favourable to the employees, but greater job security in exchange for worse working conditions (in terms of wages or working hours) are not. In other words, deviations from the collective agreement are only allowed when the change is, in a narrow sense, to the advantage of the employee (for example, higher wages) or when the collective agreement contains an opt-out clause.

Important changes have taken place in the practice of collective bargaining in Germany since 1990. Industry-wide collective wage agreements have lost importance, while, first, company-wide collective wage agreements, second, supplementary agreements at the plant level, and finally, individual wage contracts, have gained in importance in recent years. In other words, the German wage-bargaining system, in which sectoral-level agreements were highly dominant, has seen a continuous process of transformation towards more company-level bargaining. Two questions that need to be answered in the following sections arise as a result: first, why did these changes occur in the German bargaining system and, second, why did they not result in lower unemployment?

The twin challenges

Two major reasons, which are related to wage bargaining, exist as to why labour-market problems have persisted and have become worse since the 1990s: first, inappropriate adjustment to German unification caused a major rise in labour costs; and second, slow and insufficient adjustment to new structural trends have increased the need for a more fundamental reform of Germany's industrial relations system.

Problems resulting from unification

In the early 1990s, there was strong pressure to increase wages in eastern Germany to western levels. Among other things, exchanging the East German mark on a 1:1 ratio with the West German mark created the wrong expectations; these had a devastating impact on wage negotiations. This led to rapid increases in wages above and beyond increases in productivity as well as much higher unit-labour costs than in western Germany, and resulted in a rapidly rising unemployment rate and social transfers[4] from east to west Germany (Frowen, 2002; Hefeker and Wunner, 2002; Klodt, 2002). According to Morgan Stanley Equity Research (Bartsch, 2004, p. 2):

> the sharp rise in both wage and non-wage labour costs that followed the country's reunification lies at the heart of Gemany's economic malaise. [This] caused Germany's competitive position within the euro area ... to

> deteriorate by a cumulative 23 per cent in the first half of the 1990s in our analysis. Throw in around a 10 per cent appreciation of the euro against its main trading partners over the same period and the picture becomes clearer. Since the mid-1990s relative unit labour costs in the German manufacturing sector have improved only gradually ... suggesting that the bulk of the German labour cost bubble is still in place.

More recent calculations by the Bundesbank (Deutsche Bundesbank, 2005, p. 7; Weber, 2005, p. 4) show noteworthy German cost improvements since the launch of the European Monetary Union (EMU). This has been achieved by exercising, on average, cost discipline on the wage front and as a result of measures to create greater flexibility in labour utilization and more efficient production processes. For example, in 2004, relative unit-labour costs in the corporate sector in Germany compared with the other euro-area countries were 7 per cent lower than in 1998. Compared to Italy and Spain, these figures amount to 17 per cent and 14 per cent, respectively. The increasing gains in the German economy's price competitiveness, which resulted from domestic cost discipline and the fixed exchange-rate relationships among the euro-area countries, led to an expansion in German firms' market shares in the euro area by 2 percentage points, to 41.5 per cent. None the less, the figures also demonstrate that, despite the measures taken in the past few years to increase labour-market flexibility, both with regard to the institutional framework of the labour market in general and with respect to collective wage-bargaining practices and working hours, a German cost problem still remains.

In particular, in 2004 German manufacturing – especially metalworking and electrical enigneering – still had the world's shortest collectively agreed annual working hours:

> The short working hours are even more of a problem as German manufacturing has the highest labour costs in the world (with the exception of Norway). This is mainly due to large non-wage labour costs caused by Germany's high social insurance contributions and by collectively agreed benefits such as a large number of paid leave ... [However], the situation is different in the services sector, especially at banks. In the EU only Sweden and several of the new member states have a longer collectively agreed working week (40 hours) than Germany (39 hours). The EU average is considerably lower than the figures for the Germany banking sector. It must be remembered, though, that bank staff, like all employees in Germany, have an above-average number of days' leave. (Deutsche Bank Research, 2004, p. 4; see also Funk, 2004)

Moreover, it should also be noted that the cost problem is even worse in the east than in the west. In 2002, for example, east German unit-labour costs were 108.5 per cent of the west German level. This problem can partly explain the much higher unemployment level and lower economic growth from 1997 to 2003 in eastern compared to western Germany (Siebert, 2005, pp. 20–1). In spite of considerably lower actual wages[5] and earnings in the east (less than 80 per cent of the west German level), the unit-labour costs are still higher in the east than in the west as productivity in the former is considerably lower than in the latter; this is 'partly because of low capacity utilization and technological and organizational lags in East Germany' (Schnabel, 2000; Bosch, 2004, p. 94).

There is no doubt that German unification has been a shock to the German economy. This is, indeed, especially true for eastern Germany as it led to the loss of around 3.5 million jobs out of a total of 9.5 million in this part of Germany. It would be misleading, however, to assert that this is the only reason for Germany's poor economic performance. German unification took place in an environment in which new structural trends became increasingly powerful. Unification and its consequences are a specifically German problem, while the challenges arising from the evolving economic environment are also being faced by other industrialized countries. Inadequate adjustment to both of these factors hampers the solution of existing economic problems and, in all probability, aggravates them, as the Geman example demonstrates. The rest of this chapter will focus mainly on these more general trends.[6]

Problems resulting from new structural change

For some time now, a 'new' structural change (Funk, 2002, pp. 22–4) has been under way in all highly industrialized economies. This has been spurred on by a rapid decrease in transport and communication costs (which, together with the increasing openness of foreign markets, have supported global trade and foreign investment), changes in production and information technology, improvements in human capital, and changes in workers' preferences. In the words of the Deutsche Bundesbank (2004, p. 57), for example, 'the ever sharper international competition for investment in manufacturing locations and jobs means that the pressure to become more adaptable will remain strong or even increase in the future'. In a broader perspective, the new structural change is characterized by five 'mega-trends' that have several wide-ranging effects on the labour market. The following changes are, above all, characteristic (Farmer, 2000, pp. 115–20).

As a result, first, of *globalization*; second, the move towards a *service-sector economy*; and, finally, technological advances (which have paved the way for an *information* and *knowledge society*), the *demand for labour by companies has become unstable*. This has been caused by the fact that intense product-market competition has led to national comparative advantages becoming more volatile and financial markets experiencing heightened fluctuations. At the same time, *the structure of labour demand has changed*, because the increased levels of international trade as well as technological advances have required workers to have ever-higher skills levels on average. This, in turn, has accelerated structural change towards a service- and knowledge-based economy. As a result, the demand for unskilled workers in developed countries has fallen.

On the one hand, this requires employees to become more accepting of changes, either in their duties or their careers, and, on the other, increases the need for an adaptation of qualifications at the sectoral and establishment level to the altered forms of work organization. It is fundamentally true that the greater the competition, the lower the transport costs, and the more open the economic markets, the more likely it is that inflation-adjusted differences in labour-market costs between countries will only be maintained if these variations in costs reflect the differences either in the qualifications of the employees or in the general economic and institutional conditions between the various individual countries. German companies no longer have a creative or technical lead, or a general advantage with respect to know-how that would justify their comparatively high labour costs (Sinn, 2003, p. 15). As long as Germany holds one of the top positions worldwide in terms of real labour costs, the German economy will continue to see a loss of employment, at least in terms of hours worked, if Germany's innovation and productivity performance remains at best mediocre, as currently appears to be the case (Funk and Plünnecke, 2005).[7]

The *greater use of information technology* by companies and the emergence of production methods that focus on geographical proximity to the customer have *changed fundamentally the organizational structures of companies and administrations*. A considerably more unstable economic environment and the move away from standardized mass products towards mass products that are often highly individualized (and which must also be competitive on price) require a highly decentralized decision-making process. Decreasing costs for information and communication technologies have made possible more flexible forms of co-ordination and co-operation within organizations. New technologies can enable companies to optimize their products and operating procedures. A flow of information that runs more smoothly can improve the productivity and profitability of teamwork within organizations. This, in turn, can lead to teamwork gaining considerable importance. Moreover, because employees are deployed in various situations, the divisions between different occupational groups become blurred.

These developments, when taken together, are likely to lead to an increase in *companies' demand for workers with human capital that is both high and broad*. The use of new information and communication technologies, which has, by now, become universal in companies, requires workers, at the very least, to be able to process information electronically. Knowledge is, in itself, without value if it cannot be applied in a given situation. This means that the demands on human capital and on the abilities of workers to communicate with one another have increased because of, for example, more complex co-ordination problems that have arisen as a result of a broadening of the range of products offered by companies. This expectation has been confirmed empirically. In spite of differences in methods, the frame of reference and datasets, all projections up to 2020 show that the economy's structural demands for, and on, qualified workers will increase further (Reinberg and Hummel 2003, p. 39). This is connected to fundamental changes in corporate structures in the new world of work: the flattening of company hierarchies, which has been going on for some time now, has led to more opportunities for workers to become involved in, and to decide on, the production process. This has, however, also meant that they have a greater responsibility for the quality of their work. In this sense, employees also become, partially at least, co-managers. Independent working, initiative and self-reliance take on greater significance; they are therefore characteristics that are highly prized in the new world of work. As a result, training and further training must play a more central role than it has done to date. Learning to acquire a static set of knowledge, as often used to be the case, will no longer be sufficient in an environment in which career- and job-relevant information and skills are constantly deepening and changing.

The *individualization* of the supply of work has led to a *change in the structure of labour supply*. Social changes – for example, the increase in female employment (and its associated causes), as well as shifts in values, can be described as a move towards greater individualization, which, in turn, will bring about new modes of behaviour in many areas of life in general, and the economy – including, in particular, industrial relations. For example, there has been a trend towards one- and two-person households; this has promoted areas of the service sector as people buy services that, previously, would have been provided by another member of the household (often women). This development is connected with a considerable expansion of different forms of employment (part-time, fixed-term contracts, temporary work and so on). These new forms of employment, in particular low-paid, part-time jobs, have increased considerably in recent years and might appear to indicate a trend towards the direct substitution of full-time jobs, which are subject to full social security contributions, with publicly subsidized forms of employment. Up to now, however, this assumption does not appear to be justified as, in general, jobs subject to social security contributions are not being eroded in the same areas in which low-paid, part-time jobs and certain newly created government subsidized jobs are simultaneously being created. In other words, 'these new forms of employment have provided a greater degree of flexibility on the labour market which has, in turn, created additional jobs' (Deutsche Bundesbank, 2005, pp. 8, 37–40). None the less, these additional jobs have recently been restricted mainly to service sector jobs that are not subject to full social security contributions, whereas 'normal' full-time jobs, in particular in manufacturing, are disappearing.

This is causing increasing problems for the German welfare state as this is largely financed by payroll taxes.

This tendency towards individualization has also gone hand in hand with a decline in the ability to organize members of unions and employers' associations, because this new world of work requires more differentiated solutions to employees' problems and more tailored services for members of employers' associations; this compares to earlier times, when standardized services were offered to members of unions and employers' associations. However, it is precisely because of the creation of more differentiated collective agreements and because of the way in which companies can react to ineluctable social changes that there is a great need for advice and consultation (Funk, 2005a).

The demographically determined ageing of society will result in a *lower level of labour being supplied* and an *older workforce*, on average. Falling birth rates and an ageing society and workforce, together with the consequences for labour demand associated with structural changes in the economy will exacerbate further the shortage of qualified workers in parts of the economy. The potential for economic growth and innovation may be lost if appropriate measures are not taken within sectoral agreements. Companies must receive and create more incentives than has hitherto been the case, to provide their products and services using employees whose average age will be increasing (Lesch, 2004a, 107–8).

The interplay of these mega-trends combined with the adjustment problems associated with German unification have led to considerable upheavals in the labour market. In particular, the increase in instability in labour demand, which is associated with the new structural changes in the economy, requires more flexible real wages – that is, an increase, compared to earlier times, in the adaptability of wages, non-wage labour costs and the costs of regulations – if additional unemployment is to be avoided and if the existing labour-market problems are to be resolved. The changed structure of labour demand not only requires wage structures in Germany to be more flexible to a greater extent than they have been in the past between economic sectors, regions and qualifications, but it also appears to be necessary to have greater mobility between sectors, regions and careers. Apart from the high level of overall unemployment mentioned at the start of the chapter, several other indicators demonstrate a dysfunction in German labour markets, and therefore of related institutions. For example, more than half of those currently unemployed have been looking for a job for more than one year – compared to less than a third, on average, in the OECD. Unemployment is distributed unevenly across Germany, with only approximately 5 per cent out of work in some western Federal states (Bavaria and Baden-Württemberg) but more than 20 per cent in Saxonia-Anhalt and Mecklenburg-Vorpommern in the east. Despite this, the effective redistribution of workers from depressed regions to booming ones is, in contrast to more succesful countries, quite limited, and geographical mobility contributes rather little to reducing regional labour-market imbalances in Germany (OECD, 2005, pp. 73–112). Finally, in spite of high unemployment figures, skills shortages in a number of industrial sectors regularly become apparent as soon a cyclical upswing occurs; this demonstrates that labour-market adjustment problems (and inadequacies in training and education systems) exist. In other words, further labour-market-related reforms are needed if the labour potential, which until now has remained untapped, is to be put to productive use (Deutsche Bundesbank, 2004, p. 57).

The effects of the mega-trends on collective bargaining

As mentioned above, the industry-wide agreement is at the centre of Germany's system of wage bargaining. In recent years, however, there has been a tendency towards the decentralization of collective bargaining not only in eastern Germany, but across the whole of the country. Collective bargaining has gradually become more flexible. None the less, even more flexibility appears to be needed if Germnay's unemployment problems are to be solved, as wage bargaining, particularly in western Germany, must play a larger part in coming to terms with the current structural change under way in the world of work. This leads, unsurprisingly, to a debate on the direction and extent of change. Critics of the German system of wage bargaining tend to argue that the only way to respond to these mega-trends is to shift wage negotiations completely to the decentralized, establishment level. For critics, the traditional sectoral bargaining undertaken in Germany is 'ripe for the museum of industrial history' (Berthold, 2003, p. 2).

This point of view does not, however, represent a consensus among economists, as, in (western) Germany, considerable advantages can be ascribed to the dominant sectoral wage bargaining (Wagner, 1999, pp. 144–9; Gerlach and Stephan, 2005, p. 18). In particular, the following arguments in favour of sectoral collective agreements have often been put forward, and are supported by the empirical evidence:

- Sectoral collective agreements promote industrial peace within workplaces, as they take sources of conflict from the establishment or company level to the sectoral level.
- Sectoral collective agreements can provide companies with a degree of certainty, in terms of their employee relations, for their future plans. Moreover, the legal obligation not to call strikes during a period for which a collective agreement is valid enables trouble-free relationships with suppliers.
- Sectoral collective agreements mean that firms themselves do not have to engage in the costly and time-consuming process of negotiating, which, on the whole may arise if wage deals are struck with individual workers.

If collective wage agreements are made at the firm level, there is a danger that the company is too weak, and that unions can pick off employers one after the other by threatening to strike or, indeed, by taking strike action.

Collective agreements at the firm level do not automatically lead to more moderate wage bargains than sectoral collective agreements, as the example of Volkswagen (VW) has shown for a long time. Decentralization can certainly lead to greater consideration being given to the circumstances of individual establishments; however, they do tend to be geared towards the interests of employees in the company, and do not take into consideration the need for a macro-level decrease in unemployment.

Below-average wage settlements at the firm level may signal to customers and suppliers alike that the company is in dire straits. This could lead to a reassessment of their relationship with the company, and, in extreme cases, may even lead to a severing of ties.

In the post-Second World War period, until approximately the middle of the 1970s, when sectoral collective agreements were particularly widespread in West Germany, completely different economic circumstances dominated. Prior to the mid-1970s, sectoral collective agreements were characterized and strongly dominated by the following: large industrial companies, comparatively standardized forms of work, strong unions and employers' associations that had a relatively uniform wage policy, predictable career paths, and an apparently trustworthy state system of social security that helped to bridge temporary periods of low labour demand in a period that was, on the whole, noted for its full employment.

The new structural change, however, is associated with an increasing tendency to shift employee relations to the firm or establishment level. Moreover, the chronically unresolved problem of high unemployment militates against the earlier cohesive power of that institution of industrial society: the sectoral collective agreement. Therefore, more than in the past, the comparative disadvantages of centrally agreed wage agreements have come under the spotlight.

Wage agreements at the establishment level either via company-level agreements or individual contracts allow, theoretically at least, a more flexible response to the economic situation and reflect more accurately the productivity levels of the company or establishment. This may be important, as there may be differences between establishments as a result of variations in the way work is organized, or there may be regional or specific sectoral factors at play.

Sectoral collective agreements have, at the macro-level, tended to lead to wage deals that have been too high and too poorly differentiated, because, first and foremost, unions have, since the mid-1970s, tended to pursue a policy of redistribution (relatively high wages for low-skilled workers; wage policy as a 'whip' to improve productivity), and, also importantly, because policies adopted as part of collective bargains have, from a purely economic perspective, sometimes reacted incorrectly to unexpected shocks, such as the oil-price crises of the 1970s, and unification. In particular, such policies have meant that the wage costs of relatively unqualified workers have increased disproportionally; this has led, first, to a rationalization of jobs requiring unskilled workers, and, second, to the relocation of such jobs abroad. It was only up to around 1973 that the wages agreed as part of sectoral collective agreements were moderate enough to ensure, first, that there were sufficiently wide wage differentials, and, second, that positive wage drift could occur persistently. These two factors then enabled structural changes within employment to take place, while at the same time maintaining full employment.

Some sectorally agreed qualitative regulations in master labour agreements, such as working times and the choice of the optimal level at which regulations should be agreed, show, moreover, that in certain bargaining areas there is insufficient flexibility as a result of relatively centralized decision-making.

In view of the fact that the balance of advantages and disadvantages has shifted as a result of the new structural changes in the economy, so too has in many respects the optimal level for regulations to be agreed in wage bargaining. This has led to a considerable transformation of the sectoral collective bargaining system. This has been the case, as mentioned above mainly for eastern Germany, but also for Germany as a whole. This transformation has taken various forms since the 1990s (Schnabel, 2004; Schulten, 2004; Funk, 2005c).

The number of employees covered by industry-wide agreements has shown a significant decline from 72 per cent (1995) to 62 per cent (2003) in western Germany, and from 56 per cent (1996) to 43 per cent (2003) in eastern Germany, while the number of company agreements has grown continuously from 2,550 in 1990 to 7,540 in 2003. This shows that the number of companies and employees covered by a sectoral collective agreement has declined steadily. In 2003, only 43 per cent of west German and 21 per cent of east German establishments were covered by an industry-wide collective agreement (company agreements: 3 per cent and 5 per cent, respectively). Moreover, evidence demonstrates that the smaller the company, the less likely it is to be covered by a collective labour agreement. Additionally, strong variations exist between different sectors with regard to the role of collective agreements. However, it has to be taken into account that a considerable number of companies with no collective agreement use existing sectoral agreements as a point of reference for determining pay and working conditions.

The flexibility within sectoral agreements has increased significantly with the conclusion of numerous so-called 'opening clauses'. These clauses allow companies to diverge from collectively agreed standards under certain conditions. Currently, more than a third of all companies make use of an opening clause.

Many companies have established so-called 'company pacts for employment' in which employees make concessions on pay or working conditions in exchange for limited job guarantees by their employers (O'Kelly, 2004). Many of these company pacts either deal with issues not regulated by collective agreements (for example additional company payments) or adopt an existing opening clause. There are also a significant number of company pacts which more or less contravene collectively agreed standards. According to a survey conducted in the second half of 2003 by the Institute for Economic and Social Research (WSI), around 20 per cent of companies with more than twenty employees had agreements containing more working-time flexibility than was agreed in the generally binding sectoral wage agreements. This survey shows that 13 per cent of firms negotiated wage deals that allowed them to pay less than had been agreed in the area-wide wage contracts.

To sum up, all these developments have weakened the significance of sectoral regulation, to the benefit of more company regulation. Therefore, it is fully justified to speak of an erosion tendency in the system with regard to sectoral collective agreements. This transformation occurred in spite of the fact that no major changes to the legal framework in German collective bargaining have taken place during this period (Schulten, 2005). Moreover, despite these changes in the practice of collective bargaining in recent years, the debate on whether or not the German bargaining system is still too rigid has become a central issue in German politics since, in particular, 2003, as persistently high unemployment remains a central issue in Germany.

In spite of apparently moderate trends in collectively agreed wage and salary increases of around 2 per cent, on average, in 2004 (west: 1.9 per cent; east: 2.5 per cent) which was lower than the figures recorded in recent years (see Dribbusch, 2005), critics argue that problems remain in this area. According to the Deutsche Bundesbank (2004), 'no progress has been made in the past few years with regard to the wage structure according to different skill levels. In almost all cases the negotiated pay rates for all skill levels in a given sector were raised by the same percentage'. In other words, even though the unemployment rate of lower-skilled workers rose significantly in the 1990s, and in recent years in both western and eastern Germany, the wage structure with respect to qualifications has remained constant, for western Germany since the mid-1980s, and for eastern Germany since 1993. This means that low-skilled people are exposed to an increasing unemployment risk, but that relative wages have not responded to ameliorate this situation.

Moreover, if actual earnings at the macroeconomic level and at the sectoral level are considered, it is remarkable that, despite high unemployment, practically no decreases in actual earnings have been observed since the early 1990s (the sole exception was the construction sector in 1997 and 1998). This demonstrates that strong nominal wage rigidities exist in Gemany; these appear to be partly in the interests of the social partners and the result of institutional factors (for example, the validity of collective pay settlements persists even after a contract has expired or has been terminated, as the provisions remain in force until a new contract has been concluded).

Furthermore, the Bundesbank argues that, in particular, the co-ordination between regional industry-wide collective agreements does not appear to be helpful in solving labour market problems as wage increases are orientated to macroeconomic productivity increases rather than to changes in unemployment in a particular region. This is because the wage agreement by a 'pilot' sector in a particular region is used as a benchmark in other branches or regions. In almost all regions and branches, the wage agreements are orientated more or less to the wage agreements reached in northern Württemberg and northern Baden, where very profitable enterprises are located. This results, according to the Bundesbank, in a tendency for wage agreements in economically weaker regions to be 'excessive'. Taking this into account, it is no proof of appropriate flexibility in the German collective bargaining system, that 61,772 valid collective agreements were officially registered at the Federal Ministry of Economics and Labour (the 2003 figure was 59,636). Of these, 33,964 were industry-wide agreements between trade unions and employers' associations, and 27,808 were company agreements between trade unions and individual employers.

Finally, evaluating the reforms that had taken place before summer 2004, the Bundesbank noted that 'it is dubious ... whether [these] will be sufficient to reduce unemployment in Germany to any significant degree' (Deutsche Bundesbank, 2004, p. 57).

If the question 'can or should the erosion the traditional German system of wage formation be stopped?' is posed, the answer is by no means unambiguous. Recent studies show that neither sectoral collective agreements, establishment collective agreements nor individual agreements lead, in every case, to an unequivocally better solution to problems (Kohaut and Schnabel, 2003, p. 216). In spite of the erosion and decentralization tendencies, which have come to the fore, in particular, since unification, this finding – together with the increasing move towards including issues related to social policy (for example, partial retirement) within the remit of sectoral collective agreements – supports the contentions of some authors: 'That [the idea that] establishment-level agreements and works councils could, at some stage, be completely free of any links to the sectoral level appears today, as it did ten or 20 years ago, to be absurd' (Streeck and Rehder, 2003, p. 21).

However, new challenges call for new responses. In other words, even if a strategy to abolish the entire system of collective bargaining appears, at this point in time, not to be a promising alternative for efficiency or political feasibility reasons (Möschel, 2005; Ochel, 2005), 'reforms within the system are indispensable' (Gerlach and Stephan, 2005, p. 18). Whether or not these responses from the current actors, who are adapting to the new situation, will take place within institutions that, although overhauled, are basically the same as today's, or whether, in the future, totally new structures will emerge, depends ultimately on the amount of flexibility and decentralization that can now be brought into the existing framework. If the amount of flexibility and decentralization is sufficient to meet the functional requirements of the new world of work, a 'purified' collective agreement system may be stabilized. This latter reform trajectory may be most desirable as 'central elements of Germany's labour market institutions remain a source of successful economic performance' (Pugh *et al.*, 2002, p. 133).

New agenda-setting in collective agreements

The pressing problems associated with the labour market and socioeconomic change described above may lead, or at least call for, the following major changes in sectoral collective agreements. Existing trends in this direction have become amplified in recent years, particularly since 2004, and are very likely to be amplified in the future.

Lower entry-level wages, performance-related pay, and pay that takes the needs of individual establishments into greater consideration will, in particular, increase in importance. It may be necessary to re-think the situation that still prevails very often today, which requires remuneration corridors as well as 'corridor solutions' to issues such as weekly working times and overtime payments to be agreed by both unions and employers' associations. It would be more sensible to allow establishment-specific remuneration and working-time systems to be set up if the majority of senior managers, works councillors and employees agree to them. The flexibilization of the Christmas bonus in the chemical industry has set an example that others should follow. In the chemical industry, the actual amount paid out as a Christmas bonus, which is agreed at the establishment level, can vary between 80 per cent and 125 per cent of the total agreed in the sectoral agreement. Progress has also been seen in the metalworking and electrical industries; here, the bargaining partners are allowed to deviate from sectorally agreed provisions, in areas including the extension and reduction of working time, with and without wage compensation, in certain cases. Most notably, this is allowed, first, if the firm's competitiveness threatens its ability to carry out capital expenditure or innovation, or, second, if such deviations are necessary in order to ensure the sustainable development of employment in the company. A whole range of instruments related to labour remuneration are available and are used – for example holiday or Christmas supplements can be cut. However, agreements made at the production-unit level only come into force after the trade union and employers' association have ratified the agreement. An exception in this respect is made for small firms that do not maintain working-time accounts for their employees; in such businesses an agreement at the production-unit level to increase working time to a maximum of 40 hours a week is sufficient. Following the introduction of this new opt-out clause in regional wage contracts in February 2004, up to 100 company-level agreements that were reached before the end of 2004 led to increased working times in exchange for job-security guarantees, in order to boost productivity and lower wage costs. High-profile examples include accords at Siemens and DaimlerChrysler in Germany (Funk, 2005, p. 5; Lesch, 2004b, pp. 29–30; OECD, 2002, p. 80).

The importance of the qualitative aspects of sectoral collective agreements should be strengthened considerably, as tasks that require, first, highly-skilled personnel; second, the maintenance of firm-specific human capital; and, finally, the balancing of families and careers, are all becoming increasingly important. In particular, the qualitative aspects of sectoral collective agreements, such as qualifications, the way in which work is spread over people's lifetimes and the retention of staff have come to the fore much more now than under sectoral agreements in an industrial age. By contrast, the quantitative aspects of sectoral collective agreements, such as collective wage increases, and decreases in the length of the working week, have lost importance. The chemical industry is a forerunner in this regard, too. The sectoral collective agreement of 2003 on qualifications is an example for others to follow. As a purely voluntary agreement that can be made at the establishment level, it opens up a wide range of possibilities, including the introduction of long-term working-time accounts; these, in effect, enable annual working times to be changed by up to six days (Lesch, 2004b, pp. 29–30).

Against a backdrop of demographic change, the incentives to work should be increased by strengthening different instruments available within sectoral collective agreements: partial retirement options should be integrated into an overarching concept on working times that leads to an increase in the comparatively low employment rate of workers aged 55 or above. In other words, such integration needs to take into consideration not just the preferences of workers, but also the economic needs of companies and of the labour market as a whole. Policies on qualifications, which will become increasingly important, particularly for employees aged 45 or above, can also be covered by a policy on working times that views time that has been worked as a type of investment. For example, such coverage would also allow a fairer distribution, between employers and employees, of the costs associated with gaining additional qualifications (employees 'spend' some of the time that they have worked, whilst employers pay for career development schemes).

It is also, however, necessary for sectoral collective agreements to make a contribution towards removing inappropriate institutional incentives that are detrimental to the employment prospects of older workers. For example, remuneration systems based on seniority should be scrapped, the clauses in sectoral collective agreements that prevent the downgrading of older workers with long career histories with a particular employer should be weakened, and the extended employment-protection rights of such older workers should also be reduced, as all these regulations tend to increase the costs of older workers and therefore increase employers' incentives to replace them with less costly workers or machines (Funk, 2004).

Further, legislators can also play an important role in changing the framework conditions for collective bargaining by changing important elements of the current system:

> opting out of the system of collective bargaining is hampered under the current law and regulations by a relatively long validity of the prevailing contract. The alternative to resign from an employers' association should thus be facilitated for firms. Furthermore, concerning wage dispersion, an efficient opening should be enacted in the Collective Bargaining Act and be obligatory for all collective contracts with the objective to increase the flexibility and plant-level orientation of wage-setting and to enhance the possibility of differentiating wages within sectoral agreements. (Gerlach and Stephan, 2005, p. 18; see also Möschel, 2005 and Ochel, 2005).

These modifications would enhance competition between the different wage-setting frameworks that comprise the German bargaining system.

Conclusion

This chapter advocates the hypothesis that the inability of German wage-bargaining institutions to adapt sufficiently to socioeconomic mega-trends combined with the challenges posed by unification is one of the root causes of persistently high unemployment in Germany. Employees, employers and the state all have a part to play if they are to adapt to *unification, globalization*, the *increasing importance* of both the *service sector* and *information/digital technology* in the world of work, the *individualization* of life-styles, the *de-standardization* of employment forms, and an *ageing* society and workforce. If the labour-market framework were to be adjusted to the structural trends in the world of work, the opportunities would outweigh the risks, because such an adjustment would, at least in the medium term, improve Germany's economic performance considerably. This is also true as the economic costs arising from a shortage, year after year, of competitive jobs in Germany is one of the main reasons behind, first, current strains on public finances and, second and consequently, resulting low public investment expenditure as well as, in general, Germany's persistently poor economic growth rates.

Adaptation of Germany's wage-bargaining system can contribute to an improvement in this situation. Sectoral collective agreements can, when set against the backdrop of companies with very different needs, only set the broad parameters, if they are to meet the various challenges brought about by the structural change in the economy. A large part of this adaptation must therefore be undertaken within the bounds of personnel policies at the establishment level; this is especially true for policies on qualifications and working times. A cornerstone of this framework should be that sectoral collective agreements should, in the future, set genuine minimum standards as opposed to economically binding conditions that, according to many studies, contribute to Germany's problem of persistently high unemployment. Adequate opening clauses might, in addition, enable less productive companies to remain within the remit of sectoral collective agreements. Wage structures should also become even more differentiated according to the qualifications of workers – by, for example, implementing more 'introductory wage rates' for employees with relatively low qualifications and for the long-term unemployed, and by extending the amount of pay that is contingent upon performance.

Notes

1. According to the majority of the Association of German Economic Research Institutes (2004) and, amongst other, the IMF (2005) as well as Baily and Funk Kirkegaard (2004, 300–2), these reforms that reorientate German labour-market policy by, for example, merging unemployment and social assistance, may certainly make job placement more effective. Up to now, however, the long overdue reforms implemented by the Schröder government, which can become effective in the medium term only, have not yet borne fruit; instead, they appear to have seriously eroded public trust.
2. Monetary and fiscal policy are not discussed specifically in this chapter, for obvious reasons: having yielded national control over exchange rates, interest rates and deficits in order to strengthen their union, Eurozone economies such as Germany no longer have unrestricted recourse to the kinds of monetary and fiscal stimuli previously used by some of these economies to renew growth. As a result, the only option appears to be to try to reform long-standing structural difficulties to solve lasting unemployment and growth problems.
3. See, for more details, Lesch, 2004; Schulten, 2004, 2005; Funk, 2005c.
4. These social transfers are mainly financed by payroll taxes, which can be regarded as one of the major reasons for the weak labour demand in Germany as a whole (Boss and Elender, 2005).
5. The lower level of actual wages can be regarded 'a consequence of the higher share of firms not covered by collective agreements, the lower share of firms covered by collective agreements that pay above the agreed rates, and finally, nonadherence to collective agreements' (Bosch, 2004, p. 94).
6. See Michael Kaser's Chapter 13 in this volume, on the comparatively poor adjustment of the east German labour market.
7. The current relatively poor innovation and productivity results can apparently not be fully compensated by former German strengths, such as 'long-termism', the system of corporate governance and so on, although parts of the latter remain important explanatory factors for Germany's strong trade balance (Owen Smith and Funk, 1994, pp. 499–527).

References

Albeck, H. and S. J. Roth (2004) 'Regulating Competition in the Labour Market: Level Playing Field or Barriers to Entry for the Unemployed?', in J. Eekhoff (ed.), *Competition Policy in Europe* (Berlin: Springer-Verlag), pp. 63–98.

Association of German Economic Research Institutes (2005) 'The German Economy in the Autumn of 2004', available at www.diw.de (accessed 31 January).

Baily, M.N. and J. Funk Kirkegaard (2004) *Transforming the European Economy* (Washington, DC: Institute for International Economics).

Bartsch, E. (2004) 'On Offshoring, Restructuring and Reforms', *Morgan Stanley German Economics*, 9 August, pp. 1–17.

Berthold, N. (2003) 'Betriebliche Bündnisse für Arbeit – Element einer wettbewerblicheren Tarifautonomie', *Volkswirtschaftliche Korrespondenz der Adolf-Weber-Stiftung*, vol. 42, no. 4, pp. 1–4.

Bosch, G. (2004) 'The Changing Nature of Collective Bargaining in Germany', in H. C. Katz, W. Lee and J. Lee (eds), *The New Structure of Labor Relations. Tripartism and Decentralization* (Ithaca, NY London: ILR Press), pp. 84–118.

Boss, A. N. and T. Elendner, Incentives to work: The Case of Germany, Kiel Discussion Paper No, 1237, 2005.

Brandt, N. J.-M. Burniaux and R. Duval, 'Assessing the OECD Jobs Strategy: Past Developments and Reforms', *OECD Economics Department Working Paper No. 429* (Paris: OECD, 2005).

Calmfors, L. (2004) 'Activation versus Other Employment Policies – Lessons for Germany', *CESifo Forum No. 2*, vol. 5, pp. 35–42.

Deutsche Bank Research (2004) 'Germany on the Way to Longer Working Hours', *Current Issues*, August.

Deutsche Bundesbank (2001) 'Factor Prices, Employment and Capital Stock in Germany: Results of a Simulation Study', *Monthly Report*, July, pp. 49–61.

Deutsche Bundesbank (2004) 'Greater Flexibility on the German Labour Market', *Monthly Report*, September, pp. 43–57.

Deutsche Bundesbank (2005) 'Overview', *Monthly Report*, February, pp. 49–61.

Dribbusch, H. (2005) '2004 Collective Bargaining Round Examined', *eironline*; accessed at www.eiro.eirofound.eu.int/print/2005/02/feature/de0502202f.html (downloaded 20 May).

Farmer, K. (2000) 'Die Arbeitsmarktordnung der Sozialen Marktwirtschaft im Zeitalter der Globalisierung', in K. Farmer, R. Haupt and W. Lachmann (eds), *Individuelle Freiheit oder staatliche Lenkung? Markt und Staat im Licht christlicher Wirtschaftsethik* (Münster: Lit Verlag), pp. 105–36.

Frowen, S. F. (2002) 'German Monetary Unification and Its Aftermath', in J. Leonhard and L. Funk (eds), *Ten Years of Germam Unification: Transfer, Transformation, Incorporation?* (Birmingham: Birmingham University Press), pp. 229–39.

Funk, L. (2000) 'Economic Reform of Model Deutschland', in R. Harding and W. E. Paterson (eds), *The Future of the German Economy. An End to the Miracle?* (Manchester: Manchester University Press), pp. 16–35.

Funk, L. (2002) 'Towards a Transformed Federal Republic of Germany? Structural Change and the Renewal of Social Democratic Economic Policy', in M. H. Stierle and T. Birringer (eds), *Economics of Transition: Theory, Experiences and EU Enlargement* (Berlin: VWF), pp. 17–36.

Funk, L. (2004) 'Employment Opportunities for Older Workers: A Comparison of Selected OECD Countries', *CESifo DICE Report*, vol. 2, no. 2, pp. 22–33.

Funk, L. (2005a) 'Current Structural Changes: Risks and Opportunities for German Trade Unions', *The International Journal of Comparative Labour Law and Industrial Relations*, no. 1, vol. 21, pp. 59–76.

Funk, L. (2005b) 'IW Publishes New Overview of Thresholds in Labour and Job Security', *eironline*, accessed at http:// www.eiro.eurofound.eu.int/ print/ 2005/ 04/ inbrief/ de0504104n.html (accessed on 20 June).

Funk, L. (2005c) 'Recent Developments in Wage Bargaining in Germany', *International Labor Brief*, vol. 3, pp. 5–11 (published in Korean).

Funk L. and A. Pluennecke (2005) 'Deutschlands Innovationsfaktoren im internationalen Vergleich', *IW-Trends*, no. 1, vol. 32, pp. 63–76.

Gerlach K. and G. Stephan (2005) 'Wage Distributions by Wage-Setting Regime', IAB Discussion Paper No. 9 (Nuremberg: Bundesagentur für Arbeit).

Heckman, J. J. (2003) 'Flexibility and Job Creation: Lessons for Germany' in P. Aghion, R. Frydman, J. Stiglitz and M. Woodford (eds), *Knowledge, Information, and Expectations in Modern Macroeconomics: In Honour of Edmund S. Phelps* (Princeton, NJ/Oxford: Princeton University Press), pp. 357–93.

Hefeker, C. and N. Wunner (2002) 'Great Expectations, Hard Times: A Political Economic History of German Unification', in J. Leonhard and L. Funk (eds), *Ten Years of Germam Unification: Transfer, Transformation, Incorporation?* (Birmingham: Birmingham University Press), pp. 168–82.

IMF (International Monetary Fund, Germany) (2005) 'Article IV Consultation Concluding Statement of the Mission', accessed at http://www.imf.org/external/np/ms/2005/062805.htm) (downloaded 28 June).

Klodt, H. (2002) 'Public Transfers and Industrial Restructuring in Eastern Germany', in J. Leonhard and L. Funk (eds), *Ten Years of Germam Unification: Transfer, Transformation, Incorporation?* (Birmingham: Birmingham University Press), pp. 211–28.

Kohaut, S. and C. Schnabel (2003) 'Zur Erosion des Flächentarifvertrags: Ausmaß, Einflussfaktoren und Gegenmaßnahmen', *Industrielle Beziehungen*, 10 (2003), pp. 193–219.

Lesch, H. (2004a) 'Ageing Societies and Challenges for Collective Bargaining Policy', *Intereconomics*, vol. 39, pp. 102–8.

Lesch, H. (2004b) *Industrielle Beziehungen im Wandel* (Cologne: Deutscher Instituts-Verlag).

Matthes, J. and C. Schröder (2005) 'Business Regulation in International Comparison – Aggregating World Bank "Doing Business" Data', *CESifo Forum*, vol. 6, no. 1, pp. 42–9.

Möschel, W. (2005) 'Vom Regen in die Traufe', *Frankfurter Allgemeine Zeitung*, 9 July.

Nickell, S., L. Nunciata and W. Ochel (2005) 'Unemployment in the OECD Since the 1960s. What Do We Know?', *The Economic Journal*, vol. 115, pp. 1–27.

Ochel, W. (2005) 'Dezentrale Lohnverhandlungen – ein Weg zu mehr Beschäftigung?', *ifo Schnelldienst*, vol. 58, pp. 7–18.

OECD (2002) *Germany – OECD Economic Surveys* (Paris: OECD).

OECD (2005) Employment Outlook (Paris: OECD).

O'Kelly, K. P. (2004) 'Finding a Negotiated Balance Between Flexibility and Security – Pacts for Employment and Competitiveness, *Transfer*, vol. 10, pp. 326–31.

Owen Smith, E. and L. Funk (1994) 'Trade', in E. Owen Smith, *The German Economy* (London: Routledge), pp. 499–522.

Pugh, G., L. Funk and T. Lange (2002) 'Institutional Perspectives on Reforming the New German Labour Market', in L. Funk and S. Green (eds), *New Aspects of Labour Market Policy* (Berlin: VWF) pp. 133–49.

Reinberg, A. and M. Hummel (2003) 'Steuert Deutschland auf einen massiven Fachkräftemangel zu? Entwicklung des Angebots und Bedarfs an Arbeitskräften nach Qualifikationsebenen bis 2010/2015', *Personalführung*, vol. 36, no. 6, pp. 38–50.

Schnabel, C. (2000) 'The German System of Collective Bargaining Under Stress: Reforming or Abolishing the Flächentarifvertrag', in S. J. Silvia (ed.), Unemployment Ebbs in Germany: Explanations and Expectations (Washington, DC: Johns Hopkins University, American Institute for Contemporary Gemany Studies), pp. 121–39.

Schnabel, C. (2004) 'Dezentrale oder zentrale Verhandlungen – Was sagt die Empirie zur Effizienz von Lohnfindungssystemen?', in Institut der deutschen Wirtschaft Köln (ed.), *Der Flächentarifvertrag in der Kritik* (Cologne: Deutscher Instituts-Verlag), pp. 39–55.

Schulten, T. (2004) 'Collective Bargaining System under Pressure', *eirobserver*, no. 1, pp. 7–8.

Schulten, T. (2005) 'Changes in National Collective Bargaining Systems Since 1990', *eironline*, accessed at http://www.eiro.eurofound.eu.int/2005/03/study/index.html (accessed 28 July).

Siebert, H. (2005) *The German Economy Beyond the Social Market* (Princeton, NJ/Oxford: Princeton University Press).

Sinn, H.-W. (2003) 'The Laggard of Europe', *CESifo Special Report*, vol. 1, pp. 1–32.

Streeck, W. and B. Rehder (2003) 'Der Flächentarifvertrag: Krise, Stabilität und Wandel', Max-Planck-Institut für Gesellschaftsforschung Working Paper 03/6, (Cologne: MPIFG).

Streeck, W. and C. Trampusch (2005) 'Economic Reform and the Political Economy of the German Welfare State', *German Politics*, vol. 14, pp. 174–95.

Wagner, U. (1999) 'Reform des Tarifvertragsrechts und Änderungen der Verhaltensweisen der Tarifpartner als Voraussetzungen für eine wirksame Bekämpfung der Arbeitslosigkeit', *Ordo. Jahrbuch für die Ordnung von Wirtschaft und Gesellschaft*, vol. 50, pp. 143–69.

Weber, A. (2005) 'Sündenbock Euro?', *Auszüge aus Presseartikeln* (13 July) pp. 3–5.

11
Comments on Lothar Funk's Chapter

Eric Owen Smith

When unemployment reaches 5 million (or about 12 per cent of the employed population), radical policy adjustments are clearly required. Lothar Funk correctly draws our attention to the mega trends affecting all European labour markets: globalization, service-sector growth, the revolution in information technology, destandardization and individualization of employment contracts, particularly at a time when there has been a growth in company bargaining, as well as an ageing society and workforce.

Centralized bargaining, which once served the labour market well, Funk continues, is no longer able to act as an efficient allocator, although we are warned correctly against accepting the hypotheses of the neo-liberal commentators who see this system as being the exclusive cause of labour-market inefficiencies. In any case, the system is in decline, particularly in east Germany, while some remaining features are unlikely to be discarded by the parties. Moreover, centralized bargaining should continue to set *minimum* standards (my emphasis). At the same time, the importance of company and plant bargaining will inevitably grow. Such critical variables as working time and training are best determined at this level. Another response to the mega trends will be an increase in non-standard employment contracts, although this will not signal the end of normal contracts of employment. Increasing employment rates among the over-55s is also of major importance in Germany, where only half of this age group has a job. These are the major features of increased flexibility envisaged by Funk.

In other words, there is no direct reference to the wholesale removal of constraints on recruitment and, more so, dismissal – a form of 'flexibility' that is in any case legally impossible to implement in the European Union (EU). (In Germany, there are added constitutional constraints.) Yet following the tortuous and protracted implementation of Harz IV, economic adviser Franz enunciated further necessary conditions for employment creation, including 'the simplification of labour law'. Two further conditions were a reduction in corporate taxation and social insurance contributions, along with a moderation in (money?) wage growth. But corporate taxation has fallen secularly; indeed, the opposition candidate in the 2002 Federal election observed that at that juncture many large companies were not paying any tax. Further cuts in corporate taxation have now been agreed. However, the medium and small business sector has major problems. Historically, it has not been subject to *corporate* tax laws, and its chief capital market (the public-sector banks) has been required by the EU to refinance its loans in the absence of state liquidity guarantees. Both these factors increase the sector's costs. The growth in social insurance contributions also seems to have been checked, most notably in the statutory health insurance scheme. Further, examples of dampers on wage growth seem to be repeated: from the collapse of the east German engineering strike to the deals at Siemens, DaimlerChrysler, Opel, VW and Karstadt. Flexibility in both hours worked and money wage rates, with a consequent fall in labour costs, were achieved.

Another important aspect of flexibility concerns the wage structure. A relatively low-paid sector in the labour market is a necessary corollary of non-standard employment. Federal-wide part-time employment has almost doubled since 1991, to reach 30 per cent of employees. Whereas the total number of employees remained roughly stable, at 34 million, full-time employment fell to 24 million. In the west, the number of part timers grew by 60 per cent; in the east by 175 per cent. Mini jobs with a maximum wage of 400 euro per month are, of course, included in this definition. Between April 2003 and April 2004 the number of such fringe workers increased by 1.3 million, to 6 million. Employers pay 25 per cent of social insurance contributions and tax. The boost to consumption has been welcomed by the CDU/CSU political parties, while the SPD stressed the additional revenue for the social insurance funds. Students fill half of these jobs, and pensioners not registered as unemployed take up another 20 per cent. Some minimum wage protection outside the construction industry will ultimately be required. Allegedly more flexible labour markets in the EU already have such protection. At the other end of the spectrum, it has been intimated that a thoroughgoing reform of the conditions of employment enjoyed by civil servants will be undertaken. Meanwhile, holiday and Christmas bonuses have been modified in some *Länder*, and pay may legally differ between east and west. Also, at the other end of the spectrum, transparency in the pay of private-sector chief executives is being introduced.

The proverbial man from Mars could be forgiven if he thought that Germany's economic inefficiencies lay solely in the labour market. He would be misled by the public debates focused on that topic. For example, the capital market is at least as inflexible as the labour market. In consequence, employment is affected. The market for corporate control is in its infancy, witness the furore that surrounded the take-over of Mannesmann. Arguably, the largesse experienced by the sacked chief executive would be considered commonplace in the Anglo-Saxon world as a 'golden handshake'. Similarly, the EU has threatened action over the arrangement that prevents a foreign take-over of VW. Overlapping directorates also create conflicts of interests at a time when shareholder value seems to be a buzzword. However, shareholders have started to feel their feet – consider the proposed take-over of the LSE by Deutsche Börse.

Some macroeconomic aspects of German economic policy would equally perplex our man from Mars. More specifically, the shocks emanating from the process of unification and the implications of Germany's membership of the EU have both had adverse effects in employment.

It is paradoxical that consumption absorption in the east has been subsidized, while a traditionally low propensity to consume in the west has deflated aggregate demand. The German Economic, Monetary and Social Union (GEMSU) additionally meant that the two labour markets could not be segmented – otherwise there was no reason why monetary and fiscal policy should not similarly be segmented. Interest-rate and fiscal flexibility were therefore lost, and, until Harz IV, social policy provided an incentive to remain unemployed. In the latter case, an additional burden of adjustment was placed on the labour market, not least because the rises in labour and fiscal costs required to fund the social-policy integration of the east were unsustainable.

Unification was, of course, a political act with predictable and serious economic consequences. But it has been suggested that French support for unification was gained at the expense of German entry into European Monetary Union (EMU), arguably at an overvalued nominal exchange rate. Moreover, the huge economic welfare burden of the Common Agricultural Policy (CAP) will continue until at least 2013 because of German support for the French policy stance. This was at time when Germany needed to reduce its contributions to the EU's general budget. In both cases – EMU and the CAP – grist has been provided to the mill of the Eurosceptics in Britain. Although only one of the five tests for British entry into EMU is concerned with convergence, there is little hope of even this (optimum currency area) test being met. Similarly, if the British budget abatement is to be renegotiated, the CAP will have to be subjected to further reform.

Lothar Funk argues that on *purely economic grounds* wage policy reacted adversely to crude oil-price increases, free exchange-rate revaluation and unification (my emphasis). Yet, at least since 1989, policy-makers have taken unbridled decisions without regard to their economic and social implications.

Part IV

East Germany

12

Lower Firm-specific Productivity Levels in East Germany and East European Industrial Branches: The Role of Managerial Factors

Johannes Stephan

Introduction

During the socialist era, companies in East Germany became much weaker than firms in West Germany in terms of technology and competitiveness. In large part, this may be rooted in the different incentive structures of the two systems: whereas in the West, the criterion for companies' success was their ability to remain in business and generate income in a contestable market environment, firms in the East were required to fulfil a plan to which they were subjected without having their opinions considered.

Almost fifteen years since German unification, with its resulting systemic change in the Eastern *Länder* of Germany and structural adjustment in both East and West German regions, industrial firms in East Germany on average exhibit much lower levels of labour productivity than their competitors in the West; they do achieve higher levels than in Central Eastern Europe (for example, in Poland), but probably not as much as we would have expected when considering the vast financial transfers that were invested in the East German *Länder*, the importing of macroeconomic stability (in particular lower interest rates and the absence of a financial crisis) and so on. All these advantages were not available to the economies of Central Eastern Europe. Back in 1991, aggregate labour productivity levels in East German manufacturing were a mere 17.8 per cent of the West German level. By 2002, the levels between East and West Germany clearly converged, however, stagnating in their catch-up process towards the end of the 1990s (see Figure 12.1).

Research on the sources of convergence between East and West Germany suggests that the process was largely driven by increases in the share of value added in total production, and in particular by the shedding of excess labour (see, for example, Fritsch and Mallok, 1998a, 1998b).[1] When these sources of

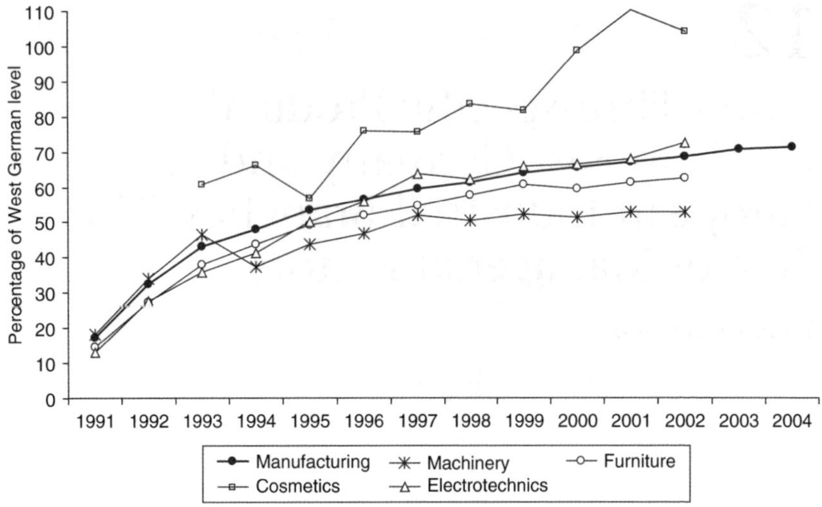

Sources: DIW (2002) and calculations by the Halle Institute for Economic Research.

Figure 12.1 Average sectoral productivity levels in east and west German manufacturing industries, 1991–2004

convergence were depleted, catch-up came to a halt, and future productivity convergence had to be based on other factors.

The analysis of this chapter sets out to ascertain the reasons for sustained lower levels of productivity at the firm level, by focusing on the management of the firm; the overarching hypothesis is that we can identify statistically significant differences, and possibly some important deficiencies in the management of East German firms, that are able to explain some of the lower levels of productivity. To achieve that objective, we make use of a unique database, generated through extensive field work using a questionnaire among firms in both West and East Germany, and for the purpose of comparison, firms in Poland, Hungary and the Czech Republic. In terms of method, we econometrically tested a simple version of a production function at the firm level, embedded in a benchmarking framework.

The chapter starts with a some ideas motivating the analysis and a brief overview of the different focuses of analysis available so far in the existing literature, which sets the agenda for our own analysis. In the next section, we describe our method of fieldwork and empirical analysis of the data generated. In subsequent sections, the results of our analysis are presented and discussed in light of the set of hypotheses we generated for possible determinants of productivity gaps at the firm level.

Motivation and prior analysis

At the most general level, reasons for those productivity gaps are manifold and include differences in sectoral structures (for example, a larger share of labour-intensive sectors), differences in functional structures (smaller share of more sophisticated tasks, labour-intensive production technology), differences in size structures (relative lack of large companies),[2] and differences in spatial structures and the resulting differences in agglomeration advantages (Kronthaler, 2005). Sectoral structures alone, however, do not account for many of the gaps between observed productivity levels at the aggregate level: a comparison at the firm level highlights that firms that belong to the same industrial branch and are comparable in terms of size still exhibit significant gaps. Such firm-specific determinants are the focus of this analysis.

Not only would we have expected a faster convergence of labour productivity levels through technology and knowledge transfer, the transfer of institutions, substantial investment in infrastructure, and the restructuring of enterprises to align to the new criterion for successful economic performance in a competitive environment of the newly integrated economic area (as in the convergence literature). Labour productivity catch-up was also among the prime political objectives with a view on calling a halt to westward labour migration and with a view to convergence in earnings and wages. While regional labour productivity differences at aggregate levels will always remain within integrated economic areas, not least because of different sectoral and functional specialization patterns, we would nevertheless expect that firms in the same industry and operating in the same markets should achieve comparable levels of productivity: inefficient firms would eventually exit the market. So far, even this narrower concept of productivity convergence still appears to be a long way off in the case of East German manufacturing.

The basic idea guiding our approach to the topic is that firms in East and West Germany could potentially achieve the same levels of productivity, if they made similar products, are of comparable size and engage on the same markets (which implicitly assumes that the co-ordinates of demand are the same: prices,[3] consumer preferences, and so on).

The objective of this assessment is to add to the body of existing research on determinants of labour productivity[4] gaps at the level of the firm by focusing explicitly on the extent and quality of strategic management at that level. In this body of literature, we can identify four main strands: the first and earliest studies focused on technology, the quality of the capital stock (for example, Lay, 1996, 1998; Mallok, 1996), and the efficient of use of capital (for example, Mallok/Fritsch, 1997). The second is on market positions and access to markets, measured in prices of sales and in procurement (for example, Eickelpasch *et al.*, 1996; Bernhardt, 1997).

Two microeconometric analyses use existing databases (for example, Bellmann and Brussig, 1998 with the Institute for Employment Research (IAB) establishment panel; and Czarnitzki, 2003, with the Mannheim Innovation Panel): the former establishes deficiencies in company organization and in the integration of the firm into the enterprise as a whole (where establishments form part of a system of enterprises with several subsidiaries). The results of the latter analysis indicate deficiencies related to innovation. This indicates in particular that differences in managerial skills and expertise probably play an important role in explaining productivity gaps. Research so far, however, has not focused on differences and possibly even deficiencies rooted in specific managerial functions. The literature on firm-specific determinants of productivity gaps therefore still lacks insight into the underlying patterns of behaviour of firm managers; that is, the extent and quality of management.

The methodology of our analysis

Research conducted at the Halle Institute (IWH) aims to close this gap. This is a unique focus in the literature, albeit difficult to measure. From the insights into growth and competition determinants from the modern development literature on the role of scale effects and specialization economies, we deduce that firms can be expected to perform well if they are able to supply the preconditions for scale and specialization economies (see, for example, Canning, 1996). We set out to examine the quality of management by focusing on:

(i) the effective, not necessarily formal, qualifications of all groups of the firm's staff and the intensity of the training of staff, as conditions for a high quality of management and work in the firm;
(ii) the intensity of strategic planning on behalf of firm managers or owners, as an input variable,
(iii) the intensity of networking with contractors and partners of the firm, on the use of a variety of modern communication technologies, and on one particular management strategy, namely product specialisation versus diversification, as output variables; and, finally,
(iv) the intensity of use of capital *vis-à-vis* labour, and the intensity of investment.[5]

During extensive fieldwork, conducted in 2002 and 2003, we used identical sector-specific questionnaires for the regions to be compared. In terms of sectors, we selected four manufacturing branches, thought to be representative with respect to our hypotheses – namely machinery, furniture, electrotechnial, and cosmetics manufacturing firms. To allow comparability of firms for the benchmarking exercise, we divided our panels into small and large firms.

The criterion for membership of either the East German or the West German panels is the location of the establishment; during the fieldwork, we attempted to interrogate firms in the East that did not have West German headquarters, but, particularly with respect to large firms, this was not always possible. Because of differences in the economic policy support schemes for entrepreneurs between the regions, we expected to find a number of Western entrepreneurs having established firms in the Eastern regions of our samples. The data generated does not allow us to distinguish between Western subsidiaries and original Eastern firms.

Our set of hypothesis

1. *Extent of qualification of personnel.* Because of the problem of comparability of formal qualification between diplomas and certificates awarded in the German Democratic Republic (GDR) and the West German education and training schemes (and the often counter-intuitive results generated in analysis simply using quantitative indicators of formal qualification), we asked firm managers to identify not only the percentage share of firms' staff with higher qualifications, but also to consider extraordinary work experience in their field when defining the qualifications of its personnel. Firms' staff were categorized in three groups (management, administration and workers). While it goes without saying that the level of efficiency of the firm will tend to increase with the relevant qualifications of its staff, we are interested in the respective relevance of the three categories.
2. *Intensity of training of personnel.* This was measured by the percentage share of employees who received training during the year previous to the interrogation of the firm.[6] We assume that not only the improvement of qualification profiles will affect productivity levels positively. We also expect that such a personnel policy will develop a heightened consideration of individual qualification profiles and hence result in a more efficient allocation of labour to the heterogeneous tasks in the firm, and improved quality of selection in the procurement of new staff.
3. *Intensity of strategic planning by the management.* This was measured by the estimated percentage share of time invested by firms' managers for non-continuous tasks targeted mainly at increasing market (shares) and exploring new markets, increasing sales prices via product or service quality, and at reducing production costs *vis-à-vis* time invested for daily operational activities aimed at improving efficiency in regularly recurring activities (both adding up to 100 per cent). We assume that the ability of firm managers to think strategically – for example, if firms have a sufficient degree of division of labour to allow managers to reflect on future opportunities in a strategic manner[7] – will be able to achieve higher levels of productivity.
4. *Intensity of networking with suppliers, customers and other stakeholders.* In our questionnaire, we asked firms to estimate the intensity of networking with suppliers, customers and other stakeholders on a scale between 0 and

100. Networking was further specified as contractual relationships with a history of at least two years. The intuition is derived from Industrial Organization Theory, where firms balance inner-firm co-ordination costs with transaction costs in their relations with other firms: networking allows firms to reduce costs associated with searching, negotiating and contracting by establishing trust and experience via long-term relationships. A high intensity of networking with suppliers and other stakeholders may not only reduce risks associated with the conditions of delivery (for example, time and quality) but also allows firms to intensify division of labour between the firm and its networking partners (for example, the outsourcing issue). Long-term networking with customers may likewise involve cost advantages but above all may form part of a marketing strategy geared towards securing prices and quantities. Advantages derived from these sources may be assumed to translate into productivity increases.

5. *Intensity of use of modern communication technologies.* This was measured in our fieldwork by the estimated intensity of the use of e-mail, the Internet, and e-business, on a scale between 0 and 100. In order to network efficiently, partners can make use of modern communication technologies. We assume that firms using such technologies more intensively also benefit more from the advantages of networking – hence are also able to achieve higher levels of productivity.
6. *Diversification versus concentration on expertise.* This was measured by the number of types of products in relation to total staff numbers. The decision on the scope of products is firm-specific, and we expect firms with a narrow line of products (that is, strong concentration) to enjoy the benefits of specialization. This does not necessarily equate to higher profits or sustainability in the market, however, because diversification can be a method of risk-reduction in case of demand shifts. The association between either of the two strategies can take a positive or negative sign, and we are interested in which strategy prevails in which industry, and whether adherence to a given strategy in fact influences productivity levels.
7. *Intensity of use of capital vis-à-vis labour as a control variable.* We are able to infer this from the fieldwork data by testing for the interaction between labour costs per number of employees in the firm and the percentage rate of automation of production (for furniture and machinery) or capital intensity (for electrotechnics and cosmetics); a positive significant interaction would indicate substitution of labour by capital in the West and the reverse in the East: do managers in firms where labour is relatively cheaper than in the benchmark region substitute capital with labour, hence deliberately and in conformity with market conditions choose a more labour-intensive production technology, which results in a lower level of labour productivity? If we were to establish this, then the labour

productivity gap between East and West Germany should not be perceived as a deficiency but rather as a conscious decision by managers.

The production function approach

Production functions are the most common method of assessing productivity. However, a production function approach effectively restricts the number of determinants to be tested (in the following: 'candidate determinants') as a large number of 'production factors' would result in insufficiently robust estimations. In our case, however, we were able to reduce the number of determinants in a preliminary step of our analysis by use of correlation analysis and partial correlation analysis to eleven regressors plus dummies for sufficiently large panels to retain the necessary degrees of freedom. Another possibility would have been to use the general method of 'matching pairs' (see, for example, Mallok and Fritsch, 1997; Czarnitzki, 2003), this was done in the prior analysis and produced largely comparable results.[8]

The theoretical production function on which we base our analysis is slightly augmented by additional production factors, such as human capital, innovation intensity and management. The production function reads:

$$\frac{Y}{L} = T \times \left(\frac{C}{L}\right)^{\alpha} \times HC^{\beta} \times Inno^{\chi} \times \prod_{i} Man_i^{\delta_i}$$

where $\frac{Y}{L}$ denotes labour productivity, T the state of technology, $\frac{C}{L}$ capital intensity, HC the extent and quality of human capital, $Inno$ the intensity of innovation, and Man_i the list of management variables that we tested. α, β, γ and δ are the usual partial production elasticities.

The levels of firm-specific labour productivities are calculated individually by the firm's gross value added per number of employees. For our OLS regression analysis, the raw data was transferred into logs; the regressions were tested individually for each panel, with identical specifications in terms of numbers of independent variables and regression method. The OLS regressions are of a cross-sectional kind and, in a first step, we wanted the analysis to treat all firms alike, that is, assuming that our list of independent variables would capture all country differences. This assumption is closest to our benchmarking hypothesis, that firms in an integrated economic area, producing the same products and of the same size, would be able to achieve similar levels of productivity – remaining gaps would then constitute 'firm-specific determinants'. In a second step, we relaxed this assumption and account econometrically for country and regional differences that are not explained by our regressors by the use of country and region dummies. We are obviously interested to find out, first, whether country dummies turn out to be significant (in particular the dummies for Germany), and second, whether the inclusion of dummies will 'soak up' the significances of our regressors.

In the analysis of data generated in our fieldwork, we first test whether the candidate-determinant of the productivity gap is a significant determinant for the dependent variable in the regression; that is, a significant determinant of firm-level productivity levels or differences.[9] What remains to be assessed in the second step is the distribution of the size of each determinant between firms in the West and in the Eastern regions and countries. In case Eastern firms are in fact weaker with respect to a determinant candidate, we hold that we positively tested this candidate as a firm-specific determinant of the productivity gap between the West German and Eastern firms within our samples.[10]

Even if, strictly speaking, results are methodologically not generalizeable because of the restricted number of firms and selection of samples, they do offer a valuable insight into firm-level conditions within the selected manufacturing branches. As long as our sample of firms, on average, achieve a productivity gap comparable with the one for the whole respective industrial branch, our results can claim some weight; this is in fact fulfilled comfortably in most panels see Table 12.1. In any case, an assessment of all firms active in the respective branches is impossible, because such data is simply not collected by statistical offices.

Table 12.1 Average labour productivity in our eight panels, in euros

	Machinery (NACE 290)		**Furniture (NACE 361)**	
	Small	**Large**	**Small**	**Large**
West Germany	89,871	81,594	72,132	88,518
East Germany	55,488	58,220	45,745	65,479
Poland	25,421	20,068	8,091	15,893
Czech Republic	20,034	21,520	24,787	16,957
Hungary	26,219	14,622	6,374	9,041
	Cosmetics (NACE 245)		**Electrotechnics (NACE 310)**	
	Small	**Large**	**Small**	**Large**
West Germany	87,199	85,019	99,912	90,557
East Germany	69,143	64,827	74,179	69,714
Poland	19,705	66,306	28,295	37,228
Czech Republic	26,270	33,609	22,581	18,919
Hungary	9,953	24,308	10,536	15,358

Note: Labour productivity levels are calculated as turnover minus intermediate consumption (corresponding to value added) per employment. The size-classes are defined as larger and smaller than 50 employees. The values have been calculated by use of all 925 firms of all panels.
Source: EEC Productivity DataBase.

Table 12.2 Distribution of sample firms according to industry, country/region and size

	Machinery (NACE 290)			Furniture (NACE 361)		
	Small	**Large**	**Total**	**Small**	**Large**	**Total**
West Germany	22	20	42	28	25	53
East Germany	22	25	47	29	20	49
Poland	17	23	40	22	20	42
Czech Republic	21	22	43	20	19	39
Hungary	69	35	104	27	21	48
Total	151	125	276	126	105	231
	Cosmetics (NACE 245)			**Electrotechnics (NACE 310)**		
	Small	**Large**	**Total**	**Small**	**Large**	**Total**
West Germany	20	16	36	17	19	36
East Germany	20	11	31	20	15	35
Poland	25	25	50	28	22	50
Czech Republic	20	19	39	19	24	43
Hungary	13	7	20	57	21	78
Total	98	78	176	141	101	242

Note: Small firms are such with less than 50 employees, large firms employ at least 51.
Source: EEC Productivity Database.

Our eight samples

The fieldwork forms part of a larger study of firm-specific determinants of productivity gaps; all data generated during fieldwork was collected via three waves of questionnaires: the first wave was used as a pre-test, and the second and third were focused on a 'cleansed' set of questions and number of industrial branches.[11] Most of the interrogations were carried out via the telephone, but some firms preferred to fill out the questionnaires on paper or via the Internet. In all cases, full confidentiality was guaranteed.

In each country or region, we set ourselves a target to collect at least twenty completed questionnaires for each of the eight panels, categorized by the product group (or industrial branch at a NACE 3-digit level) and by the size of the firm or establishment. In total, we were able to collect completed questionnaires from a total of 959 firms (see Table 12.2).

The results of the analysis of generated data

On a broader sectoral level of aggregation, the average labour productivity level of all East German machinery manufacturers of NACE 29 (measured as value added per employment) amounts to some 53 per cent of the levels achieved by West German firms in 2001 (DIW, 2002). This is well represented by our panels, with labour productivity levels of small Eastern firms reaching some 62 per cent of the levels of their Western pairs and some 71 per cent by large firms (see Figure 12.2). However, our machinery manufacturer panels appear to be slightly biased towards more successful firms.

In the panels of furniture manufacturers, the sectoral aggregated labour productivity level of all Eastern NACE 36 firms amounts to some 61 per cent of the levels achieved by West German firms in 2001 (DIW, 2002). In our samples, the gaps were comparably high, with small Eastern firms reaching a level of some 63 per cent of their Western pairs and around 74 per cent by large firms. Here, the bias is only significant for large firms.

The productivity gap between our sample West German and East German cosmetics manufacturers (NACE 245) amounts to some 79 per cent of the West German level for small firms and 76 per cent for large firms. This compares to a *negative* sectoral aggregated labour productivity gap of −4 per cent of the West German level for East German firms, because a few very large firms (as, for example, to the south-west of Leipzig) received vast foreign investment, enabling them to instal the latest technology. Hence, our data, including small- to medium-sized firms, achieves a much lower level.

With regard to the electrotechnical industry (NACE 310), the aggregate sectoral difference in levels amount to the East achieving some 73 per cent of the West German level, whereas our small East German electrotechnical firms achieve some 74 per cent of the West German average, and our large firms around 77 per cent. This comfortably matches the sector's aggregate, although our field work data is arguably slightly biased upwards for large firms.

Machinery manufacturers are producers of typically non-mass products. While their final products are often not comparable between firms, their production processes *are*. Hence, the method of benchmarking is viable. Machinery manufacturers often produce a small number of very specific, non-standard products, tailored to the demands of the customer. This is particularly pronounced in smaller firms. In the new WIFO taxonomy, machinery manufacturers typically employ highly qualified personnel (Peneder, 1999, pp. 36–7). In terms of competitive management strategies, such industries would typically focus their attention on horizontal integration (that is, networking may be more intense with other stakeholders than with suppliers and customers), and innovation through new technology (Kaniovski/Peneder, 2001). Within our sample, firms mainly produce special-purpose machinery for packaging, harnessing of material, for printing and publishing and so on, as well as equipment for production lines.

Furniture manufacturers typically produce more standardized products; in some cases probably even mass-produced, large-scale products. In this industry, products and production processes are sufficiently comparable to warrant the use of a benchmarking analysis. Furniture manufacturers are

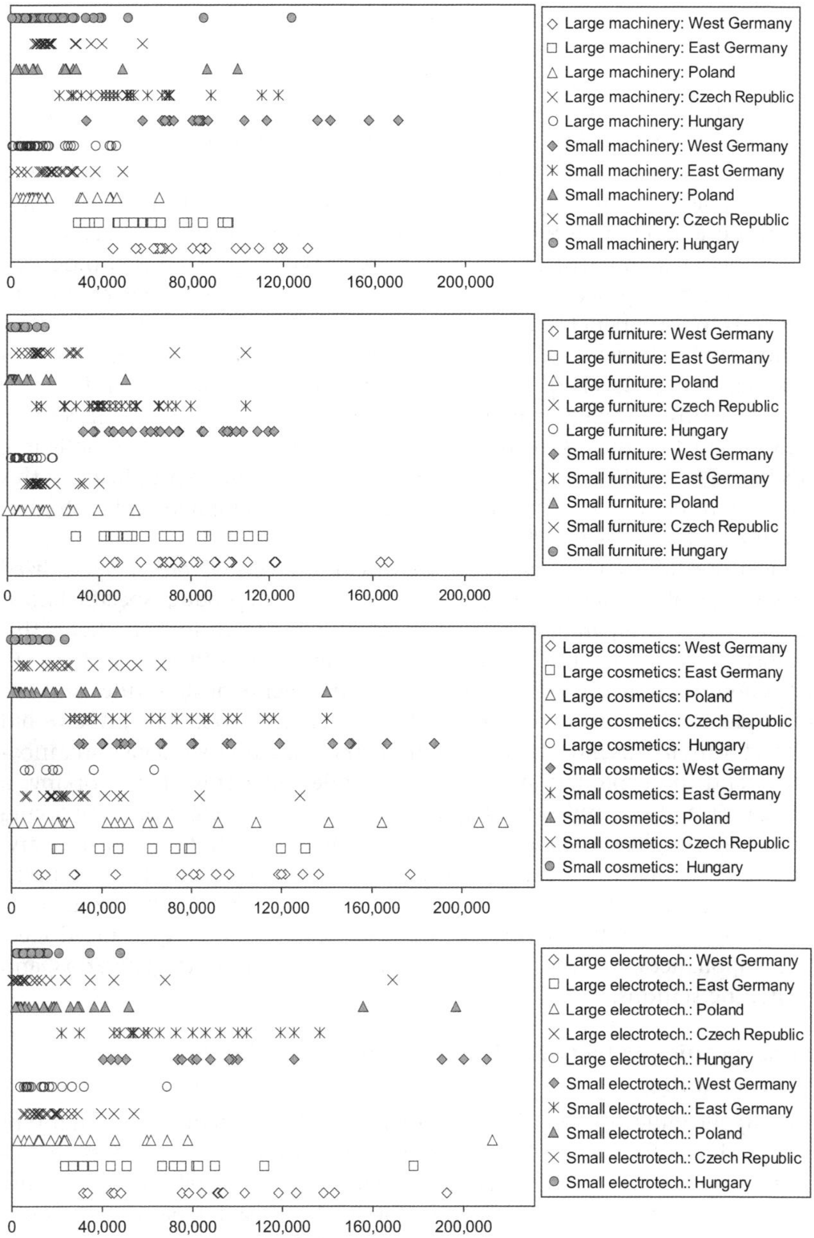

Figure 12.2 Distribution of labour productivities in each of our panels, in euros

typically considered as being rather labour intensive with a comparatively less skill-intense personnel, and typically derive their endogenously created firm-specific advantages from intangible investments in marketing (Peneder, 1999, pp. 36–37). In terms of their competitive strategy, firms in this industry can be expected to favour innovation through variety and brand creation, as well as by vertical integration, either within the firm or via networking, predominantly with suppliers and customers (Kaniovski/Peneder, 2001). Within our sample, firms mainly produce goods such as kitchen furniture, office furniture, and other furniture – for example, living room chairs and tables.

Cosmetics manufacturers are producers of typically diversified products, and production processes between lines of business are similar enough to allow us to use a benchmarking framework of analysis. Cosmetics manufacturing can be characterized as a market-driven industry employing personnel with fairly high levels of qualification (Peneder, 1999, pp. 36–7). In terms of competitive strategy, this industry would typically focus on inventing new products – that is, technological development – and on establishing it's brand name. With respect to networking, we would expect firms in this industry rather to focus on vertical integration with suppliers and customers (Kaniovski and Peneder, 2001).

Electrotechnical manufacturers are also producers of rather specialized products, making use of firm-specific knowledge and product-specific know-how. While, comparability across firms is less straightforward here, this industry does constitute an important one with sufficient features in common, such as the rather high skill requirements of personnel and the often demanding technological input (Peneder, 1999, pp. 36–7). We would expect firms in this industry to focus in their competitive strategies on innovation and the exploitation of scale economies. In terms of networking, a typical firm in this industry, may place considerable weight on networking with both suppliers and customers as well as with firms in the same industry, and in particular the machinery industry, where larger and more complex components are produced (Kaniovski and Peneder, 2001). The products of firms in our samples in this industry are mainly rather specialized electrical appliances, including electrical engines, trafo stations, generators, and switching stations.

Firm-specific productivity determinants in machinery manufacturing

Among the indicators we selected, the strongest firm-specific determinants of the productivity levels between our Eastern and Western machinery manufacturers pertain to their intensities of strategic planning (elasticity of 23 per cent for large firms and 45 per cent for small firms: a 1 per cent increase in the intensity of strategic planning is predicted to increase productivity levels by 23 per cent and 45 per cent, respectively) (see Table 12.3). If we also include country-dummies, however, the results become insignificant: all

Table 12.3 Firm-specific determinants of productivity levels for our machinery firms

	Machinery industry							
	Large firms		small firms		Large firms		Small firms	
	Coeff.	*t*-stat.	Coeff.	*t*-stat.	Coeff.	*t*-stat.	Coeff.	*t*-stat.
Constant	8.87	6.92***	8.21	20.90***	10.50	9.08***	11.00	24.99***
Control variable	0.09	1.14	0.01	1.13	0.01	0.14	0.02	1.72*
Specialization/ diversification	−0.08	−1.22	−0.03	−1.19	−0.07	−1.30	−0.03	−1.37
Quality management	−0.29	−2.20**	0.01	0.32	0.07	0.54	0.03	1.82*
Quality workers	0.03	1.27	−0.02	−1.60⁻	0.01	0.41	0.00	−0.25
Training of personnel	0.07	2.01**	0.04	2.97**	0.05	2.55**	0.03	3.59***
Investment	0.19	4.16***	0.14	2.49**	0.16	2.93***	0.05	0.92
Strategic planning	0.23	2.02**	0.45	3.63***	−0.07	−0.76	0.03	0.31
Innovations	0.04	2.43**	0.01	0.26	0.00	0.11	−0.01	−0.57
Networking	0.04	2.21**	0.05	3.18***	0.03	2.04**	0.03	1.73*
Communication tech.	0.11	5.37***	0.00	0.02	0.04	2.75***	−0.02	−0.85
Country dummies	-without dummies-				GE, CZ, HU, PO		GE, CZ, HU, PO	
	R^2 adj.	0.55	R^2 adj.	0.33	R^2 adj.	0.66	R^2 adj.	0.64
	n	89	n	105	n	89	n	105

Notes: Levels of significance are denoted by: *** error probability less than 1 per cent; ** less than 5 per cent; * less than 10 per cent, and ⁻ less than 15 per cent. The list of dummies only includes those tested to be significant. GE: East Germany, Cz: Czech Republic, Hu: Hungary, Po: Poland.
Source: EEC Productivity Database.

four country dummies, including the East German one, are significant, suggesting that the differences in intensities of strategic planning are a rather country-specific feature and not related so much to productivity differences. The second factor we identify as being an important determinant is the intensity of investment – again, this holds irrespectively of the size of the firm and – at least for large firms – also irrespective of whether we include country dummies or not. Third in the ranking list turn out to be training of personnel: here, coefficients are significant for all sizes of groups, and both specifications with respect to country dummies.

The qualifications of workers and management, however, either turn out to be insignificant or to bear a counter-intuitive sign–only in the group of small firms is the qualification level of management significant, and only for the specification with country dummies. Consistently significant results are also obtained for the test of networking intensities as a determinant of productivity levels, with elasticities between 4 per cent and 5 per cent for the specification without country dummies, and 3 per cent with country dummies. For the intensity of use of modern communication technologies (e-mail, Internet and e-business), the regression models only produce significant results for the group of large firms; the size of elasticities fall from 11 per cent for the specification without country-dummies to 4 per cent with country-dummies. The variable controlling for the intensity of use of capital *vis-à-vis* labour (the factor-substitution test) only turned out to be significant in the model specification with country dummies and for small firms, and the test of whether the degree of product specialization versus diversification did not produce any significant results: the productivity gaps of the Eastern firms *vis-à-vis* the West German firms can in fact be interpreted as competitive disadvantages – reasons explaining gaps must lie among the other factors, including the ones assessed above.

Having established the most important determinants of productivity levels in the machinery manufacturing industry, we assess in the second step the distribution of the size of each determinant between firms in the West and in the Eastern regions and countries. In fact, the average intensity of strategic planning across our firms from all the Eastern countries and regions reaches around only half the intensity of our West German firms, whereby the East German firms perform much better. Nevertheless, the intensity of strategic planning may therefore be considered an important determinant of productivity gaps between Eastern and Western machinery manufacturing firms. While investment in fixed assets turned out to be a significant determinant of productivity levels, its intensity proved to be much higher on average among East German firms compared to the average between West German firms. This is not too surprising, as we know that investment in East Germany was generously supported by transfers from the West. We therefore conclude that investment activity, though undoubtedly important for productivity levels, is not a determinant of productivity gaps between East and West German machinery manufacturers. The intensity of training of personnel also turns out to be much lower on average across all our Eastern firms, but small East German firms apparently invested more in training than their Western competitors, and the gap between large firms is small. Also with respect to training, we can only hold that this may be considered a weak determinant of productivity gaps between East and West Germany for large machinery manufacturers.

Networking intensities are much weaker on average in all Eastern firms, and here, our East German firms are by no means more active networkers compared to other East European firms. The largest gaps appear for the group of small firms and for networking with other stakeholders. Subsequently, the productivity-gap determinant of networking activities plays a more important role for small firms than for large ones. It is, however, important to note that a lower intensity of networking in the East may not be attributed exclusively to managers' skills and expertise in reaping potential benefits: the East German industrial environment is often still characterized by a general lack of spatial concentration of interrelated activities. This will make it more difficult for East German managers to establish new and lasting networks of activities beneficial to the firm.[12] The intensity of use of modern communication technologies, having turned out to be a significant determinant of levels only among the group of large firms, not only appears to be lower in the whole group of Eastern firms, but the gap is also slightly larger for large firms. The gaps we identify for our East German firms alone are clearly lower than the all-Eastern average, but still significant and between some 25 per cent for e-mail and Internet, and 40 per cent for e-business. Hence the use of communication methods did prove to be an important determinant of productivity gaps between East and West German machinery manufacturers.

We furthermore tested our hypothesis that managers of firms under intense competition might increase their efforts in terms of strategic management (the pro-competitive effect). Among our machinery manufacturers, we could support this hypothesis most for product innovations: the more intense the competition, the more product innovations were generated. In the group of small firms, the correlation coefficient turned out to be 0.40, and in the large-firm group 0.38. With firms in the East experienced on average a much lower intensity of competition, and with Eastern firms being less innovative, we can conclude that some insufficiency in the reaction of managers to intense competition contributes to explaining productivity gaps in both size groups of our machinery manufacturers. Other means of strategic management as a counter-measure against intense competition, however, produced mixed results: a higher intensity of training of personnel was only significant for the group of large machinery manufacturers (with a coefficient of 0.35), and small firms in a particularly competitive environment appear to have larger product portfolios.

Firm-specific productivity determinants in furniture manufacturing

Despite the fact that labour costs per employee in East Germany on average reach only 57 per cent of the costs in our Western firm of the group of small furniture manufacturers, and 67 per cent in the case of large firms, the capital–labour substitution test again suggests that differences in labour productivities are rooted in other determinants (see Table 12.4). In contrast to the machinery manufacturing panels, robust results can only be identified for three determinants: investment intensities turn out to be significant in all four tests, with elasticities ranging from 35 per cent for large firms and the specification without dummies to 12 per cent for small firms in the specification with country dummies. And in three out of four cases, the use of modern communication technology also turned out to be significant, more so for small firms (with elasticities between 13 per cent for 'without

Table 12.4 Firm-specific determinants of productivity levels for our furniture firms

	Furniture industry							
	large firms		small firms		large firms		small firms	
	coeff.	*t*-stat.	coeff.	*t*-stat.	coeff.	*t*-stat.	coeff.	*t*-stat.
Constant	8.05	8.82***	8.84	27.07***	10.54	22.16***	10.36	40.49***
Control variable	0.08	1.02	−0.01	−0.48	0.04	1.38	0.01	0.98
Specialization/ diversification	−0.06	−1.44	−0.03	−0.36	−0.04	−1.82*	0.08	1.39
Quality management	0.01	0.15	−0.02	−1.59^{-}	0.05	1.95***	0.01	1.13
Quality workers	0.04	2.56**	0.01	0.72	0.01	0.65	0.01	1.43
Training of personnel	0.06	3.13***	−0.02	−1.22	0.02	1.86*	−0.01	−0.74
Investment	0.35	4.87***	0.27	3.89***	0.14	2.12**	0.12	2.09**
Strategic planning	0.06	3.28***	0.01	0.35	0.01	0.96	−0.01	−0.46
Innovations	−0.01	−0.36	−0.03	−1.40	0.02	1.60^{-}	0.01	1.21
Networking	0.01	0.38	0.07	2.83***	−0.02	−1.09	0.02	0.91
Communication tech.	0.05	1.78*	0.13	5.69***	0.00	0.04	0.06	2.96***
Country dummies	-without dummies-				GE, CZ, HU, PO		GE, CZ, HU, PO	
	R^2 adj.	0.46	R^2 adj.	0.50	R^2 adj.	0.79	R^2 adj.	0.78
	n	70	n	68	n	70	n	68

Notes: Levels of significance are denoted by: *** error probability less than 1 per cent, ** less than 5 per cent, * less than 10 per cent, and $^{-}$ less than 15 per cent. The list of dummies only includes those tested to be significant. GE: East Germany, CZ: Czech Republic, Hu: Hugary, Po: Poland. GE: East Germany, Cz: Czech Republia, Hu: Hungary, Po: Poland.
Source: EEC Productivity Database.

dummies' and 6 per cent with country dummies); in the specification with country-dummies, however, this determinant becomes insignificant for large firms. Again, the inclusion of country dummies not only 'soaks up' some of the significance levels but also tends to reduce elasticities as well; the dummy for East Germany is significant in both regressions for the furniture manufacturers.

Training of personnel also appears to be a significant determinant for productivity levels among furniture manufacturers, yet only in the group of large firms (with elasticities of 6 per cent and 2 per cent, respectively, in the two specifications of regressions). The indicators for the quality levels in the two personnel groups produce sketchy results and even one counter-intuitive sign – results not robust enough to warrant interpretation. The intensities of strategic planning and of networking both produce significant results in only one of the two size groups (large firms for the former and small firms for the latter), but those significances vanish in the specification that includes the country dummies. Interestingly, the determinant-test for specialization versus diversification produces a significant result for large firms, but only in the specification including our country dummies and with a negative sign, suggesting that large furniture manufacturers benefit in terms of productivity levels if they specialize in a smaller number of products per employee – quite in line with our expectations from the characterization of this industry.

The comparison of average investment intensities between East and West reveals that gaps for all Eastern firms taken together are particularly pronounced for small firms; small East German furniture manufacturers in fact achieve a much higher intensity than their West German competitors. We therefore conclude that investment activity can be held to explain some of the productivity gap only between large East and West German furniture manufacturers. Intensities of use of modern communication technologies are also lower among all Eastern furniture manufacturers, the gaps being largest for the use of e-business, with gaps of over 60 per cent. East German firms have caught up slightly more than their Polish, Czech and Hungarian competitors, yet gaps of around 15–20 per cent still prevail for e-mail and the use of the Internet, and 30 per cent for e-business. Having turned out to be significant as an explanation of differences of productivity levels only for small firms, we establish that a lower intensity of use of modern communication technologies is in fact an important determinant of productivity gaps between East and West German furniture manufacturers of a smaller size – that is, with fewer than 50 employees.

Training intensities also exhibit large gaps for the average of all Eastern furniture firms of our samples, with gaps of around 70 per cent for large firms and half that size for small firms. Our East German firms have already more-or-less caught up with training intensities among small firms, but a large gap of nearly 40 per cent remains for large firms. Because our regression analysis only produced significant results for the group of large firms with respect to training intensities, we conclude that lower intensities of training of employees does contribute strongly to the explanation of labour productivity gaps between large furniture manufacturers in East and West Germany. In terms of product specialization, the average Eastern firms of both size groups manage a much larger number of products per employee than their competitors in West Germany, and this also holds true for our East German firms. Insufficient depth of product specialization, having been established as significant determinant of levels in the group of large firms, can hence also explain some of the productivity gaps for this industry and size group.

Our test concerning the pro-competitive effect resulted in ambiguous results: while among the small firms, competition was felt to be fiercer in the East, the opposite is true for large firms. Yet, within the large firm-panel, we could establish a significant correlation between intensity of competition and long-term strategic planning, with a considerably large coefficient of 0.57. No other correlations turned out to be significant. Hence, our results could not establish inadequate strategic behaviour of managers as determinants of productivity gaps between East and West.

Firm-specific productivity determinants in cosmetics manufacturing

Among our cosmetics manufacturing firms, the productivity levels of large firms can in fact be explained significantly by firms substituting relatively more expensive capital by cheaper labour with elasticities in the range of some 37 per cent: a large share of labour productivity gaps are hence a conscious decision of managers and should not be perceived as a deficiency. The remaining differences in labour productivities in this industry can again be traced back to differences in intensities of strategic planning which turned out to be significant in all four tests; that is, for large and small firms, and for the specification with and without country dummies.

Investment intensities also turned out to be significant explanatory determinants of productivity levels, yet the test for large firms in the specification with country dummies turned out to be insignificant. In the group of small cosmetics manufacturers, the level of qualification among managers also significantly explains some of the productivity-level differences; networking intensities are significant only for small firms, and the use of modern communication technologies only among large cosmetic firms. The dummies are significant for all countries among large firms, but in the group of small firms, only the dummies for the Czech Republic and Hungary turn out to be significant – interestingly, belonging to the groups of East German firms does not contribute to explaining productivity differences of small firms between East and West. Also, dummies appear not to 'soak up' as much in terms of significances and elasticities as was the case in the two industries above.

Augmenting those results with an assessment of the distribution of the size of each determinant between firms in the West and in the East shows that the intensity of strategic planning in fact not only significantly explains differences in levels, but also that East German firms of both size groups in fact invest less time in planning strategies to increase market (shares) and explore new markets, increase sales prices via product or service quality, and to reduce production costs (with gaps of around 23 per cent between East and West German firms (see Table 12.5)). We hence conclude that the lower levels of intensity of strategic planning among East German cosmetics manufacturers does explain some of the productivity gaps observed between the two region-specific groups. Investment intensities again turn out to be lower in the East only for the group of small firms: small East German firms' investment intensity only reaches only 74 per cent of the intensity observed for our West German competitors. Large cosmetics manufacturers in East Germany in fact spent more in terms of gross investment per fixed asset, amounting to some 122 per cent of the corresponding West German intensity. Investment intensities can hence be held to contribute to explaining productivity gaps only between small East and West German cosmetics manufacturers.

Table 12.5 Firm-specific determinants of productivity levels for our cosmetics firms

	Cosmetics industry							
	large firms		small firms		large firms		small firms	
	coeff.	*t*-stat.	coeff.	*t*-stat.	coeff.	*t*-stat.	coeff.	*t*-stat.
Constant	4.60	2.50**	8.97	5.82***	8.07	3.16***	10.22	5.62***
Control variable	0.37	4.06***	0.02	0.32	0.34	3.29***	−0.02	−0.44
Specialization/ diversification	0.04	0.24	−0.17	−1.67⁻	−0.03	−0.16	−0.12	−1.34
Qualatiy management	−0.02	−0.54	0.11	3.57***	−0.11	−1.68⁻	0.05	1.82*
Quality workers	0.01	0.21	−0.01	−0.18	0.00	0.04	−0.01	−0.15
Training management	0.01	0.19	0.01	0.23	−0.01	−0.42	0.02	0.72
Training workers	−0.02	−0.45	0.03	1.24	−0.04	−0.94	0.00	0.02
Investment	0.25	1.76*	0.11	2.18**	0.09	0.80	0.12	2.13**
Strategic planning	0.04	2.01*	0.51	2.98***	0.10	2.91***	0.37	1.69*
Innovations	0.04	0.58	0.02	0.56	0.08	1.20	0.03	1.18
Networking	−0.32	−1.08	0.07	2.56**	−0.63	−1.56⁻	0.07	1.78*
Communication tech.	0.09	1.83*	−0.06	−0.82	0.06	1.78*	0.02	0.32
Country dummies	-without dummies-				GE, CZ, HU, PO		GE, CZ,	HU, PO
	R^2 adj.	0.39	R^2 adj.	0.79	R^2 adj.	0.57	R^2 adj.	0.82
	n	35	n	48	n	35	n	48

Notes: Levels of significance are denoted by: *** error probability less than 1 per cent, ** less than 5 per cent, * less than 10 per cent, and ⁻ less than 15 per cent. The list of dummies only includes those tested to be significant. GE: East Germany, CZ: Czech Republic, Hu: Hungary, PO: Poland.
Source: EEC Productivity Database.

While the qualification of management turned out to significantly explain differences in productivity levels at least for the small-firm group, the small East German cosmetics manufacturers in fact have similar average qualification levels in this personnel category, hence personnel qualification does not contribute to explaining productivity gaps. The same applies to networking: here, the intensity of networking with suppliers and customers among small East German firms of this industry in fact compares to the average level among small West German firms. Only for networking with other stakeholders can we identify a significant gap of some 10 per cent, suggesting that a lower intensity of networking with other stakeholders might go some way to explain productivity gaps. The intensity gaps exhibited by large East German cosmetics firms in terms of the use of modern communication technologies are rather small for e-mail and Internet (around 2–4 per cent), and only for the use of e-business platforms could we establish both a significant and positive elasticity and simultaneously a large enough gap in the intensity of its use (to the tune of 43 per cent) between large East and West German cosmetics manufacturers to conclude that the use of e-business is an important determinant of productivity gaps.

Firm-specific productivity determinants in electrotechnics manufacturing

As was the case for our large cosmetics manufacturers, the productivity levels of electrotechnical firms of both size groups can in fact be explained significantly by firms substituting relatively more expensive capital with cheaper labour, with elasticities in the range of 20–30 per cent (see Table 12.6) (slightly lower than for our large cosmetics manufacturers). We therefore again conclude that we can identify some of the labour productivity gaps as being rooted in a rather rational decision of managers. Our regression tests furthermore reveal that the remaining differences in

Table 12.6 Firm-specific determinants of productivity levels for our electrotechnical firms

	Electrotechnical industry							
	large firms		**small firms**		**large firms**		**small firms**	
	coeff.	***t*-stat.**	**coeff.**	***t*-stat.**	**coeff.**	***t*-stat.**	**coeff.**	***t*-stat.**
Constant	5.17	4.42***	2.27	2.18**	5.29	3.37***	4.62	2.22**
Control variable	0.28	4.15***	0.30	4.83***	0.20	3.36***	0.22	3.54***
Specialization/ Diversification	−0.34	−2.23**	0.22	1.14	0.03	0.25	0.20	0.90
Quality management	−0.01	−0.20	0.00	0.05	0.01	0.54	−0.01	−0.61
Quality workers	0.03	0.74	0.17	5.55***	−0.04	−2.12**	0.16	5.66***
Training management	−0.03	−1.14	0.02	1.39	0.03	1.76*	0.02	1.29
Training workers	−0.01	−0.32	0.02	1.78*	−0.02	−2.30**	0.02	1.13
Investment	0.19	1.99*	0.15	2.51**	0.15	2.03*	0.09	1.01
Strategic planning	0.24	1.91*	0.23	1.55⁻	0.26	1.64⁻	0.10	0.73
Innovations	0.04	1.38	0.01	0.87	0.05	3.13***	0.01	0.78
Networking	−0.02	−1.46	0.05	2.27**	−0.02	−1.07	0.06	1.97*
Communication tech.	0.23	1.72*	−0.01	−0.68	0.27	3.01***	−0.02	−1.36
Country dummies	-without dummies-				GE, CZ, HU, PO		GE, CZ,	HU, PO
	R^2 adj.	0.67	R^2 adj.	0.71	R^2 adj.	0.82	R^2 adj.	0.75
	n	44	n	55	n	44	n	55

Notes: Levels of significance are denoted by: *** error probability less than 1 per cent, ** less than 5 per cent, * less than 10 per cent, and ⁻ less than 15 per cent. The list of dummies only includes those tested to be significant (the ones in brackets are significant only at the 15 per cent level). CZ: Czech Republic, PO: Poland, HU: Hungary.

Source: EEC Productivity Database.

labour productivity levels in this industry may lie with a lower intensity of investment, albeit including country dummies (of which, in the group of large firms, only Poland and (weakly) the Czech dummies, and in the group of small firms only the Hungarian – even if only weakly – turned out to be significant), but the significance disappears for small firms. The intensity of strategic planning did produce a significant result for large firms and a rather weakly significant result for small firms,[13] and the results become even weaker when the country-dummies are included. The intensity of networking turned out to be consistently significant for small firms in both specifications of our regression models (with elasticities of 5–6 per cent), and the intensity of use of modern communication technologies is similar for large firms (with 23 per cent and 27 per cent, respectively, for the specification without and with country dummies). The significant result for the specialization versus diversification test among large electrotechnical manufacturers disappears in the specification that includes our country dummies, and the results for qualification levels and training intensities are rather sketchy, with some counter-intuitive signs: all we can read from these results is that the level of qualification of workers appears to be a significant determinant of productivity levels among only small electrotechnical manufacturing firms (which is a consistent result for both model specifications).

Not only did the intensity of investment turn out to be a significant determinant of productivity levels, large East German electrotechnical firms did in fact invest less in terms of fixed assets. Albeit for the small-firms group, East German companies again surpassed the levels of the in West German competitors in an attempt to renew obsolete capital stocks. We can hence conclude that investment intensities can only explain some of the productivity gaps between East and West German electrotechnical firms in the large-firms group. The gaps in time invested for strategic planning are also rather small – less than 10 per cent – still, they contribute to explaining some of the productivity gaps. The largest gaps for intensities in networking in the small-firm group again appear for other stakeholders (with some 20 per cent), and much less for customers (less than 8 per cent) and suppliers (less than 4 per cent). Among communication technologies for large firms, the gaps are largest again for e-business (with East German firms exhibiting intensities of some 84 per cent of their Western competitors), around 95 per cent for e-mail and insignificant for the intensity of use of the Internet. Again, this helps to explain some of the productivity gaps we observe between East and West Germany among small electrotechnical manufacturers. With respect to the level of qualification of workers, our analysis and data (elasticity of 16 per cent and gap between East and West Germany of 27 per cent) suggests that this determinant does explain a large share of the productivity gaps for small electrotechnical manufacturing firms.

Summary and discussion of main results

To sum up, our research results turned out to be not always in line with our assumptions derived from related research and plausibility assumptions. In particular, we expected the furniture and the electrotechnical industries to thrive on a strategy of product specialization, and the cosmetics industry rather on a strategy of product diversification. Despite the fact that large productivity gaps exist between East and West German competitors in those industries, we were only able to establish the expected strategic orientation for the furniture industry, and here only in the case of large firms (see Table 12.7).

Furthermore, we expected machinery, cosmetics and electrotechnical manufacturers to draw some of their competitive advantages from the high qualifications of their employees. Our analysis, however, did not establish this factor as a determinant of productivity gaps for the machinery or the cosmetics industries, but it did for the electrotechnical industry, but even here only for large firms. Some explanation for this shortcoming might lie in the fact that levels of qualifications have been estimated differently between Eastern and Western managers of our firms.[14] As a further test variable, the intensities of training did provide some weak indication for the expected result for large machinery manufacturers (but also for large furniture manufacturers, whom we expected to be rather less skill-intensive).

Table 12.7 Summary of firm-specific determinants of productivity levels

	Machinery	Furniture	Cosmetics	Electrotechnics
Control variable	weak (s)		strong (l)	strong (s, l)
Specialization/ diversification		strong (l)		
Qual. management				
Qual. workers				strong (s)
Training management	weak (l)	strong (l)		
Training workers				
Investment		strong (l)	strong (s)	strong (l)
Strategic planning	strong (s, l)		strong (l)	weak (s, l)
Innovations				
Networking	strong (s, l)		strong for stake holders (s)	strong for stake holders (s)
Communication tech.	strong (s, l)	strong (s)	strong for e-business (l)	strong for e-business (s)

Notes: The distinction between strong and weak is at the author's discretion and reflects the sizes of elasticities, possible significance weaknesses, and the sizes of gaps between East and West.
Source: EEC Productivity Database.

Then we generated expectations on the particularly important networking partners for each industry. In fact, networking turned out to be an important determinant in four out of our eight samples, often with a bias towards networking with 'other stakeholders', as expected for machinery firms and possibly electrotechnical firms, but not so for the other industries. The raw data collected, however, clearly shows that this result is the case mainly because networking with stakeholders is typically less developed in the East in general.

The use of modern communication technologies, which we expected to be important regardless of size and industry, did turn out to be an important determinant in five out of the eight samples and across all industries. The intensity of investment in fixed assets did turn out to be important in three out of the eight cases, and the intensity of strategic planning in five out of eight cases (of which, however, two results are rather weak).

The variable controlling for the possibility that labour productivity gaps are a result of a rational choice of managers substituting capital for relatively cheaper labour did uncover this gap determinant in four out of our eight samples (even if in one case only weakly). We therefore hold that the main reasons for productivity gaps between East and West German manufacturing firms may lie with (in the order of ranking of importance):

(i) the intensity of use of modern communication technologies;
(ii) the intensity of strategic planning by management;
(iii) the intensity of networking with suppliers, customers and other stakeholders;[15]
(iv) the rational choice of substituting capital by relatively cheaper labour;
(v) the intensity of investment in fixed assets;
(vi) the training of management and workers, and the quality of skills of personnel; and finally,
(vii) the intensity of product strategies such as specialization or diversification.

In general, we may finally conclude that some of the productivity gaps are rooted in factors that we can trace back to the quality and expertise of management: management functions that yield more than purely on organization of the production process play a dominant role in explaining firm productivity levels, and because, in our samples, East German firms exhibited on average lower levels of productivity, such management functions are apparently still relatively less developed among East German firms than West German firms. In particular, with respect to these latter determinants, we have to interpret the results carefully, because our method cannot establish causalities. Our results do suggest that deficiencies in market orientation and strategic planning still prevail among firms in East Germany. Apparently, the shift in paradigms brought about by the systemic change of the East German economy from a planned system in the GDR to one that is governed by competition and markets in unified Germany, has not yet been incorporated fully at the level of management among East German firms. While this result was already hinted at by previous research, our fieldwork and analysis is the first to test this assumption explicitly. If our results in fact capture the most important reason for lower levels of productivity among firms in East Germany, then the prospects for a swift catch-up are rather less bright: more than ten years after the systemic change and the steep restructuring of the East German economy (demise of COMECON as the previous market orientation and the submission of East German firms to unfettered competition with the West), the individual learning curve will become increasingly flatter with diminishing returns. Without intensified eastward migration, the East German manufacturing economy might well need many more years to catch up.

The main caveat of our analysis pertains to the causality issue. Of significant importance for the robustness of our results is also the fact that we are unable to identify which of our East German firms are just Western subsidiaries and hence can benefit from expertise originating in their close association with their West German headquarters. Those caveats are rooted in the limitations associated with the methodology of large-scale field work, and further research can serve to deepen and complement our results.

This suggests that future research may increase our understanding of the roots of productivity levels by investigating more deeply the role of strategic planning, the use of communication technologies and the intensity of networking: with respect to strategic planning, we could dig deeper by investigating not only its intensity but also its (time-) efficiency; with respect to the use of communication technologies, we could attempt to retrieve quantitative information on, for example, the endowment of the firm with computers, points of access for the Internet, the number of hours spent by employees servicing web-pages for the firm and so on. (in this respect, the author's attention was drawn towards Electronic Data Exchange by an anonymous referee as an additionally important communication method); with respect to the intensity of networking, we could try to control for differences in location differences of firms (spatial concentration and agglomeration advantages). Those issues, however, cannot be tested satisfactorily by using large-scale questionnaire-based fieldwork, but rather necessitates deep-level structured interviews with the generality limitation typically associated with this method.

Notes

1. This corresponds, incidentally, to experience in Central Eastern European manufacturing (see, for example, Stephan, 2003).
2. See Ragnitz (1999, 2001) and Ragnitz *et al.* (2000) for a review of results of empirical studies as well as for their own assessments of determinants conducted in a larger project. The analysis and results presented here form an extension of

this project. We built on the questionnaire and the methods used in one subset of that research project.

3. With respect to prices, previous research suggests that East German firms achieve on average slightly lower prices (to the tune of about 10–20 per cent lower on average in manufacturing industries in 1998: Ragnitz *et al.*, 2000, p. 184). Reasons for this, however, are not to be found in a general preference for West German products; rather, the lower prices achieved in the East are thought to have their roots in insufficient market orientation and can hence be treated as firm-specific in our analysis.
4. This research focuses on apparent labour productivity; the efficiency of the use of capital has not been assessed, mainly because firms were reluctant to provide that kind of data, and because of difficulties in the precise valuation of capital stocks.
5. It would have been desirable also to measure the extensiveness and effectiveness of marketing efforts, and the intensity of R&D activity, but this proved to be impossible in pre-tests of our field work. Product and process innovations produced ambiguous results (as is often the case: see, for example, Czarnitzki, 2003) and are hence not reported here.
6. Because of the problem of low rates of return in a field studies using questionnaires we were unable to devise a quantitative indicator for training (such as, for example, the amount of time spent in training programmes, or the total amount spent on training programmes by firms).
7. This conceptualization is the result of several test runs of field work. It obviously remains riddled with the problem that we have to assume comparable efficiency in the use of time for either task between East and West German firms, and within sub-samples.
8. The method of 'matching pairs' originates from clinical surveys in which treatment effects are controlled for by use of a non-treatment control group. It is a non-parametric approach which allows us to analyse field data without prior assumptions on functional distributions. For a description of the method, and an early application for British and German manufacturers, see, for example, Daly *et al.* (1985).
9. Without, however, being able to establish the direction of causality: is the firm's performance relatively weaker because of the lower intensity in a positive determinant, or is the intensity of this determinant lower because of the difficult situation of the firm? This caveat is inherent to the methodology applied here and we can only rely on plausibility in interpreting results.
10. Another caveat of our method is that our regression analysis only tests for linear associations: if productivity first increases with the value of a determinant candidate but then falls again with even higher determinant values (hat-shaped correspondence), our method would reject our hypothesis. It is conceivable that with respect to determinants like *e.g.* the intensity of use of capital or investment activity, there could exist single or multiple optimal intensities.
11. In our fieldwork, we also collected completed questionnaires from some construction firms (38), computer retailers (3), meat processing firms (12), transport (logistics) firms (23), textile manufacturers (1), and hotels (15). Because of their low number and because we adjusted the questionnaire, these do not form part of our 'CEE firm-specific database'.
12. In a related empirical study using official statistical data, Kronthaler (2005) concludes that spatial concentration is lower in all East German regions compared

to West German ones, and that within East Germany, only regions like Greater Berlin, Dresden and Leipzig can be considered to offer significant agglomeration advantages. Along the same lines, spillover effects between foreign and domestic firms seem to be rather low (Günther and Gebhardt (2005). This means that the results of this empirical analysis – unable to establish causality – have to be interpreted with due care.

13. The interpretation of results with an error probability of between 10 and 15 per cent is debatable. Yet, because we are analysing cross-sectional data that was generated in fieldwork, and because we do not have too many observations, it might be justifiable to use those as indicative results.
14. Because the results were generated from field study using questionnaires, we are unable to determine whether firms in fact assessed their own qualifications in terms of 'work experience' rather than 'formal qualifications'. It is a well-established fact that the East German population commands a much higher level of formal qualifications, but which, however, do not necessarily match the necessary qualifications requested by their current occupation: often, firm managers and owners in the East have technical qualifications that do not serve any real purpose in management and market-related activities. As in most panels, we – inspite of this – monitored a lower quality of human capital in East German firms, so our results and their interpretation are all the more robust.
15. Although we have to consider that location specifics in the East, namely a lesser spatial concentration, can be assumed to make it more difficult for firms in the East to establish long-term networks of activities and to reap benefits from spillover effects in terms of technology and knowledge.

References

Arbeitskreis volkswirtschaftliche Gesamtrechnung der Länder (2002) *Reihe 1 Länderergebnisse* (Stuttgart: Statistisches Landesamt Baden-Württemberg).

Beer, S. (2004) 'Die Entwicklung ostdeutscher Industriezweige von 1991 bis 2003 – aktualisierte Branchenskizzen', Halle Institute for Economic Research (IWH), Discussion Paper No. 199 (IWH, Halle).

Bellmann, L. and M. Brussig (1998) 'Ausmaß und Ursachen der Produktivitätslücke ostdeutscher Betriebe des verarbeitenden Gewerbes', *Mitteilungen aus der Arbeitsmarkt- und Berufsforschung,* vol. 31, no. 4, pp. 648–60.

Bernhardt, M., H. -G. Vieweg and R. Heisig (1997) 'Maschinenbau im Freistaat Sachsen', *ifo-Dresden Studien,* vol. 16, p. 80.

Brinkmann, U. (1996) 'Magere Bilanz: Neue Managementkonzepte (NMK) in transformierten ostdeutschen Betrieben', in M. Pohlmann and R. Schmidt: (eds), *Management in der ostdeutschen Industrie* (Opladen: Leske & Budrich), pp. 215–48.

Canning, D. (1996) 'Specialisation, Scale Economies and Economic Development', *Economic Letters,* vol. 52, pp. 95–100.

Czarnitzki, D. (2003) 'Extent and Evolution of the Productivity Gap in Eastern Germany', Centre for European Economic Research (ZEW) Discussion Paper No. 03-25 (Mannheim: ZEW).

Daly, A., D. Hitchens and K. Wagner (1985) 'Productivity, Machinery and Skills in a Sample of British and German Manufacturing Plants', *National Institute Economic Review,* vol. 111, pp. 48–62.

DIW (2002) *Vergleichende Branchendaten für das verarbeitende Gewerbe,* German Institute for Economic Research (Berlin: DIW).

Eickelpasch, A., V. Lessat, I. Pfeiffer, C. Grothe, J. Moeller and D. Wirth (1996) *Untersuchung der Bezüge und Lieferungen der Brandenburger Wirtschaft von und zu Unternehmen innerhalb des Landes, mit Berlin und dem übrigen Bundesgebiet sowie zum Ausland, Gutachten* (Brandenburg: Ministeriums für Wirtschaft Mittelstand & Technologie).

Fritsch, M. (1997) 'Die ostdeutsche (Maschinenbau)Industrie im Transformations- und Globalisierungsprozess', in R. Pohl and H. Schneider (eds), *Wandeln oder weichen*, Halle Institute for Economic Research (IWH) Sonderheft No. 3/1997 (Halle: IWH), pp. 133–61.

Fritsch, M. and J. Mallok (1998a) 'Surviving the Transition: The Process of Adaptation of Small and Medium-sized Firms in East Germany', in H. Brezinski, E. Frank and M. Fritsch (eds), *The microeconomics of Transformation and Growth* (Cheltenham: Edward Elgar), pp. 163–84.

Fritsch, M. and J. Mallok (1998b) 'Wie es vorangeht – Die Entwicklung mittelständischer Industriebetriebe in Ost- und Westdeutschland 1992–1995', in J. Schmude (ed), *Neue Unternehmen in Ostdeutschland – Neuaufbau und Umstrukturierung der Unternehmenslandschaft* (Heidelberg: Physica-Verlag) pp. 154–79.

Fritsch, M., F. Meyer-Krahmer and F. Pleschak (eds) (1998) *Innovationen in Ostdeutschland. Potentiale und Probleme* (Heidelberg: Physica-Verlag).

Günther, J. and O. Gebhardt (2005) 'Eastern Germany in the Process of Catching-up: The Role of Foreign and Western German Investors in Technological Renewal', *Eastern European Economics*, vol. 43, no. 3, pp. 80–105.

Günther, J. and H. Lehmann (2004) 'Is East Germany Successful in Catching Up? An Empirical Investigation of the Technological Capability in Manufacturing Industry', *VEST Journal for Science and Technology Studies*, vol. 17, no. 1, pp. 24–40.

Hachmann, K., W. Kühn and K. Schuldt (1998) *Zur Lage der Metall- und Elektroindustrie in Ostdeutschland – Gesamtwirtschaftliche und strukturelle Rahmenbedingungen sowie betriebliche Eckdaten für die Metall-und Elektroindustrie Ostdeutschlands*, Gutachten for the Otto Brenner Stiftung, November (Berlin: Otto Brenner Stiftung).

Hitchens, D., K. Wagner and J. E. Birnie (1993) 'The Comparative Productivity of East German Manufacturing: A Matched Plant Comparison' Wissenschaftszentrum Discussion Paper No. FS I 93–310 (Berlin: Wissenschaftszentrum).

Hitchens, D., K. Wagner, J. E. Birnie, J. Hamar and A. Zemplinerová (1995) 'The Comparative Productivity of Manufacturing Plants in the Czech Republic and Hungary', *Economic Systems*, vol. 19 no. 3, pp. 187–218.

Kaniovski, S. M. and M. Peneder (2001) 'On the structural dimension of competitive strategy', Östereichisches Institut für Wirtschaftsforschung (WIFO) Working Paper No. 145 (Vienna: WIFO).

Kronthaler, F. (2005) 'Economic Capability of East German Regions: Results from a Cluster Analysis', *Regional Studies*, vol. 39, no. 6, pp. 741–52.

Lay, G. (1996) *Sachsens Investitionsgüterindustrie im Regionalvergleich – Trotz Modernisierungsschub unterdurchschnittliche Produktivität*, Mitteilungen aus der Produktionsinnovationserhebung, No. 3 (Karlsruhe: Fraunhofer Institut für Systemtechnik und Innovationsforschung).

Lay, G. (1998) 'Modernisierung und Produktivität in der Investitionsgüterindustrie Ostdeutschlands', in M. Fritsch and F. Pleschak (eds), *Innovationen in Ostdeutschland* (Heidelberg: Physica-Verlag) pp. 43–59.

Mallok, J. (1996) *Engpässe in ostdeutschen Fabriken. Technikausstattung, Technikeinsatz und Produktivität im Ost-West-Vergleich* (Berlin: edition sigma).

Mallok, J. (2005) Produktivitätsfortschritte im ostdeutschen Maschinenbau – Ergebnisse einer Benchmarking-Studie (1992–2002), *Zeitschrift für wirtschaftlichen Fabrikbetrieb*, vol. 100, no. 4, pp. 202–7.

Mallok, J. and M. Fritsch (1997) Die Intelligenz der Technikausnutzung. Zur Bedeutung des Maschinenparks und seiner Einsatzweise für die betriebliche Leistungsfähigkeit', *Schmalenbachs Zeitschrift für betriebswirtschaftliche Forschung*,vol. 49 no. 2, pp. 141–59.

Peneder, M. (1999) 'Intangible Investment and Human Resources, the New WIFO Taxonomy of Manufacturing Industries', Österreichisches Institut für Wirtschaftsforschung (WIFO) Working Paper No. 114 (Vienna: WIFO).

Pilat, D. (1998) 'The Impact of Competition on Productivity', *Wirtschaftspolitische Blätter*, vol. 1, pp. 38–47.

Ragnitz, J. (1999) 'Warum ist die Produktivität ostdeutscher Unternehmen so gering?', *Zeitschrift für Konjunkturpolitik*, vol. 3, pp. 165–87.

Ragnitz, J. (2001) 'Produktivitätsrückstand der ostdeutschen Wirtschaft: Eine zusammenfassende Bewertung', *Wirtschaft im Wandel* vol. 7–8, pp. 181–9.

Ragnitz, J., G. Miller and M. Wölfl (2000) *Produktivitätsunterschiede von Wirtschaftsräumen – Das Beispiel der neuen Länder*, Halle Institute for Economic Research (IWH) Endbericht (Halle: IWH).

Stephan, J. (2003) *Evolving Structural Patterns in the Enlarging European Division of Labour: Sectoral and Branch Specialisation and the Potentials for Closing the Productivity Gap*, Halle Institute for Economic Research (IWH) Sonderheft No. 5/2003 (Halle: IWH).

13

East Germany's Economic Transition in Comparative Perspective

*Michael Kaser**

> ... by jingo if we do,
> We've got the ships, we've got the men, we've got the money too
> (Music Hall song, G. W. Hunt, 1878)

Territorial expansion – a psychic public good

Net transfers from the western to the eastern *Länder* from the date of unification to 2003 aggregated €1,200 billion euros, a sum almost equal to the Western *Länder* GDP on the eve of unification[1]; they are being tapered out, but the 'solidarity package' beginning this year assures €156 billion for infrastructure investment in the eastern *Länder* through to 2015. No other process of imperial or national consolidation involved so heavy a cost to the expanding power – in the nineteenth century the British expenditure on its empire, and the unifications of Germany (where the transfer was east to west) and of Italy (north to south), the latter resumed strongly in the 1950s in the Mezzogiorno Plan.[2] The utility gained by the donor state was described as jingoism in Victorian England and promoted as national duty by leaders such as Bismarck and Garibaldi. Commentators on the German transfers of the 1990s have called them the conversion of capital 'from being a factor of production to being an economic good' (Page, 2003, p. 18), 'a historical necessity' (Hall and Ludwig, 1995, p. 495) and yielding for West Germans a 'psychic income' (Headey and Headey, 2003).[3] From the standpoint of the recipient, no other national transfer was so large at its peak in domestic consumption; Western *Länder* transfers equalled a quarter of the Eastern *Länder*'s consumer demand in 1998. Economics has two concepts to explain such voluntary renunciation of resources in favour of others. The broader one is altruism, on which there is an extensive literature – the International Economic Association organized two recent conferences, reviewing and adding to it (Gérard-Varet *et al.*, 2000; Agarwal and Vercelli, 2005) – and the narrower, psychic valuation.

Among many manifestations of psychic income[4] is that enjoyed when two entities or people differ in wealth or income, and the richer weighs the benefit received by the poorer against the opportunity cost of the surrendered resources.[5] A psychic disutility may be suffered in parallel by the poorer by reason of their status as recipient. Both apply to the contemporary inner-German case, where the east is poorer than the west. Three measures of psychic income were used between 1990 and 1997 by Headey and Headey (2003) in surveys of households in the respective regions, questioning their respondents on three psychic fields. Within a capital account, they recorded perceptions of holdings of physical and financial assets, human capital (measured by years of education) and marital/partner status; within a current account, they recorded paid work and hours of leisure per week; and within psychic income they enquired about life satisfaction, health satisfaction and household-income satisfaction (p. 108). Over the seven years, former West Germans had gained on their capital account, with former East Germans considering themselves constant. Trends on current accounts, however, diverged, 'Wessies' losing on work but gaining on leisure, while 'Ossies' gained on work but lost on leisure. All felt a deterioration in psychic income with the former East Germans perceiving themselves as 'second class citizens, at least somewhat dissatisfied with their lives in the Federal Republic' (p. 136). A correlation of macroeconomic and psychic income trends is well documented: GDP growth with psychic gains, and GDP recession and higher unemployment with psychic losses have been found for a quarter of a million Europeans and Americans sampled between the 1970s and the 1990s.[6]

Regional disparity within Germany

The western relativity in wealth and income is, however, a relatively recent characteristic of the German economy. Although the nineteenth-century growth nexus of Silesia is not within the present Eastern *Länder*, it influenced the industrialization of Saxony and Thuringia (the optical industry in Jena was world-famous).[7] The later development of the Ruhrgebiet, notably its expansion for armaments for the First World War, contributed to bringing the present Western *Länder* into approximate equality with the present Eastern by the 1930s. Having been constrained temporarily by Versailles Treaty restrictions on German munitions capacity, the area which after the Second World War was to form the Western *Länder* was, by the time Hitler reoccupied the Rheinland, a little ahead of the Eastern. The author's calculation for 1936 shows GDP per capita of the West to be 7 per cent greater than that of the East (Kaser, 1987: 138). This study compared the respective GDPs with that of the USA in 1936 and 1980. The GDP of the present area (excluding West Berlin) was 29.7 per cent of the contemporary USA in 1936,

Table 13.1 Eastern and western *Länder* GDP, in 1995 prices

Year	GDP growth (% p.a.)	GDP (€bn)				Index (1989=100)	
	East DE	East DE 1	East DE 2	West DE	All DE	East DE	West DE
1989				1,346.1	1,617.3	100.0	100.0
1990	−30.5	121.3	98.8	1,422.8	1,669.1	69.5	103.2
1991	−2.2	118.6	96.6	1,495.4	1,710.8	68.0	105.8
1992	7.4	127.4	103.8	1,520.3	1,749.1	73.0	108.1
1993	5.8	134.8	109.8	1,481.4	1,730.1	77.2	107.0
1994	8.5	146.3	119.1	1,501.8	1,770.7	83.8	109.5
1995	5.3	154.0	125.4	1,523.1	1,801.3	88.2	111.4
1996	2.0	157.1	127.9	1,532.3	1,815.1	90.0	112.2
1997	1.7	159.8	130.1	1,556.1	1,840.4	91.5	113.8
1998	2.1	163.1	132.8	1,591.5	1,876.4	93.5	116.0
1999	2.0	166.4	135.5	1,624.8	1,914.8	95.3	118.4
2000	1.0	168.1	136.9	1,675.9	1,969.5	96.3	121.8
2001	−0.1	167.9	136.7	1,694.1	1,986.0	96.2	122.8
2002	0.1	168.1	136.9	1,695.2	1,987.6	96.3	122.9
2003	0.2	168.4	137.1	1,693.6	1,985.2	96.5	122.7
2004	1.4	170.8	139.0	1,723.1	2,018.2	97.8	124.8

Notes: East DE 1 are data of the Statistische Bundesamt and include East Berlin; East DE 2 are calculations by Professor Ludwig and include East Berlin; West DE and All DE are data of the Statistische Bundesamt and include East and West Berlin.
Source: Professor Udo Ludwig, IWH, University of Halle.

but 32 per cent in 1980, while that of the present Eastern *Länder* represented 11.7 per cent of US GDP in 1936, but only 3.9 per cent in 1980.

The causes of the divergence of economic growth between 1945[8] and 1990 in the Eastern and Western *Länder* are outside the scope of this study.[9] As the foregoing indexes show, the GDP of the GDR was estimated at 12 per cent of the then Federal Republic in 1980; in 1990 it was only 7 per cent (see Table 13.1). Both are in striking contrast to the 39 per cent indicated for 1936.

Comparative experience in early transition

After the collapse of communism throughout Central and Eastern Europe in late 1989, all affected countries suffered a recession, but its extent was most severe in the GDR, which became the eastern *Länder* of the Federal Republic after unification. As Table 13.2 shows, GDP in the latter fell by 30.5 per cent, but by only 1.2 per cent and 3.5 per cent in the Czech Republic and Hungary, respectively; the cutback was somewhat larger in Poland – GDP fell by 11.6 per cent, the rate by which output in the Czech Republic and Hungary

Table 13.2 Index numbers (1989 = 100) and annual percentage changes of GDP in eastern and western *Länder*, Poland, Czech Republic and Hungary, constant prices

Year	East DE	West DE	PO	CZ	HU	East DE	PO	CZ	HU	New EU-10
1989	100.0	100.0	100.0	100.0	100.0					
1990	69.5	103.2	88.4	98.8	96.5	−30.5	−11.6	−1.2	−3.5	
1991	68.0	105.8	82.3	87.3	85.0	−2.2	−7.0	−11.6	−11.9	−9.6
1992	73.0	108.1	84.4	86.8	82.4	7.4	2.6	−0.5	−3.1	−2.8
1993	77.2	107.0	87.6	86.9	81.9	5.8	3.8	0.1	−0.6	0.2
1994	83.8	109.5	92.1	88.8	84.3	8.5	5.2	2.2	2.9	3.6
1995	88.2	111.4	98.6	94.1	85.5	5.3	7.0	5.9	1.5	5.5
1996	90.0	112.2	104.5	98.1	86.6	2.0	6.0	4.3	1.3	4.7
1997	91.5	113.8	111.6	97.4	90.6	1.7	6.8	−0.8	4.6	4.7
1998	93.5	116.0	116.9	96.3	95.1	2.1	4.8	−1.0	4.9	3.6
1999	95.3	118.4	121.7	96.8	99.0	2.0	4.1	0.5	4.2	3.1
2000	96.3	121.8	126.6	99.9	104.2	1.0	4.0	3.3	5.2	4.1
2001	96.2	122.8	127.9	103.0	108.1	−0.1	1.0	3.1	3.8	2.4
2002	96.3	122.9	129.7	105.1	111.9	0.1	1.4	2.0	3.5	2.4
2003	96.5	122.7	134.6	109.0	115.3	0.2	3.8	3.7	3.0	4.0
2004	97.8	124.8	141.9	113.1	119.9	1.4	5.4	3.8	3.9	5.1

Notes and Source: Statistisches Bundesamt data supplied by Dr Johannes Stephan (IWH) and UN Economic Commission for Europe, *Economic Survey of Europe*, 2005, no. 2, tables A.1 and A.10. CZ = Czech Republic, Hu = Hungary, Po = Poland.

declined the following year. The start of substantial supportive measures by the Federal Republic to its eastern *Länder* staunched the decline, which was only 2.2 per cent in 1991 and, apart from a blip in 2001, growth has subsequently remained positive. Although Poland resumed positive growth at the same time, the Czech Republic and Hungary took longer to bottom out; the upturn in the first came in 1992 and in the second in 1993. The annual gains continued in the eastern *Länder* until 1995, when a GDP gain of 5.3 per cent was matched by the average of the group of ten states that were to join the EU in April 2004 (5.5 per cent). Subsequent experience has been dismal for the eastern *Länder* in comparison with those ten: by 2003 they exhibited a mere 0.2 per cent growth, whereas the ten gained 4.0 per cent (Table 13.2).

In the GDR, as in other Soviet-type economies, unemployment had been 'kept behind the factory gate'; that is, by maintaining staff at low productivity in order to fulfil the ideological priority of full employment under socialism. The opening of the economy to competitive market forces and the determination of the Federal government to maintain only competitive enterprises brought expectedly high unemployment. As Table 13.3 shows, the experience of eastern *Länder* was not dissimilar to that of Poland with regard to high unemployment. Indeed, apart from in the mid-1990s, when Poland showed a lower incidence, the rate of unemployment in the

Table 13.3 Unemployment rate in eastern and western *Länder*

Year	East DE	West DE	All DE	PO	CZ	HU
1993	15.0	7.3	8.9	14.0	4.4	6.8
1994	15.3	8.2	9.6	14.4	4.4	6.1
1995	14.1	8.3	9.4	13.3	4.1	5.6
1996	15.7	9.0	10.3	12.3	3.9	9.6
1997	18.3	9.8	11.4	10.9	4.8	9.0
1998	18.1	8.9	10.6	10.2	6.3	8.4
1999	16.4	8.3	9.7	13.4	8.6	6.9
2000	16.7	7.5	9.1	16.4	8.6	6.3
2001	17.1	7.4	9.1	18.5	8.0	5.6
2002	18.1	7.8	9.5	19.8	7.3	5.6
2003	18.9	8.6	10.3	19.2	7.8	5.8
2004	18.8	8.6	10.2	18.8	8.3	5.9

Notes and Source: See Table 13.2 on page 232.

two has been similar. On the other hand, the Czech Republic and Hungary have to date consistently exhibited a lower incidence than the eastern *Länder* and (apart from the Czech Republic in 2000 and 2001) lower than the average for the euro area. Unemployment in the western *Länder* was through the decade to 2003 lower than the euro area mean, and for that period half of that in the eastern *Länder*.

Capacity closure in the Eastern *Länder*

No other transition economy underwent the radical privatization undertaken by the Treuhand (June 1990 to December 1994), whose policy was characterized, with only a little exaggeration as 'Sell or slaughter'. Of the 13,815 state enterprises entrusted to it, only 63 firms were unsold when its mandate ended.[10] Transactions were overwhelmingly within Germany: 85 per cent of the firms sold went to western *Länder* owners, nearly all in the same industry and hence implying that the purchase was to forestall competition as well as to facilitate the intra-firm transfer of technology and managerial expertise. Fewer than 6 per cent were bought by eastern *Länder* residents, and fewer than 10 per cent being bought by foreigners, although they undertook proportionately much higher obligations on maintaining employment and investing new capital than did German buyers.[11]

The extensive closure of productive facilities was attributable to three causes. First, much equipment had been manufactured within the GDR or purchased from other Comecon producers, and Comecon formed a region of preference for self-sufficiency, further inhibited from purchases of contemporary Western technology by NATO embargo (exercised through CoCom).[12] Second, the GDR had operated, like others of the Soviet type, a 'shortage economy', wherein the annual plan dictated the production of a state and co-operative enterprise on the basis of correspondingly planned inputs. Because those inputs, by both misjudgement and deliberation, were frequently inadequate to assure the target outputs, almost any capital or intermediate good was accepted by a state or co-operative enterprise. For consumer goods, repressed inflation assured the purchase by households of the supply made available. When the ties of trade with Comecon states were dissolved, eastern *Länder* exporters lost their 'soft' markets. Demand also dropped for defence goods when the GDR armed forces were disbanded and orders from allies in the Warsaw Pact also ended. Eastern *Länder* households, with DM in their hands after the currency exchange, ceased to buy domestic products as soon as products from the west were available – the boycott of eastern *Länder* goods was close to total in those first two years. Low prices for both producer and consumer goods, which assured the disposal of planned production, had been maintained by heavy subsidization, which could not be continued under a market economy. The productive profile was not that of a modern economy: in 1988 'it resembled that of West Germany in the mid-1960s, with some 11 per cent of the GDR's 9.7 mn workforce still employed in agriculture, 38 per cent in industry, 10 per cent in retail and merely 32 per cent in transportation and services (including the state)'.[13]

The productivity gap

These capital and demand factors affected all post-communist economies, but the longer-term factor that related only to the eastern *Länder* was on the supply side, in the much lower labour productivity in wage costs whereby eastern *Länder* enterprises were burdened by the one-to-one rate of exchange of Ostmarks to DM. Whereas all the other transition countries devalued their currencies early in the transition period, the GDR currency was revalued. The relationship was that large fiscal deficits were incurred in those other states, mainly because of the dismantling of the revenue sources appropriate to a centrally-planned, state-run system, while expenditure rose (partly as a result of increased demand for social benefits as a result of unemployment); because no structure of public borrowing was in place, the deficits were monetized, and with the liberalization of prices (after the long periods of control) rapid inflation was induced.

Thus in 1991 the consumer price index rose by 56.7 per cent in the Czech Republic, by 35 per cent in Hungary and by 70.3 per cent in Poland, while in the western *Länder* it rose only 4.1 per cent. Triple-digit inflation characterized other transition states that year – Bulgaria 338.5, Lithuania 216.4, Estonia 202.0, Latvia 172.2, Romania 170.2, Croatia 124.2, Serbia 122.0, Slovenia 115.0, Bosnia 116.2 and Macedonia 110.8; the average for the twelve states of the CIS was 148.9. Thus the Russian rouble fell to a quarter of its real value against the US dollar[14] in the first four months after price decontrol, but the GDR currency, by the one-to-one conversion rate, quadrupled against the DM.[15] As market forces were around the same time pushing the DM upwards, the effect was magnified. Between the end of 1990 and the end of 1992, the DM appreciated by 5.2 per cent, and by 8.6 per cent in relative unit costs in manufacturing.

The arguments at the time for a one-to-one exchange are well known: the revaluation of money assets (only above a certain maximum were savings converted 2:1) gave political support both for unification and for the government party in the subsequent elections, and inhibited massive migration of labour from east to west. But eastern *Länder* labour productivity was around a third of that of the western *Länder*. Worse, under 'social unification' the western *Länder* trade unions embraced the eastern and began to press for wage rises towards western levels, ostensibly helping eastern workers but in fact seeking to protect their members against eastern competition. Average wages were 67.5 per cent of those in the West in 1993, 70.4 per cent in 1994 and 72.5 per cent in 1995. As Ludwig (1999, p. 16) shows, both wage and labour productivity convergences were rapid in the earlier years and then slackened.

Comparative economic growth

Subject to the usual caveats about comparing economic aggregates in a planned economy within a controlled and subsidized price mechanism with those in a market economy, Poland was the first of these countries to regain its 1989 level of output (1996), Hungary the next (2000) and the Czech Republic the last (2001); that level has at the time of writing not quite been reached in the eastern *Länder*. The western *Länder* did not, of course, undergo any recession in the 1990s (a blip in 1993 excepted) and by 2004 its GDP was 25 per cent above that of 1989. In 2004, Poland was 42 per cent above 1989, the Czech Republic 20 per cent, and Hungary 13 per cent.

The weaker dynamics of the eastern as against the western *Länder* has disproved the so-called 'two per cent rule', formulated by Barro and Sala-i-Martin (1995, p. 413), that empirically poor regions have displayed a rate of growth 2 per cent greater than that of the richest region(s) of the same country. Such convergence was displayed among US states, Japanese prefectures and within eight European countries. Lange and Pugh (1998, pp. 136–9) point out the varying circumstances of the eastern and western *Länder* and compare the record of convergence among western *Länder*. In the most dynamic post-war period, 1950–90, the best-performing of the *Länder* that were the most lagging in 1950 closed the gap in per capita GDP with the Federal average by only between 5 and 18 percentage points. Thus the experience of these forty years or so indicates how much longer it would take for the eastern *Länder*, starting from a per capita GDP of about half that of the western *Länder*. Lange and Pugh (1998, pp. 140–1) also show that the catch-up of the six poorest Italian regions, the Mezzogiorno, over 1950–90 was only trivially positive (less than 1 percentage point), again despite substantial north-to-south transfers. Boltho *et al.* (1999) perceive that the German authorities have avoided some of the negative factors that influenced the non-convergence between the Mezzogiorno and the rest of Italy, a process badly affected by 'the large scale divergence of massive transfers into rent-seeking activities' (1999, p. 342). They commend the large western investment into the eastern economy and restraint on claims for wage parity while productivity differentials persisted. Much of the investment went into infrastructure: Lange and Pugh (1998, p. 137) show that between 1991 and 1995 per capita infrastructure investment as being 75 per cent higher in the eastern *Länder* than in western ones.

Prospects worsened around the start of the twenty-first century, as the eastern *Länder* rate of GDP growth became negative (–0.1 in 2001) and was very modest in the following two years. Only in 2004 did the rate exceed 1 per cent: at 1.4 per cent this was less than the western rate of 1.7 per cent, thus widening the margin and further delaying convergence.

Longer-run consequences

As an economic study, this chapter only touches on social effects. Attitudes of psychic income and psychic unease have been noted above and must have been affected further by the differing experience of unemployment, also described briefly above. Among other examples, Corak *et al.* (2005) show that child poverty was downward-trending in the 1980s in the western *Länder* but began to rise in the 1990s, and child poverty rates are higher in the eastern *Länder*. Demographic experience has also been worse.

Breu (2000, 2001) and Breu and Benwell (1999) analysed extensive surveys among managers in over sixty eastern *Länder* companies and found that, after a general expression of euphoria as the state-run industrial economy was dismantled, managers were confronted by an environment (to them novel) of unpredictability, to which a process of self-assessment led to the continuing supportiveness of transformation. These findings confirm an early forecast by Hall and Ludwig (1995), that the gainfully-occupied population accepted 'market adaptation', but they go on to observe in some branches social unease caused by displacement by senior western personnel (such as in university posts and in management). They note that migration to the western *Länder* posed longer-term problems for the eastern stock of human capital.

The application of human resources is just one aspect of the longer-run issue still confronting both the eastern *Länder* and comparable post-transition states of the EU – the Baltic States, the Czech Republic, Hungary, Poland, Slovakia and Slovenia. This is the need to catch up in productivity at the microeconomic level. Two recent investigations have used a measurement technique different from the standard factor productivity approach, essentially by matching factory-level productivity with that of corresponding western *Länder* enterprises. A team study led by Stephan (2005) identifies the extent of 'catch-up productivity' still needed in the Czech Republic, Hungary and Poland.

Under conditions of high unemployment in the eastern *Länder* and Poland, the question needs to be posed as to whether 'extensive' policies favouring more employment should take precedence over 'intensive' policies promoting labour productivity, a ranking recommended for the euro area by an IMF paper (Estavão, 2004), which evokes 'focusing a bit less on productivity growth and bit more on increasing labor market utilization' when examining lower productivity in the euro area than in the USA. Given the 'psychic unease' generated by high unemployment, social considerations may in the medium term be preferable to strictly economic ones. It is somewhat ironic that the 'extensive' labour utilization that characterized the GDR has returned to present-day prominence – effectively on the same social (though very different political) criteria.

Notes

*I thank Dr Karin Breu (Fellow of Templeton College, Oxford), Professor Udo Ludwig and Dr Johannes Stephan (both Halle Institute for Economic Research) for help in identifying valuable papers and data for this study.

1. Aggregate to 2003 from *Financial Times*, 3 July 2004, annual rates from *The Economist*, 7 December 2002 and 'solidarity package' from *Financial Times*, 23 June 2001. Western *Länder* GDP in 1989 was €1,350 billion in 1995 prices (see Table 13.1), hence broadly comparable to the net transfer, which is at current prices.
2. Conclusion reached in discussion of relevant magnitudes with Professor Patrick O'Brien (London School of Economics), acknowledged with appreciation.
3. Burkett (2003) defines psychic income as 'enjoyment of life' and traces it to Marx's distinction between 'labour value and use value'. A contrary perception, 'psychic unease' is traced by Gilbert (1997) to Adam Smith's *Theory of Moral Sentiments*.
4. But note the caution expressed by Thurow (1978).
5. Young (1989) models a person's 'psychic reward' from the act of donation to voluntary or not-for-profit organizations.
6. Reference is to the household sector in DiTella *et al.* (2003), who also observe that the welfare state weakens the relationship because 'higher unemployment benefits are associated with higher national well-being' (p. 209). For the enterprise sector, the theory of rational expectations operates for cyclical economic activity, but cyclical behaviour can also be described in terms of a psychic climate among producers (Kraft and Weise, 1987).
7. The author found no quantitative historical study, but benefited from the advice of Professor Anthony Nicholls (St Antony's College, Oxford).
8. The Soviet Zone of Occupation became the GDR in 1949.

9. Among other studies, Ross (2000) cogently explains the investment and productivity factors in industry and the disincentives of farm collectivization, and Biedenkopf (1994, pp. 129–42) the obsolescence of productive capital and infrastructure. For an analysis while the GDR was in existence, see Brus (1986).
10. Among an extensive literature on eastern *Länder* privatization are Carlin (1994), Carlin and Richthofen (1995), Brücker (1995), and most chapters in Hölscher and Hochberg (1998).
11. Foreigners' labour pre-commitments were 10.3 per cent of the total, but employment was 5.7 per cent; capital obligated was 12.2 per cent of the total, compared with the enterprises' 8 per cent of sales (Kaser, 1998, p. 62).
12. See in Kaser (1967), chs 4 and 8.
13. Büchtermann and Schupp (1992, p. 91), quoted by Breu (2000, p. 13). Breu (2000: pp. 12–17) provides a concise summary of the GDR economy and the problems of unification.
14. The real exchange rate is the nominal rate adjusted for inflation in the two countries compared.
15. One DM had been exchanging against four Ostmarks, reflecting the purchasing-power parity rate.

References

Agarwal, B. and A. Vercelli, (eds) (2005) *Psychology, Rationality and Economic Behaviour* (Basingstoke: Palgrave/Macmillan).

Barro, R. J. and Sala-i-Martin, X. (1995) *Economic Growth* (New York: McGraw Hill).

Biedenkopf, K. (1994) *Einheit und Erneuerung: Deutschland nach dem Umbruch in Europa* (Unity and Renewal: Germany after the Upheaval in Europe) (Stuttgart: Deutsche Verlags-Anstalt).

Boltho, A., W. Carlin and P. Scaramozzino (1999) 'Will Eastern Germany Become a New Mezzogiorno?', in J. Adams and F. Pigliaru (eds), *Economic Growth and Change. National and Regional Patterns of Convergence and Divergence* (Cheltenham: Edward Elgar), pp. 323–48.

Breu, K. (2000) *East German Managers in Transition. A Study into Individual Change in Transformative Contexts, Arbeit, Organisation und Personal im Transformationsprozess, Vol. 10* (Munich: Rainer Hampp Verlag).

Breu, K. (2001) 'The Role and Relevance of Management Cultures in the Organizational Transformation Process', *International Studies of Management and Organization*, vol. 31, no. 2, pp. 28–47.

Breu, K. and M. Benwell (1999) 'Modelling Individual Transition in the Context of Organisational Transformation', *Journal of Management Development*, vol. 18, no. 6, pp. 496–520.

Brücker, H. (1995) 'Selling Eastern Germany. On the Economic Rationale of the Treuhandanstalt's Privatisation and Restructuring Strategy', *MOCT-MOST*, vol. 5, no. 4, pp. 27–53.

Brus, W. (1986) Chapters 23 to 26 in M. Kaser (ed.), *The Economic History of Eastern Europe 1919–75, Vol. 3* (Oxford: Oxford University Press).

Büchtermann, C. and J. Schupp (1992) 'Repercussions of Reunification: Patterns and Trends in the Socio-economic Transformation of East Germany', *Industrial Relations Journal*, vol. 23, no. 2, pp. 90–106.

Burkett, P. (2003) 'The Value Problem in Ecological Economics: lessons from the Physiocrats and Marx', *Organization and Environment*, vol. 16, no. 2, pp. 137–67.

Carlin, W. (1994) 'Privatization and Deindustrialization in East Germany', in S. Estin (ed.), *Privatization in Central and Eastern Europe* (London: Longman), pp. 127–53.

Carlin, W. and P. Richthofen (1995) 'Finance, Economic Development and the Transition: The East German Case', *Economics of Transition,* vol. 3, pp. 169–95.

Corak, M., M. Fertig and M. Tamm (2005) 'A Portrait of Child Poverty in Germany', Institute for the Study of Labour, Bonn, Discussion Paper No. 1528.

DiTella, R., R. MacCulloch and A. Oswald (2003) 'The Macroeconomics of Happiness', *Review of Economics and Statistics*, vol. 85, no. 4, pp. 809–27.

Estavão, M. (2004) 'Why Is Productivity in the Euro Area So Sluggish?', IMF Working Paper No. 04/200 (Washington, DC: IMF).

Gérard-Varet, L., S.-C. Kolm and J. Mercier Ythier (eds) (2000) *The Economics of Reciprocity, Giving and Altruism* (Basingstoke: Palgrave Macmillan).

Gilbert, G. (1997) 'Adam Smith on the Nature and Causes of Poverty', *Review of Social Economy*, vol. 55, no. 3, pp. 273–91.

Hall, J. and U. Ludwig (1995) 'German Unification and the "Market Adoption" Hypothesis', *Cambridge Journal of Economics*, vol. 19, pp. 491–507.

Headey, B. and D. Headey (2003) 'German Reunification: Welfare Gains and Losses East and West', *Social Indicators Research*, vol. 64, no. 1, pp. 107–38.

Hölscher, J. and A. Hochberg (eds) (1998) *East Germany's Economic Development since Unification: Domestic and Global Aspects* (London: Macmillan).

Kaser, M. (1967) *Comecon. Integration Problems of the Planned Economies* (Oxford: Oxford University Press).

Kaser, M. (1998) 'The Eastern Länder as a Transition Economy' in J. Hölscher and A. Hochberg (eds), *East Germany's Economic Development since Unification: Domestic and Global Aspects* (London: Macmillan), pp. 53–78.

Kaser, M. (1987) 'The Economic Dimension', in Edwing Moorton (ed.) *Germany between East and West* (Cambridge: Cambridge University Press) pp. 123–40.

Kraft, M. and P. Weise (1987) 'Eine Formalisierung on Spiethoffs Theorie der wirtschaftlichen Wechsellagen (A formalization of Spiethoff's business-cycle theory), *Schweizerische Zeitschrift für Volkswirtschat und Statistik,* vol. 123(4), pp. 531–42.

Lange, T. and G. Pugh (1998) *The Economics of German Unification: An Introduction* (Cheltenham: Edward Elgar).

Page, W. (2003) 'Germany's Mezzogiorno Revisited: Institutions, Fiscal Transfers and Regional Convergence', Deutsche Bank Research Working Paper Series No. 9 (13 June).

Ross, C. (2000) *Constructing Socialism at the Grass-roots: The Transformation of East Germany, 1945–65* (Basingstoke: Palgrave).

Stephan, J. (2005) *Report to the European Commission of Productivity Catch-Up* (Halle: IWH).

Thurow, L. (1978) 'Psychic Income: Useful or Useless?', *American Economic Review,* vol. 68, no. 2, pp. 142–5.

Young, D. (1989) 'A "Fair Share" Model of Public Good Provision', *Journal of Economic Behavior and Organization*, vol. 11, no. 1, pp. 137–47.

Part V
Conclusion

14
Investment in Germany – Flop or Top?

*Norbert Walter**

After reading newspapers and listening to academic and economic discussions these days, it almost seems cynical to talk about investments in Germany. Why should anyone in their right mind think about investing their precious money in an inflexible, high-wage economy? No German and nobody in international circles would admit publicly that they saw sizeable potential in 'the sick man of Europe'. In the case of 'locusts', as foreign investors now seem to be called in Germany, this is understandable, as they want to keep prices for assets at a low level and buy cheaply. It is much harder to understand the mental state of the Germans themselves, however, being the biggest exporting country worldwide. Why is Germany so obsessed with bad news? This chapter is an attempt to put some of the facts in a more positive light, and to show that Germany is still a place where people work hard and where it is still possible to make money.

The economic basis

Demand prospects

Germany is still the most populous country in Europe, with about 80 million consumers. The absolute numbers continue to speak in favour of Germany as a huge customer market. GDP totals no less than €2,207 trillion, making the country by far the biggest economy in the region and representing approximately 30 per cent of the euro area. The weak point is the future development of GDP and the population. It is clear that Germany is not in for a big increase in its number of inhabitants. Obviously, the ageing of the population will eventually result in the population shrinking. This trend does not compare favourably with the USA, France or the UK, and certainly not with the emerging markets, which have a totally different demographic structure.

Another weak point is that GDP per capita now approximately matches the EU average (PPS: Germany 108 versus EU-25 100). Back in 1995 it was 11 points higher. There have been several reasons for this, including Germany's unfavourable demographic development and the catch-up efforts of other countries (convergence, more reform). However, German reunification has played a part. The already huge costs of remodelling a socialist economy became prohibitively expensive with the adoption of the West German social security system in the new *Länder*. These costs are still one reason for the high social contributions that are so harmful to growth.

GDP development still does not look overly rosy and the potential annual growth rate appears unlikely to exceed 1.5 per cent for the next 15 years. Nevertheless, there is a good chance that we are underestimating potential growth. Germany could probably do substantially better if all the reform plans were put in place. A growth rate of 2 per cent would then be within reach.

Potential growth results from the use of available capital and labour as well as from productivity increases. On all these fronts, Germany has shown progress and should do so for some time. Besides real effects there are also some problems in knowing how to measure improvements in productive capacities. In the future, the physical part of the capital stock will lose its crucial role and be replaced by intellectual capital. The measurement of knowledge in the national accounts is far less simple than the measurement of performance for a factory or a machine. But in the service world of tomorrow, investment in knowledge may bear more fruit than investment in infrastructure or other physical assets.

One reason for the low potential growth is the inefficiency of the use of capital, and low labour participation. In the past, Germans were quite slow to embrace technological developments, and companies were also rather hesitant to invest in their future. This means that, in comparison to the USA, there is still some room for productivity improvements. Bearing this in mind, and the fact that Americans work 1,900 hours/year and Germans only 1,580/year, it is easy to see that there is still considerable potential in the German labour force. As well as the low number of working hours, potential is also trapped in the high unemployment rate, which means that Germany could add 5 per cent of the workforce into the production process over the next few years. With more labour market flexibility, all this could lead to a growth rate of 2.5 per cent without any risk of inflation for a good number of years.

The problem is, though, that the German public is not in the mood for shopping. The high unemployment rate is one of the main reasons for the general scepticism. People are afraid of losing their jobs, and this has led to a rise in the savings ratio as they want to be prepared for an unstable and unsafe future. Another reason for the high level of the savings ratio, it is hoped, could be that the German public is finally listening to the experts and making provision for old age. As these savings are not being used for consumption and real incomes are also not growing, the result is stagnating consumption. With a little more confidence in the future, it should be easy to move away from this situation of paralysis.

Comparative advantage

Benchmarking and ranking have become the standard methods of comparing different countries. During the past few years, every time such a report or ranking was published it was quite a sad and depressing experience for Germany. For example, in the IMD World Competitiveness Ranking 2005, Germany again lost 2 ranks and found itself in 23rd position. In the defence of the country, one must say that these rankings are also partly based on surveys. As Germans are hard to satisfy and just love to complain it is not surprising that in some categories the rankings show amazingly negative results. To illustrate, in the 2003 IMD report, Germany was ranked below Colombia on the criterion of government efficiency. A more recent study by the Wissenschaftliche Hochschule für Unternehmensführung (WHU) and the relocation advisory firm Contor says that Germany has regained attractiveness compared to the UK and Italy, especially becasue of lower unit-labour costs.

The facts taken from more traditional statistics also paint a distorted picture. The current account surplus is growing each year. It is already bigger than that of China, and it is just a matter of time before people realize that it will soon reach the magical mark of €100 billion. This means that Germany is still able to add value. It is just sad that the country seems to have lost the ability to be proud of itself: 82 million Germans are able to export more products and services than 120 million Japanese, 1.3 billion Chinese or 250 million Americans – quite an achievement, especially in the face of a strong euro at the same time.

Germany is still able to produce goods that are appreciated by customers. It is true that imports have risen. But to complain that this smacks of a 'bazaar economy' seems wrong. Adam Smith and David Ricardo showed us a long time ago that specialization and division of production are to the mutual benefit of all participants. In the case of Germany, they helped the country to regain competitiveness in global markets.

European environment

The pressure to reach Lisbon targets (employment rates, productivity goals) has the potential to spur growth and reform in Germany. But recent developments (Germany's resistance to the Stability Pact and the Services

Directive) show that the public is less willing to sacrifice short-term comfort for long-term, EU-dictated goals.

The declared focus on promoting growth and jobs is not convincing, as many social and environmental goals were brought into play through the back door. The Stability and Growth Pact has been diluted substantially, if not buried altogether. The commitment to structural reforms on the part of member states is still rather vague. The envisaged national reform programmes – monitored by the European Commission – was presented as late as 2006. This may help to get the priorities right and increase pressure on member states to push through reforms. This may also be helpful to make Lisbon part of the national political debate. But procedure and governance cannot substitute for reform commitment by the member states themselves. Therefore, the question is whether the European governments will agree on additional reform measures under the aegis of the new Lisbon Agenda.

A disappointing element is the EU Services Directive. Liberalizing the provision of cross-border services is the best single measure to boost growth in Europe. But the member states concluded that the Commission draft of early 2004 had to be rewritten. There is a big political risk of dilution as several member states, in particular France and Germany, as well as the European Parliament, have strongly criticized the Directive for causing 'social dumping'.

However, this is a pity, as the EU is miles away from a genuine single market in the services sector, and services account for almost 70 per cent of GDP and jobs. Politicians ignore the fact that growth is generated mainly through new and/or better-functioning markets. The Services Directive would have given new freedoms to, for example, consultants, employment agencies, retailers, architects, travel agencies and healthcare providers. Studies estimate that a net increase of about 600,000 jobs could be achieved by freeing up the service sector. This would be especially interesting for Germany with its qualified workforce and high standard of knowledge.

Why go to the land of beer and sauerkraut?

What will the German position be in the future?

Recently productivity growth in Germany has been mediocre: from 1998 to 2003 GDP per hour grew only by 1.6 per cent versus 2.4 per cent in the USA or 2.1 per cent in Japan. As productivity growth often springs from technological progress it is always useful taking a look at innovation and R&D culture. R&D expenditure does not look that bad in comparison with Germany's international competitors. Yet it is worthwhile taking a closer look.[1]

An important indicator of the deployment or availability of R&D-specific human resources is research and development (R&D) personnel intensity; that is, the share of a country's total workforce employed in research and experimental development. This covers not only scientists and engineers, but also administrative and support staff at R&D departments in government and industry – together they form the backbone of the innovation system. By international standards, Germany still holds a good position here (for example, it ranks fourth in terms of R&D personnel intensity in companies). The development of R&D personnel intensity in Germany over time is similarly encouraging. It did drop in the first half of the 1990s (as part of the course of reunification), but then rose again through 1999. Germany makes a similar – although not quite as good – showing in respect of the total funds spent domestically on R&D: in terms of their share of GDP (that is, R&D intensity) they do at least put Germany in the upper-middle range, at not quite 2.5 per cent (2001), and the trend has been nudging upwards for some years. In terms of expenditure on R&D by industry – which, as in most industrialized countries, accounts for roughly two-thirds of total R&D spending – Germany holds a similar international position with total expenditures. But unlike the USA and Japan, for example, Germany has not yet made good the severe decline that took place in the first half of the 1990s. It is still too early to say whether this has been caused by short-term repercussions of slack business activity, or whether the country has moved into a generally lower gear. What is certain, however, is that the intensification of R&D activity since the mid-1990s stems from a stronger commitment by industry. Despite a nominal increase, public R&D spending has fallen behind GDP growth. Although R&D personnel intensity and R&D intensity are the measures applied most frequently to quantify innovation input, they do not fully describe it. In addition to invention and prototypical realization as such, their implementation in a company (process innovation) or market (product or service innovation) is an essential element of the innovation process. As well as R&D spending itself, this also involves the costs of serialization, design, marketing and so an. Innovation expenditure (as a percentage of sales) is therefore taken as an estimator of the total funds put up by a company in the innovation process. Here too, the data available point to a comparatively good position for Germany by international standards. In the services sector, Germany puts on an even better performance here than in manufacturing. Also striking is that, as a proportion of sales, this expenditure in Germany has remained broadly constant on a company-wide average in recent years.

Innovation input and basic conditions are ultimately the major determinants of innovation output. The production of scientific knowledge is a measure of output by an important part of the innovation system. It can be estimated with reference to the number of publications per inhabitant. In this respect, Germany does not play in the premier international league, although it does hold a firm position. In addition to quantity, the quality of publications by German scientists, while sound, generally falls short of that produced by the world leaders. Quality can be gauged approximately by the citation impact, for example.[2]

How well is the knowledge used?

Germany has a strong record of patent output. In terms of the number of triadic patents – patent families registered with the European and Japanese Patent Office and granted by the US Patent and Trademark Office – per capita, Germany belongs to the leading group internationally. In absolute figures, the USA, Japan (JP) and Germany (DE) are together responsible for three-quarters of all OECD patents (USA, 36.4 per cent; JP, 25.3 per cent; DE, 13.4 per cent). In recent years, after an initial post-reunification downturn, German patent output has followed the general uptrend in most OECD countries. But when assessing patent data it should be remembered that the importance of this kind of intellectual property protection varies considerably from industry to industry.

Finally, there is also something moderately positive to report on German companies' business success with innovation. This can be assessed, first, by considering the share of novel market products in total corporate turnover, and, second, with reference to the share of process innovations in total cost reduction. In both areas, following a downturn in the first half of the 1990s, the German manufacturing industry almost doubled its innovation-induced share in the second half. The respective shares also edged up in the services sector during the same period (data from 1997). The most recent figures (dating from 2001) show sales data for market innovations trending upwards again slightly, and those on cost-cutting through process innovations showing a little.

To summarize briefly the initial overview: the proportion of R&D personnel is high by international standards; governments and companies spend substantial sums on generating basic knowledge; so far companies have kept on track with expenditure on market realization; and the framework conditions are rated comparatively positively. Scientific output is solid; patent output still ranks among the best in the world; and the economic success of innovation is not slowing.

One problem is the translation of this knowledge into practice. As already mentioned, Germans are not early adopters of new technologies. This trait has been reinforced by the low level of corporate investment, which is one of the biggest challenges Germany has had to face in recent times. The creation of human capital does not grow at the same rate there as in other countries. Investment in education and training has to be intensified, so that the newest technologies can be used and transformed into higher productivity.

Strong financial position of companies

The strong profit and cash-flow positions of domestic and foreign firms in Germany reflect investment opportunities. Current sluggish investment is explainable by weak consumption growth and the lagged effect of poor 2003 and pre-2003 profits.

Investment in machinery and equipment is fell short of hoped-for levels in 2005 (growing some 3 per cent). Still there is some optimism that investment will pick up more strongly in 2006 and expand by a good 6 per cent. The scenario of export growth leading to increased investment spending, which had been predicted and anticipated since 2003, is in fact not supported by historical data. In previous recoveries it was private consumption that gave the economy growth momentum. Nevertheless, there is widespread disappointment regarding current anaemic investment spending. But the growth of investment spending has only been stronger during the recoveries in the 1970s and 1980s. The current lack of investment is similar to the recovery in 1993/4. As explained in a study[3], the current sluggish investment is not caused by structural changes. It is explainable in particular by current weak consumption growth and the lagged effect of poor 2003 profit growth.

The continued decline in the investment ratio caused by the correction of the 1999/2000 over-investment will stop. The surge in 2004 profits and exports will trigger stronger investment growth in 2006. Entrepreneurs have been accused of raking in surging profits while at the same time not investing. These accusations have gained in bitterness as restructuring continues in tandem with a further decrease in jobs. But the turnover composition of DAX companies shows that the bulk of for 2004 and 2005 profits were earned abroad, where the economic conditions look much more favourable. An increasing difference between the mood of these larger companies and that of smaller, more domestically-orientated companies suggests that domestic profits are still not looking very bright, probably because of low volume growth. Larger companies, with their experience and know-how in international investments, are probably more inclined to invest in more dynamic regions which contribute strongly to demand and profits. According to surveys, increasing numbers of smaller and medium-sized companies are investing abroad, or thinking about making this step. It would, however, be too early to conclude that this will be redirecting capital from domestic investment to foreign activity. In the past, German foreign direct investment was positively correlated with investment in Germany. Given this year's mediocre 0.5 per cent growth in private consumption and only a modest rise in investment, GDP growth reached only 0.8 per cent after 1.6 per cent in 2004. In 2006 the domestic recovery – namely consumption and investment– will gain breadth and depth, especially if the mid- and small companies regain their confidence in the government and overcome their hesitation to invest further.

Politics

The SPD–Green government took several steps in the right direction to address some of Germany's most pressing problems. The reform of the tax system was a substantial achievement of the year 2000, when the government started to reduce the 'punishment' meted out to companies that achieved good business performance and financial success. Corporate taxation has definitely become more business friendly. It is obvious that the German job market was able to gain a little momentum as a result of the improvement in some social legislation, especially the implementation of the Hartz I–IV programmes. These changes may lead to a more adaptable and dynamic workforce. Another sector where far-reaching reforms took place was in the financial markets. Finance Minister Hans Eichel succeeded in overcoming the opposition of the Bundesbank and put in place a modern supervisory structure.

Considering that the demographic problems mentioned earlier are sure to engulf Germany in the coming years, the SPD–Green government was the first to take tentative steps in the right direction to deal with the fourthcoming challenges. The famous phrase 'the pensions are safe' uttered by Norbert Blüm, Minister of Labour and Social Affairs under the previous CDU/CSU government, was finally laid to rest where it belongs – in the land of dreams. The creation of a second pillar for old age provision by his successor, SPD Labour Minister Walter Riester, was unfortunately not as successful as had been desired. Nevertheless, Germans started to understand the importance of saving for their old age.

The SPD's Agenda 2010 was another step that held promise of mastering future developments. Politicians have accepted the need for reform, but have not managed to push for further action and to convinc the public. More labour market reforms and an overhaul of the full social security system are strongly needed.

Citizens

Germans are willing to try harder. Workers have reduced their wage expectations; recent collective wage bargaining has had reasonable outcomes; working time increases and sick leave are at all-time lows; and the de facto pension age has risen by almost two years. Labour relations are still intact and working days lost because of strikes are at the very lowest end of international statistics. Besides this, the German workforce is highly educated and the dual education (apprenticeship) system delivers specialists of various kinds. It is not surprising that German craftsmen are the symbol of quality work and are in high demand in, for example, the UK and Norway.

Nevertheless: the public remains very sceptical about Germany's future economic performance and is thus afraid to spend on consumption and unwilling to support more far-reaching reforms.

Infrastructure

A part from its central location in the heart of Europe, Germany also has a very highly developed infrastructure. The *Autobahn* (motorway) system is still a stable backbone for the economy. Of course, considerable investments have to be made to close the remaining holes in this dense network and to reconnect the new EU members to the rest of Europe. The existing network also needs more money, as a general overhaul cannot wait much longer. The recent introduction of a toll system for trucks is a first step to rebase the financing of roads on a more stable and fairer foundation. Going to the east of Germany you can already see what German engineering skills can do to improve an ailing transportation system.

German *Autobahns* are famous, but the train system has also reached a new level of quality. All big cities are connected by the high-speed ICE network. It is now possible to travel by train from Hamburg to Berlin in less than two hours. With this fast network the workforce has also become very mobile. For companies, this means that the pool of skilled labour has grown as their catchment area may now cover several big cities.

The German sky is a battlefield of low prices. It is also very well connected to the rest of the world. Apart from the unfortunate example of Berlin, most of the country's airports have modernized and are delivering high-class services to the rest of Europe. It is not surprising that several logistics companies chose Germany as their base. This economy, in the new middle of Europe, boasts high-quality networks that are also well interconnected with one another.

EU enlargement

The recent accession of ten new members to the EU has been very effective in terms of putting pressure on Germany to overhaul its economy. At the same time, the new members have become reliable customers for high-quality goods of German origin. Exports of machinery and technology have gained in importance as the new members modernize their economies. But not only goods are in high demand. German knowledge has also become an important factor in relations with the new members. Further enlargement will work in the same direction and provide Germany with more markets where superior-quality goods and services will be needed. Because of their geographical proximity the delivery chains will be short and the cheap labour of the new countries may help to increase the competitiveness of German industry. Germany is now in the middle of Europe and well connected to all important markets. As home to 3 million Turkish immigrants, Germany is also very well prepared to gain a large share of the Turkish market.

Where to invest in Germany

East Germany is a springboard to Eastern Europe: cross-border value chains are reducing production costs substantially while allowing companies to keep one foot in a technologically advanced country. East Germany's geographical location alone gives it a considerable advantage over the competition in the quest to conquer the Eastern European market. DHL, BMW and Porsche have all discovered the hidden charms of Saxony.

Germany's competitiveness as a business location can be illustrated impressively by looking at the automobile industry. In 2004, the value of output was nearly 85 per cent higher than in 1993, the last year of recession. Unit car exports grew by more than three-quarters during the same period; the export ratio is now around 70 per cent. The strong growth was also driven by the auto-parts industry, which has more than doubled the value of its output in the domestic market since 1993. As well as outsourcing, the key factor was qualitative growth, which is a reflection of better-equipped vehicles and the trends towards higher-quality niche models and more expensive diesel passenger cars.

Of course, it has to be borne in mind that many vehicle parts are now imported from Eastern Europe and other countries. But in the days of globalization this is quite common, and is a sign of how Germany can respond to new competitive situations and capitalize on the location opportunities on its doorstep. Another major point is that German parts makers are well integrated into the global sourcing of international vehicle manufacturers.

The fact that Germany's vehicle manufacturers and their suppliers have set up new factories in east Germany shows that the location is very attractive. True, this region was given a shot in the arm by government subsidies. Nevertheless, the availability of, for example, skilled labour, good transport and telecommunications infrastructure, and the proximity to the important western European customer markets, all argue for Germany. Germany's high wage costs are a negative point, but this is less important in capital-intensive car production. Given the wage restraints of the past few years and the related improvement in Germany's relative price competitiveness, the label 'cars made in Germany' should continue to enhance the country as a business location – and for foreign investors.

Germany is not just cars, though. There are a lot of hidden champions. The Dräger Group, a medical and safety products conglomerate based in Lübeck, invested heavily in research and has now reached a level of expertise unchallenged by its competitors.

But you will also find successful models in other countries too. Retail is in a lamentable state in Germany, but Aldi and Lidl are showing how to succeed in a tough market and are now trying to export their model to other areas. The Green members of the government coalition helped to ensure that

German businesses became leading suppliers of environmental technology in energy, recycling, water treatment etc.

Why German real estate will continue to attract foreign investors

Germany boasts the largest volume of real estate assets in Europe, with their gross value totalling some €9 trillion. They represent more than 80 per cent of total gross fixed assets in Germany. Over the past few years, both the housing market and numerous regional markets for commercial property have been sluggish. In the residential segment, house prices have been declining since 2003 and today they are no higher on average than they were in the early 1990s. In the office segment the slide has been even more pronounced: dotcom euphoria triggered a boom in the construction of new complexes, particularly in the urban agglomerations of west Germany, and the surge in supply coincided with a fall in demand. As a result, vacancy rates reached record highs in early 2005. At the time of writing, Frankfurt an Main has an office vacancy rate of 17 per cent, Dusseldorf nearly 15 per cent and Munich over 10 per cent. At the same time, rents have tumbled: back in 2001 tenants were paying over €50 per square metre for office space in prime locations in Frankfurt. At the time of writing, landlords in the banking district consider themselves fortunate if a new tenant pays €30. Dusseldorf, Munich and Hamburg have also witnessed more than a 20 per cent decline in rents in prime locations since 2003. Since the German economy does not look set to gather much momentum in the short term, and since demographic trends will weigh on the German real estate market in the long term, there seems to be little to say for investment in German property at present. That is why some market watchers are surprised at how much interest Anglo-American private equity funds are taking in German residential property. Around 300,000 housing units were sold to foreign investors in 2004; a further 200,000 changed hands by the end of the first half of 2005. This interest is, of course, partly attributable to the low cost of borrowing and partly to the dearth of really attractive investment alternatives abroad. Other factors in favour of the German market are that the number of housing completions has been very low over the past few years, suggesting that rents will rise in the medium term, and above all that the home ownership rate is very low. Nearly 60 per cent of all households live in rented accommodation, but many of them wish they owned their own homes. This mismatch is the basis for the strategy of the foreign funds: they acquire large housing portfolios from big companies or the public sector and then sell the individual flats to the tenants. Over the next few years more local authorities and companies are likely to reduce the size of their portfolios – partly to raise revenue in the short term, and partly to focus more strongly on their core business. As long as current owners are willing to sell, interest in the German housing market is unlikely to ebb.

Besides housing, it is also worthwhile considering German commercial property, as here too the market is witnessing a quiet, steady shift towards international benchmarks. The owner-occupancy rate for the corporate sector also far outstrips the international mean. Estimates vary, but it is said that two-thirds to three-quarters of the real estate in Germany is on the users' books. In the UK the share is less than half, and in the USA only a third. German corporates are realising increasingly that this is another area where disinvestment will enable them to focus more strongly on core activities. This means that the supply side of the investment market will become more liquid. Since many German investors are still keen on diversifying their portfolios internationally and – logically – steering clear of their home market, foreign investors in particular should find a window of opportunity here. This will hold above all if Germany allows the establishment of real estate investment trusts (REITs). As they are a common standard internationally, foreign investors will have reduced transaction costs since they are already familiar with and understand the vehicle.

When to invest in Germany

It is hard to imagine a better time for investment in Germany. European interest rates are at record lows. The prices of real estate and stocks are still reasonable. The stock market seems to have overcome the depression that set in when the tech stock bubble burst. The high profits of the DAX blue-chip companies will lead to higher dividend payments. And another fact worth noting is that the price–earnings ratio in Germany is, at 11.5 lower than in the US market (15). It is true that growth rates of the USA and Asia are a lot more convincing than those of old Europe and Germany. However, global imbalances are forcing investors to look for diversification. The first movers have already appeared on the scene. Foreign investors have been puzzled to hear a leading member of the governing party make reference to them in connection with the biblical story of the 'plague of locusts'. These 'locusts' are very keen to find promising investment locations as their customers are demanding a high return on the capital with which they have entrusted them. Smart people should ask themselves why these archetypal members of Anglo-American capitalism have started to take such an interest in sclerotic old Germany, 'the sick man of Europe'. They seem to have discovered the potential to earn money in this country. So every investor should think about whether he wants to join in before the party is over.

Notes

*Thanks to Werner Becker, Eric Heymann, Jan Hofmann, Tobias Just, Jörn Quitzau and Stefan Schneider.

1. The next paragraph is taken from the DB Research study 'Innovation in Germany: Mind the Gap!' published October 2003.
2. Language – that is, the dominance of English in the Ivy League – might discriminate against German people and Germany.
3. The 2006 German Investment Recovery, *Deutsche Bank Research*, 25 April 2005, current issues.

Name Index

Subject Index